MOON HANDBOOKS®
BELIZE

SIXTH EDITION

CHICKI MALLAN & JOSHUA BERMAN

© DANIELLE VAUGHN

Ⓐ AVALON TRAVEL

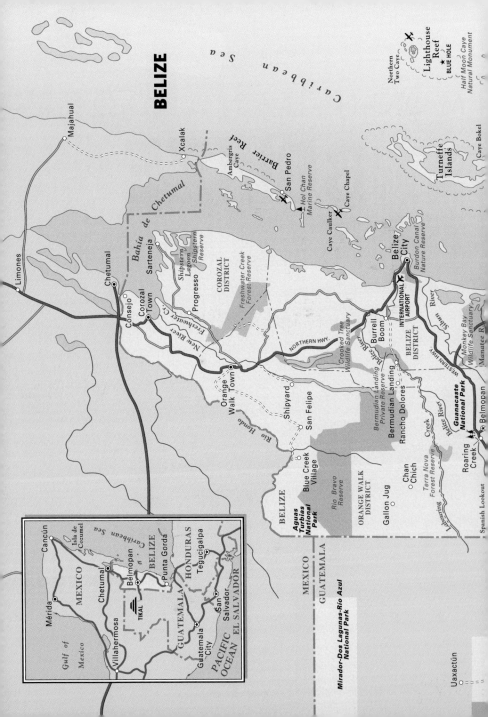

CONTENTS

Discover Belize

Explore Belize

Belize District

The Northern Cayes

Belmopan Area and the Hummingbird Highway

Cayo and the Mountain Pine Ridge

Know Belize

MAPS

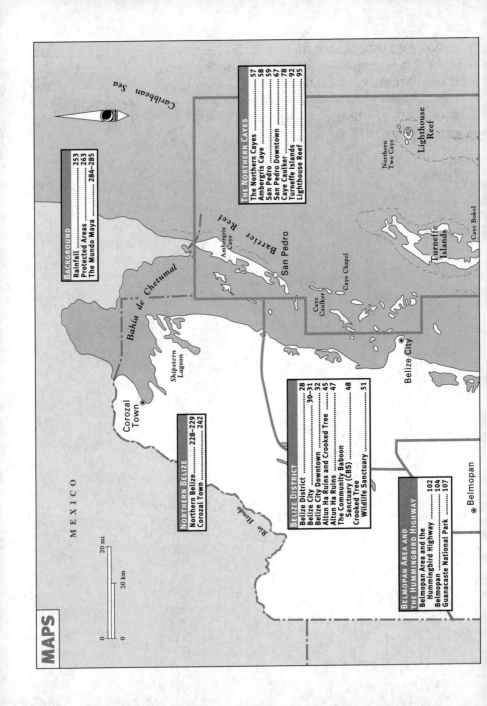

MEXICO

20 mi
20 km

Caribbean Sea

Bahía de Chetumal

Rio Hondo

Corozal Town

Shipstern Lagoon

Barrier Reef

Ambergris Caye

San Pedro

Caye Chapel

Caye Caulker

Belize City

Belmopan

Northern Two Caye

Turneffe Islands

Caye Bokel

Lighthouse Reef

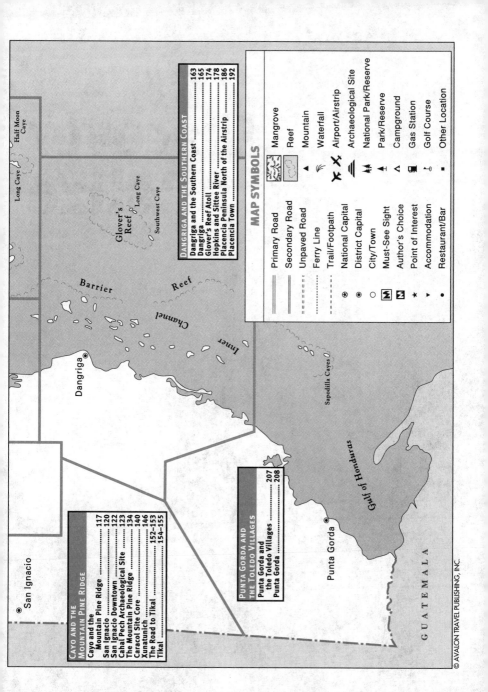

MAP SYMBOLS

═══	Primary Road	〰️	Mangrove
───	Secondary Road	🪸	Reef
═ ═ ═	Unpaved Road	▲	Mountain
· · · · ·	Ferry Line	💧	Waterfall
- - - - -	Trail/Footpath	✈ ✕	Airport/Airstrip
⊛	National Capital	🔺	Archaeological Site
◉	District Capital	🌲	National Park/Reserve
○	City/Town	♠	Park/Reserve
🄼	Must-See Sight	⋀	Campground
🄼	Author's Choice	⛽	Gas Station
★	Point of Interest	⛳	Golf Course
▶	Accommodation	▪	Other Location
●	Restaurant/Bar		

San Ignacio

Half Moon
Cave

Long Cave

Glover's
Reef

Long Cave

Southwest Cave

Barrier

Reef

Inner Channel

Dangriga

Sapodilla Cayes

Punta Gorda

GUATEMALA

Gulf of Honduras

© AVALON TRAVEL PUBLISHING, INC.

Discover
Belize

To understand Belize, one must first appreciate the various identity crises that this up-and-coming corner of the continent has yet to resolve: for example, is this Latin America or the Caribbean? Is the country's future in the direction of the hyper-developed industrial tourism of cruise ships and Cancún, or is it aligned with the more sustainable successes of Costa Rica? Is Belize capable of making big self-governing decisions, or will its fate always be at the mercy of more powerful nations and foreign corporations?

At the same time that Belize's government and tourism industry ask these questions, some 260,000 Belizeans continue to seek a way to place at least six distinct cultures under one national identity. Belize, formerly British Honduras, gained independence only in 1981 and, like many impetuous youngsters in their mid-20s, it continues to learn and grow in the face of all kinds of challenges—from ancient ones like hurricanes and forest fires, to modern ones like the effects of a globalized economy, the illegal drug trade, and AIDS.

Despite having to deal with such typical developing-world struggles, the word is out: Belize is hot. People are coming—from the steady stream of backpackers and divers who have been enjoying this Central American "backwater" for decades, to the rich and famous who first heard the country's name mentioned on trashy "reality" television. Belize is the only country within the Caribbean to experience consistent increases in overall tourist arrivals since 1998—*including* post-9/11, a period that devastated other tourism-dependent areas.

No wonder. Belize's English-speaking, affable people make things easy here; its proximity to the United States and Canada makes it close; and its tiny area (no bigger than Massachusetts or Belgium) is jam-packed with adventure travel opportunities, making it a practical—and exciting—destination.

Belize is ripe and bursting with adventure travel and learning opportunities for all ages and abilities. The hard part is deciding which ones to choose in your limited amount of vacation time. It's helpful to keep in mind the style of travel you like, your physical ability, and whether you will be bringing children. Some folks enjoy getting dirty and being tested to the limits of their physical abilities; others like to stay clean and experience the outdoors in a softer fashion. Some travelers like to trek through miles of muddy jungle in hopes of seeing a tapir or jaguar; others prefer to sight one at the Belize Zoo. While some travelers choose to participate in a jungle research project, others are fascinated by a short visit to some excavated Maya ruins and a guided tour. All of the above are available in Belize and can be arranged through travel agents, guides, hotels, and lodges—or on your own.

Museums are a rarity in Belize (although there are a couple of small, interesting ones in Belize City and elsewhere) and "sightseeing" is much more of an active experience: hiking through Maya archaeological sites, paddling, swimming, diving, snorkeling, horseback riding, caving, and so on. Of course, you can also lay low, spending your vacation reading in a hammock and listening to the surf.

Once you've got an idea of what kind of Belize trip you're looking for, you've got to plan your time. If you only have 7–10 days, be careful not to overextend yourself. Because of Belize's uniquely compact size, many resorts and campgrounds serve well as bases to explore the surrounding sea and mountains in all directions, making moving from hotel to hotel unnecessary. You may consider choosing only one or two regions that suit your needs, then after you've arrived, planning your day trips from there. There are also some great loop trips to be had in Belize, especially for the independent traveler. And if you've got several weeks or more, you'll have no problem spending them all in Belize.

It's not necessary to plan out your activities before arriving in-country, nor is it necessary to have your hotels completely booked before departing home— except during high season in popular areas like San Pedro, Caye Caulker, and Placencia. Plan on everything—especially road travel within Belize—taking more time than you expect. Indeed, Belize starts to seem a lot bigger during those long bus rides, as distances stretch along with the local concept of time. Renting a car speeds things up, but can be prohibitively expensive for some. Flying within the country is a cinch, and Belize's two national airlines can help save many precious hours, with regular service and reasonable rates between the most popular towns and islands.

Most visitors look at a combination of their available vacation time and Caribbean climate trends when planning when to take their trip. Some plan around the bigger events of the year, like Garinagu (Garifuna) Settlement Day in November or the Ruta Maya Challenge Canoe Race in March. High season (meaning an increased number of tourists and hiked prices) is generally mid-December through May, a period many travel agents and guidebooks will tell you is the "dry season" in a vain effort to neatly contain Belize's weather. In many years, this is true, with this time of the year enjoying sunny skies and vegetation still green from the rainy season. Mother Nature, however, enjoys making things a bit more unpredictable, especially in these times of uncertain global climate. November can be dry as a bone and sunny, while December, January, and even February can play host to wet cold fronts that either blow right through or sit around for days.

Your best bet? Be prepared, both with clothing and attitude! A week of stormy weather may ruin a vacation planned solely around snorkeling, but it could also provide the perfect setting for exploring the rainforests or enjoying a hot tub and fireplace in the Mountain Pine Ridge.

June, July, and August technically fall in the rainy season—rain during these months may mean just a quick shower each afternoon, or it may go on for days. Those who travel to Belize during this time are rewarded with significantly discounted prices at most accommodations. August is the big month for European backpackers and travelers, while December and February are dominated by North Americans. Some tourism businesses shut down completely during the months of September and October, the peak of hurricane season.

WHAT TO TAKE

CLOTHING

In general, pack for hot weather (both humid and dry) and the occasional cool front; at least one pair of pants, long sleeves, and a light shell jacket are recommended (rainy season can push all the way into February when it wants to, and June through November are guaranteed to be damp). Cayo and the Mountain Pine Ridge can get down to sweater weather in any part of the wet season. Don't forget a swimsuit—and a sarong or wrap for that stylish saunter to the beach bar.

PAPERWORK

Make a photocopy of the pages in your passport that have your photo and information. When you get the passport stamped in the airport, it's a good idea to make a photocopy of that page as well, and store the copies somewhere other than with your passport. This will facilitate things greatly if your passport ever goes lost or stolen. Also consider taking a small address book, credit cards, travelers checks, your insurance policy, and an international phone card for calling home. Be discreet when using a money belt—the best option is to buy one that looks like a regular belt instead of a money belt.

LUGGAGE

If you plan to hitchhike or use public buses and collective taxis, don't use a large external-frame pack. For rain and theft concerns, it's preferable to have your luggage inside the vehicle with you, and this will be harder to ensure if you bring a monster backpack—instead, strive for something smaller. A bag that fits on your lap is a good parameter. A strong bike cable and lock can secure the pack to a bedpost and a small padlock can shut zippers.

CAMPING GEAR

A few of Belize's campgrounds offer tents and pads for rent, but not all, so if you're looking to do a lot of camping, pack a lightweight tent and other items like a small shovel for burying waste. A light, summer-weight rated sleeping bag should be more than enough, or even just a cotton or silk sleep sack or sheet. Don't forget a water bottle. Finally, if you leave the road with a map, compass, and/or GPS unit, make sure you also have the knowledge to use these tools—or better yet, go with a local guide.

MISCELLANY

Bring a small first aid kit (see the Practicalities chapter for suggestions), a flashlight or headlamp, plenty of plastic bags and zip-locs for protection during rain or boat travel, and a cheap set of ear plugs for the occasional early morning rooster or karaoke concert. Don't worry if you forget reading material—most hotels and lodges have a large selection of abandoned or traded books in English. Consider bringing a couple of photos of home to show Belizean hosts and friends who will invariably be interested in your life "up there."

BELIZE DISTRICT

This swath of coastline, islands, and lowlands is where the country was born, in the area surrounding Belize City, where mahogany poles floated down from upcountry and were loaded onto ships bound for the rest of the world. Today's ocean-side "city" of 60,000 or so is a steamy, 21st-century version of those raucous old days, and it boasts just enough sights and goings-on to make it worth a one- or two-day visit. If you don't appreciate the grit and grime of Belize's one-time capital, the surrounding district offers several remote experiences, all well under an hour from the airport. Shack up at the Community Baboon Sanctuary, Crooked Tree or Monkey Bay Wildlife Reserves, or near the Altun Ha ruins. You can stay in any of these places, or you can book a room in Belize City, make day trips to the above parks, and enjoy the evening Caribbean breeze over your Belize City happy hour by night.

THE NORTHERN CAYES

Pronounced "keez," these dozens of islands consist of everything from the most deserted spit of sand and palms to Ambergris Caye, the original Isla Bonita and home of San Pedro, the most developed and swankiest side of Belize tourism. San Pedro Town and the reef-facing beach resorts that stretch north and south from it are still wonderfully small-scale compared to nearby Mexican and Caribbean destinations, and comprise the most luxurious, expensive, and well-known part of the country. In fact, Ambergris is the only part of Belize that some tourists ever see, spending their entire vacation in San Pedro, so enraptured are they by the chic restaurants, beach bars, shopping, and—oh yeah, world-class diving and snorkeling just minutes offshore. Then there's the more budget-oriented Caye Caulker, just down the reef, with its own rasta-tinted vibe and equally incredible activities. There are also far-off Turneffe Island and Lighthouse Reef Atolls, geographical phenomena that feature spectacular wall diving and Jacques Cousteau's old favorite, the Blue Hole; these atolls are accessed by day trips from Belize City, Ambergris, or Caulker, or from a handful of upscale, on-site lodges.

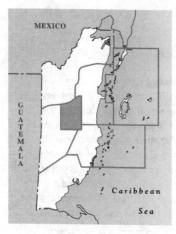

BELMOPAN AREA AND THE HUMMINGBIRD HIGHWAY

Belize's relatively new capital, Belmopan, is nothing more than an annoying bus layover for most travelers. The surrounding countryside, however—and the beautiful Hummingbird Highway that snakes through it—is not to be missed, whether as stunning scenery from your bus window, or as a memorable morning backdrop when you emerge from your cabin or tent on a bluff above the Caves Branch River. Some of the country's most famous adventure lodges (Ian Anderson's Caves Branch, Jaguar Paw, and Banana Bank) occupy various riverbanks in the area, as does Belize's only mainland golf course on Roaring Creek. The area's accommodations are destinations in themselves, and are also used as bases for forays into the west and south. There are homestay programs in some of the villages along the Hummingbird, as well as trails and guides to take you around Guanacaste, Blue Hole, and Five Blues Lake National Parks.

CAYO AND THE MOUNTAIN PINE RIDGE

Go west, young traveler! Belize's interior is vast and wild, serviced by only a couple of roads and a growing number of unique lodges and camps. The area, which borders Guatemala's mighty Petén Wilderness, can be toured on hiking trails, lazy rivers, horseback, and single track. Clean mountain water awaits you in dozens of caves, waterfalls, swimming holes, and maybe even a hot tub. This is not an area to blow through in just a day or two—not if you'd like to experience its many highlights: ruins, caves, rivers, and waterfalls aplenty. Save a day each for the Xunantunich and Caracol Archaeological Sites, and another 2–3 days to pop over to Guatemala's Tikal. Smaller archaeological sites abound, as do unique ways of getting there—ask your lodge about guided horseback and mountain bike expeditions. You can also paddle up the Macal River from the mellow town of San Ignacio to the Belize Botanical Gardens, then float back down in time for dinner. Cayo is home to one of the world's largest cave systems, as well as the refreshing heights of the Mountain Pine Ridge.

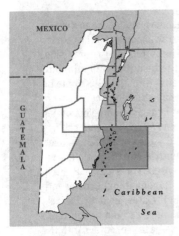

DANGRIGA AND THE SOUTHERN COAST

The cultural center of Belize's Garinagu (or Garifuna) population, the town of Dangriga makes an unassuming base for exploring the surrounding islands and a handful of national parks in the nearby Maya Mountains. There's not much to see in Dangriga Town except a typically multi-ethnic array of Belizeans going about their daily lives and occasionally dancing the night away. Still, many travelers are glad they chose to spend a night in 'Griga on their way to or from Tobacco Caye, Southwater Caye, or Glover's Reef. Many also bump down the coast to lazy Hopkins and Sittee River, farther south to one of the many accommodations along the Placencia Peninsula, or stay in a tent in the Cockscomb Basin Wildlife Sanctuary. This is Stann Creek District, and you can easily spend a week or more here, especially if you make it out to the cayes, where there are plenty of opportunities for kayaking, fishing, diving, snorkeling, and sailing.

PUNTA GORDA AND THE TOLEDO VILLAGES

They used to call this the "forgotten corner" of Belize and, to some extent, it still is. The Southern Highway is paved now—mostly— and boat access to and from Guatemala from the tiny, relaxed port town of Punta Gorda (PG) makes Toledo District a natural stopover for a growing number of backpackers. Still, PG is a long bus ride from Belize City, and the long-awaited investment boom remains just around the corner. Toledo's offshore cayes, upland villages, caves, rivers, and waterfalls are tucked away, and you'll need at least a few days to see them (plus a day of travel on either end if you need to get back to Belize City), especially if you elect to participate in one of the renowned guesthouse or homestay programs. Planned and coordinated from offices in PG, the Toledo Ecotourism Association and Dem Dat's Doin' programs will send you up into the hills to learn a few phrases of Q'eqchi' Maya and how to make a corn tortilla.

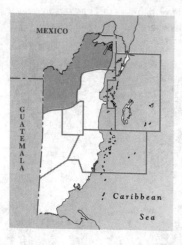

NORTHERN BELIZE

Seldom a main focus of most travelers' attention, Orange Walk and Corozal Districts are, more often than not, just driven through—unless, of course, you've heard about Chan Chich or Lamanai Outpost Lodges, both consisting of gorgeous upscale accommodations amid fascinating archaeological sites set deep in the wildlife-choked bush. These areas are must-stops for any serious bird-watcher. You may also have heard about the sleepy streets of Corozal, a gentle Caribbean town, just across the bay from the lights of Chetumal, Mexico, and a possible launching pad to Ambergris Caye.

The 21-Day Best of Belize

If you have the means for a three-week trip to Belize, you will not be let down. In fact, you'll be surprised that the deeper you go in this relatively small country, the deeper there is to go. Following is an extremely active and mobile tour of Belize; you can easily double or triple the time allotted to each of the destinations listed below and still stay busy. Feel free to follow this itinerary in any order and, when you tire of traveling, stop anywhere along the suggested trail and soak it in.

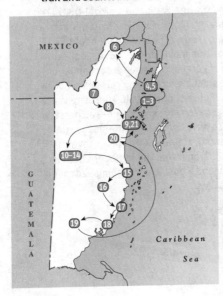

Caye Caulker

DAY 1

Arrive at Philip Goldson International Airport and transfer to the Water Taxi Terminal in Belize City; take a 40-minute boat ride straight to Caye Caulker to ease into things.

DAY 2

Wake up late and spend the day strolling the sandy streets and selecting a dive or snorkel shop. Be sure to reserve a front-row Lazy Lizard barstool for the sunset scene at The Split, followed by a beachfront lobster dinner.

DAY 3

Rise with the sun for an early morning guided nature hike, then dive or snorkel off the reef during the afternoon.

DAY 4

Take a morning boat to San Pedro to kick things up a notch. Check in, scope the scene, and pop over to Hol Chan Marine Reserve for the famous snorkel tour and to rub flippers with nurse sharks and rays.

Altun Ha

DAY 5
Spend the day diving or snorkeling—or shopping and soaking in one of several spas. End it with a beach barbecue surrounded by an intriguing array of expat characters.

DAY 6
Hop a boat (or plane) back to the mainland at Corozal, where you'll appreciate the lack of crowds and easy access to the Maya museums in Chetumal, Mexico, which can be explored in a day.

DAY 7
From Corozal, head south and west to the Lamanai Outpost Lodge for a day of serious bird-watching and exploring.

DAY 8
Relax at the ruins for a day, or day-trip over to Altun Ha or Crooked Tree for more birds and maybe a hot mud treatment at Maruba Jungle Resort and Spa.

DAY 9
Transfer to Belize City and walk the old streets and canals, soaking up modern Belizean culture and a few heaping plates of typical food.

DAY 10
Go for one more morning stroll, then board an express bus for Cayo District. Find a budget hotel in San Ignacio, drop off your bags, then head out for a tour of the Iguana Exhibit, followed by an excellent vegetarian dinner.

DAY 11
Book a guided canoe trip up the Macal. Depending on the water level, you may make it up to the famous Chaa Creek and duPlooy's Lodges, both with a number of attractions, including a nature center, butterfly farm, and botanical garden. Float back downstream for another relaxed San Ignacio evening—enjoy those well-worked shoulders.

DAY 12
Go for a lazy float trip on the Mopan River, then

Xunantunich

spend the night outside of San Ignacio, at the Trek Stop in San José de Succotz or one of the funky riverside budget lodges in Bullet Tree.

DAY 13

Hit the Xunantunich or El Pilar archaeological sites, either by foot, montain bike, or horseback. When you get back, ask your host to set up a trip to Caracol for the next day.

DAY 14

Enjoy the ride along the Mountain Pine Ridge to Caracol, then the swimming hole tour on the way back. Stop for a wood-stove pizza at Coppola's Blancaneaux Lodge, or a photo op at Thousand Foot Falls, one of the highest in Central America.

DAY 15

Transfer to Dangriga, but spend the day stopping,

bird-watching, and sightseeing along the Hummingbird Highway. Check into a simple hotel or the Pelican Beach Resort, right on the water.

DAY 16

Arrange a ride to the Cockscomb Basin Wildlife Sanctuary and spend the night in a cabin, guest-house, or tent. Go for a guided afternoon hike with a Maya guide who grew up in this forest—or better yet, go at night.

DAY 17

Continue south to Placencia Village, where you'll find more fun in the sun, beach bars, and maybe a massage before a big fish dinner.

DAY 18

Take a day trip to Monkey River and back, or else take a boat to Mango Creek, then catch a bus south to Punta Gorda. Spend the night, but arrange for a trip to a Maya village the following day, if transportation allows.

DAY 19

Spend a night upcountry, experiencing cultural immersion, waterfall hikes, and maybe some more ruins at Lubaantun or Nim Li Punit. Accommodation options range from dirt-floor homestays to upscale jungle lodges.

DAY 20

Start the trip back north. Consider a night at Monkey Bay Wildlife Sanctuary, where you can wind down and still get in one last hike (or a trip to the nearby zoo) before your return home.

DAY 21

Transfer to Philip Goldson International Airport for your departure flight.

Belize is one of the undisputed adventure travel capitals of the world, and although you are free to hole up in any of Belize's resorts and lose yourself in a stack of novels, you'll no doubt begin to feel left out as you watch your fellow guests return each day from all kinds of exciting excursions.

Most travelers come to Belize with at least a few activities they'd like to learn or practice. For many, diving is the focus. Here's a quick overview of a few of the more popular water activities you'll find available in Belize.

DIVING

Belize was a Western Hemisphere diving mecca decades before it became the romantic and trendy destination it is today. Hundreds of miles of reefs, atolls, caves, coral patches, and rugged coastline harbor the unknown, as do shipwrecks with hundreds of years of secrets. Swimming among the curious and brazen fish puts you literally into another world—theirs. This is raw excitement and, combined with the sensation of zero gravity, there's really nothing like it. Dive shops exist everywhere there is access to the reef and cayes in Belize—this means San Pedro and Caye Caulker, Belize City, Sittee River, Placencia, and more shops and dive resorts scattered throughout the islands and atolls.

Belizean dive stories include swimming with dolphin, swarms of horse-eye jacks or massive tarpon, and dozens of eagle rays at one time. Some divers go strictly to photograph the eerie underwater beauty and color, or to get that elusive whale shark photo in March or April, when they come to these waters to breed during the full moon. Speaking of breeding, others enjoy the January full moon when hundreds of groupers gather at their primeval mating grounds on the reef; some tell of so many groupers gathering that the reef face is covered with these thick-lipped fish, releasing sperm and eggs in such a fury and quantity that you cannot see two feet in front of you.

INTRODUCTORY DIVE COURSES

You're in Belize on vacation and want to dive—but you don't want to spend four precious days getting certified. What can you do? How about a "resort course"—a one-day introduction to using scuba to enter the underwater world. Also called "discovery" courses, they usually include one tank of air and cost around US$75.

OTHER CERTIFICATION COURSES

The full menu of PADI- and NAUI-accredited courses are offered at most dive shops. You'll have no trouble finding a shop; in fact, you may have quite the time choosing between so many options. Throughout this book, we've tried to identify dive shops with the best reputation for safety practices and quality of instruction and gear. In most cases, prices are more or less uniform between shops, but it pays to do a bit of shopping around. Expect to pay US$60–75 for a two-tank fun dive and US$250–300 for certification courses (Open Water and Advanced).

LIVE-ABOARD DIVE BOATS

Several excellent live-aboard vessels based in Belize City are designed for scuba divers, but can also accommodate an avid diver's companion if he or she is a sea lover or a casual angler. Nondivers pay less. Your luxury hotel and chef travel with you to some of the most scenic and best diving spots in the tropical world. Fees are usually all-inclusive. Here are a few options: *Belize Aggressor III* (120'), US tel. 985/385-2628 or 800/348-2628, fax 985/384-0817, belize@aggressor.com, www.aggressor.com; *Offshore Express* (50'), tel. 501/226-2817, forman@btl.net; and *Sun Dancer II* (138'), Peter Hughes Diving, US tel. 305/669-9391 or 800/932-6237, dancer@peterhughes.com, www.peterhughes.com.

boating

© JOSHUA BERMAN

BOATING

Whitewater, lagoons, open ocean, surf, lazy rivers, underground water systems—Belize's paddling terrain is as varied as every other part of the country's amazing geography, and there is an enormous fleet of canoes, open and closed kayaks, and other small craft with which to float it all. A spectacular array of flora and fauna can be seen along the riverbanks, and night paddles reveal just as much wildlife activity. Stunning sea kayaking trips (day trips and overnight island-hopping) are available on Glover's Reef, Placencia, and from other coastal towns as well.

canoeing

© JOSHUA BERMAN

Experienced sailors and yachties find abundant anchorages among the cayes and coastal villages of Belize. The Belize Barrier Reef provides calm inshore waters, with none of the crashing surf or large swells of the open ocean. Sailing charters are available up and down Belize's coast—with or without a captain. Boat owners take note: Vessels traveling to the area must have permission from the Belize Embassy in Washington, D.C.

FISHING

Fly-fishing the flats of Belize has become one of the biggest fishing attractions in the Caribbean; wet that hook in search of tarpon, bonefish, permit, and barracuda. In the mangroves, anglers are likely to snag a snook, tarpon, mangrove snapper, or mutton snapper. Outside the reef, it's deep-sea fishing for red snapper and the big trophies such as marlin, sailfish, giant grouper, and tuna.

San Pedro, Caye Caulker, and Placencia are home to fabled Belizean fishing guides who have been featured in international angling magazines and on ESPN. Most resorts offer fishing trips, and a few specialize in fishing packages.

THE SURF-N-TURF VACATION

This is the classic Belizean combo, often pre-booked in a pair of upland–lowland sister resorts and offering all kinds of "best-of-both-worlds" activity packages for both short and lengthy stays. Those who don't enjoy the whirlwind-tour style of travel, staying in a new hotel every day, will appreciate only having to make one move: between the hills and the ocean breeze. Beach-and-reef-oriented lodges are found on Ambergris, Caulker, the Atolls, near Dangriga, and up and down the Placencia Peninsula. Soak up the salt for four or five days, then move west, where your daily adventures will be shaded by a ceiling of lush, bird-filled canopy instead of the shiny surface of the Caribbean to which you've become so accustomed on your scuba outings. A large number of interior jungle resorts and adventure camps are available in Toledo, Cayo, and Orange Walk Districts, depending on your budget and preferred activities. Always ask about surf-n-turf packages, which sometimes include some kind of discount.

Depending on your desires, you can make either surf or turf the more active part of your vacation, then relax during the other half. For instance, if you begin in the mountains, going out on vigorous paddling and walking tours every day, you can choose to treat the latter, beach half of your trip as a kind of "reward," relaxing sore muscles, working on your tan, and swapping war stories with fellow guests. Or vice versa: dive, snorkel, and dive some more for four or five days, then head upcountry to watch birds from your balcony all day and ponder the remarkable similarities between reef and rainforest.

The 10-Day Bird-Watching Tour

Bird-watching is spectacular throughout Belize, drawing novice and experienced bird-watchers from all over the world. Many Belizean guides possess a truly amazing wealth of knowledge to supplement the bird-spotting skills they learned growing up in these hills. Most lodges offer casual bird-watching in their backyards, and some areas really cater to the pro bird-watcher. Bird-watchers with a serious agenda often sign up with bird-watching-based tour operators who handle the logistics of a country-wide tour so you can keep your eyes glued to those binocs (check with individual resorts in the areas listed below, or look into specific operators like www.birdinginbelize.com).

Bring binoculars and wear boots, lightweight long-sleeved shirts, and trousers if you plan to go bird-watching in jungle areas. Don't forget your bird guide, although several good ones can be purchased in Belize, as can local and national bird lists.

The Belize Audubon Society (BAS) is active in managing many of Belize's reserves, and has a number of bird lists and field guides available in the central office in Belize City, as well as at the various visitors centers they operate throughout the country. Hidden Valley Inn, whose 7,200 acres encompass several bird habitats, maintains a downloadable and updated bird list on their website, www.hiddenvalleyinn.com. Of course, seeing the most number of birds means visiting the most number of habitats—from marsh to forest to riverine to jungle.

DAY 1

Arrive at Philip Goldson International Airport and transfer to one of three accommodations in Crooked Tree Village, a quick drive north.

DAY 2

Spend the day on a guided boat tour of the wetlands (much of which dry up in April and May), with a spectacular variety of water fowl and migratory birds.

DAY 3

Transfer to the Lamanai Archaeological Zone and on-site lodge in Orange Walk District, considered a cornerstone of any Belizean bird-watching tour.

toucan

juvenile blue heron

DAY 4

Plan on early morning guided hikes, exploration of the nearby ruins, and some wonderful meals as your checklist grows longer by the day. Spend another night and get ready for the trip west tomorrow.

DAYS 5 AND 6

Make your way up to the Mountain Pine Ridge—a rented 4WD will come in handy here. Any of the fine resorts along these highlands offer hundreds of bird species, but only the grounds of the Hidden Valley Inn are home to the rare orange breasted falcon, king vulture, and stygie owl. Spend at least two days hiking or biking the many miles of trails and private swimming holes. Pook's Hill is another of the many area lodges specializing in bird tours.

DAY 7

Head down to the Southern Coast: Spend the entire day park-hopping down the length of the Hummingbird Highway, ending up at Sittee River, where a private cabin and a night paddle up Boom Creek await.

DAY 8

Tour the Cockscomb Basin Wildlife Sanctuary, where you'll undoubtedly see more birds than cats.

DAY 9

Celebrate the week with a final two nights on the beach—treat yourself to a bungalow on the Placencia Peninsula and be content with pelicans and frigates, seen from your hammock.

DAY 10

Fly or drive back to Philip Goldson International Airport for your flight home, triumphant and tanned.

Even with Belize's increased name recognition around the world, it still doesn't take much to drop off the beaten path, and for those whose preferred "scene" is no scene at all, here are some ideas. The two-week adventure suggested below is an entirely mainland one. To add some Caribbean time to your trip, consider inserting several days on Caye Caulker, followed by Raggamuffin Tours' three-day sailing trip to Placencia; this unique tour includes fishing, snorkeling, and camping on tiny islands before they drop you off at the tip of the peninsula. From Placencia, you can visit Laughing Bird Caye National Park, spend a night in Monkey River Village, or hop a boat bound for Puerto Cortés, Honduras. Many figure out a way to get to Glover's Reef Atoll, an unparalleled Caribbean experience. Another alternative is to make it to Punta Gorda, as listed below, then instead of the village homestay, find a way out to the Sapodilla Cayes or Livingston, Guatemala for a few nights.

Of course, the most important items you'll want to pack for any of these trips are an open mind, extra patience, and the ability to scrap the entire plan when you feel the adventure pulling you in its own direction.

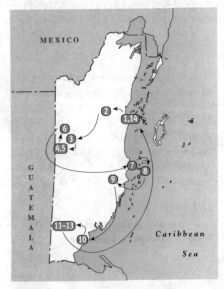

DAY 2

Catch a bus to the Community Baboon Sanctuary at Bermuda Landing, where you are guaranteed howler monkey sightings and can stay in a tent or cabin or with a local family.

DAY 3

After a morning hike, take a bus out to the Western Highway and catch another ride up to San Ignacio in Cayo District. Continue through town and stay at one of the budget places toward the Guatemala border, like the Trek Stop or Clarissa Falls. If staying at the Trek Stop, you should have time for a round of disk golf and a tour of the Tropical Wings Butterfly Farm before bedtime.

DAY 4

Spend the morning at the Xunantunich archaeological site, climbing pyramids and convening with the spirits. In the afternoon, arrange a pickup in Benque Viejo to take you to one of the funky places down the Hydro Road: Maartz Farms or Chechem Ha.

DAY 1

After arriving at Philip Goldson International Airport, transfer to Belize City and enjoy your first heaping plate of rice, beans, and stew chicken while reggae blasts all around you.

You're guaranteed a monkey sighting at the Community Baboon Sanctuary.

DAY 5

Spend the day hiking, horseback riding, caving, and spouting poetry inspired by the awesome views of the upper Macal River Gorge. Spend a second night in your tent, cabin, or waterfall-enhanced tree house.

DAY 6

Get a ride back to Benque, then travel to Bullet Tree via canoe or kayak—plan on five hours of easy paddling and mellow riffles down the Mopan River; when you arrive, take out and have a cabin and meal waiting for you at Cohune Palms or Parrots Nest Lodges.

DAY 7

Roll into town and take a morning to enjoy the San Ignacio vibe, maybe the Cahal Pech ruins, then bus it toward Dangriga, getting off in the village of St. Margaret's for a homestay and some hearty hiking in Five Blues Lake National Park.

DAY 8

Make your way to Hopkins for a few beers and a Garinagu drumming workshop. You'll likely have to spend a few hours in Dangriga on the way, so feel free to get sidetracked out to Tobacco Caye for a night or two.

DAY 9

Get back to the Southern Highway and check into low-key Mama Noots Jungle Resort, the best base for exploring Mayflower, Belize's newest national park.

DAY 10

Continue south to Punta Gorda (PG) and check into a seaside room. Arrange a homestay in the hills for the following days (ask for the remotest village they have), then dine on a gourmet soybean feast at Gomier's.

DAYS 11, 12, AND 13

Go deep into the Toledo bush, living among the Maya or Garinagu. Hire guides, listen to stories, music, and the river. On the last day, transfer back to PG.

DAY 14

Fly back north to Philip Goldson International Airport and begin writing your memoirs as your return flight takes off.

There's a giddy, childlike feeling one gets while climbing 1,000-year-old stone structures in the middle of the God-blessed jungle—a fairytale, Tolkienesque mood of mystery as you scramble over winding, crooked staircases and tunnels while strange creatures hoot and holler from the surrounding forest canopy. Belize offers dozens of such sites to explore, some fully excavated and restored, others still hidden under a carpet of dense vegetation.

Archaeologists estimate that at one time, between one and two million Maya lived in the area that is now called Belize—a fantastically huge number when compared to the relatively tiny population of today. More domestic, ceremonial, and agricultural sites are discovered each year, and it's quite common for Belizean families to have ruins in their backyards without official archaeological knowledge. These are often small oratorio-style buildings or caves with artifacts that date back hundreds of years. As money becomes available, whether from the government or outside universities, more discoveries are made and it becomes apparent that Belize is a veritable treasure chest of Maya culture.

You'll find that nearly every destination in Belize offers at least one day trip to a Maya archaeological site, and that may be enough for you. If you're on San Pedro or Caye Caulker, this means making a boat-bus commute to and from a site like Altun Ha or Lamanai—by nightfall, you'll be back in your beach chair. If you'd rather get closer and wake up to a Maya dawn, consider a stay in Chan Chich, Lamanai, or Pook's Hill, all accommodations built among the ruins themselves. You'll have easy access to archaeological sites from any other lodge on the mainland, many specializing in trips to the ruins closest to them.

The most spectacular and exciting sites include Caracol, Xunantunich, and Lamanai, where impressive excavations have been done in recent years, making these ceremonial centers more accessible to tourists. Most sites now boast visitors centers that act as both mini-museums and interpretive centers. Although many sites are quite accessible (especially Altun Ha, where the parking lot is on even ground with the main plaza), many more require at least some level of physical activity to reach, and can be explored by foot, horseback, canoe, or mountain bike.

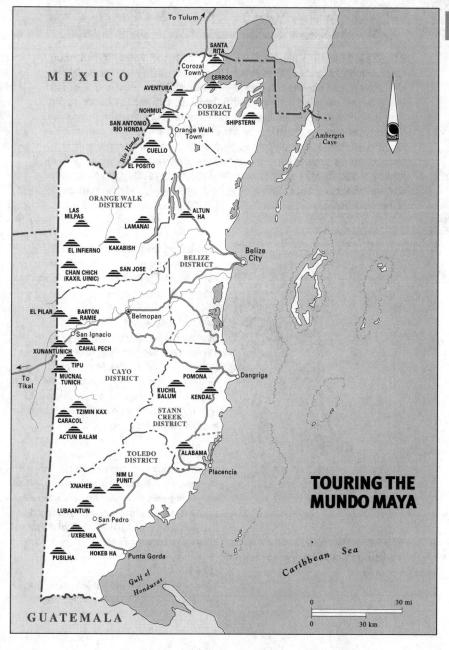

To Tulum

SANTA RITA

MEXICO

Corozal Town

CERROS

AVENTURA

COROZAL DISTRICT

NOHMUL

SHIPSTERN

SAN ANTONIO RÍO HONDA

Orange Walk Town

Ambergris Caye

CUELLO

EL POSITO

ORANGE WALK DISTRICT

ALTUN HA

LAS MILPAS

LAMANAI

EL INFIERNO

KAKABISH

Belize City

BELIZE DISTRICT

CHAN CHICH (KAXIL UINIC)

SAN JOSE

EL PILAR

BARTON RAMIE

Belmopan

San Ignacio

XUNANTUNICH

CAHAL PECH

TIPU

To Tikal

MUCNAL TUNICH

CAYO DISTRICT

POMONA

Dangriga

KUCHIL BALUM

KENDAL

TZIMIN KAX

CARACOL

STANN CREEK DISTRICT

ACTUN BALAM

TOLEDO DISTRICT

ALABAMA

Placencia

NIM LI PUNIT

XNAHEB

LUBAANTUN

San Pedro

UXBENKA

PUSILHA

HOKEB HA

Punta Gorda

Caribbean Sea

Gulf of Honduras

TOURING THE MUNDO MAYA

GUATEMALA

0   30 mi

0   30 km

Pack the kid-friendly sunscreen and load up the brood. Family-friendly tours, accommodations, and activities abound throughout Belize and at all budget levels—long-haired parents still truck their flower children down from California in VW buses, camping through Belize, while executive baby boomers conduct their own tours, spending a bit more but often visiting the same sites. Some areas and resorts in Belize are tailored specifically for romantic escapes or adult-level expeditions, so always ask your tour operator and/or accommodations provider specific questions concerning how welcome little Johnny and Susie will be. Try typing "family" into any search you do of Belize and see what comes up; many lodges cater specifically to families on all different budgets.

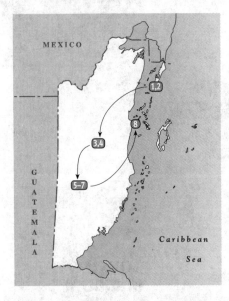

DAY 2

Hang out on the island, book a family-friendly snorkeling or manatee-watching tour, maybe even a sunset cruise to top it off (make sure it won't be a drunkfest though).

DAYS 3 AND 4

Head back to the mainland (by boat or plane), rent a vehicle, and make your way to one of the lodges in the Central Belize area. Stop at the Belize Zoo on the way, then check into your desired jungle hut. The lodges near Belmopan have great activities for kids, including cave tubing, horseback riding, and canoe trips.

DAYS 5, 6, AND 7

Transfer to another lodge in the Cayo District. Many have special family-oriented itineraries that include butterfly tours, boating, and easy caving trips. Maya ruins will make parents feel child-like too, with the mystery in the air and all the scrambling up and down pyramids.

DAY 1

Arrive Philip Goldson International Airport. Board a puddle-jumper to San Pedro, a good place to ease into paradise.

DAY 8

Transfer back to the airport; if you missed the zoo on the way up, save an hour to fit it in here.

Explore
Belize

Belize District

Here on the banks of Haulover Creek, the country was founded, its hopes kindled, its successes forged, and many of its problems born as well. In addition to boasting a rich pot of ethnic diversity, Belize District also encompasses a variety of habitats, including mangroves, pine savannah, marshes, broadleaf forest, and a couple hundred Caribbean cayes. It juxtaposes Maya ruins with the modern commotion of Belize City. Belize District is the most populated in the country, comprising nearly a quarter of all Belizeans.

You'll almost certainly pass through this district, whether you're exploring some of the region's unique reserves, plunging into Belize City itself, or just traveling between the cayes and the inland.

PLANNING YOUR TIME

A self-guided, daytime walking tour of Belize City is a must for anyone wishing to get a complete understanding of the country—even if you only have a few hours between bus and boat connections. Think about spending a night or two, though. You can see everything you need to in one rushed day or two relaxed ones. Although Belize City certainly doesn't have the restaurant scene of some of the more tourished parts of the

Must-Sees

© JOSHUA BERMAN

Altun Ha

M Fort George Area: When you first arrive in Belize City, take a stroll through this pleasant neighborhood with its beautiful colonial homes and up-scale hotels. Start out at the lighthouse along the waterfront to enjoy the sea breezes and views of cayes and ships (page 34).

M Art Galleries: Check out Belize's exciting art scene, starting at The Image Factory Shop and Gallery. In addition to browsing, you can learn about concerts and cultural events in the city. Also visit the Fine Arts Gallery, right on Front Street, then skip to the Southside and walk by the Bliss Institute and Government House/House of Culture just down the seawall (page 35).

M Gales Point: The path less traveled lies to the south, along the Manatee Road to the Southern Lagoon, a vast, wild estuary, and to this peaceful fishing village on the ocean (page 44).

M Altun Ha Ruins: Head north to this ancient Maya trading center, the most extensively excavated ruins in all of Belize. You might even combine this trip with a visit to the **Maruba Resort Jungle Spa** (page 45).

M The Community Baboon Sanctuary: A visit guarantees monkey sightings—the area is thick with black howlers who wander just outside a num-

ber of simple Creole villages. This community-managed eco-tourism venture offers an excellent menu of wildlife hikes and canoe trips (page 48).

M Crooked Tree Wildlife Sanctuary: Drive an hour north to this habitat for hundreds of resident and migratory birds for a full day of bird-watching on a boat tour (page 51).

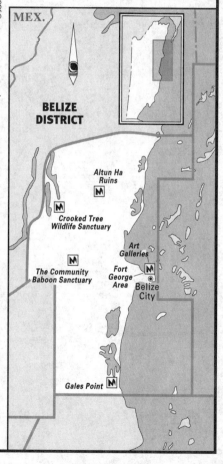

MEX.

BELIZE DISTRICT

Altun Ha Ruins M

Crooked Tree Wildlife Sanctuary M

The Community Baboon Sanctuary M

Art Galleries M

Fort George Area M

Belize City

Gales Point M

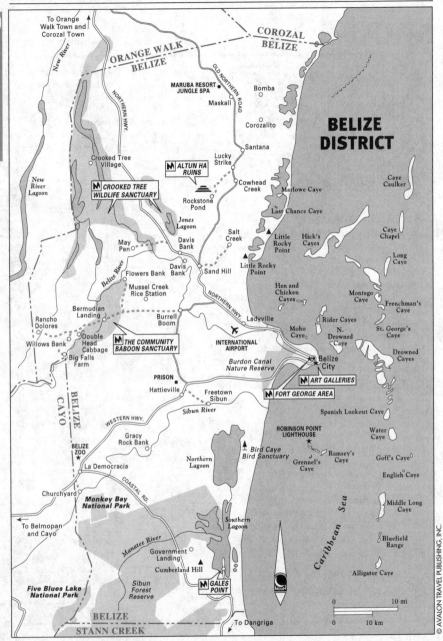

To Orange Walk Town and Corozal Town

ORANGE WALK BELIZE

COROZAL BELIZE

New River

NORTHERN HWY.

OLD NORTHERN ROAD

MARUBA RESORT JUNGLE SPA

Maskall

Bomba

Corozalito

Santana

New River Lagoon

Crooked Tree Village

M *ALTUN HA RUINS*

Lucky Strike

Cowhead Creek

BELIZE DISTRICT

Marlowe Caye

Caye Caulker

M *CROOKED TREE WILDLIFE SANCTUARY*

Rockstone Pond

Last Chance Caye

Jones Lagoon

Salt Creek

Little Rocky Point

Hick's Cayes

Caye Chapel

May Pen

Davis Bank

Belize River

Davis Bank

Sand Hill

Little Rocky Point

Long Caye

Flowers Bank

Mussel Creek Rice Station

NORTHERN HWY.

Hen and Chicken Cayes

Montego Caye

Frenchman's Caye

Rancho Dolores

Bermudian Landing

Burrell Boom

Ladyville

Moho Caye

Rider Cayes

N. Drowned Caye

St. George's Caye

Willows Bank

Double Head Cabbage

M *THE COMMUNITY BABOON SANCTUARY*

INTERNATIONAL AIRPORT

Drowned Cayes

Big Falls Farm

Burdon Canal Nature Reserve

Belize City

CAYO

PRISON

Hattieville

Freetown Sibun

M *ART GALLERIES*

M *FORT GEORGE AREA*

WESTERN HWY.

Sibun River

Spanish Lookout Caye

Gracy Rock Bank

BELIZE ZOO ★

La Democracia

COASTAL RD.

Northern Lagoon

ROBINSON POINT LIGHTHOUSE

Water Caye

Bird Caye Bird Sanctuary

Ramsey's Caye

Goff's Caye

Churchyard

Monkey Bay National Park

Grennel's Caye

English Caye

To Belmopan and Cayo

Southern Lagoon

Middle Long Caye

Manatee River

Government Landing

Bluefield Range

Five Blues Lake National Park

Cumberland Hill

Sibun Forest Reserve

M *GALES POINT*

Caribbean Sea

Alligator Caye

BELIZE

STANN CREEK

To Dangriga

MOON

0   10 mi

0   10 km

country, there are a handful of excellent restaurants and a plethora of cheap, local eateries to keep you happy. If you find the tropical bustle of the streets and the daily swinging of the bridge intriguing, stay a couple of extra days. There are easily accessible dive, snorkel, bird-watching, and ruins trips from the city and a number of interesting accommodations.

Belize City

Okay, so "city" might be stretching it, but there is no doubt that the biggest concentration of Belizeans in the world is here (about 55,000). In fact, Belizeans the country over usually refer to the former capital simply as "Belize," which can be a bit disorienting until you get used to it. And while it's true that there are no high-rises, only three traffic lights, and more faded paint and rotten wood than you'd expect to see in the country's most important population center, it's also true that Belize City is a bustling and exciting cluster of cultures that alternately throbs and stews under the tropical sun, wind, and rain.

The town straddles Haulover Creek (named when cattle were attached to each other by a rope wrapped around their horns and "hauled" across the river), soaking in the breezes off the Caribbean Ocean (or, occasionally, the stink from the street gutters). Visitors should know that Belize City is no Caribbean "paradise," as it may or may not be presented in cruise ship brochures. The city appears at first glance to be old and run-down, and, though it's perched on the edge of the gorgeous Caribbean, it is without beaches. Antiquated clapboard buildings on stilts—unpainted, weathered, tilted, and streaked with age—line the narrow streets, but are slowly being replaced by concrete structures. If Captain Lafitte, the pirate of old, came swaggering down the street today, he'd fit right into some of these neighborhoods. The banks of the Belize River and Haulover Creek, meandering through the middle of the city, are often dirty and smelly.

The people, for the most part, are friendly, and their future more hopeful than that of the residents of many other cities in Central America. Schools are everywhere, shops are popping up, and some of the simplest bars are gathering places for truly interesting people. There's also an electricity in the air, buzzing with growth, dreams, plans—history in the making.

Hub of the Nation

Belize City has direct access to rivers, ocean, and three of the five major roads in the country. The city is ideally located for reaching any part of Belize within a couple hours' time. Because of this access, Belize City is also where you'll find the headquarters of the bus lines, rental car agencies, and airlines, as well as water taxis to get to the cayes.

ORIENTATION

Arriving from the islands, you'll find yourself on Front Street, near the Swing Bridge. Arriving by most buses will put you at the main Novelo's Bus Terminal, about a 10-block walk from the Swing Bridge (from Novelo's, cross the canal and stay on King Street till you reach Albert Street, then make a left; continue for three blocks to the Swing Bridge). This is a walk that should not be attempted at night, but is usually safe during the day. Remember, when in doubt, take a cab.

SIGHTS

An early morning stroll through the weathered, clapboard buildings of Belize City gives you a genuine feeling of the city. This is when people are rushing off to work, kids are all spiffed up on their way to school, and housewives are out and about doing their daily shopping. The streets are crammed with small shops (many operated by East Indian and Chinese merchants), a stream of pedestrians on the occasional sidewalks, and lots of traffic.

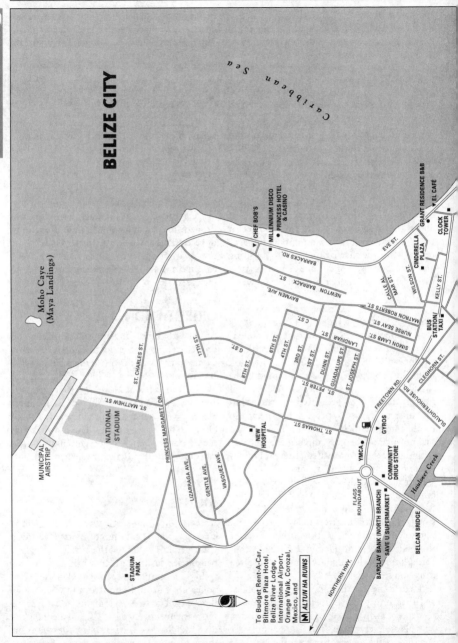

BELIZE CITY

Caribbean Sea

Moho Caye
(Maya Landings)

MUNICIPAL
AIRSTRIP

NATIONAL
STADIUM

ST. MATTHEW ST.

ST. CHARLES ST.

17TH ST.

G ST.

8TH ST.

4TH ST.

C ST.

BAYMEN AVE.

NEWTON BARRACK ST.

BARRACKS RD.

EVE ST.

CALLE AL
MAR ST.

WILSON ST.

CINDERELLA
PLAZA

KELLY ST.

CLOCK
TOWER

GRANT RESIDENCE B&B

EL CAFÉ

CHEF BOB'S

MILLENNIUM DISCO

PRINCESS HOTEL
& CASINO

PRINCESS MARGARET DR.

LIZARRAGA AVE.

GENTLE AVE.

VASQUEZ AVE.

NEW
HOSPITAL

ST. THOMAS ST.

ST. PETER ST.

ST. JOSEPH ST.

GUADALUPE ST.

DUNN ST.

1ST ST.

3RD ST.

LANDIVAR ST.

SIMON LAMB ST.

NURSE SEAY ST.

MATRON ROBERTS ST.

FREETOWN RD.

BUS
STATION/
TAXI

CLEGHORN ST.

SLAUGHTERHOUSE RD.

YMCA

GYROS

COMMUNITY
DRUG STORE

FLAGS
ROUNDABOUT

BARCLAY BANK (NORTH BRANCH)

SAVE U SUPERMARKET

BELCAN BRIDGE

Haulover Creek

NORTHERN HWY.

STADIUM
PARK

To Budget Rent-A-Car,
Biltmore Plaza Hotel,
Belize River Lodge,
International Airport,
Orange Walk, Corozal,
Mexico, and

ALTUN HA RUINS

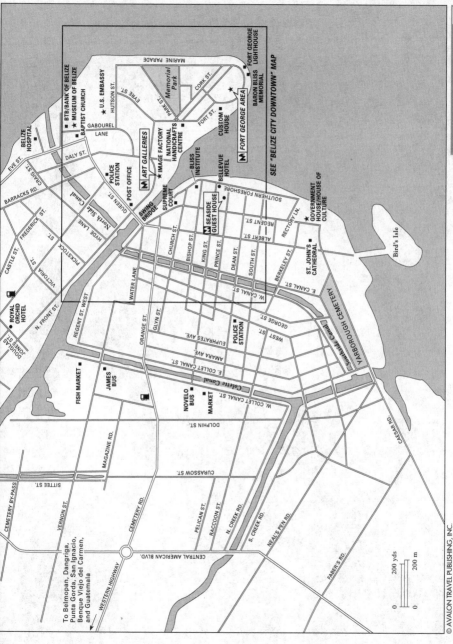

SEE "BELIZE CITY DOWNTOWN" MAP

FORT GEORGE LIGHTHOUSE
BARON BLISS MEMORIAL
FORT GEORGE AREA
MARINE PARADE
MARINE PARADE
Memorial Park
CORK ST.
CUSTOM HOUSE
FORT ST.
HUTSON ST.
EYRE ST.
PARK ST.
U.S. EMBASSY
BTB/BANK OF BELIZE
MUSEUM OF BELIZE
BAPTIST CHURCH
GABOUREL LANE
BELIZE HOSPITAL
EVE ST.
CRAIG ST.
DALY ST.
BARRACKS RD.
ART GALLERIES
IMAGE FACTORY
NATIONAL HANDICRAFTS CENTRE
BLISS INSTITUTE
BELLEVUE HOTEL
POLICE STATION
POST OFFICE
QUEEN ST.
North Side Canal
HYDE LANE
SWING BRIDGE
SUPREME COURT
FREDERICK ST.
PICKSTOCK ST.
CASTLE ST.
VICTORIA ST.
ROYAL ORCHID HOTEL
N. FRONT ST.
DOUGLAS ST.
SONG'S ST.
REGENT ST. WEST
WATER LANE
CHURCH ST.
BISHOP ST.
KING ST.
PRINCE ST.
DEAN ST.
SOUTH ST.
W. CANAL ST.
SEASIDE GUEST HOUSE
SOUTHERN FORESHORE
REGENT ST.
ALBERT ST.
RECTORY LN.
GOVERNMENT HOUSE/HOUSE OF CULTURE
BERKELEY ST.
ST. JOHN'S CATHEDRAL
E. CANAL ST.
YARBOROUGH CEMETERY
Collette Canal
Southside Canal
Bird's Isle
FISH MARKET
JAMES BUS
MAGAZINE RD.
ORANGE ST.
GLYN ST.
E. COLLET CANAL ST.
AMARA AVE.
EUPHRATES AVE.
POLICE STATION
WEST ST.
GEORGE ST.
NOVELO BUS
MARKET
W. COLLET CANAL ST.
DOLPHIN ST.
CURASSOW ST.
CEMETERY RD.
PELICAN ST.
RACCOON ST.
N. CREEK RD.
S. CREEK RD.
NEAL'S PEN RD.
CAESAR RD.
FABER'S RD.
CENTRAL AMERICAN BLVD.
SITTEE ST.
CEMETERY BY-PASS
VERNON ST.
WESTERN HIGHWAY
To Belmopan, Dangriga, Punta Gorda, San Ignacio, Benque Viejo del Carmen, and Guatemala

0   200 yds
0   200 m

© AVALON TRAVEL PUBLISHING, INC.

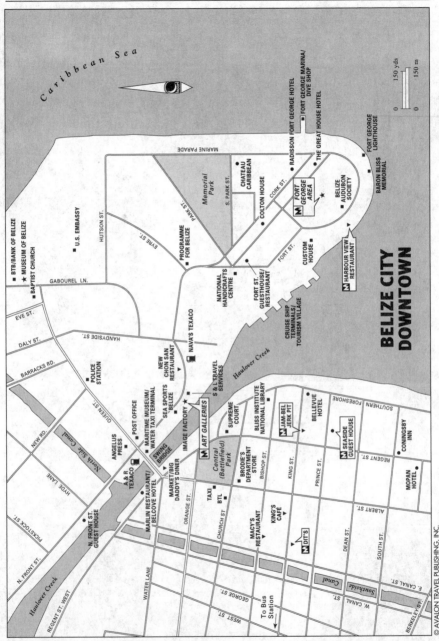

BELIZE CITY DOWNTOWN

© AVALON TRAVEL PUBLISHING, INC.

parade on North Front Street

The Swing Bridge spans Haulover Creek, connecting "Northside" to "Southside," and is the most common landmark in Belize City.

On the bridge's south end, Regent and Albert Streets "V" apart from each other, and are the core of the city's banking and shopping activity. There are a few old government buildings here too, as well as Battlefield (Central) Park and a couple of guesthouses. Southside has a seedier reputation than across the way, but the area immediately east and south of the Swing Bridge is relatively safe.

Here you'll encounter even more traffic and more local color. Vendors sell fruits, vegetables, clothes, incense, jewelry, and cold drinks along the southeast side of the bridge. Bliss Promenade skirts the waterfront and eventually brings you to the newly renovated **Bliss Institute;** social functions and seminars are held here. It is also the location of a theater, museum, and library, as well as the **National Arts Council.**

In the main business section of Regent and Albert Streets (originally called Front and Back Streets—the only streets in 18th-century Belize City) you'll see old brick slave houses, with timber-and-shingle second floors. Slaves were kept in chains in the brick basements when they were not working in the fields.

North of the creek, Queen and Front Streets are the crucial thoroughfares. As you face the bridge, a look to the right will reveal the Texaco Station; a look to the left reveals the **Water Taxi Terminal** and the **Caye Caulker Water Taxi Association,** whose boats take you to the cayes. Across the street from them you'll find the new post office and library, with a quiet sitting room in which to write some letters.

Moving east on Front Street, on your right you'll find several art galleries. Continuing on brings you into "Tourism Village," the hopeful, Dinsey-esque name used for the Cruise Ship Terminal environs.

Supreme Court Building

Sitting in front of Battlefield (Central) Park, this structure is decorated with a graceful white-metal filigree stairway that leads to the long veranda overlooking the square. An antiquated town clock is perched atop the white clapboard building.

St. John's Anglican Cathedral

This lovely old building, the only typically British structure in the city, is surrounded by well-kept green lawns. In 1812, the slaves in Belize helped to erect this graceful piece of architecture using bricks brought as ballast on sailing ships from Europe. Several Mosquito Coast kings from the Waiki tribe were crowned in this cathedral with ultimate pomp and grandeur; the last was crowned in 1815.

Government House/House of Culture

Behind St. John's Cathedral, at the southern end of Regent Street and also on Southern Foreshore, is the House of Culture museum in the old Government House, which, before Hurricane Hattie and the ensuing construction of Belmopan, was the home and office of the governor general, the official Belizean representative of the Queen of England. (Today the governor general can be found in Belmopan at Belize House.) For a long time it was used as a guesthouse for visiting VIPs and a place for social functions. Queen Elizabeth and Prince Philip were houseguests here on their visit in 1994. The old wooden buildings (built 1812–14) are said to have been designed by acclaimed British architect Christopher Wren, and until recently were described as "as elegant as it gets." It's surrounded by sprawling lawns and wind-brushed palms facing the sea along Southern Foreshore.

Wander through the wood structure and imagine the private lives of rulers and politicians of days gone by. Antique lovers will enjoy the period furniture as well as the silverware and glassware collections—plus a selection of modern painting and sculpture by Belizean artists. On the water's edge, stroll the grounds and enjoy the solitude of the city. Open 8:30 A.M.–4:30 P.M. Mon.–Fri., admission US$2.50.

Maritime Museum

This museum, at the Water Taxi Terminal by the Swing Bridge, has displays of fish and local marine life downstairs; upstairs are models of various boats used past and present in Belize, as well as photos and bios of local fishermen and boatbuilders. Open 8 A.M.–5 P.M. daily, admission US$2.

Fort George Area

In general, the Fort George area is one of the most pleasant in Belize City. Meander the neighborhood and you'll pass some lovely homes and a few that have become charming old guesthouses. The **Baron Bliss Memorial** and **Fort George Lighthouse** stand guard over the old, stately goings-on of upscale hotels, embassies, and restaurants.

The sea breeze can be very pleasant here as you glimpse numerous cayes as well as ships at anchor offshore. Once you round the point, the road becomes Marine Parade and runs past the modern Radisson Fort George Hotel and **Memorial Park,** a grassy salute to the 40 Belizeans who lost their lives in World War I, and ends at Hutson Street. The **U.S. Embassy** sits at the end of the block on the right. The old colonial house was built in New England, dismantled, and transported to Belize as ship's ballast. It was reconstructed 120 years ago and houses the entire U.S. Embassy, which has been in Belize since 1840.

From the **Radisson Fort George dock** you'll get a good view of the harbor. Originally this was Fort George Island; until the 1850s it was the location of the army barracks. The strait separating the island from the mainland was filled in during the early 1920s and dedicated as a memorial park for the dead of World War I. Today, it is the site of the Baron Bliss Memorial and the Radisson Fort George Hotel. After World War II, visiting dignitaries from England surveyed the country armed with plans for various agricultural projects to help the people, but they couldn't find a place to stay. So, accommodations went to the top of their priority list and became one of the first postwar projects in the colony. An easygoing, low-key charmer with excellent service and tasty meals, Fort George was the best hotel in town. Today, the hotel is part of the Radisson chain and has

CRIME AND THE CITY

Like many other countries, Belize has its share of problems with drugs and crime. Over the last several years, violent crime has increased noticeably in Belize City. The government has taken steps to battle crime, including stiffer enforcement of the law and a new force of special Tourist Police, who are here specifically for the protection of tourists and can be recognized by their khaki shirts and green pants. They are especially active around Tourism Village, while hotel owners on the Southside complain that their neighborhood is not patrolled enough.

Use the same common sense as you would apply in any city. Before you venture out, have a clear idea of how to get where you're going, and stick to the main streets if you're walking. Always ask a Belizean—like your hotel hosts, or restaurant waiters—whether or not your plan is reasonable. At night, don't walk if you are at all unsure; taxis are plentiful. Don't flash money, jewelry, and other temptations, but if threatened, hand them over.

taken over the Villa Hotel across the street, one block off the waterfront.

Museum of Belize

Housed in the old city jail (Her Majesty's Prison was built in 1857), this impressive display includes city history artifacts, Maya relics, and rotating displays, like "Insects of Belize." Open 8:30 A.M.–5 P.M. Mon.–Fri., tel. 501/223-4524, US$3.

Art Galleries

Start with the House of Culture (see listing earlier in this chapter), then make your way to **The Image Factory Shop and Gallery,** a few doors down from the Maritime Museum, where there's a great book store and gallery space for frequent openings (usually Friday evenings at happy hour). The **Bliss Institute** also has revolving displays of artwork.

The **Fine Arts Gallery** (9:30 A.M.– 4 P.M. Mon.–Fri.), right on Front Street in front of the Wet Lizard and between the cruise ter-

minals, has an incredible collection of paintings and crafts.

Inside the Fort George compound is **Rachel's Art Gallery,** which carries prints and original art by various artists, including Rachel herself.

RECREATION
Diving and Snorkeling

Don't listen to anyone who tells you there is no diving from Belize City. There are four cayes minutes from the city, all with excellent wall dives and idyllic snorkeling; the main reef and Turneffe Island are both easily accessed as well. In addition to the live-aboards discussed in the Discover Belize section, there are two top-notch dive shops to get you there: Try **Sea Sports Belize** (83 N. Front St., tel. 501/223-5505, info@seasportsbelize, www.seasportsbelize.com) or **Hugh Parkey's Dive Connection** (US tel. 888/223-5403, Bel. tel. 501/223-5086 or 223-4526, hugh@belizediving.com, www.belizediving.com). The latter offers a full-service PADI dive shop at the Radisson Fort George Hotel's marina. Snorkel and dive trips are offered on the newest and biggest day-trip boat fleet to the surrounding cayes, as well as day trips to the Blue Hole.

Sailing

Ask at any of the tour companies, marinas, or dive shops to see what's available; there should be a decent range of charters available, plus day trips and sunset cruises. There are also interesting sailing/snorkeling trips available to Caye Caulker (US$50), plus sunset cruises to Ambergris Caye (US$25) on a "Belizean Authentic Gaff Rig Sloop" (tel. 501/603-0434 or 226-2340).

Spectator Sports

The basketball court on Bird Isle used to be packed to the gills during local championship games. Ask around to see if any scheduled games are coming up. Catch a soccer (called football here) match at the stadium Sundays at 3:30 P.M. through mid-December or so. There's loud, booming music pre-game, and lots of security. The stadium is located across the street from the Princess Hotel.

BARON BLISS, BELIZE'S BENEFACTOR

Henry Edward Ernest Victor Bliss, also known as the "Fourth Baron Bliss of the former Kingdom of Portugal," was born in the County of Buckingham, England. He first sailed into the harbor of Belize in 1926, though he was too ill to go ashore because of food poisoning he had contracted while visiting Trinidad. Bliss spent several months aboard his yacht, the *Sea King*, in the harbor, fishing in Belizean waters. Although he never got well enough to go ashore, Bliss learned to love the country from the sea and its habitués—the fishermen and officials in the harbor all treated him with great respect and friendliness. On the days that he was able only to languish on deck, he made every effort to learn about the small country. He was apparently so impressed with what he learned and the people he met that before his death he drew up a will that established a trust of nearly US$2 million for projects to benefit the people of Belize.

So far, more than US$1 million in interest from the trust has been used for the erection of the Bliss Institute, Bliss School of Nursing, and Bliss Promenade, plus contributions to the Belize City water supply, the Corozal Town Board and Health Clinic, and to buy land for the building of Belmopan.

An avid yachtsman, Bliss stipulated that money be set aside for a regatta to be held in Belize waters, now a focal point of the gala Baron Bliss Day celebrations each March. The baron's white granite tomb is at the point of Fort George in Belize City, guarded by the Bliss Lighthouse and the occasional pair of late-night Belizean lovers.

Massage and Bodywork

If you're in a bind and can't make it to any of the resort spas around the country, try some "traditional Maya therapy" at the **Oltsil Day Spa** (148A Barrcaks Rd., tel. 501/223-7722, oltsil@yahoo.com), with a long menu of treatments. Or put yourself in the strong hands of **Harold Zuniga,** a U.S.-trained physical therapist and masseuse (85 Amara Ave., tel. 501/207-1137, haroldzuniga@yahoo.com).

ENTERTAINMENT AND NIGHTLIFE

Friday nights are big in Belize City, especially those that fall on a payday; ask around to find out where the happening Happy Hour of the Week is being held—often with live music and free *bocas* (usually some kind of deep-fried appetizer). There's usually some form of entertainment from Wednesday to Saturday as well, although serious dancing usually doesn't get started till after 11 P.M.

Lil Jay's Bar & Grill is a good open-air, low-key bar to get things started, right across the street from the glitz of the Princess Hotel

(11 A.M.–10 P.M. Tues.–Sat., closed 2 P.M.–6 P.M., from US$5). The Radisson's **Baymen's Tavern** features exotic cocktails, live lounge music, and happy hour specials on weekends.

When it is finally time to dance, there's the **Copa Cabana Latin Club** (Daly St. and Queen St.) for merengue and salsa; otherwise, it's a standard mix of dancehall reggae, *punta* rock, and American pop. Most Saturday nights belong to the disco at the **Bellevue Hotel,** where the views of the harbor are great at sunset and music often goes on until the wee hours of the morning.

SHOPPING

There are a number of gift shops, craft stalls, and street vendors lining Front Street near Tourism Village, as well as just south of the Swing Bridge. In the Fort George area, check out the **Belize National Handicraft Center** (2 South Park St., tel. 501/223-3636, open 8 A.M.–5 P.M. Mon.–Fri., till 4 P.M. Sat.). It's near the Radisson and has an interesting selection of crafts. There is a **Flea Market** at the Catholic Church on North Front Street Satur-

© JOSHUA BERMAN

days at 7 A.M. Seek out the **Mennonite Furniture Market** at 47 North Front Street, open Friday and Saturday during daylight hours. They won't arrange shipping, but you can get nice, basic, handmade wooden furniture for reasonable prices.

ACCOMMODATIONS
Under $25

Despite the occasional cockroach, the **M Seaside Guest House** (3 Prince St., tel. 501/227-8339, seasidebelize@btl.net, www.seasidebelize .com, dorms US$12, private rooms US$20/30 s/d) is still the best of the budget options. The rooms are tiny but comfy, and the social space is ideal for meeting travelers from the world over. There is hot water in the community bathroom, a breeze on its ocean-facing porch, and a friendly, family-run atmosphere. A breakfast of beans, eggs, toast, orange juice, and tea or coffee is available for US$4. If you know you're coming to town, make a reservation—it'd

be great if there were more budget options of this caliber, but there aren't, so they fill up fast.

Another option on the Southside is the **Belcove Hotel** (9 Regent St., tel. 501/227-3054, belcove@btl.net, www.belcove.com), centrally located on the southern bank of Haulover Creek, just west of the Swing Bridge. There are 13 rooms on three stories; options include US$16/22 s/d shared bath, US$22/27 private bath, US$43 s/d for the works (a/c, TV). The porch over the creek is an excellent vantage point, and cheap, lively eats are right next door at the Marlin. The only disadvantage is the seedy stretch of Regent Street between the hotel and the Swing Bridge; take a cab to and from the hotel door.

There are a handful of budget places on the Northside, just west of the Fort George neighborhood. The **Downtown Guesthouse** (5 Eve St., tel. 501/223-2057, US$7.50–22.50) has some rooms with a/c and private bath. The rooms are minimalist and small, but with a nice balcony overlooking the street. The Baptist elementary school is next door. **Freddie's Guest House** (86 Eve St., tel. 501/223-3851) charges US$25 shared bath, $30 private bath for one of its three immaculate, very private rooms. It's like staying in your Grandma's basement, with no social scene at all.

Three Sisters Guest House (55 Eve St., tel. 501/203-5829, US$20–30) has clean rooms plus a quiet common space. The **North Front Street Guest House** (124 N. Front St., tel. 501/227-7595, US$15), located across from Haulover Creek, offers eight rooms with shared basement bath. The rooms are, well, you get what you pay for. The neighborhood isn't the greatest—definitely take a taxi at night.

$25–50

The **Hotel Mopan** (55 Regent St., tel. 501/227-7351, www.hotelmopan.com) is a longstanding standby that got a major facelift in Fall 2003. Its 14 rooms, some with ocean view, all with modern private bath, TV, phone, go from US$34/45 s/d fan, US$10 more with a/c; the bar has been known as a meeting place for both locals and travelers for decades.

© JOSHUA BERMAN

"The Best of the Budget," the Seaside Guest House on Prince Street.

$50–100

Coningsby Inn (76 Regent St., tel. 501/227-1566, fax 501/227-3726, coningsby_inn@btl.net, US$50 s/d, $54/59 with a/c) has 10 beautiful rooms with TV, private bath, and mini-bar. There's a plush second-story bar and restaurant; breakfast is US$5.

The **Royal Orchid Hotel** (tel. 501/223-2783, wchang@btl.net, US$50) is a safe, four-story hotel on the corner of Douglas Jones Street and New Road. All rooms have hot and cold water, private baths, a/c, and TV.

Located in Belama, a residential area three miles from downtown and seven miles from the International airport, **D'Nest Inn** (tel. 501/203 0443, 501/223 5416, info@dnestinn.com, www.dnestinn.com) is a two-story Caribbean-style structure surrounded by an English garden. The three spacious rooms are decorated with Be-

lizean antiques, have private bath, a/c, TV, and data ports for your laptop; from US$50/60 s/d plus tax.

Chateau Caribbean (6 Marine Parade, tel. 501/223-0800, chateaucar@btl.net, www.chateau caribbean.com, from US$80) is a bit pricey for the condition. This old wooden building has great porches and catches wonderful breezes, but is in need of some TLC. The rooms are worn but have private baths, cable TV, and a/c. The restaurant has a variety of tasty dishes and pleasant servers. If you value character, this may be your place.

The Belize Biltmore Plaza (US tel. 800/528-1234, Bel. tel. 501/223-2302, biltmore@btl.net, www.belizebiltmore.com, from US$89) is Belize's local Best Western, located three miles north of the city center and seven miles south of the international airport on the Northern Highway. The Biltmore is comfortable and attractive, with 92 midsize rooms surrounding a lush garden, pool, and bar. Rooms have cable TV, phones, and modern baths; there's also Internet service, an excellent gift shop (called Papaygayo), and a popular upscale dining room and lounge.

The **Bellevue Hotel** (5 S. Foreshore, tel. 501/227-7051 or 608-5150, bellevue@btl.net, US$65–85) is a charming landmark that was built as a private home in the early 1900s. The family that built this hotel has owned and operated it for the past 46 years. Most of the rooms are large, with private bathrooms, a/c, and telephones. The hotel features a garden and pool, restaurant, bar, and a lively disco with a live band on Friday nights plus happy hour and karaoke.

The **Villa Boscardi Bed & Breakfast** (6043 Manatee Dr., tel. 501/223-1691, boscardi @btl.net, www.villaboscardi.com, US$65) has six rooms; it's a small, quaint, comfortable inn (they boast "European elegance") in a safe, quiet residential area, a block away from the Caribbean. There's easy access to the international airport, marinas, and downtown Belize City. A full breakfast is included in the room rate, plus free drop-offs or pickups from the airport, excluding Sundays.

$100–150

The Great House (13 Cork St., tel. 501/223-3400, grreathouse@btl.net, www.greathousebelize.com, from US$110) is a beautiful colonial structure, built in 1927 and recently renovated to show off its twelve unique, colorful rooms, with both tiled and hardwood floors to offset the pastel walls and modern furniture. Downstairs, you'll find car rental and tour services, plus a high-end real estate company, business service center, and the Smoky Mermaid Restaurant.

The **Princess Hotel and Casino** (US tel. 800/233-9784, Bel. tel. 501/223-2670, resprincess@btl.net, www.princessbelize.com, from US$100, suites US$180) has 118 concrete rooms, all with the same a/c, cable TV, and typical bland look. Aside from the casino riff-raff downstairs, this is a good place for families and also features Belize's only cinema and bowling alley. Everything you need is here: pool, gift shop, beauty salon, conference facilities, bars, restaurants, and a tour desk. Great views of the city. An on-site marina has docking facilities and various water-sport rentals.

Over US$150

One of the oldest upscale hotels in Belize City is the **Radisson Fort George Hotel** (US tel. 800/333-3333, Bel. tel. 501/223-3333, amin.dredge@radisson.com, www.radisson.com, from US$150), with nicely appointed rooms, private baths, a/c, TV, and mini-bars; ocean views are more expensive. This grand, resort-style hotel has lots of amenities, including two swimming pools, poolside bar, the **Stone Grill** (outdoor restaurant where you grill your own meat), and fine dining and a breakfast buffet in **St. George's Dining Room.** All the restaurants offer special events from time to time. Full catering facilities and banquet rooms are available. All kinds of tours, from diving to caving to golfing, are organized right out of the hotel.

Near the Airport

Embassy Suites (tel. 501/225-3333, embassy@btl.net, US$50) is not an embassy-type hotel and has been in need of some serious TLC for years, but it's the only hotel located this close (100 yards) to the international airport. The owners are nice, helpful people. They have passenger vans and will arrange tours for their guests. They also rent cars at comparable prices. The hotel caters to school and church groups, and gives groups over eight good rates on meals and rooms. Rooms have private bathroom, a/c, and TV, and are a bit musty and dismal. Ask about their theater, featuring Friday night Christian movies and secular Saturdays, and their live-aboard boat for rent, especially for groups.

FOOD

Belize City has a decent range of eateries and, at press time, still only one North American fast-food chain, a welcome relief from other Americanized cities in Mexico and Central America.

Cheap and Belizean

The cheapest food in Belize City is undoubtedly the free *bocas* (usually deep-fried appetizers) during Friday night happy hour at the Radisson and many other bars—and the free midnight buffet in the Princess Casino (get in line early and consider lining your stomach with a shot of Pepto Bismol against the grease). After that, there are a number of taco vendors in the streets, as well as "fast-food" stands and shacks scattered throughout the city.

Bill's Place (7:30 A.M.–3 P.M.) is located on Front Street where it meets the Swing Bridge. Here you'll find Belizean and American staples like burgers, local beer, and a variety of fresh-squeezed juices in a glass-enclosed air-conditioned corner room.

Big Daddy's Diner, on the top floor of the public market, has good eggs and fry jacks for breakfast, as well as a nice view of the water taxis in the creek below. Massive buffet-style lunches deliver bang for the buck. The **Deli** in Brodie's supermarket has sandwiches, ice cream, and more.

Macy's Restaurant (18 Bishop St.) is a good bet for Creole food at reasonable prices, as is **M Dit's**

on King Street. It's always packed with Belizeans—a good sign.

Deep Sea Marlin's Restaurant & Bar (Regent St. West, 7 A.M.–9 P.M.) is located on Haulover Creek, next to the Belcove Hotel. It's a cheap, cool, and sometimes raucous fishermen's joint, with Belizean and American staples for US$3.

Cafés

King's Café (7:15 A.M.–8 P.M. Mon.–Sat.) is a great Belizean espresso bar, ice cream shop, and tamale joint, with breakfasts from US$2.50, and a counter to sit at while you read the latest *Amandala*. A bit more European in flavor is **Le Petit Café** (6 A.M.–8 P.M. daily), belonging to the Radisson right across the street. Delicious pastries, cakes, and ham-and-cheese croissants are available.

The **Smokin Balam** (59 North Front St., 7 A.M.–5 P.M.) is a café, gift shop, cigar room, and Internet hub. There are great views of Haulover Creek from their back porch.

Pizza

Not many options here, but try **Pepper's** (tel. 501/223-5000, 11 A.M.–10 P.M.), with free delivery within city limits. The same is true at **Carol's** (tel. 501/203-0430, 10 A.M.–9 P.M.).

Chinese

You'll find a lot of Chinese food in Belize City. The highest-rated by expats who have been here awhile is **Chon Saan** on Kelly Street. There's a new Chinese place near the Seaside Guest House that is good as well: **Mandefu Café.** Also try the **Chateau Caribbean Hotel** or **Timmy's Place.**

International Food

The 🅜 **Jam-Bel Jerk Pit** is only half international, combining Jamaican with Belizean recipes to produce a savory menu in a great atmosphere. It's located on King Street, just one block over from the Seaside Guest House, and is open for lunch and dinner, with Internet access on-site.

Belize City's Arab community assures a few authentic Lebanese restaurants in town; **Gyro and Crepe** (south of the flag traffic circle, 10 A.M.–10 P.M. daily) has lots of Middle Eastern veggie and meat options, with US$6 gyros and

falafel for US$5. Then there's **Manatee Landing,** before the entrance to the international airport; watch dolphins swim by in the Belize River while you enjoy your hummus.

For Indian, check out **Natraj, Gateway of India** (5 Amara Ave.), where you'll find a menu that includes chicken tikka, mutton egg fry, and fish baryani. The **Sea Rock Restaurant** (190 New Town) also features a large selection of Indian dishes.

Fine Cuisine

Chef Bob's (164 Newtown Barrack St., tel. 501/223-4201) is a short walk from the Princess Hotel, and very popular with upscale travelers. **The Smokey Mermaid** (tel. 501/223-4780, 6:30 A.M.–11 P.M.) has a built-in smokehouse and specializes in smoked fish, meats, and assorted fresh breads. Breakfast, lunch, and dinner featuring Belizean cuisine, and fresh-baked Creole bread are server, and there's a dining patio under thatch roofs set around a porcelain mermaid. Among the better small restaurants is the **Fort Street Restaurant** (4 Fort St., tel. 501/223-0116), a popular spot with an excellent menu for a special candlelight dinner; but don't give short shrift to their breakfast and lunch.

The **Bellevue Hotel** is known for good food and a bar upstairs that overlooks the water. The **Radisson Fort George Hotel** serves a beautiful buffet with a multitude of tasty seafood delicacies, and the **Princess Hotel** has a whole selection of dining experiences on the premises.

The 🅜 **Harbour View Restaurant** (tel. 501/223-6420) is right on the water in the Old Customs House, open for lunch Monday–Friday, and for dinner every night. This is one of the nicest dining rooms in town, featuring beautiful sunsets behind the city, sea breezes, and a scrumptious and clever menu: Argentine steaks, cinnamon-crusted grouper, snapper, and more from the Filipino chef (US$7–30 per entrée). Their drink list includes Chilean and Californian wines, as well as top-shelf imported spirits and liqueurs. Once you get clean from the jungle, this is a good spot to welcome yourself back to civilization.

INFORMATION AND SERVICES

Tourist Information

The central office of the **Belize Tourism Board** (BTB, tel. 501/223-1913, info@travelbelize.org, www.travelbelize.org) is in the shiny new Central Bank building on Gabourel Lane, behind the Museum of Belize. There's also the **Belize Tourism Industry Association** (10 North Front St., tel. 501/203-1969, or 10 North Park St., tel. 501/223-3507). Both can answer many of your questions and give you lodging suggestions, as can any tour company and many hotel front desks. There are lots of hotel ads, brochures, and an information desk at the Water Taxi Terminal that might prove helpful.

Money

Most of the city's banking is clustered in one strip along Albert Street, just south of the Swing Bridge, and includes **Atlantic Bank** (tel. 501/227-1255), **Bank of Nova Scotia** (tel. 501/227-7027), **Barclay's Bank** (tel. 501/227-7211), and **Belize Bank** (tel. 501/227-7132). Most banks keep the same hours and days: 8 A.M.–1 P.M. Monday–Thursday, 8 A.M.–1 P.M. and 3–6 P.M. Friday. The **Casas de Cambio,** whose purpose is to change money in an effort to retain U.S. dollars in the country, only function regularly in Corozal and San Pedro. In Belize City and other towns, their usefulness is questionable, as they offer a significantly lower rate than the oft-used black-market changers, easily found in most "Hindu shops" on Albert Street.

Health and Emergencies

For police, fire, or ambulance, dial 90 or 911.

    Belize Medical Associates (5791 St. Thomas St., tel. 501/223-0302, 223-0303, or 223-0304, bzmedasso@btl.net, www.belizemedical.com) is the only private hospital in Belize City. They provide 24-hour assistance and a wide range of specialties. Or, try **Karl Heusner Memorial Hospital** (Princess Margaret Dr., tel. 501/223-1548 or 223-1564). Also look under "Hospitals" in the BTL yellow pages.

shoe shine on King Street

© JOSHUA BERMAN

Internet Access

Like elsewhere in the country, an increasing number of hotels and guesthouses offer at least a single dial-up computer, and a few broadband cafés are opening as well, though not nearly as many here as in San Ignacio or San Pedro.

    On the Southside, try **KGS Cybercafe** (near the corner of King and E. Canal Sts., 9 A.M.–5 P.M. Mon.–Sat., US$3/hr.). It's a bit dark and dingy but has fast cable connections. **Mailboxes Etc.,** across from the water taxi terminal, has excellent DSL connections and will let you plug your laptop into their landline. A few doors down, the **Community Computer Center** (9 A.M.–5 P.M. Mon.–Fri., "sometimes" closed for lunch), located in a narrow, tucked-away room above the library, has nine super-fast computers for a bargain US$2 an hour, but no laptop docks. No doubt more options will be springing up across the city, especially around Tourism Village.

Library and Bookstores

A quiet reading room and two stories of books are found on Front Street at **Turton Library** (tel.

501/227-3401, 9 A.M.–7 P.M. Mon.–Fri., 9 A.M.–1 P.M. Sat.), a wonderfully quiet respite from the chaotic rush just outside. Stop in to enjoy the day's newspaper at one of the long, open tables, or dig into their archives for a look at the past.

A few stores have small but pertinent book selections, featuring several shelves of Belizean and about-Belize books. The newest is the **Image Factory** on Front Street. **Angelus Press,** right around the corner on Queen Street, has a complete corner of books and maps, back behind all the office supplies. Across the Swing Bridge, you'll want to hit the second-story **Book Center,** open 8 A.M.–5:30 P.M. Monday–Saturday, 8 A.M.–9 P.M. Friday.

Groceries and Sundries

Brodie's (Albert and Regent Streets, tel. 501/227-7070, 8 A.M.–7 P.M., earlier on weekends) is a department store, supermarket, sub shop, drug store, and more—a Belizean institution. Across the street is another supermarket, **Ro-Macs.**

Stock up on your way into or out of town on the north edge at **Sav U Supermarket.** This modern, air-conditioned market sells everything any supermarket in the United States would carry, and it's reasonably priced.

Post Office

The old post office in the Paslow Building (corner of Queen and Front Sts., by the north end of the Swing Bridge) was burned down in 2002 by an embezzling employee trying to hide the evidence (he's now serving time in the "Hattieville Marriott" for his efforts), but the new one is right next door to the razed lot (tel. 501/227-2201, 8 A.M.–5 P.M. Mon.–Fri.). There is a smaller branch around the corner on Queen Street called the Philatelic Bureau (tel. 501/227-2201 ext. 35, same hours as above but closed for lunch); a third post office is at Queens Square on the Southside of the city (tel. 501/227-1155).

Travel Agents

If you prefer to delegate the logistics of your trip, local travel agencies can book local and interna-tional transportation, tours, and accommodations across the country. These agencies can get you all the information you need, and when rooms are tight (a not-too-infrequent situation Feb.–Apr.), they are more likely to be able to get you accommodated.

S & L Travel and Tours (91 N. Front St., tel. 501/227-7514 or 227-7593, fax 501/227-7594, sltravel@btl.net, www.sltravelbelize.com) is easy to find, next door to the Image Factory, and also with a booth in the Water Taxi Terminal. Belizean owners Sarita and Lascelle Tillet run a first-class and very personable operation; they've been in business for over 25 years. They can get as creative as you like, whether you want a custom vacation, a photo safari, a bird-watching adventure, or anything else you can imagine.

Belize Global Travel Services Ltd (41 Albert St., tel. 501/227-7185 or 227-7363, bzadventur@btl.net, www.belizeglobal.com) is one of the more established travel consultants in the city, offering a full range of Belizean tours, packages, and custom trips. A TACA Airline counter and the country's only official American Express window are located in the same office. The Continental Airlines office is found at 80 Regent Street (tel. 501/227-8309, kimflyco@btl.net, 8 A.M.–5 P.M. Mon.–Fri., 8 A.M.–noon Sat.).

Laundry

G's Laundry (22 Dean St. between Albert and Canal, tel. 501/297-4461, 8 A.M.–8 P.M., 8 A.M.–1 P.M. Sun.) charges US$4 to wash and dry.

Luggage Lockers

Visit the **S & L Travel and Tours** kiosk in the main Water Taxi Terminal to rent a locker for your pack or arrange for longer storage (US$1/hr, US$5/day).

Haircuts

How 'bout a little reggae with your haircut? Loud music blasts all day long at the **Ras Tash Barber Shop** on King Street (8:30 A.M.–8 P.M. Mon.–Sat., plus Sun. mornings, US$5 cut and shave) and don't be surprised if your barber sings and bops while sculpting your 'do. If you're not into incredibly loud reggae music, choose from one of the (seemingly) thousands of other barber shops within a three-block radius, all with their own personality and similar prices.

GETTING AROUND

Much of what may interest you is close together in Belize City, and you can walk from the Southside's House of Culture to the National Museum near the U.S. Embassy in about 15 or 20 leisurely minutes. This route is considered safe during the day, especially if you are traveling in a group.

By Taxi

To hail a taxi, just look for the green license plates, or ask your hotel to call you one. From the international airport to Belize City, the fare is US$20; from the municipal airstrip expect to pay US$5 or less. The fare for one passenger carried between any two points within Belize City (or any other district town) is US$3–5. If you plan to make several stops, tell the cabbie in advance and ask what the total will be; this eliminates lots of misunderstandings. Taxis can be hired by the hour (about US$20) for long trips out of town.

GETTING THERE AND AWAY

Belize City is very much the transportation hub of the country, by land, sea, and air.

By Air

Belizean commuter planes provide a great service in and out of Belize City to the outlying airports all over the country. Call for current schedules and prices. Two airlines offer regularly scheduled flights to all districts in Belize: **Tropic Air** (US tel. 800/422-3435, Bel. tel. 501/226-2012, reservations@tropicair.com, www.tropicair.com) and **Maya Island Air** (US tel. 800/225-6732, Bel. tel. 501/223-1140, mayair@btl.net, www.mayaislandair.com). Daily flights leave Belize City's municipal and international airports for Caye Caulker, San

Pedro, Dangriga, Placencia, Punta Gorda, and most recently, San Ignacio. There are a few charter services at the municipal airport.

By Bus

Domestic bus service is handled almost entirely out of the **Novelo's Terminal,** located at the western terminus of King Street. International service to Guatemala and Mexico is offered by a handful of companies with offices in the main Water Taxi Terminal. For more information on domestic and international buses, please see Getting Around in the Practicalities chapter.

To San Pedro, Caye Caulker, and Other Islands

The main Water Taxi Terminal is located on North Front Street at the foot of the Swing Bridge. Here you'll find regular daily service to and from the more popular destination cayes to the east. The terminal is owned by the Belize Tourism Board (BTB), managed by the Belize Tourism Industry Association (BTIA), and serviced by 22 boats, the captains of which are all members of the **Caye Caulker Water Taxi Association.**

Boat transit to Caye Caulker takes about 45 minutes, then it's another half hour to Ambergris Caye. The trip to Caulker costs about US$10 one-way, US$15 round-trip; to San Pedro US$14 one-way, US$25 round-trip. Most boats will stop at Caye Chapel or Long Caye (US$7.50 one-way to either) on their way to Ambergris if you alert the captain as you board. The trip is pleasant on calm, sunny days, but be prepared for a cold and wet ride if the sky to the east is dark. A few of the boats are covered; others will pass out a plastic tarp if it's really coming down.

The (roughly) hourly departures begin at 8 A.M., with the last boat leaving at 4 P.M. (another boat at 5:30 P.M. will get you as far as Caye Caulker). Two daily trips to St. George's Caye (US$12.50 one way) leave at 10:30 A.M. and 4:30 P.M. The *Thunderbolt* runs boats to the cayes at 8 A.M., 1 P.M., and 4 P.M. It's about the same price as the others, but quicker if it doesn't have to stop at Caulker.

Near Belize City to the South

M GALES POINT

A small village originally established by logwood cutters sits on a two-mile-long peninsula that juts into the Southern Lagoon; both are called Gales Point. Gales Point is about 15 miles north of Dangriga in Stann Creek District and 25 miles south of Belize City. To get to Gales Point by car, choose either the Manatee Highway (Coastal Road) or the Hummingbird Highway and make sure it's not raining! Going by way of the Hummingbird is about 25 miles longer.

Access from Belize City by boat is a pleasant way to Gales Point. The boat winds through mangrove-lined canals and across the Sibun River before going through the Northern and Southern Lagoons.

Southern Lagoon

The lagoon is part of an extensive estuary surrounded by thick mangroves. Their tangled roots provide the perfect breeding grounds for sport fish, crabs, shrimp, lobster, and a host of other marine life. Rich beds of sea grass line the bottom of the lagoon and support a population of man-atees. These gentle mammals are often seen basking on the surface of the water or coming up for air (which they must do about every four minutes). This is a popular spot for boaters to bring visitors to observe the manatees.

Accommodations

Manatee Lodge (US tel. 877/462-6283, Bel. tel./fax 501/220-8040, from US$75) caters to bird-watchers, fisherfolk, and independent travelers who enjoy the outdoors. The lodge is on the northern end of Gales Point, and visitors here have access to a completely different wildlife habitat that exists in the broad expanse of shallow brackish water and mangroves called the Southern Lagoon. The nine rooms of the lodge are spacious, have private bathrooms, and are connected to the main buildings by elevated walkways. The number of shorebirds and waterfowl is impressive, and to encourage guests to see local wildlife, the lodge provides each room with a canoe. Binoculars and bug repellent are a must. Children under six are free, ages 6–12 half price. Moderately priced meals are available.

Near Belize City to the North

Driving the Northern Highway

If you are driving to Bermudian Landing from downtown Belize City, leave town on Freetown Road. You'll pass through the intersection with Central American Boulevard (to the left) and Princess Margaret Drive (to the right). Continue straight out of town. As you cross this major intersection, the road becomes the Northern Highway; set your trip odometer just a couple of hundred yards farther, where the road begins a gentle bend to the right.

Expect a good deal of traffic in the mornings and afternoons on the stretch past the Bella Vista suburb and the Belize Biltmore Hotel. You'll encounter lots of school buses, vehicles pulling over to pick up riders, and speed bumps. The **Belize**

ALTUN HA RUINS AND CROOKED TREE

© AVALON TRAVEL PUBLISHING, INC.

River is off to the left. At about Mile 5.5, you'll come to **Haulover Bridge** (one-way traffic at a time) and continue skirting the river northward on Northern Highway.

ⓜ ALTUN HA RUINS

Altun Ha (tel. 501/609-3540, 9 A.M.–5 P.M., US$3 per person), a Maya trading center as well as a religious ceremonial center, is believed to have accommodated about 10,000 people. Archaeologists, working in the midst of a community of Maya families that have been living here for several centuries, have dated construction to about 1,500–2,000 years ago. It wasn't until the archaeologists came in 1964 that the old name "Rockstone Pond" was translated into the Maya words "Altun Ha." The site covers an area of about 25 square miles, most of which is covered by trees, vines, and jungle.

A team led by Dr. David Pendergast from the Royal Ontario Museum began work in 1965 on the central part of the ancient city, where upwards of 250 structures have been found in an area of about 1,000 square yards. So far, this is the most extensively excavated of all the Maya sites in Belize. For a trading center, Altun Ha was strategically located—a few miles from Little Rocky Point on the Caribbean and a few miles from Moho Caye at the mouth of the Belize River, both believed to have been major centers for the large trading canoes that worked up and down the coasts of Guatemala, Honduras, Belize, Mexico's Yucatán, and all the way to Panama.

Near Plaza B, the **Reservoir,** also known as **Rockstone Pond,** is fed by springs and rain runoff. It demonstrates the advanced knowledge of the Maya in just one of their many fields: engineering. Archaeologists say that for centuries, an insignificant little stream ran through the jungle. No doubt it had been a source of fresh water for the Maya—but maybe not enough. The Maya diverted the creek and then began a major engineering project, digging and enlarging a deep, round hole that was

A tour of Altun Ha ruins is a popular day trip from Belize City.

then plastered with limestone cement. Once the cement dried and hardened, the stream was rerouted to its original course and the newly built reservoir filled and overflowed at the east end, allowing the stream to continue on its age-old track. This made the area livable. Was all of this done before or after the temple structures were built? Is the completion of this reservoir what made the Maya elite choose to locate in this area? We may never know for sure. Today Rockstone Pond is surrounded by thick brush and the pond is alive with jungle creatures, including tarpon, small fish, and turtles and other reptiles.

The concentration of structures includes palaces and temples surrounding two main plazas. The tallest building (the **Sun God Temple**) is 59 feet above the plaza floor. At Altun Ha, the structure bases are oval and terraced. The small temples on top have typical small rooms built with the Maya trademark—the corbel arch.

Pendergast's team uncovered many valuable finds, such as unusual green obsidian blades, pearls, and more than 300 jade pieces—beads, earrings, and rings. Seven funeral chambers were discovered, including the **Temple of the Green Tomb,** rich with human remains and traditional funerary treasures. Maya scholars believe the first man buried was someone of great importance. He was draped with jade beads, pearls, and shells. And it was next to his right hand that the most exciting find was located—a solid jade head now referred to as **Kinich Ahau** ("The Sun God"). Kinich Ahau is, to date, the largest jade carving found in any Maya country. The head weighs nine pounds and measures nearly six inches from base to crown. It is reportedly now housed far away, in a museum in Canada.

Altun Ha was rebuilt several times during the Pre-Classic, Classic, and Post-Classic periods. Scientists believe that the site was abandoned due to violence and the desecration of the structures.

Tour Guides

A couple of local tour guides will be waiting for you at the entrance. They charge about US$10 per group per half hour and are well worth it, especially Ann-Marie Avona. If you're coming to Altun Ha as part of a package, consider insisting that your tour provider use a local guide. This is important to ensure that local communi-

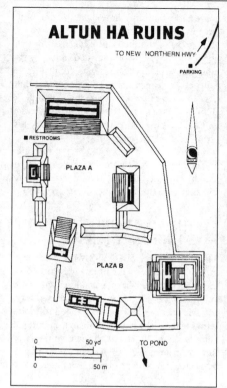

ALTUN HA RUINS

TO NEW NORTHERN HWY

PARKING

■ RESTROOMS

PLAZA A

PLAZA B

TO POND

0   50 yd
0   50 m

© AVALON TRAVEL PUBLISHING, INC.

and Caye Caulker. There is a gift shop and toilet facilities at the entrance.

Note that Altun Ha is a popular destination for cruise ship passengers, so if you don't want to share your experience with 40 busloads of gawking Midwesterners, be sure to check with the park before coming.

Accommodations and Food

There are several budget-oriented lodgings in the area, but few travelers choose to stay here, probably because there's not much offered in the area apart from a short hike through the nearby ruins and the tranquil sounds of the jungle. **Mayan Wells Restaurant** (till 5 P.M. Tues.–Sat., opening times vary) is close to the ruins and offers typical Belizean fare.

MARUBA RESORT JUNGLE SPA

By any standards, Maruba Resort Jungle Spa (US tel. 800/552-3419, Bel. tel. 501/322-2199, maruba@btl.net, US$175–425) is an interesting sight in the middle of the forest, located at Mile 40.5 on the Old Northern Highway, about a mile out of Maskall Village. Many visitors come just for the day—it's a popular stopover for Altun Ha visitors who have decided to enjoy lunch and a mud mask before heading back to San Pedro, Belize City, or other nearby destinations.

The resort focuses on pampering the body and soul, as is evidenced by the focal points spread around the grounds. A tiny, glass-decorated chapel; a palapa-covered stone chess table; a pool that seems to spring from the jungle, complete with small waterfalls.

The rooms are spread out on the grounds for privacy and are addressed by name—Moon, Fertility, and Bondage, to name a few. All continue the eclectic motif—carved masks, mosaic tile floors, standing candles, cement fountains, tiled tubs, screened and shuttered windows, and fresh flowers on the massive feather beds and in the bathrooms. Each is different, but all have a private bath and electricity.

The restaurant often offers wild game in addition to standard fare, and at the bar, you will

ties receive something other than a crumbling road. To that end, you'll most likely find tables of artisan vendors with decent crafts for sale.

Visiting the Ruins

From the Northern Highway, continue past the Burrell Boom turnoff (to the Baboon Sanctuary) and continue to about Mile 19, where the road forks; the right fork is the Old Northern Highway and leads to Altun Ha and Maskall Village. Ten and a half miles from the intersection, you'll reach the Altun Ha entrance. The road is in horrible condition and is not getting any better with the increased traffic, mainly from long parades of buses carrying cruise ship passengers.

The ruins of Altun Ha have become one of the more popular day trips for groups and individuals venturing from Belize City, Ambergris Caye,

Belize District

find viper rum with a warning label that reads for "real men only." Instructions on how to properly down a shot of this potent rum will be given by owner/bartender Nicky.

Massages, mud wraps, manicures and pedicures are all available, plus a free-weight gym. Packages are available with tours to the reefs, ruins, and inland destinations.

Getting to Altun Ha and Maruba

For those who want to bus it, ask at your hotel for current schedules and make sure there is a return bus the same day if you do not plan on staying in the area. Altun Ha is close enough to the city that a taxi is your best bet, or try a tour operator that specializes in these trips. Those going to Maruba should ask at the hotel about transfers when making reservations.

BURRELL BOOM

This is the gateway village to the Community Baboon Sanctuary and the destination of a popular day trip that involves taking a boat from Belize City up the Belize River and landing at the **Olde River Tavern,** where passengers find crafts, food, and beverages. Talk to the hustlers in

Belize City's Tourism Village about this one, or to any tour operator in the city.

This is also the site of **El Chiclero Inn** (tel. 501/225-9005, US$60 plus tax), a locally famous six-room hotel known more for their huge American-style menu, with everything from chili dogs to pizza to pastas, steaks, and Cajun pork chops—oh yeah, and they've allegedly got the only cashew pie in the country. The restaurant is open 7 A.M.–9 P.M. daily.

The rooms are spacious and bright, with a/c, TV, and private bathroom. El Chiclero is often used by business travelers, as it is located a mere 11 miles from the international airport.

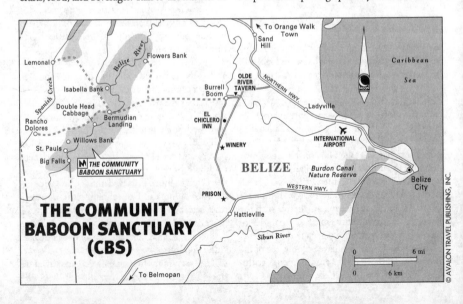 THE COMMUNITY BABOON SANCTUARY (CBS)

The sanctuary (tel. 501/220-2181, baboon@btl .net) is the result of the unique efforts of 220 members in nine local communities who have voluntarily agreed to manage their land in ways that will preserve their beloved baboon (the local term for the black howler monkey). Because of community-based efforts to preserve the creature, there are now 4,000 individuals waiting to be spotted and photographed by curious travelers.

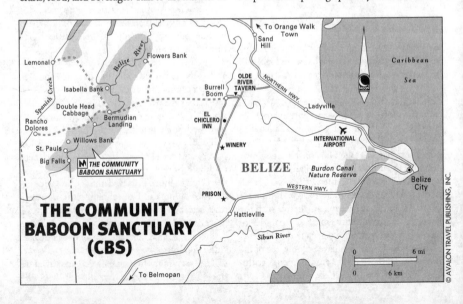

© AVALON TRAVEL PUBLISHING, INC.

CBS feels remote, but in reality, it is only 26 miles from Belize City and 13 miles from the international airport, making it both a popular day trip *and* a common destination for tent-schlepping backpackers who'd rather wake up to the throaty roars of the Belizean baboon than the smelly bustle of Belize City.

History

One of the six species of howler monkeys in the world, the black howlers are the largest monkeys in the Americas. Zoologist Robert Horwich from the University of Wisconsin at Milwaukee was the first zoologist to spend extended time in the howler's range, which covered southern Mexico, northeast Guatemala, and Belize.

The results of his study were disturbing. In Mexico, the monkeys were being hunted by the locals for food, and their habitat was fast being eliminated with the destruction of the rainforest. Conditions in Guatemala were only slightly better. Here, too, the monkeys were hunted by locals in the forests around Tikal, and as the forest habitat shrank in the country, so too did the numbers of howler monkeys.

In Belize, however, in the village of Bermudian Landing, the communities of monkeys were strong and healthy, the forest was intact, and the locals seemed genuinely fond of the noisy creatures. This was definitely the place to start talking wildlife reserve.

Horwich, with the help of Jon Lyon, a botanist from the State University of New York, began a survey of the village in 1984. After many meetings with the town leaders, excitement grew about the idea of saving the "baboon." Homeowners agreed to leave the monkey's food trees—hogplums and sapodillas—and small strips of forest between cleared fields as aerial pathways for the primates, as well as 60 feet of forest along both sides of waterways.

An application was made to World Wildlife Fund USA in 1985 for funds to set up the reserve. Local landowners signed a voluntary management agreement set forth by Horwich and Lyon—and a sanctuary was born. At last count, the number of participants had grown to 220 landowners in nine villages covering 18 square miles along a 20-mile stretch of the Belize River.

Continuing Results

According to sanctuary manager Fallett Young, the monkey population has grown to a whopping 4,000. There have been successful attempts to relocate some of the troops around the country, especially to southern areas like the Cockscomb Basin Wildlife Sanctuary, where howlers haven't been heard since they were decimated by yellow fever decades ago.

One of the outgrowths of this innovative plan in Belize is the knowledge that educating people about conservation and arousing in them a basic fondness for all of nature has been much more successful than enacting a stringent hunting law. The managers of the sanctuary are local villagers who understand their neighbors; much of their time is spent with schoolchildren and adults in interested villages. Part of their education includes basic farming techniques and sustained land use that eliminates the constant need to cut forest for new *milpas* (cornfields); this might be the most important lesson for the forest inhabitants.

Another result is the unhindered growth of 100 species of trees, vines, and epiphytes. The animal life is thriving as well—anteaters, armadillos, iguanas, hicatee turtles, deer, coati, amphibians, reptiles, and about 200 species of birds all live here.

However, all is not perfect in this baboon paradise. Occasionally, people from urban areas still come to the sanctuary to kidnap baby monkeys to sell for pets. The only way anyone can kidnap a baby howler is by killing the mother, since she will never relinquish her young without a fight. A lively debate continues among traditional conservationists about allowing people to live within a wildlife preserve. However, Belize's grassroots conservation is proving that it can succeed. Other countries such as Australia and Sierra Leone are watching carefully to see how this same concept can be adapted to the needs of their own endangered species without disturbing the people who have lived on the land for many generations.

Activities

There are enough trails, rivers, and guided tours to keep you busy here for a couple of days. It's always a thrill to watch the bright-eyed black monkey as it sits within five feet of you on a wild-lime tree branch, happily munching the leaves. They seem to know they're protected here.

All activities are arranged through the CBS Visitor Center in Bermuda Landing (group trips and/or guides from local hotels are also available). The most basic is the 45-minute nature walk that is included with your US$5 entrance fee to the Natural History Museum. You are 100 percent guaranteed to see wild monkeys, as there is a troop of seven that lives in a tree right across the road.

There is also a three-hour canoe tour and a two-hour walking tour of some of the different sanctuary villages. Overnighters should absolutely take advantage of the nighttime trips, including a 3.5-hour crocodile canoe trip up Mussell Creek or a two-hour night hike into the surrounding forest.

Be aware that the trails are on private land, and visitors should not infringe on private property. A trail is maintained and it's required that all visitors have a guide for orientation. The trails are marked with numbered signs that correspond with information provided in a book, *Community Baboon Sanctuary*, which is available in most gift shops or at the sanctuary.

Accommodations and Food

A popular choice for adventurous travelers is the homestay program, where you'll stay with a local family in primitive conditions, bathing with a bucket, and talking with your host family in the evening. Arrange your stay in one of these "Bed-and-Breakfasts" (about US$13 pp, meals around US$4) at least 24 hours in advance through the Visitor Center at Bermudian Landing.

If you've got a tent, you can pitch it on the Visitor Center grounds, or down by the river, for US$5 pp. Eat at the on-site restaurant, or arrange a meal with a local family; both options are under US$5 per meal. There are privies, but shower facilities are still in the making.

A couple notches up in comfort and price, and right next to the Visitor Center, is the **Nature Resort** (tel. 501/220-2121) with eight cabanas, ranging from US$15/27 s/d for a shared bath to US$53 d with a full kitchenette and hot/cold private bathroom. The cabins are new, well-kept, and well-equipped.

Just a bit up the road is the **Howler Monkey Lodge** (jungled@btl.net), which has received bad reviews since ownership shifted a few years back. Many guests have arrived and opted to stay elsewhere, but you're welcome to inspect for yourself. Accommodations are simple, some with porches that overlook the river.

Getting There and Away

Bermuda Landing is only 26 miles from Belize City; the bus ride takes about an hour. Four early-morning buses leave Bermuda Landing from 5 A.M. to 6:45 A.M., and depart Belize City at noon, 4 P.M., 5 P.M., and 5:15 P.M. Catch the bus two blocks east of the main Novelo's Terminal at the corner of Euphrates and Amara Avenues. There are no buses in either direction on Sundays.

The sanctuary is close enough to the city or either airport that you can consider a taxi or an escorted tour for a day trip. Negotiate taxi prices ahead of time.

Spanish Creek Wildlife Sanctuary

Located seven miles farther up the road, this is a brand new protected area, rich in wildlife, but short on infrastructure so far. Ask at Bermuda Landing for more details.

Crooked Tree

Both the island village and wildlife sanctuary (that also encompasses the bird-bursting freshwater lagoon that surrounds the area) of Crooked Tree are only a 36-mile drive from Belize City and a primary destination for all serious bird-watchers who visit Belize. Others will enjoy paddling through the water, hiking various trails, or reveling at the annual cashew festival. Most visitors to the area also enjoy the simple pleasure of mingling with the islanders—most of whom grew up here—perhaps at one of the weekly cricket matches.

Crooked Tree is a network of inland lagoons, swamps, and waterways. **Crooked Tree Lagoon** is up to a mile wide and more than 20 miles long. Along its banks lies the town of Crooked Tree. An island surrounded by fresh water, accessible only by boats traveling up the Belize River and Black Creek, it was settled during the early days of the logwood era. The waterways were used to float the logs out to the sea.

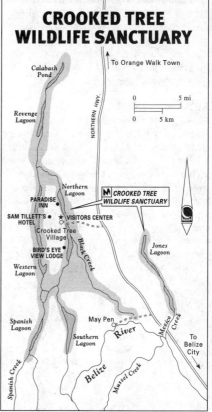 CROOKED TREE WILDLIFE SANCTUARY

The 16,400 acres of waterways, logwood swamps, and lagoon provide habitat for a diverse array of hundreds of resident and migratory birds—all year long. Explore the area by paddle power in a rented canoe or kayak, motor through on a guided tour, or hike the system of boardwalks through lowland savannah and logwood forests, with observation towers providing wide views across the lagoons.

The reserve was established by the Belize Audubon Society to protect its most famous habitant, the jabiru stork. It's the largest flying bird in the Western Hemisphere, with wingspans of up to eight feet. Multitudes of other birds (285 species, at last count) find the sanctuary a safe resting spot during the dry season, with enormous food resources along the shorelines and in the trees. After a rain, thousands of minuscule frogs (no more than an inch long) seem to drop from the sky. They're fair game for the agami

heron, snowy egret, and great egret—quick hunters with their long beaks. A fairly large bird, the snail kite uses its particular beak to hook meat out of the apple snails.

Two varieties of ducks, the black-bellied whistling duck and the Muscovy, nest in trees along the swamp. All five species of kingfishers live in the sanctuary, and you can see osprey and black-collared hawks diving for their morning catch.

On one trip, we watched from our dory (dugout canoe) as a peregrine falcon repeatedly tried but failed to nab one of a flock of floating

American coots. Black Creek, with its forests of large trees, provides homes to monkeys, Morelet's crocodiles, coatimundi, turtles, and iguana. A profusion of wild ocher pokes up from the water, covered with millions of pale pink snail eggs. Grazing Brahma cattle wade into the shallows of the lagoon to munch on the tum tum (water lilies), a delicacy that keeps them fat and fit when the grasses turn brown in the dry season.

Hunting and fishing are not permitted.

Audubon Society

Although several organizations had a hand in founding the park with financial aid, ongoing credit for supervision goes to the Belize Audubon Society (tel. 501/223-5004, base@btl.net, www.belizeaudubon.com). The organization, with the continued help of devoted volunteers, maintains a small visitors center on the right just after you cross the causeway. Do sign in; this validates the sanctuary and gives the society a reason to sponsor it. It's also obligatory, as is the US$4 pp entrance fee; the office is open 8 A.M.–4:30 P.M. 365 days a year. You will always find a knowl-edgeable curator willing to answer questions about the birds and flora encountered at the sanctuary.

THE VILLAGE

The village is divided into three neighborhoods: Crooked Tree, Pine Ridge, and Stain, with a total population of under 1,000. Villagers operate farms, raise livestock, and have a small fishery. Visitors will find the village spread out on the island, with more cattle trails, half-roads, and fence line than actual public roads. There are a few well-grazed athletic fields, four churches, and scores of neat wooden houses (many on stilts) in the middle of large, well-kept plots of land, each with its own tank to catch rainwater. It's a tranquil community.

Crooked Tree mainly attracts nature lovers, but visitors will find barefoot boys going home for lunch with fishing poles over their shoulders as well as women with floppy hats gabbing over back fences. And if you indulge in conversation, you'll have a chance to hear the lovely soft Creole

CROOKED TREE CASHEW FESTIVAL

The namesake of this relaxed, inland island village is the cashew tree, which grows prolifically throughout the area. The unique nut has always contributed to the community's economy, especially for its women, who have been able to secure additional income for their households by selling cashew products. The situation is even better today, as the product is more often sold directly to local consumers and tourists rather than to distributors in Belize City, as it was in the past.

To celebrate the bent branches and their heavy fruit, the people of Crooked Tree Village throw a big cashew harvest festival on the first weekend in May. It's a lot of fun, a hometown fair with regional arts, music, folklore, dance, and crafts. And of course it's a chance to sample cashew wine, cashew jellies, stewed cashews . . . you get the picture. Just make sure the "hometown fair" picture in your head includes *punta* music, fry jacks, and johnnycakes.

Seek out the demonstrations showing how the cashew nut is processed—interesting stuff. The fruit, or the cashew "apple," is either red or yellow, with the seed hanging from the bottom of the apple. The seedpod is roasted in an open fire on the ground, and the meat of the apple can be stewed or made into jam or wine. When roasting the cashew, the fire stabilizes the highly acidic oil, at the same time making the pod brittle for cracking. The nut is partially cooked during this step in the processing. The seeds are raked to cool evenly and quickly.

The cashews are then cracked by hand, one at a time. The shell contains a highly irritating poison that for most people causes blisters and inflammation. Those who handle the nuts wear gloves (processing removes all poison). The fruit is juicy and makes delicious jelly and wine.

patois that is common throughout the country. While strolling through the village, you might see local children playing football, racing horses, or whacking a ball around the cricket pitch.

Chau Hiix Ruins

Archaeological site Chau Hiix is being studied nearby. Archaeologists have made some startling discoveries, including a ball court and ball-court marker, along with small artifacts. Preliminary studies indicate the site was occupied from 1200 B.C. to A.D. 1500. **Sapodilla Lagoon** is south of Crooked Tree on Spanish Creek.

GUIDES AND TOURS

The recommended way to visit Crooked Tree is to hire a local guide who really knows his digs. Options include boat, horseback, and walking tours. The best way to really experience the lagoon is by boat, and there are all kinds available at each hotel. Ask Sam Tillet at Sam Tillett's Hotel and Tours (see next section for contact information) if he's available to paddle you around the lagoon in his dugout canoe (a dory); this silent transport (with a trawling motor) enables you to get very close to the shoreline without getting tangled in the thick plants, such as water lilies (called tum tum), that grow on the surface of the lagoon.

If you can't get in touch with Sam, check with the people at the Belize Audubon Society office in Belize City, who will be happy to have a guide and boat waiting for you when you arrive.

ACCOMMODATIONS AND FOOD

This is a low-key tourist area with just a few locally run and owned accommodations and tiny cafés, usually an extension of someone's home. All will allow you to camp on their grounds for US$5 pp.

As you approach the island on the causeway, on the shoreline off to your left, you'll see the buildings of the **Bird's Eye View Lodge** (tel. 501/203-2040, birdseye@btl.net, US$50–80 for a couple). This hotel stands above the rest in

modernity and dependable service, and this is reflected in its higher rates. The 18 rooms all have private bath and various comforts, including the option of air conditioning—something you may be happy for if visiting in April or May. Miss Verna will take good care of you; the rooftop bar and patio is a wonderful spot to take in the breeze and keep on bird-watching, even after your four-hour, daybreak bird-watching boat cruise on the lagoon—or a hike along the shore. Meals are US$7 for breakfast and lunch, dinner US$10. Boat rentals, tours, and airport pickups can be arranged.

Sam Tillet is old-school Crooked Tree, and the quality of his guiding services is acknowledged and respected throughout the country. **Sam Tillett's Hotel and Tours** (tel. 501/220-7026, samhotel@btl.net) may be located inland, away from the lagoon's edge, but it offers a charming, family-style feel with its small group of rooms—from a tiny one with a shared bath (US$15) to a very nice thatch-roof A-frame with private bath (the "Jabiru Suite") for US$55. All rooms have hot/cold water. Meals consist of typical Belizean food: stew chicken, vegetable salads, local fish, fry jacks, and johnnycakes (breakfast and lunch US$4–6, dinner US$8).

Everyone is welcome to dine at **Triple J's**, and **Suzette's Burger Bar** is a fine little spot for burgers and hot dogs. Both are found by walking into Crooked Tree Village, and their hours vary depending on demand. A small gift shop across from Sam's Tillett's Hotel specializes in locally made herbal skin and beauty products.

On the shore of the lagoon, to the north of the causeway, lies the Crawford family's **Paradise Inn** (US tel. 888/875-9453, Bel. tel. 501/225-7044 or 606-7659, info@wildsidebirding.com, www.wildsidebirding.com, US$40/50 s/d tax included, camping US$8 pp). All seven of the inviting, rustic cabanas are made of natural materials, and have private bath, hot/cold water, and porches facing the water. Student groups are welcome. A cold-water shower and bathroom are available for campsite users.

Getting There

By car, drive north to Mile 33, turn left, and

continue until the dirt road turns into the earthen causeway that will carry you into Crooked Tree. (Be prepared to give way to allow vehicles coming from the opposite direction to pass.) Or, catch the **Jex Bus** to Crooked Tree in Belize City at 34 Regent Street. From Crooked Tree to Belize City, buses depart only in the mornings; ask about times. This is fine for those who plan to spend the night; other options are to go by taxi or with a local tour operator. Check with the Audubon Society for further transportation information, rates, and an updated schedule.

The Northern Cayes

By the 17th century, pirates had found the cayes around the Belizean mainland perfect for laying low, riding out a storm, drinking rum, and replenishing water and food supplies before setting sail for another round of pillaging and sacking. No doubt modern-day travelers to Belize's largest and most visited islands engage in at least some of the same activities. Caulker, Ambergris, St. George's, Chapel, Half-Moon, Lighthouse, and Moho—these islands (and dozens more) are classic, Caribbean Belize. From dots of sand to extensive mangrove forests, all are surrounded by the same crystal blue waters and coral rainbows that so attracted the original Maya inhabitants—followed by buccaneers and now you, 21st century castaway.

The Northern Cayes are rightly considered the crown jewels of Belize's tourism industry. They have the most experience catering to visitors, have developed several different scenes between them, and continue to be the most popular destinations in the region. By one estimate, more than 70 percent of visitors to Belize come to at least one of these islands during their trip. It's not hard to imagine why, with immediate access to world-class fishing, diving, and snorkeling; contact with hospitable Belizean islanders and fellow travelers from around the world; and an

Must-Sees

Look for **M** to find the sights and activities you can't miss and **M** for the best dining and lodging.

M **Hol Chan Marine Reserve:** Belize's famous Barrier Reef, less than a mile offshore from both Caye Caulker and Ambergris, is marked by this famous "cut," or break, in the reef where the mixing water from the open ocean (and bait thrown in from tour boats) ensures plenty of wildlife. Other snorkel and dive sites include nearby Shark Ray Alley and Mexico Rocks (page 62).

M **Swallow Caye Wildlife Sanctuary:** One of many ocean-bound excursions available from Belize's Northern Cayes, this protected area is visited by a number of guides who offer manatee- and bird-watching tours (page 81).

M **The Elbow:** The steep drop-off and clashing currents at Turneffe Island's southern tip is a unique dive site because of the deep-water fish that frequent the area, as well as a thriving population of interesting sponges (page 91).

M **Half Moon Caye Wall:** This beautiful crescent-shaped island is at the southeast corner of **Lighthouse Reef Atoll.** The wall just offshore is one of Belize's most fascinating sites, with numerous tunnels and and canyons in the reef crest, all swimming with wildlife (page 96).

M **Spanish Lookout Caye:** Lose the crowds at this 187-acre mangrove island, located at the southern tip of The Drowned Cayes, just east of Belize City. Spanish Lookout is part of a unique tropical ecosystem that includes seagrass beds, mangrove islands, and coral reefs, and boasts excellent snorkeling and diving (page 98).

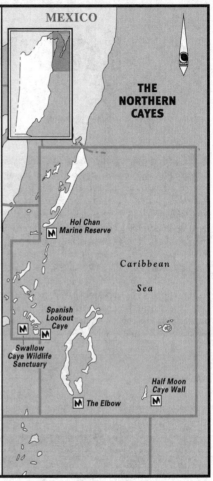

MEXICO

THE
NORTHERN
CAYES

Hol Chan
M Marine Reserve

Caribbean

Sea

Spanish
Lookout
Caye

Swallow
Caye Wildlife
Sanctuary

Half Moon
Caye Wall

M The Elbow

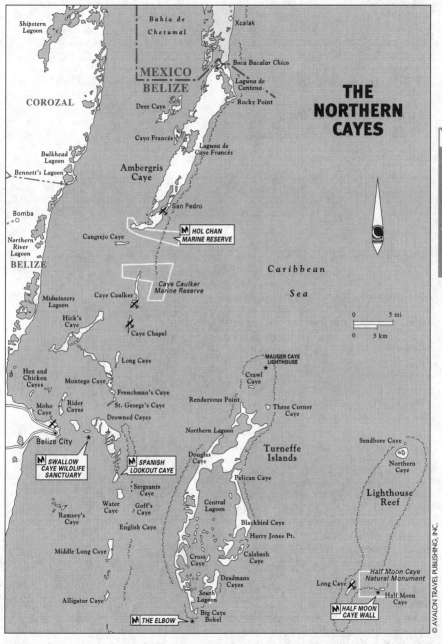

THE NORTHERN CAYES

Shipstern Lagoon

Bahía de Chetumal

Xcalak

MEXICO
BELIZE

COROZAL

Boca Bacalar Chico

Laguna de Cantena

Deer Caye

Rocky Point

Cayo Francés

Laguna de Cayo Francés

Ambergris Caye

Bulkhead Lagoon

Bennett's Lagoon

San Pedro

Bomba

Cangrejo Caye

HOL CHAN MARINE RESERVE

Northern River Lagoon

BELIZE

Caribbean Sea

Midwinters Lagoon

Caye Caulker Marine Reserve

Caye Caulker

Hick's Caye

Caye Chapel

Long Caye

MAUGER CAYE LIGHTHOUSE

Crawl Caye

Montego Caye

Frenchman's Caye

St. George's Caye

Rendezvous Point

Three Corner Caye

Hen and Chicken Cayes

Moho Caye

Rider Cayes

Drowned Cayes

Northern Lagoon

Belize City

Douglas Caye

Turneffe Islands

Sandbore Caye

SWALLOW CAYE WILDLIFE SANCTUARY

SPANISH LOOKOUT CAYE

Pelican Caye

Northern Caye

Lighthouse Reef

Sergeants Caye

Water Caye

Goff's Caye

Central Lagoon

Ramsey's Caye

English Caye

Blackbird Caye

Harry Jones Pt.

Middle Long Caye

Calabash Caye

Cross Caye

Half Moon Caye Natural Monument

Alligator Caye

Deadmans Cayes

South Lagoon

Long Caye

Half Moon Caye

THE ELBOW

Big Caye Bokel

HALF MOON CAYE WALL

0   5 mi
0   5 km

The Northern Cayes

© AVALON TRAVEL PUBLISHING, INC.

amazing selection of small, personable resorts and restaurants from which to choose. Then, of course, there's that desert-island feeling—the palms, rum punches, boat rides, clear blue ocean, and long, easy island time.

Enjoy and repeat after the locals: "Go Slow!"

PLANNING YOUR TIME

What should we do today, honey? Go diving again? Snorkeling? Did you want to try the kayak trip around the island? The Pittmans invited us on that sunset sailing cruise this evening. What about a day trip to the mainland? Wanna get a massage? Go shopping? Deep-sea fishing? No? Nothing? I guess you're right, we do have all week . . .

Most visitors to Caulker, Ambergris, or the outlying atolls book their entire vacations there and are not disappointed—especially fishing and diving freaks on a mission. You can easily kill seven to ten days on any of these islands, no problem. Then there are the surf-n-turfers, who do five days in the cayes and five days upcountry, gettin' their jungle on. More mobile wanderers with wings on their backpacks often only include a couple of days in the North Cayes (or at least long enough to get scuba certified) before continuing on their country-wide tours. If you focused your vacation elsewhere in the country and only have a day or two, it's still worth the trip to either Caulker or Ambergris, both under an hour by boat from Belize City and worthy of the quickest of glimpses.

San Pedro and Ambergris Caye

San Pedro is the only town on Ambergris and has long been the most-visited destination in Belize—in fact, for years it was the *only* developed part of the country's tourism industry. It has a population of about 9,000 Belizeans and an ever-fluctuating mob of gringos that numbers from the hundreds to about 1,000 at any one time. Foreigners own about 60 of Ambergris's 70 accommodations—good for island economy, or the "new colonialism"? You decide.

THE LAND

Ambergris Caye is Belize's largest island, jutting south from the Mexican Yucatán mainland, stretching 24 miles into Belizean waters and interrupted by an ages-old canal. In fact, if it weren't for this "cut," dug by the Maya, Ambergris could easily have ended up part of Mexico. As for its name, *ambergris* is a waxy substance originating in the intestines of the sperm whale. Don't laugh—the rare and valuable substance used to be used in the manufacture of perfume and went for top dollar.

The island sits only 35 miles east of Belize City and only three-quarters of a mile west of the Belize Barrier Reef, visible from most beachfront

AMBERGRIS CAYE

MEXICO
BELIZE

Boca Bacalar Chico

Inner Channel

Laguna de Cantena

Deer Caye

Basil Jones

Rocky Point

Cayo Pajaros

Punta Arul

Laguna de Cayo Francés

Palermo Point

Blackadore Caye

SALAMANDER HIDEAWAY

MEXICO ROCKS

Ambergris Caye

CATALAN ROCKS

Caribbean Sea

Punta Arena

Laguna de San Pedro

Buena Vista Point

San Pedro

ENTRANCE THROUGH THE REEF

HOL CHAN MARINE RESERVE

Congrejo Caye

0   5 mi

0   5 km

© AVALON TRAVEL PUBLISHING, INC.

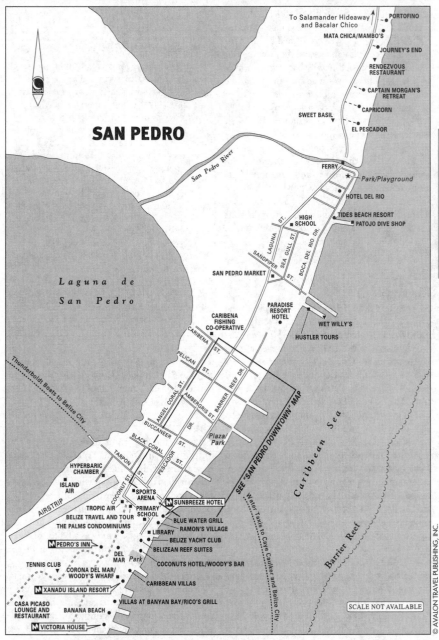

© AVALON TRAVEL PUBLISHING, INC.

hotels. Ambergris's beach runs parallel to the reef except at Rocky Point, where they briefly come together. Ambergris Caye was formed by an accumulation of coral fragments and silt from the Río Hondo as it emptied from what is now northern Belize. The caye is made up of mangrove swamps, 12 lagoons, a plateau, and a series of low sand ridges. The largest lagoon, fed by 15 creeks, is 2.5-mile-long **Laguna de San Pedro** on the western side of the village.

San Pedro Town sits on a sand ridge at the southern end of the island. Over the years, the constant wind, rain, tides, and occasional battering of a hurricane have reduced the shoreline and beachfront of the village by 30 feet. This is normal for barrier islands, which naturally shift position—but it's a bummer for we humans who like to build things in the sand.

HISTORY

The Maya

As with the rest of Belize, the first people on the caye were the Maya. They managed to fight off the invading Spaniards as early as 1508. Very little is known about these Maya. However, a small Post-Classic site in the Basil Jones area and a few jade and carved ornaments have been found along with obsidian flakes and fragments of pottery. Remnants indicate that Ambergris Caye was an important hub for trading. It is possible to visit these sites; transportation and guides are widely available.

At the southern end of the caye, the ruins of Marco Gonzalez are also considered of strategic importance. It is presumed that because of the location of Ambergris Caye (in the center of the sea-lane) it was a stopover for Maya traders traveling up and down the coast. And because of its close proximity to Mexico, no doubt it had great military value as well.

Four and a half miles north of Rocky Point, at Boca Bacalar Chico, a narrow channel separates Belize and Mexico. The Maya dug the strait by hand so that they could bring their canoes through rather than go all the way around the peninsula (now Ambergris Caye). In dry years when the water receded, it was impossible to get

---

TURTLE PENS TURNED SWIMMING POOLS

In the days when pirates roamed the high seas for months at a time, they had regular stopping places: Islands with abundant supplies of water were probably the most important. St. George's Caye was a favorite spot to pick up giant sea turtles. The seamen built large square pens (called kraals) at the end of wooden docks and would keep the captured turtles there until they left for the bounding main. Several turtles were taken on board and fed, kept mostly on their backs and out of the way (they would live that way for a month or two), until they were slaughtered for their meat. Often, turtle was the only sweetmeat the crews would eat for many months.

Over the years, the pirates dwindled and St. George's Caye became the unofficial capital of Belize. Many more homes were built along the waterfront, and kraals became "crawls," swimming areas for people. Today, many of the bright-white wooden houses still have these small "pools" at the ends of their docks.

---

a boat through, so in 1899 the Mexican government expanded the channel to, like the Native Americans before them, allow its ships easy access to the other side of the peninsula.

The Blakes

Between 1848 and 1849, during the Caste War on the Yucatán Peninsula, Yucatecan mestizos migrated to Belize, and four families were the first permanent residents of what has developed into present-day San Pedro on Ambergris Caye. Before long, there was a population of 50 self-sufficient fishermen, who were also growing corn and vegetables. Life was idyllic for these people—until 1874 and the coming of the Blake family.

James Blake paid the Belize government BZE$650 for Ambergris Caye (taking over every parcel of land except one set aside for the Catholic church) and began collecting rent from people who had been there for many years. After this, the history of the island was tied up with the fortunes of the Blakes and their in-laws, the Parhams and Alamillas. Their story reads like a script from a novel, including love affairs, illegitimate children, unlikely marriages, and (some say) power trips. The Blakes controlled everybody and everything on the island, including the coconut and fishing industries, though in the end (after almost 100 years) the good guys won out—or so it seems today. After many years, the rule of the Blake family came to a close when the Belizean government stepped in and made a "forced purchase" of San Pedro. It redistributed the land, selling lots and parcels to the same islanders who had been living on the land for generations.

The Fishing Industry

The caye saw industry change according to the political climate: from logwood to *chicle* to coconuts, and then to lobsters. Before 1920, the spiny lobster was thrown away and considered a nuisance, constantly getting caught in fishing nets. That all changed in 1921 when the lobster became a valuable export item. Though the fishermen were getting only a penny a pound, the business became lucrative when freezer vessels and freezer-equipped seaplanes began flying between the cayes and Florida. After struggling long and hard, the islanders established fishing cooperatives. Once they shook off the human "sharks," the fishing industry on the cayes became successful, with the benefits finally going to the fishermen.

Today's Ambergris

The island is rich in lore, some of which still reaches out and taps the modern islander on the shoulder. The establishment of the fishermen's co-op enabled the population of Ambergris to develop a good middle-class economy over the years. The financial upswing has allowed the town to improve the infrastructure of the island, which in turn has created a good atmosphere for tourists. Lots of stores, cafés, and hotels are waiting to be enjoyed, and the streets are becoming crowded with golf carts as the island develops.

The earliest tourists came to Ambergris Caye aboard the boat *Pamelayne* in the 1920s. By 1965, the first real hotel was established, and

San Pedro's Front Street, the hippest strip in Belize

the industry has been growing ever since. The caye is considered the most developed and successful tourism area of Belize. It boasts 24-hour-a-day electricity, modern telephone communication to anywhere in the world, and medical services.

There is a steady, mellow buzz to San Pedro Town, becoming a bit hectic and trendy at holiday times. If you visit during **El Dia de San Pedro,** June 26–29, you'll get a good local festival in as well. There is no doubt that Ambergris is quickly developing in an upscale direction, but don't be fooled—it's doing it Belizean style. You'll have to come down to find out what that means for yourself.

ORIENTATION

Whether arriving by air or sea, your trip to Ambergris begins in San Pedro Town. There are three roads running north-south and paralleling both the beach, on the island's east side, and the reef,

SEARCHING FOR SUNKEN TREASURE

Allied in the early 1950s, a group of Mexican divers (CEDAM—Conservation, Exploration, Diving, Archaeology, and Museums) from nearby Quintana Roo has salvaged several old vessels along the reef. The booty from these old ships wasn't gold treasure, but other practical items such as equipment, kitchen implements, tools, arms, beads, and an occasional coin, all contributing to our understanding of another era.

The first ship discovered and explored was *Mantanceros*. It was named for Punta Mantanceros, the point off the Quintana Roo beach close to where it's believed the ship went down. On February 22, 1742, the Spanish ship ended up in a skirmish with a British ship. The British ship was part of the Admiral's fleet that ducked into the protection of Belize and engaged in blockading any ships along the coast. The Spanish galleon was loaded with 270 tons of mixed cargo bound for New World ports. Many years after CEDAM salvaged the ship, information about it was discovered in the Archives of the Indies in Seville, Spain. The real name of the ill-fated ship was *Nuestra Señora de los Milagros* ("Our Lady of the Miracles"). Again, no gold, but many fascinating artifacts from 18th-century Spain.

Another doomed ship was *La Nicolasa*, believed to be the flagship of the fleet of Montejo, who was one of the conquerors of the Maya. And at Chinchorro Banks, a favorite dive spot just off the southern Mexican shore, a 40-cannon mystery wreck has for years defied efforts to make a definitive identification.

---

visible just offshore. Most locals still refer to the streets by their historic names, so that's what we do most of the time here. They are: **Front Street** (Barrier Reef Drive), **Middle Street** (Pescador Drive), and **Back Street** (Angel Coral Street). Another common landmark is the north end of town, where the San Pedro River flows through a navigable cut. This spot is often referred to as **"the cut"** or "the ferry," the latter referring to the hand-drawn barge that crosses back and forth all day, carrying pedestrians, bicycles, and golf carts for a small fee.

You'll often hear the term "south of town," both on the streets and in these pages. This refers to the continually developing area beyond the airstrip, accessed by traveling south on Coconut Drive.

SIGHTS

Beaches

Don't expect the wide open, clean beaches you've seen in other Caribbean destinations. A few hotels have good sand; most don't. But the ocean is as beautiful as ever, and when you want to swim, small docks are provided where it

might be difficult. In some areas, you need to wade through some sea grass to get to deep water, but it's worth it.

Hol Chan Marine Reserve

Once a traditional fishing ground, back when San Pedro was a sleepy village of a few hundred people, Hol Chan is now the most popular dive and snorkel site in Belize, with 75,000 visitors a year. Once you visit, you'll quickly understand the popularity of the reserve, and why it is important to help preserve it for years to come. Please follow the simple reef etiquette guidelines (see the sidebar "Reef Etiquette" in the Know Belize chapter), and help to lessen the impact humans have on these fragile ecosystems.

Declared in 1987, this marine park was established in order to preserve a small, but complete, section of the Belize Barrier Reef. Because of the no-fishing restrictions near the reef, the site boasts an amazing diversity of species. The reserve focuses its energy on creating a sustainable link between tourism and conservation, protecting the coral reef while allowing visitors to experience and learn about the beauty of the marine life living there.

The Hol Chan Marine Reserve office is on Caribena Street in the center of town and features an interactive visitors center, information on the reserve, and displays detailing the various zones of the reserve and its species.

Nearly all tour operators have trips to the Hol Chan cut and Shark Ray Alley.

Other Sights

Most of the other noteworthy sights in the area are under water. Every dive and snorkel operator has their own list of secret spots where they'll take you. Ask about ruins and cuts around the northern part of Ambergris Caye.

For many, the main attractions of Ambergris include the shops and boutiques in central San Pedro and the chain of resorts stretching north and south from the island. Walking, biking, or golf-carting in either direction can be a great half- or full-day activity, as you hop from one swanky hotel bar to the next, sampling different cuisines, moods, and color schemes, all with a view of the reef just offshore.

ENTERTAINMENT AND NIGHTLIFE

San Pedro boasts the best nightlife in the country, whether your idea of fun is dancing up a storm, drowning in alcohol, hearing live music, or watching chickens shit—it's all here. Wednesdays and Saturdays are the biggest nights out, and water taxis actually change their schedules to accommodate revelers. In general, the hotspots don't get going until 11 P.M. or midnight, with lots of warming up in the various bars before the bumpin' and grindin' begins.

Bars

Diving by day and drinking by night is the standard Ambergris scene—although with a number of proud under-achievers, you can replace the diving with a full day of cocktails. The bar at **BC's** (on the beach, back from the airstrip) is a particularly popular spot at which to drink your breakfast (and other meals), open at 9 A.M. daily and ragingly popular for its Sunday afternoon BBQ (bar food available). The standard tourist hangout is found in **Fido's Courtyard, Cannibals,** or the **Purple Parrot Bar.** The latter is in Ramon's Village and is apparently a favorite of Jimmy Buffet. Fido's often has live music. The **Rehab Bar** is next to the Jaguar's Temple disco, open daily, and on an open corner—great for people watching.

Local musician Barefoot Skinny's got a place of his own now, the **Hammock House** (11 A.M.–11 P.M. daily), all the way up by the north end ferry (right across the cut), featuring live music and jams five nights a week, and happy hour 4–6 P.M. daily. **Cholo's Sport Bar** is one of the mellower local hangouts. The **Casa Picasso** restaurant turns into a sensually lit martini lounge at 9 P.M., with half-price martinis to wash down their scrumptious tapas.

Of course, you'll have to catch a Wednesday night **Chicken Drop,** 6 P.M. at the **Pier Lounge** (in the Spindrift Hotel)—this is a local cultural event in which bets are placed as to which numbered square a caged chicken will choose to soil. Also ask if the crab races are still happening on Mondays, and warm up at the 2-for-1 happy hour, 4 P.M.–6 P.M.

Ambergris also has **The Palace,** a casino that lets you lose your money at slots and blackjack. They open every day at 2 P.M. but are closed Wednesday.

Crazy Canuck's Beach Bar has live *punta* music and dancing on Mondays, and all kinds of games (dice, cards, horseshoes, dominoes), including Saturday-afternoon Scrabble competitions.

Dancing

Wednesdays feature ladies night at **Wet Willy's,** and the Saturday scene really gets going when Fido's closes at midnight and everyone wanders across the street to the **Jaguar Temple,** open from 9:30 P.M. Thursday, Friday, and Saturday. The night often ends up at **Big Daddy's Disco,** on the edge of the park and the ocean at Ambergris Street. Music and dancing can easily go until 3 A.M., sometimes later. The **Barefoot Iguana Disco,** south of town on Coconut Drive, just changed ownership and seems to be steered toward an older, rock 'n' roll menu of entertainment; definitely look into it, as they plan to import all kinds of music and other entertainment.

Movies

The only real movie theater in the country is in the basement of the Princess Hotel in Belize City; the nearest modern cinema is just across the lagoon in Chetumal, Mexico. Here in San Pedro, however, you can enjoy the intimate setting of the **Brown Sugar Cinema** (located across from Fido's on Front St., tel. 501/608-6110, US$6), projecting DVDs on a big screen (bigger than your television, anyway); swing by their video rental shop down the block for a schedule.

SHOPPING

Gift shops abound in San Pedro, especially on Front and Middle Streets; many are fond of reminding you that you are, in fact, on the island from Madonna's song, *La Isla Bonita.* They've got your postcards, shells, swim-and beach-apparel, towels, hats, T-shirts, and the rest of the usual knickknacks. Some are more than just souvenir shops and have displays of gems or fascinating crafts—San Pedro has several artists who create world-class art with excellent portrayals of life and nature in Belize on canvas, and at least one artist who works in clay. Following are just a couple of notable shops.

You'll find **Belizean Arts** (tel. 501/226-2638) in Fido's Courtyard, featuring native art by local and neighboring-country artists as well as a great variety of crafts. If you're looking for more than the run-of-the-mill T-shirts, this store might be worth checking out. **Mambo Chill,** right next door, is the hip spot for expensive women's clothing. The sale sections at the **Toucan 1** and **Toucan 2** stores are treasured by local thrifters.

Ambergris Art Gallery is worth a look, with two stores: one on Middle Street near the men's clothing store Moonbreeze, the other in the Sunbreeze Hotel. There's a stained glass gallery south of Victoria House, and another interesting art gallery north of the cut, past Sweet Basil's.

Get your rocks on at the **Ambergris Maya Jade and History Museum** (located across from Town Hall, tel. 501/226-3311, ambergris-jade@aol.com, 9 A.M.–6 P.M. daily). Also a retail jade shop, it's designed "to give visitors an overview of 3,000 years of Mesoamerican jade and its importance to the cultures in the region." When you're finished, check out **Ambergris Emeralds,** just a few doors down.

RECREATION

Diving

There are *many* dive shops on the island. Almost every hotel on Ambergris employs the services of local divers, and some have on-site dive shops and dive masters. They all offer pretty much the same thing: resort courses, PADI and/or NAUI certification classes, day trips, and snorkel trips. Some also offer things like night dives, and a few have NITROX capabilities. What really makes the difference is the instructor or dive master. Prices are pretty standard around the island. It's worth it to shop around, but in general expect the following: two-tank dive US$60 plus rental fee and tax; open water certification US$250–350; three-tank dive to the Blue Hole US$185, to Turneffe US$150.

Amigos del Mar (tel. 501/226-2706, amigosdive@btl.net), located on the pier off of Cholo's Bar, is a bustling place with top-notch gear and a solid reputation as one of the best and safest operations on the island. **Patojo's** (tel. 501/226-2283, patojos@btl.net), located on the pier off Boca del Rio Drive, has an equally excellent reputation for professional service.

The Victoria House (victoria@btl.net) has the **Bradley brothers,** great dive masters who lead a very personal and educational tour—they enjoy their jobs and want you to enjoy their environment. The **Coral Beach Dive Shop** (tel. 501/226-2013) not only has been around for a long time, but also has the *Offshore Express,* the only live-aboard based in San Pedro. **Bottom Time** dive shop is a full-service facility at the Holiday Hotel.

Boating, Snorkeling, and Fishing

Take a boat ride. Explore the Caribbean Sea in and around the many cayes of the area. Some vessels are glass-bottom boats, such as the *Reef*

SNORKELING SAN PEDRO

Most visitors to San Pedro snorkel at least once during their stay. With such an abundance of fine sites—from docks to the Belize Barrier Reef—you will not have to look far, and nearly all tour operators run trips to the following areas.

For starters, grab your snorkel, mask, and fins, and take a swim around the dock at **Ramon's Village Resort.** With an artificial reef that is home to a wide variety of small reef fish, this spot is a favorite swimming hole for locals.

© JOSHUA BERMAN

Float, watch, and don't forget to breathe: World class snorkel sites abound throughout Belize's waters.

For those anxious to see real live coral, the most popular sites are **Mexico Rocks** and the **Hol Chan Marine Reserve.** Mexico Rocks is on the reef north of town and is the place to go to see a huge diversity of coral formations. Only twelve feet at its deepest, there is an abundance of coral, and the channel nearby brings in a lot of marine life, especially small reef fish. There aren't as many big fish here as in Hol Chan, but for some that's a plus. A little bit south of this area is **Tres Cocos,** a site gaining popularity because of the likelihood of seeing spotted eagle rays. Most tour operators have trips to both areas.

The crown jewel of San Pedro snorkeling is the Hol Chan Marine Reserve, located four miles southeast of San Pedro Town. Visitors are taken to the Hol Chan cut, a 30-foot deep natural break in the Belize Barrier Reef. Snorkelers stay in the shallow inner reef area, but can swim through the cut. Because of the movement through this area between the ocean and the inner reef lagoon, it is high in nutrients and allows for marine animals of all types to thrive and increase in size. Be on the lookout for spiny lobsters, black groupers, nurse sharks, moray eels, and a plethora of reef fish showing off their bright colors. Rangers patrol the area during the day and help ensure the safety of visitors. Listen to your guide, though—the current at Hol Chan can be strong!

Another site, **Shark Ray Alley,** is also part of the reserve and is a mile south of the Hol Chan cut. This site offers visitors the rare opportunity to snorkel alongside southern stingrays and nurse sharks that frequent the area in search of food (which is kindly provided by your tour operator). Remember—only tour guides are allowed to feed these big fish, and please . . . no touching! Large schools of horse-eyed jack and snapper also come here for the free handouts. There are spectacular coral formations on the back reef for snorkelers, and the fore reef gives scuba divers the chance to dive the Amigos Del Mar tug boat wreck.

When you step back onto dry land, stop in at the Hol Chan Marine Reserve office on Caribena Street in the center of town. The interactive visitors center has information on the reserve, as well as displays detailing the various zones of the reserve and species. Not sure what you saw? Stop in and ask the staff—they're happy to answer questions and give more details on the reserve.

(Contributed by Laurie Smith, a Peace Corps Volunteer who worked for two years to help educate both locals and visitors alike in proper reef etiquette in and around San Pedro's snorkel and dive sites.)

The Northern Cayes

Seekers (tel. 501/226-2802), so the non-swimmer can enjoy the beauty of the sea too. Two trips daily, 9 A.M. and noon. Snorkeling is also part of the activity on many boats, and gear is readily available.

Blue Hole (at the Spindrift Hotel, tel. 501/226-2982, www.bluedive.com) offers all the standard caye and inland tours. **Captain Rick Bevan** charters a 42-foot catamaran from his dock behind BC's Bar (tel. 501/226-3168, www.belizecharters.com).

A day-boat with a long history of success is the *Rum Punch II,* run by brothers Tony and George. A snorkeling stop at the **Coral Garden,** lunch at Caye Caulker, and captivating stories make a pleasant day. True to the boat's name, rum punch is served throughout the trip. For a romantic evening, check out various sunset cruises.

Most dive shops and snorkeling guides also do fishing trips. Ask around the docks (and your hotel) for the best guides. **Rubie's Hotel** has a shack on the beach, and the guys working there are rumored to be excellent guides. The area within the reef is a favorite for such fish as tarpon and bonefish. Outside the reef, the choice of big game is endless. Most hotels and dive shops will make arrangements for fishing, including boat and guide. One resort, **El Pescador Lodge,** specializes in fishing packages that include all types of angling (see Accommodations for contact information).

Fitness

The **Isla Bonita Tennis Club** (toward the south end of the airstrip, tel. 501/226-2683) has an air-conditioned, fully equipped (if small) workout room in an interesting, modern building. There are also aerobics and yoga classes, two tennis courts, a 200,000-gallon pool designed to accommodate both lap swimmers and frolicking children, volleyball, and horseshoes. Use of the facilities for tourists costs US$5 half-day, $10 full-day, or $50/week (special rates for locals). The low-key restaurant and bar offers omelets and other breakfasts, burgers, steaks, and lighter options from US$7. From here you can watch the planes take off and land all day.

On the opposite end of town, almost at the ferry, you'll find the working-man's gym at **Oscar's Fitness Center** (tel. 501/226-2239), with a magazine-plastered free-weight room, only US$2.50 per workout.

Yoga and Massage

Today's San Pedro offers much more than the marathon drinking bouts it has been famous for in the past, and there is an ever-growing number of healthy activities to choose from. Yoga is usually a wandering affair in San Pedro, with individual instructors roaming from resort to resort, but Leslie Soukup (tel. 501/226-3024, leslie_inbox@hotmail.com) is making a more permanent go at it; call for details on her morning classes, or keep an eye out for her flyer.

There are numerous massage therapists in San Pedro, and a few studios, but prices are no cheaper than in the States or Europe (massages roughly US$65 an hour).

Sol Spa (tel. 501/226-2470, www.solspa-belize.com) is just north of the airstrip, offering treatment for your "spirit, mind, and body;" ask about the special "Honeymoon Bliss" and "Solar Therapy" treatments. **Synchronicity Healing Arts** (tel. 501/226-2936) is more about energy and healing work than merely pampering spa treatment; proprietress TP Pas is a licensed masseuse as well as a yoga and Pilates instructor, and can arrange private or group sessions in her studio, located next door to the *San Pedro Sun* office, south of town; ask about her "flower essence therapy."

Rosie Uejbe runs **Ambergris Massage** (tel. 501/606-2127). **The Art of Touch** (tel. 501/226-3357) is in the entrance to the Sunbreeze Hotel; then there's **Tropical Touch** (tel. 501/266-4666), Master Lee, and other options. Check the Salamander Hideaway resort as well.

ACCOMMODATIONS
Under US$25

Finally—a cheap hostel on Ambergris! ꟿ **Pedro's Inn** (tel. 501/226-3825, pedroback2000@yahoo .com, US$12.50) has 40 beds in a stilted barn-like dormitory. The rooms, which only have two

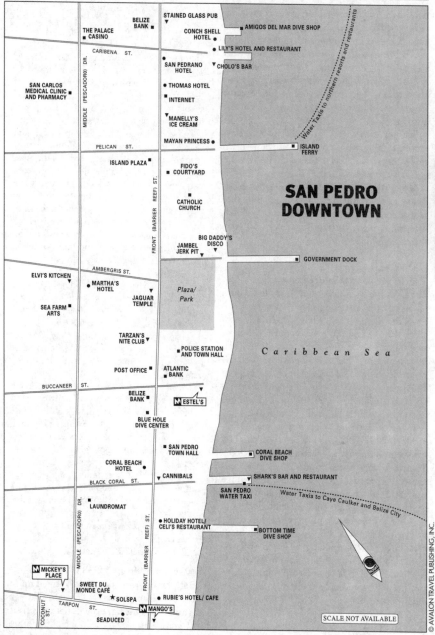

STAINED GLASS PUB

BELIZE BANK

THE PALACE CASINO

AMIGOS DEL MAR DIVE SHOP

CONCH SHELL HOTEL

LILY'S HOTEL AND RESTAURANT

CARIBENA ST.

SAN PEDRANO HOTEL

CHOLO'S BAR

MIDDLE (PESCADORO) DR.

THOMAS HOTEL

SAN CARLOS MEDICAL CLINIC AND PHARMACY

INTERNET

MANELLY'S ICE CREAM

PELICAN ST.

MAYAN PRINCESS

ISLAND FERRY

Water Taxis to northern resorts and restaurants

ISLAND PLAZA

FIDO'S COURTYARD

SAN PEDRO DOWNTOWN

FRONT (BARRIER REEF) ST.

CATHOLIC CHURCH

BIG DADDY'S DISCO

JAMBEL JERK PIT

GOVERNMENT DOCK

AMBERGRIS ST.

ELVI'S KITCHEN

MARTHA'S HOTEL

Plaza/ Park

SEA FARM ARTS

JAGUAR TEMPLE

Caribbean Sea

TARZAN'S NITE CLUB

POLICE STATION AND TOWN HALL

POST OFFICE

ATLANTIC BANK

BUCCANEER ST.

BELIZE BANK

ESTEL'S

BLUE HOLE DIVE CENTER

SAN PEDRO TOWN HALL

CORAL BEACH DIVE SHOP

CORAL BEACH HOTEL

CANNIBALS

SHARK'S BAR AND RESTAURANT

BLACK CORAL ST.

SAN PEDRO WATER TAXI

Water Taxis to Caye Caulker and Belize City

MIDDLE (PESCADORO) DR.

LAUNDROMAT

HOLIDAY HOTEL/ CELI'S RESTAURANT

BOTTOM TIME DIVE SHOP

FRONT (BARRIER REEF) ST.

MICKEY'S PLACE

SWEET DU MONDE CAFÉ

SOLSPA

RUBIE'S HOTEL/ CAFE

COCONUT ST.

TARPON ST.

MANGO'S

SEADUCED

SCALE NOT AVAILABLE

© AVALON TRAVEL PUBLISHING, INC.

beds each, are partitioned-off stalls, comfy with lamp and fan. Shared bathrooms are clean and adequate. A seven-minute walk to the town center, Pedro's also offers cheap Internet, onsite bar and BBQ, big kiddie pool, and discounted tours.

Walk the backside of the island to find other cheaper and less formal rooms, like **Stone's Rooms** (tel. 501/206-2441), just behind the airstrip.

Ruby's Hotel (tel. 501/226-2063, rubys @btl.net) may have lumpy beds and oddly angled sinks, but it's an excellent central location and you can sip coffee with the fishermen as the sun rises over Ruby's Cafe (Ruby's just bought a guesthouse a few minutes' walk away on the other side of the island as well). Rooms with great balconies and private baths go for US$35–50, with shared bath US$16.

US$25–50

The classic **N Hotel San Pedrano** (tel. 501/226-2054, sanpedrano@btl.net, US$30 w/ fan, US$40 a/c) offers six rooms less than a block from the ocean. The Pedrano is the self-proclaimed "top of the low end," popular with business travelers. From the breezy upstairs veranda, it's easy to eat a bite, read a book, or watch the street life below. It's a favorite of both European and American travelers, who offer nothing but favorable comments. Each room has hot/cold water, private bath, and ceiling fan or a/c.

It isn't very pretty, but **Thomas Hotel** (tel. 501/226-2861, US$32 fan, US$38 a/c, plus tax) has seven cheap rooms. **Martha's Hotel** (Middle St. across from Elvi's, tel. 501/226-2053, julian@btl.net, from US$35) is two blocks from the waterfront. Rooms are upstairs, clean, with private baths, ceiling fans, and linoleum floors.

Right on the beach and around the corner from Hotel San Pedrano, **N The Conch Shell Hotel** (tel. 501/216-2062, conchsehll@btl.net, from US$40/55 s/d) has simple rooms with private baths, ceiling fans, linoleum floors, woodpaneled walls, and simple furnishings. Some have kitchenettes.

US$50–100

Tides Beach Resort (tel. 501/226-2283, pa-

CHOOSING A HOTEL

The only accommodations options for economy travelers on Ambergris Caye are located within San Pedro Town or on the outskirts by the airstrip. If you have budgeted more than US$25 per night per couple, you have more options and should be aware of a few things before beginning your search. First off, when discussing downtown hotels, condos, and apartments, the word "beachside" is, in fact, referring to the narrow strip of sand (sometimes crowded with boats and vendors) that is kept hard-packed by a constant flow of foot traffic in both directions. Only on the north and south ends of town do you start seeing people actually lounging in the sand. Then, as you move farther from town in either direction along the caye, the beaches fronting the resorts become more and more exclusive (even though, officially, they all still belong to the Queen).

Of course, what you give up in beach quality, you get back in location: "in town" means in the middle of cafés, bars, boutiques, dive shops, dancing, and dining. If you're more into privacy, the action is easily accessible from any resort on the island—if you choose the best of both worlds in one of these resorts, you'll pay for it in cold, hard cash.

Keep in mind that the special rates and extra taxes discussed in the Accommodations section of the Practicalities chapter apply to all hotels in San Pedro. Always verify seasonal rates and whether or not they include taxes before paying! We've tried to identify these, but hotels advertise rates differently and keeping track is difficult.

Ambergris has an astounding number of accommodations (70!) and their reputations and quality of service often comes and goes with the tide (and eternal flow of new managers and owners). Please let us know if you find a hotel not listed here that should be, or vice versa.

tojos@btl.net, from US$85/100 s/d) is a friendly, family-run guesthouse located on the beach, away from the center of town. The eight light and airy units have tile floors and private bathrooms. This is also the home of the Jumping Frijoles beachside bar and Patojos Scuba

Center, one of the most respected outfits on the caye.

The **Coral Beach Hotel** (tel. 501/266-2013, coralbeach@btl.net, US$50/57 s/d w/ fan, about $10 more for a/c) offers 19 clean, small rooms, each with private bath, hot/cold water, and a/c or fan. There's a nice veranda overlooking the action on Front Street. Meal plans are available.

Lily's Hotel (tel. 501/206-2059, lilies@btl.net, US$65) has 10 rooms offering decent value for private bath, a/c, and very nice verandas on beach. The simple hotel is run by the Felipe Paz family—friendly, long-time residents of San Pedro. Lily's is located on the main, reef-facing beach strip, near the dock where the *Triple J Shania* is tied up. Lily's has been known for years for offering excellent local food in plentiful family-style servings, and they offer complimentary coffee every morning.

On the north end of town toward the cut, the **Hotel del Rio** (tel. 501/226-2286, www.ambergriscaye.com/hodelrio) is one the best bargains on the island. Accommodations range from basic economy rooms with shared baths and cold water (US$30 a couple) to bigger casitas built of natural materials (US$75 for a king or two queen beds; sleep up to five people for US$125). Anglers, take note: The owner's husband, Fido, is a well-known fishing guide with his own 28-foot boat.

At the north end of Front Street, you'll find the entrance to the compound of **Paradise Resort Hotel** (tel. 501/226-2083, paradise@btl.net). With a pleasing range of amenities and a good location on a sandy beach with its own dock and beachside bar, it conveys a relaxed, "barefoot" feeling. You'll find a deli, gift and dive shops, and you can make all fishing arrangements on the premises. You'll have your choice of a thatched cabana, a villa, or a mini-suite with a/c, all built with natural materials—a nice break from all the cement in many San Pedro hotels. Cabanas start at US$100 with fan and rates for the various units go up from there.

US$100–150

The pleasant **San Pedro Holiday Hotel** (tel. 501/226-2014 or 226-2103, www.sanpedrohol-iday.com, US$103 plus tax) was the island's first hotel and, still under the original management, keeps getting better. The 17 somewhat spacious rooms all have a/c and fans, private bath with hot/cold water, and beachfront verandas. Some have refrigerators. Lots of water sports and boats are available. **Celi's Restaurant** serves delicious lunch and dinner.

The **N SunBreeze Hotel** (tel. 501/226-2191 or 226-2345, www.sunbreezehotel.com, US$120/130 s/d, deluxe rooms US$160) is a beautiful, conventional style hotel with 42 rooms built in a U-shape around an open sand area and swimming pool, all of them with an ocean view and many comforts: two queen beds, a/c, TV, tile floor, local artwork, large private bath, and quick access to the restaurant's upscale island cuisine. Front Street starts next door, and the entrance is right across from the airstrip, so it's an easy walk to almost any point in town; on-site dive shop.

One of the island's biggest, the **Banana Beach Resort** (tel. 501/226-3848, info@bananabeach.com, www.bananabeach.com, from US$125) has a huge range of options among its 66 units, from smallish standard hotel rooms to deluxe four-bedroom suites. There's a pool, gift shop, bar, and steakhouse on-site, and lots of packages are available.

The northernmost resort on Ambergris, **N Salamander Hideaway** (tel. 501/606-5922, info@salamanderbelize.com, www.salamander-belize.com, US$120–140) has eight simply and elegantly furnished cabanas near a handsome common lodge. All of it is swimming distance from the Belize Barrier Reef, with some of the most beautiful and untouched snorkel and dive sites on the island. Sea kayaks, sailboards, and other water sports are available, free of charge. The spa is in a Native American tepee where a wide range of body treatments, energy work, and facials are offered. Also, on-site yoga and meditation is often available at sunrise on the dock. This is a bit more rustic and isolated than other places on the island, but it's still only a 10-mile boat ride back to town.

Three miles north of San Pedro, the **Capricorn Resort** (tel. 501/226-2809, www.ambergriscaye.com/capricorn) offers intimate beachfront

© JOSHUA BERMAN

The majority of Ambergris's beachfront accommodations are still small and eclectic, as seen here at Salamander Hideaway.

seclusion in one of three cabanas. Under fresh, new management, Capricorn has enjoyed a bright, tasteful makeover and your young, Texan hosts will make you feel at home—and so will the 15 staff on hand (do the math: that's five per cabana). Rates include a continental breakfast and Capricorn's restaurant is one of the best (considered *the* best by many) on the island. The small beach bar serves lunch for those not wanting to hop a water taxi into town.

Caribbean Villas (tel. 501/226-2715, c-v-hotel @btl.net) is a luxury suite group (11 units) a 15-minute walk from town and popular among birdwatchers for its four-story wooden "people perch" on the edge of the bush offering a canopy-eye view of the wildlife. Non-guests are welcome to use it; please check in with the front desk beforehand. The fully furnished suites start at US$100 and there are some higher-priced deluxe options.

Inside an elegant three-story building of tropical colonial design, on the corner of Sandpiper Street and the ocean, are the 14 suites comprising the **Blue Tang Inn** (US tel. 800/337-8203, Bel. tel. 501/226-2326, www.bluetanginn.com, US$125–160). All suites have fully decorated bedrooms, living rooms, and kitchens with h/c water, private baths, ceiling fans, and a/c, and can accommodate up to six adults; third-floor rooms have whirlpool tubs.

US$150–200

Occupy your own pleasure dome at **M Xanadu Island Resort** (tel. 501/226-2814, www .xanaduresort-belize.com). These monolithic domes are among the strongest and best-insulated structures in the world, the only hurricane-proof buildings on the island. The rounded walls and thatch shade roofs give a hobbit-hole feeling, except Bilbo Baggins never had so much space, wicker furniture, or kitchen appliances—nor did he live elevated above a white-sand beach and pool. The one-bedroom lofts start at US$160; 2- and 3-bedroom options cost a bit more.

A full-service resort, **Ramon's Village** (US tel. 800/624-4215, Bel. tel. 501/226-2071, www.belizeisfun.com) has a fantastic 500-foot beach, barely south of San Pedro, with attractive surroundings, good restaurant and bar, a myriad of activities, and a long pier with a *palapa* at the end. The recreational pier features two dive shops with boats, guides, and all diving equipment available for reef trips. The pool is steps away from the cabanas and one end of it is a whirlpool tub. Ramon's offers 20 fully equipped apartment units starting at US$185. The restaurant is one of the best on the island (dinner averages about US$24, and room service is available). Recreational rentals include sailboards, aqua cycles, speedboats, bicycles, and golf carts.

The **Belize Yacht Club** (US tel. 800/688-0402, Bel. tel. 501/226-2777, www.belizeyachtclub.com). is a 10-minute walk south of town; the complex boasts a friendly staff, pier/marina, gift shop, manicured lawns, pool, dive shop, and its 40 units are among the plushest suites on the island. Rates for the fully equipped suites start at US$165 and climb from there.

Over US$200

The handsome  **Victoria House** (US tel. 800/247-5159, fax 713/224-3287, Bel. tel. 501/226-2067, www.victoria-house.com) is the best of the best, presenting the colonial elegance you'd expect from its name. Located on a well-manicured, lush piece of property about two miles south of town, Victoria House's 35 units include 10 stucco and thatched casitas with tile floors, ocean views, private bathrooms, and ceiling fans or a/c (US$250), state rooms (US$170), and luxurious "plantation suites" (US$340). Multi-bedroom, mansion-like villas are also available—as is a pool, full-service dive shop with private guides, the Admiral Nelson Bar, and one of the top-rated restaurants in the country.

Rent a plush villa at **Banyan Bay** (also south of town, tel. 501/226-3739, www.banyanbay.com);

The lap of luxury: Victoria House is only one of Belize's class acts.

this "luxury family resort" offers all the amenities in their 70 suites, including a whirlpool tub in every room. Lots of activities and lessons for children available; full dive/inland trips arranged. Suites from US$250 s/d; two couples can go in on a beachfront unit for US$375. There's a great on-site dock restaurant, Rico's.

Guests at **Captain Morgan's Retreat** (US tel. 888/653-9090, Bel. tel. 501/226-2567 or 226-2207, www.belizevacation.com, from US$250, plus tax) will find 32 units, including clean, attractive thatch-roof casitas with a/c and fully equipped villas with kitchen and a/c. There's an on-site pool complete with swim-up bar, and a restaurant with decent food. Some say the Cap'n is every bit as cheesy as you would expect a place to be that brags about its participation in trashy television.

True to its name, **El Pescador Lodge** (US tel. 800/245-1950, Bel. tel. 501/226-2975, www.elpescador.com, from US$200), three miles north of San Pedro, is focused on fishing packages, though some come just to get away from it all. The resort has 12 rooms and one suite, all with private baths in a large colonial building. A long veranda faces the sea within sight of the reef, just 200 yards offshore.

A little more than four miles north, **Mata Chica Beach Resort** (tel. 501/220-5010, matachica@btl.net, from US$230) has fourteen spacious casitas and luxury villas, exquisitely and personally styled by the owner. The resort, which draws numerous guests from a swanky Hollywood scene, specializes in "grand or intimate weddings, honeymoons, and secluded getaways."

Still not luxurious enough for you? Jump across the lagoon from San Pedro's west side to **Cayo Espanto** (US tel. 888/666-4282, www.aprivateisland.com) where you'll find five units, each with king-size bed, terry robes, private pool, and yes, your own personal butler. Rates from US$995, or what the hell—rent the entire island for US$8,000 a night.

FOOD
Cheap Belizean
The least expensive eats in town are undoubtedly at the row of fast-food shacks near the park, where you can eat three meals a day (burritos, rice and beans, stew chicken, etc.) for less than US$3 a meal. Walking the streets (especially the back streets), you'll find a plethora of fast-food and local eateries with similar Mexican and Belizean options. Grab a quick pastry or stuffed croissant at **La Popular Bakery,** with a big building near the cut and a small shop in the middle of town, around the corner from the post office.

A local favorite for breakfast is **Ⓜ Estel's.** The people are very cool, and the breakfast burrito massive. Located behind the Atlantic Bank, on the beach. For inexpensive Mexican food, try the **Reef Restaurant,** next to Elvi's on Pescador Drive. **Tropical Takeout,** across the street from the airport and next to the SunBreeze Hotel, has great homemade salsa, super-cheap breakfasts, and other treats—you know you're getting good value when all the cabbies hang out here. **Cannibals** serves three meals a day and offers a bit of everything—salads, marinated chicken (US$5), and

breakfast burritos (US$4), baked potatoes with various fillings, and nachos.

Ruby's has good pastries and coffee early in the morning. Other reputable spots are **Ambergris Delights** and **Celi's Deli,** near Ruby's. Ⓜ **Mickey's Place** on Tarpon Street is home of the huge Wednesday special burrito for US$4; Mickey's has an ample menu of local fare as well and offers a bit more ambience than the other Belizean places.

Cafés
Café Olé, across from the airstrip, has coffee drinks and smoothies, and the porch is a good spot to eavesdrop on local gossip as you watch the town's characters cruise by in their golf carts. There's also a full Italian menu (entrees from US$14). Across the schoolyard, the **Sweet du Monde Cafe** (7 A.M.–6 P.M., closed Sun.) has breakfast and lunch sandwiches, including bagels and lox for US$9. Go to **Manelly's** on Front Street for homemade ice cream.

Sweet Basil (tel. 501/226-3870, 11 A.M.–6 P.M. Tues.–Sun.) is a posh, upscale café serving pastas, vegetarian meals, salads, sandwiches, and gourmet burgers, as well as a full, sinful dessert menu and many coffee drinks and wine—all in quiet isolation about a 15-minute walk north of the cut.

Pizza
Pizza is available for delivery at a number of places. In a week-long, island-wide poll of expats and tourists, Ⓜ **Pepperoni's** (tel. 501/226-4515, 5 P.M.–10 P.M. Sun.–Thurs.) was the unanimous choice for both quality and price—a large 16" specialty pie goes for US$20. Call for delivery anywhere south of the ferry—or pick it up or dine in on their outdoor patio, located south of town. Just north of the airstrip, **Pauly's** (tel. 501/226-2651) has a delicious shrimp pizza and other creative slices (plus subs and appetizers).

Barbecues
A rotating schedule ensures a beach barbecue nearly every night of the week, starting with **BC's** on the beach, 11 A.M.–3 P.M. Sunday; your choice of chicken, ribs, or fish (US$5–10). Also on Sun-

day, **Crazy Canuck's** throws in live music and a horseshoe tournament. The **Holiday Hotel** has live music to accompany its beach barbecue on Wednesday night; the **Lions Club** donates the money it makes from its Friday and Saturday night barbecues to those who need medical help and can't afford it, and **Ramon's** has a Tuesday and Friday barbecue.

Caribbean and More

The cozy reggae-fueled kitchen of the **JamBel Jerk Pit** offers Jamaican flavors like coconut curry and jerk chicken dishes from US$7.50. Open for lunch and dinner, located right in front of the playground.

Caliente has waterfront Mexican and seafood. Open 11 A.M.–9:30 P.M. (but closed Mon.), they are famous for their lime soup at lunch and generous lobster dinners (US$22); other entrees start at US$12.

For Chinese, try the **Jade Garden** (.25 mile south of the airstrip, tel. 501/226-2506 for deliveries); open for lunch and dinner daily, entrees from about US$10.

For delicious Cajun/Caribbean cuisine, go to M **Mango's,** sandwiched on the beach between Ruby's and the library. The menu features 140 items, including gumbo (US$5 a bowl), shrimp jambalaya (US$15), and all kinds of smoothies and froufrou drinks.

The **Stained Glass Pub** gives a faraway English-bar feeling, offering cider drinks and "Home cooked comfort foods and nouvelle cuisine" in a classy, cozy setting. Dinner entrées from US$15, with great lunches and soups.

Papi's Diner offers cheap breakfasts and lunches, and is very popular with locals. This is one of the better locally owned Caribbean joints in San Pedro, and the hike up to the north end of town is worth it—or order in (delivery tel. 501/226-2047, 7 A.M.–10 P.M. daily). Fish dinners from US$10, or try the seafood platter with generous chunks of lobster, shrimp, and fish for US$17.50.

Celi's Restaurant, at Holiday Hotel, delivers icy piña coladas and some of the best conch ceviche on the island, plus a full menu, of course. It's been locally owned for many years. **Tastes**

of Thailand (reservations and take-out tel. 501/226-2601, 6 P.M.–10:30 P.M., closed Wed.) gets rave reviews for its 60 authentic dishes.

Fine Island Cuisine

San Pedro is blessed with an ever-evolving selection of locally trendy restaurants offering international fare and flair; if you don't pay for such indulgence with an expanded waistline, you'll surely pay for it in cash. If you're *really* dining out—appetizer, couple of drinks, entrée, and dessert—expect to pay as much as you would in New York City, from US$35–60 per person or more if you like your wine—better savor every scrumptious bite. Reservations are recommended at all of the following, at least in the high season.

Some of the best dining ambience on the island is found at **Elvi's Kitchen,** on the corner of Middle Street and Ambergris Street since 1974. The seafood specials, like Maya fish (US$12.50), are especially good, and the frozen key lime pie is famous; live local music on Thursday.

At Capricorn Resort's acclaimed restaurant, your table is yours for the night.

Of the finer restaurants, **Blue Water Grill** (at the SunBreeze Hotel, tel. 501/226-3347) is known to offer some of the best value and biggest portions; the chef brings his experience in Hawaii and Southeast Asia to your table and prides himself on an awesome presentation. Sushi on Tuesday and Thursday, pizza on Sunday (entrees about US$18). **El Divino,** at Banana Beach Hotel, is a reputable steakhouse, and **Rico's,** on the water behind Banyan Bay, is also highly rated.

Casa Picasso (tel. 501/226-4507 or 610-4056, from 5:30 P.M. Mon.–Sat.) fills a unique niche, with its tapas, pastas, desserts, and good tunes. You'll have to seek this place out, located out of the way near the south end of the airstrip, but you'll be glad you did—there are veggie options, fresh bread, and a huge drink and martini menu (tapas US$5–11 each, pasta bowls from US$10).

Capricorn (tel. 501/226-2809), three miles north of San Pedro, offers an intimate, beachfront dining experience that is gourmet in every sense of the word. Reservations are a must; your table is yours for the night. Feast on fish, Italian or French cuisine, and daily specials like stuffed grouper, crab cakes, and seafood crepes. Capricorn's fisherman goes out each morning to catch that day's entrees. Save room for desserts like creamy rum chocolate cake.

The **Rendezvous Restaurant** (tel. 501/226-3426) holds a stellar reputation for its blend of Thai and French cuisine. Start with escargot with lemon-garlic butter sauce for an appetizer (US$10); then grilled shrimp (US$22) or chicken with coconut red-curry sauce (US$15). They serve lunch and dinner; you'll need to take a water taxi here.

Up the coast a couple more miles, **Mambo's,** at the Mata Chica Resort, is pure indulgence, serving rich and artful heaps of seafood paella, glazed shrimp, lobster, and calamari (or a bleu cheese–encrusted filet mignon); save room for the to-die-for chocolate mousse.

The chef at **Victoria House** (tel. 501/226-2067) has won numerous awards, including first place in the annual "Taste of Belize" contest—try her famed "snapper tower" or, if you miss it (the three dinner menus rotate throughout the week), consider the bacon-wrapped, rum-glazed shrimp, served atop a bed of Caribbean rice and grilled pineapple. Wow.

DIVING ABBREVIATIONS

Don't know what the hard-core divers are talking about? Here are a few abbreviations explained so you'll be in the know.

NAUI—National Association of Underwater Instructors
NITROX—oxygen-enriched air (more than 21 percent oxygen) used as breathing gas for deep water dives
PADI—Professional Association of Dive Instructors
SCUBA—Self Contained Underwater Breathing Apparatus

INFORMATION

Things change quickly in San Pedro. Before your trip, be sure to take a good look at **www.ambergriscaye.com.** This is by far the best portal to all things Ambergris, including a lively message board filled with opinionated characters. You'll find links to over 120 island businesses, as well as Ambergris's two weekly papers, *The San Pedro Sun* (tel. 501/226-2070, www.sanpedrosun.net) and *Ambergris Today* (tel. 501/226-3462).

Once you arrive, you'll want to find the latest free copy of *The Green Guide,* a handy pocket guide with schedules, maps, and local ads (tel. 501/226-3825, greenguideac@hotmail.com). Another source of information is the **Ambergris Caye Chamber of Commerce** (tel. 501/226-3245, acchamber@hotmail.com).

Diving

For diving information, start with **www.scubadivingbelize.com,** and try to find the latest annual Belize issue of *Skin Diver* magazine, usually out in June.

SERVICES

The **post office** is on the corner of Front and Buccaneer Streets, open 8 A.M.–5 P.M. Monday–Friday. It's always fun to choose from Belize's beautiful, artistic, and often very large postage stamps; they make great gifts for the folks back home and are perfect for framing or for the traditional stamp collector.

Nellie's Laundry (on Pescador Dr., tel. 501/226-2454, 7 A.M.–8 P.M. daily, US$6 a load) offers free pick-up and delivery.

Belicolor one-hour photo (tel. 501/226-3304) is in the Island Plaza.

Travel & Tour Belize (just north of the airstrip, tel. 501/226-2137 or 226-2031, www.travel-tourbelize.com, 8 A.M.–5 P.M. Mon.–Fri., plus Sat. morning) is the oldest and only full-service travel agent in San Pedro; they'll handle all your bookings, both local and international, and can help with weddings and events too.

Money

Change money at the **Casa de Cambio,** where you'll get the same rates for travelers checks (near Town Hall, 8 A.M.–5 P.M. Mon.–Sat.). **Milo's Money Exchange** is another option (on Middle St., tel. 501/226-2196, 8 A.M.–5 P.M. Mon.–Fri. and 9 A.M.–noon Sat., closed lunchtime during the week). It exchanges Belizean, U.S., Guatemalan, Mexican, Canadian, and British currencies (and is also a Western Union branch).

The Atlantic Bank is next to the Spindrift Hotel. The Belize Bank is across the street and south of Buccaneer Street.

Medical

Prescriptions and other medicines can be found at **R&L Pharmacy** (tel. 501/226-2890, open daily) by the airstrip. If you need medical attention, there's **Dr. L Rodriguez Medical Services** (tel. 501/226-3197) and the **San Carlos Medical Center** (tel. 501/226-2918).

Internet Access

Click on to the end of the speedy DSL line in **Coconet** (on Front St., 7 A.M.–10 P.M.), with a full bar, breakfast treats, coffee, and a brand new network. New owners may make some changes, but Coconet will undoubtedly remain a solid, mellow option. Up the block, a Bulgarian couple runs the **Caribbean Connection Internet Café** (7 A.M.–10 P.M. daily), which is air-conditioned and has phone service and espresso drinks.

Island Internet may be located a bit out of the way, on the road south of town (actually it's not out of the way at all for those staying at south-end resorts), but they know how to attract customers: free alcohol and caffeine. That's right, come surfing on Island's speedy machines (DSL with satellite backup), and you'll receive a complimentary beer, rum drink, espresso, or other beverage, for every 15 minutes you're logged on—you do the math (US$1 per five minutes, US$11/hr).

Groceries

There are plentiful medium-sized supermarkets located throughout San Pedro Town, the cheapest is **Super Buy** on Back Street. The best selection is at **Island Supermarket** (on Coconut Dr., delivery tel. 501/226-2972). For fresh fruit and vegetables, try **D & L Produce** on Back Street, or the **Greenhouse** on Front Street. **Wine De Vine** (tel. 501/226-3110) has the finest selection of foreign wines and cheeses in all of Belize, and also offers daily free tastings. It's located in the Vilma Linda Plaza, just north of the airstrip.

GETTING AROUND

Walking is feasible within the town of San Pedro itself; it's about a 20-minute stroll from the airstrip to the ferry. Once you start traveling between resorts to the south or north, however, you may wish to go by bike, golf cart, taxi, or boat. At one time, cars were a rarity, but more are showing up on the sandy roads. However, since the government eliminated the duty on electric golf carts, hundreds of these quiet vehicles—instead of cars—are now on the island.

Many resorts have free bicycles for their guests, others have them for rent, as do a handful of outside shops. Rentals are available by the hour (about US$5), day (US$7.50), and week (US$25). Minivan taxis (green license plates) are

DRIVE YOUR OWN GOLF CART

If you like to do your own driving, rent one of the hundreds of electric golf carts used on Ambergris Caye. Just follow one of the many advertisements leading you to a rental place, or start with **Moncho's**, closest to the airstrip and boasting one of the island's largest fleets (tel. 501/226-3262). There's also **Cholo's** (tel. 501/226-2406) on Jewfish Street in town, and **Polo's** (tel. 501/226-3542). Polo's is near the north end of Front Street and has bicycle rentals as well. There are plenty more options; most resorts outsource to one rental company. Rates are pretty standard: about US$50 for 8 hours, US$250 for the week.

When driving your cart, carry a valid driver's license and follow all normal traffic laws. As the *Green Guide* advises: "Don't count on the golf carts around you to have brakes. They're designed for lush fairways with a few sprinklers, not for high tides and potholes. When driving, please don't run over the children, or splash pedestrians, and note all the one-way streets on the town map."

Front Street closes down to all but pedestrian traffic on Friday, Saturday, and Sunday. Also, make sure you park on the correct side of the street (it alternates every few weeks, just do what the locals are doing).

---

found running north and south along the island at most hours; just wave one down and climb in, and expect to pay about US$6–7 to travel between town and points south. There are seven drivers that you (or your front desk) can call as well, including **Airstrip Taxi** (tel. 501/226-2076), **Isabel Chi** (tel. 501/614-9591), and **Jesus Wiltshire** (tel. 501/226-3653). Taxis cannot take you anywhere north of the ferry.

Usually the smoothest and quickest way to travel up and down the island, water taxis are available from the **Island Ferry** dock at Fido's Courtyard (tel. 501/226-3231). Boats leave for points north on the hour, from 7 A.M.–10 P.M., with special late-night schedules on big party nights (Wed.–Sat.). The price depends on how far you are going, but is roughly US$5–10 each way.

GETTING THERE

By Air

The 2,600-foot-long runway is located practically in downtown San Pedro (although there's been talk for years of moving this strip to a 550-acre spot south of town). Belize's two airlines each run a dozen daily flights between San Pedro, Caye Caulker, and Belize City—and another five to and from Corozal. For schedules and prices contact **Maya Island Air** (US tel. 800/225-6732,

Bel. tel. 501/223-1140, mayair@btl.net, www.mayaislandair.com) or **Tropic Air** (US tel. 800/422-3435, Bel. tel. 501/226-2012, reservations@tropicair.com, www.tropicair.com).

The flight from Belize City (international airport) to San Pedro takes about 15 minutes and costs about US$75 round-trip. Leaving from Belize City's Municipal Airport (as opposed to the international airport) is cheaper.

By Boat

The **Caye Caulker Water Taxi Association** (tel. 501/226-2194 or 226-0992) runs seven daily trips between Belize City and Ambergris, a 75-minute ride that costs US$14 one way. In Belize City, you'll find the Caye Caulker Water Taxi Terminal at the north end of the Swing Bridge, with boats leaving between 9 A.M. and 4:30 P.M. Boats depart San Pedro from Shark's Pier from 7 A.M. to 3:30 P.M. Always check the schedule before making plans; usually there are extra boats on weekends and holidays.

Thunderbolt boats (tel. 501/226-2904, 614-9074, or 614-9075, US$12.50 one-way) are the fastest way to make the trip, as they do not stop in Caye Caulker (45–60 minutes each way). In Belize City, you'll find their boats docked upstream from the Swing Bridge (walk west on Front St.). There are three daily trips from Belize

City: 8 A.M., 1 P.M., and 4 P.M., and boats depart San Pedro (from the west side of the island) at 9 A.M., 2 P.M., and 5 P.M.

No regularly scheduled trips are available between cayes other than Ambergris and Caye Caulker, but ask about stopping at St. George's Caye or Caye Chapel.

Caye Caulker

About 800 or so native Jicauqueños (hee-kaw-KEN-yos, from the Spanish Cayo Jicaco, which evolved into Caye Caulker), or "Caulker Islanders," reside on this island 21 miles northeast of Belize City, just south of Ambergris Caye, and less than a mile west of the Belize Barrier Reef. The island is four miles from north to south, but the developed and inhabited part is only a mile long, from the Split to the airstrip. The land north of the Split is uninhabitable, consisting mostly of mangrove swamps with a narrow strip of land along the east coast. Commercial fishing is still very important on Caye Caulker, supplying most of San Pedro's lobsters.

Yes, there have been changes and some development on the island as it figures out its place in Belize's evolving tourism economy, but Caye Caulker is still *way* cheaper than San Pedro and still as *tranquilo* as everybody says. It ain't for nothin' that Caye Caulker is one of the old-time anchors in Belize's backpacker trail.

During the rainy season, May–September, sand flies and mosquitoes can get pretty fierce, though some years are better than others.

HISTORY

Most historians agree that Caye Caulker was not permanently inhabited during the time of the pirates, but they did stop here—an anchor dating from the 19th century was found in the channel on the southern end of the island, and a wreck equally as old was discovered off the southern end of Caye Chapel. The island was known to be visited by Mexican fishermen during those centuries—for generations they handed down stories of putting ashore at Caye Caulker for fresh water from a "big hole" on the caye.

The island was uninhabited as late as the 1830s. It wasn't until the outbreak of the Yucatán Caste War in 1848, when refugees (Spanish and mestizos) fled across the border into Belize by the thousands, that many permanently settled on Ambergris Caye, and a few found their way onto Caye Caulker. Many of today's Jicauqueños can trace their family histories back as far as the Caste War and even know from which region in Mexico their ancestors originated.

Exact dates of settlement on Caye Caulker are uncertain, but one of the remaining families on the island, the Reyes family, tells of their great-grandfather, Luciano, who arrived in Mexico from Spain and worked as a logwood cutter along the coast of Yucatán and later fled south to avoid the bloodletting in Mexico. He first settled in San Pedro on Ambergris Caye and decided it was going to be his permanent home. Then, when land fever erupted, he competed in the intense bidding for Ambergris Caye, only to lose out to James Blake, who became the owner with a bid of BZE$650. Reyes decided to buy Caye Caulker instead and, with BZE$300, became the owner of the small caye. Over the years, land was sold to various people; many descendants of the original landholders are still prominent on Caye Caulker.

Early Economy

Though the town developed into a fishing village, *cocales* (coconut plantations) were planted from one end of the caye to the other. Though no written records have been found, it is believed the original trees were planted in the 1880s and 1890s at about the same time as those planted on Ambergris Caye. It took a lot of capital to plant a *cocal,* and involved a great deal of time-consuming, laborious work. Reyes was one of the original planters. His workers would begin at the northern end and stack the coconuts all along the shore, where they were picked up by boats. When

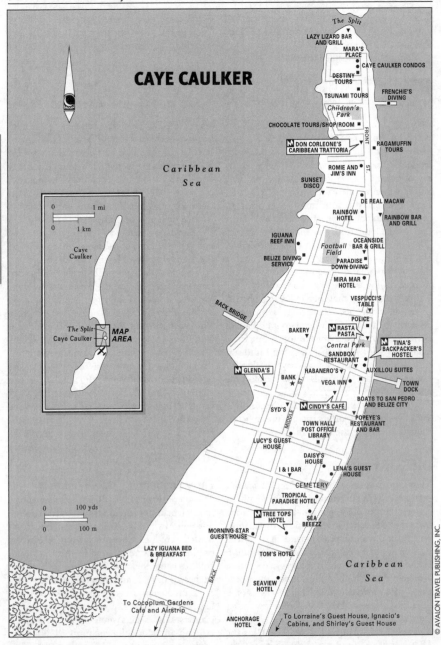

CAYE CAULKER

the workers finished their sweep of the island, it was time to begin again—the trees produced continually.

Slavery was never a part of the Caulker economy, which prevented the development of the stereotypical plantation hierarchy based on race and class that was so common in other parts of the Caribbean. Laborers earned a cash (albeit small) wage, enabling them to use their income to buy the necessities to supplement their subsistence fishing. The people were very poor. Some of the older folks remember their grandparents and great-grandparents working long days and making only pennies.

Maybe because of the economic conditions, the families on the caye began helping each other out early on. When one man got a large catch of fish, his family and neighbors helped him with it and, in turn, always went home with some. When one man's fruit trees were bearing, he would share the fruit, knowing that he would benefit later. This created very strong ties, especially between families and extended families.

Independent fishermen liked being their own bosses and, as a result, to this day Jicauqueños are independent thinkers with a lot of self-assurance. They take pride in their early roots on the island. Today, longtime fishing and lobstering families on Caulker make an above-average living, and many of them add to it by providing some type of service to the tourists that are coming more regularly every year.

The Future

Three words: fresh water supply. As accommodations grow to serve the increasing number of visitors (400 beds for tourists in 52 hotels at last count), Caye Caulker's thin lense of groundwater (plus whatever rainwater has been collected) will be stretched even thinner.

Several years ago, points of disagreement were the sewage treatment plant and the building of the airport. Seventeen acres of crocodile and bird-nesting lands were destroyed with their construction, and stresses were put on the 120 species of birds that nest on the southern end of Caye Caulker. The next discussion was over sand dredging. Sand was brought from the backside of

the island and dumped and spread along the front side.

As for landownership, Caye Caulker islanders don't want to "lose" their island as they believe the San Pedranos have lost theirs on Ambergris Caye.

ORIENTATION

Caye Caulker is cut into two pieces. The **"split"** or **"cut"** separates the southern inhabited part of the island from the northern mangrove swamps. This feature earned its name after Hurricane Hattie widened the channel in 1961. Travelers and locals alike come to enjoy the water (and Lazy Lizard Bar) here.

Moving south from the split on Front Street, the street that skirts the eastern shore (there are two more north-south streets, inland), you'll find seven sandy roads that run east to west, crossing three blocks to the other side of the island and Back Street.

On the western pier, there's a fuel pump. Sailors exploring the nearby cayes anchor in the shallow protected waters offshore. The body of water here is open ocean, but is still often referred to as a "lagoon."

Front Street dead-ends by the cemetery; turning right and then cutting to the left one street over, you'll find another dusty avenue that leads to the airstrip. Turn left at the airstrip until you reach the beach where you can loop back past Shirley's and Tree Tops Hotel until you reach Front Street again.

SPORTS AND RECREATION
Diving

Many people enjoy the day trips out to the Blue Hole and Turneffe Island, even though they'll spend over four hours (two each way) on a boat in open ocean. There is much fantastic diving much closer, right along the reef: Most shops run trips to the Caye Caulker Marine Park, Caye Chapel, St. George's Caye, Spanish Bay, Sergeant's Caye, and Hol Chan. Again, there is no "best" dive site, as every diver is looking for something different—just be sure to discuss the various options before booking the trip (and

main street "bustle" on Caye Caulker

© JOSHUA BERMAN

make sure you're comfortable with their boat and gear).

There are presently four dive shops on Caye Caulker, all of which offer similarly priced local diving (US$60–75 for two tanks), Blue Hole/Turneffe day trips (US$150 for three tanks and transport), certification courses (US$250 for Open Water and Advanced, US$75 for a single-tank resort course), as well as a variety of snorkeling excursions and other trips. **Frenchie's** (tel. 501/226-0234, www.frenchiesdiving.com) has a rock-solid reputation for quality service and is owned by a native islander who has been diving these waters since he was a child. Frenchie's guarantees smaller groups (no more than 10 divers per boat), ensuring lots of personal attention from your dive master. At **Belize Diving Services** (located behind the soccer field, tel. 501/226-0143, www.belizedivingservices.com), gringa owners Dawn Williams and Kathy Dalton offer three boats, PADI certification, and an on-site classroom.

Paradise Down Scuba (tel. 501/226-0437, www.paradisedown.com) is located right on Front Street and has the biggest dive boat on the island—important when making the two-hour crossing to the Blue Hole. Their day trips include all equipment fees, breakfast, and lunch. **Big Fish Dive Center** (tel. 501/226-0450, www.bigfish-dive.com) is locally owned and reputable.

Snorkeling and Swimming

Mask and fins are available for US$5/day and can be used off almost any dock or at the island's most popular beach and snorkel spot: the split. You'll see flocks of sunbathers here an any given day, lounging like reptiles atop the various chunks of sand and cement, getting up only to splash on some more oil or order another Panty Ripper at the Lazy Lizard, who provides mellow music for the scene.

Be aware that swimming in the channel can be dangerous; this is a shallow and heavily trafficked area. The pull of the current can be enough to overpower children or weak swimmers. Also, be very careful of boat traffic, as serious accidents have occurred here. Around the bend only a few yards out of the channel, the water is calm and safer. However, old construction materials have been dumped here for fill, so be careful where you step.

At least a dozen shops on the island rent gear and offer snorkeling trips to farther destinations: usually to the nearby reef, Hol Chan Marine Reserve, and a number of local cayes (see the sidebar "Snorkeling San Pedro"). Following are a couple of reputable operators, but many more are available. **Carlos Tours** (tel. 501/226-0058 or 600-1654, carlosayala@hotmail.com) offers an uncommon level of personal attention and focus on safety, and for this, Carlos has earned an excellent reputation. His office is on Front Street next to the Sand Box. **Anwar Tours** (tel. 501/226-0327), run by a pair of local brothers who specialize in snorkel trips to the local reef, Shark Ray Alley, and Hol Chan Reserve also gets good reviews. Also check out **Seagull Tours.**

Tsunami Adventures (tel. 501/226-0462, www.tsunamiadventures.com) not only provides local snorkel excursions and a range of inland trips, but they serve as a travel agent as well. With an office located up toward the split, they can also book your dive trip.

Some of the best, most sought-after snorkel and trip guides on the island actually prefer not to be mentioned in guidebooks for various personal reasons. They still work and are well-known; seek them out by asking around Front Street.

Boating

Say L King (tel. 501/226-0489, www.saylking.com) has a handful of small sailboats, kayaks, and canoes for rent (US$10/hr), located right on the beach just past Tina's. A bit farther north, look for **Toucan Canoe and Kayaks Too,** where you can rent boats (US$5/hr or US$23 for six hours) or sign up for a sunset paddle, bird-watching trip, or "round da caye" expedition. Many people do the island circumnavigation on their own—it should only take a couple of hours, but you should have some idea of what you're

doing. **EZ Boy Tours** rents kayaks for US$10/hour or US$60/day.

Fishing

Inquire at your hotel about making arrangements with a fisherman (tackle provided) to take you on a hunt for the sweetest seafood in the Caribbean. Or, take a walk to the backside of the island, where you'll find fishermen cleaning their fish, working on lobster traps, or mending their nets in the morning. Many will be willing to take you out for a reasonable fee. The main trophies are groupers, barracuda, snapper, and amberjack—all good eating. Small boats are available for rent by the hour.

Check with Mark Nicholas at **Destiny Tours** (near the split, tel. 501/610-2962 or 226-0275) for all kinds of custom trips that include tackle, bait, and fishing and, if you want, you can arrange for Mark to grill up your catch at the end of the day. (Inland cave tubing and other trips are available as well.)

You can also seek out **Porfilio Guzman** (tel. 501/226-0152) a well-known fishing guide for reef or flats fishing. **Rolando "Roly" Rosado** (tel. 501/226-0190 or 226-0058) offers fishing and diving charters. He'll take you to the reef to dive, or on daylong fishing expeditions. Talk to Roly or his brother, Ramon. **Raul Young** (tel. 501/226-0133) takes travelers snorkeling or fishing on the reefs and is known for flats fishing.

Swallow Caye Wildlife Sanctuary

Captain Chocolate is a local legend in the trade; he was the first guide to take people on trips to a nearby caye to see manatees, and was instrumental in the creation of this sanctuary in July 2002. The protected area is comprised of approximately 7,500 acres of sea and mangrove around the Northern Drowned Cayes and Swallow Caye, just a few miles east of Belize City.

The sanctuary is co-managed by Friends of Swallow Caye and the Government of Belize's Department of Natural Resources. The numerous manatees who live here now enjoy limited motorboat and anchor traffic—now they need only put up with curious, photo-taking

WHERE THE MANATEES ROAM

Manatees are mammals: They are warm-blooded, nurse their young with milk, breathe air, and have hair. Commonly referred to as the "gentle giants of the sea," they are large and bulky—weighing 300–500 kilograms (600–1200 lbs.) with a flattened, rounded tail and dexterous paddle-shaped forelimbs. Along with their Indo-Pacific cousin, the dugong *(Dugong dugon),* manatees belong to Order Sirenia, a group of four species that represents the only herbivorous marine mammals living today. There are three species of manatees: the Amazonian manatee *(Trichechus inunguis),* the West African manatee *(Trichechus senegalensis),* and the West Indian manatee *(Trichechus manatus).* The two subspecies of the West Indian manatee include the Florida manatee *(T. m. latirostris)* and the Antillean manatee *(T. m. manatus).*

© CAROLYN SELF-SULLIVAN

Belizean waters comprise one of the last strongholds for the endangered "sea cow."

Belize is considered the last stronghold for West Indian manatees in Central America and the Caribbean. One of only three extant species, West Indian manatees are found year-round in Florida, are sparsely distributed throughout Central America and the Caribbean, and are also found as far south as Brazil. The Antillean subspecies (which excludes the Florida animals) is Red-Listed by The World Conservation Union (IUCN) as vulnerable, in continuing decline, with severely fragmented populations. The U. N. Caribbean Environmental Programme considers Antillean manatees an endangered and protected species of regional concern.

With a relatively short coastline extending from the Gulf of Honduras in the south to Chetumal Bay in the north, Belize reports the largest number of Antillean manatees in the Caribbean region. Why? Perhaps because of the extensive seagrass, mangrove, coastal, and riverine habitat within the Belize Barrier Reef Lagoon system; or perhaps because manatees have been protected by local laws since the 1930s and are currently listed as endangered under The Wildlife Protection Act of 1981. But, more likely, it's because the people of Belize exhibit a strong conservation ethic and care deeply about their wildlife and other natural resources.

Even so, manatees in Belize are increasingly threatened by anthropogenic impacts, including poaching, boat strikes, entanglement in fishing gear, and habitat degradation. Because manatees are elusive, endangered, and have slow reproductive rates, long-term studies in Belize are necessary to evaluate and monitor their relatively healthy status and develop practical conservation plans to insure survival of the population, and ultimately the sub-species.

One such study has been ongoing since 1998 in the Drowned Cayes area near Belize City. The project, which focuses on manatee ecology and behavior, is currently funded by the

Earthwatch Institute and offers a unique opportunity for travelers to donate their vacation time to participating in the daily research activities (for more information on the cost and available dates, see www.earthwatch.org).

The Drowned Cayes area has long been designated as an important manatee habitat, but is increasingly impacted by growing tourism, originating from Belize City, Caye Caulker, San Pedro, and most recently, the cruise ship industry. Data provided by the Earthwatch project were influential in including a portion of the Drowned Cayes in Swallow Caye Wildlife Sanctuary (SCWS), an 8,970-acre manatee-protected area and the premier location for manatee tours. The SCWS lobbying efforts began in the early 1990s and were spearheaded by Chocolate Heredia, of Caye Caulker. With tears in his eyes, the 73-year-old Captain Chocolate accepted his personal copy of the statutory instrument at a special ceremony in July 2002.

But designating protected areas is just the beginning; much work is still in progress as diverse stakeholders attempt to come to a consensus on setting and enforcing rules and regulations for the sanctuary. The reserve is co-managed by Friends of Swallow Caye (an NGO founded by Chocolate in 1998) and the Department of Natural Resources.

Indeed, Belize has designated several wildlife sanctuaries and protected areas for the benefit of manatees and other marine life, including Swallow Caye Wildlife Sanctuary, Corozal Bay Wildlife Sanctuary, Southern Lagoon Wildlife Sanctuary, Bacalar Chico National Park & Marine Reserve, South Water Caye Marine Reserve, Burden Canal (part of the Belize River system), and Port Honduras Marine Reserve. Belize was also one of the first Caribbean countries to establish a National Manatee Working Group and a National Stranding Network, and to adopt a Manatee Recovery Plan. Many local Belizeans, including national manatee researchers Nicole Auil and Angeline Valentine, have dedicated years of work to a country-wide research program and the stranding network. With the help of both local and international NGOs, the stranding network has successfully rescued and rehabilitated three manatee orphans: Hercules, Woody, and Tiny. Hercules and Woody have been released back into the wild in Southern Lagoon, and Tiny is currently being cared for by Wildtracks in Sarteneja.

A number of other individuals and organizations are doing ongoing manatee research, education, and conservation work in Belize (in addition to those mentioned above). The Conservation Division of the Forestry Department, Department of Natural Resources is the official participating government agency; Wildlife Trust, Northern & Southern Lagoon (Gales Point Manatee) does radio and satellite tracking, annual health assessments of tagged animals, monitoring of known mother-calf pairs, soft release program for rehabilitated manatees, and genetic and acoustical research. On Ambergris Caye, GreenReef has country-wide educational outreach programs, and Greg Smith has been doing long-term monitoring and a photo-ID project documenting the seasonal occurrence of known male manatees at Basil Jones Cut since 1994. The Oceanic Society, on Turneffe Atoll, conducts boat surveys, aerial counts, and ecology of manatees (contact: Dr. Ellen Hines).

(Contributed by Caryn Self-Sullivan, a marine scientist who, since 1998, has been studying manatee ecology and behavior in the Drowned Cayes area near Belize City.)

The Northern Cayes

tourists, and they sometimes swim right up to your boat to "pose."

Manatee and Wildlife Trips

Chocolate's Manatee Tours (tel. 501/226-0151, chocolate@btl.net) continues to rack up all kinds of environmental and tourism awards for providing quality trips to hundreds of tourists per season. The all-day excursion first stops in an open area where it is possible to approach manatees in their element, while being careful not to disturb or harm the gentle creatures. After viewing the manatees for an hour or two, Chocolate heads to the white-sand island of Sergeant's Caye for an afternoon of snorkeling.

Jim and Dorothy Beveridge of **Sea-ing Is Belizing** (tel. 501/220-4079, tourism@cayecaulker .org.bz) offer nature walks that explore and explain the mangrove forests as well as the trees and critters of the island. They give slide presentations on topics ranging from the local ecosystems to marine birds. They also specialize in organizing custom trips for academic groups and wildlife photography buffs. Signs are usually posted for the slide shows. If you've ever wanted to see crocodiles, they do a morning nature walk that includes a croc watch. The walk starts at sunrise, lasts about three hours, and costs US$20 pp.

Multi-Sport and Overnight

Although it is tempting to place **Raggamuffin Tours** (tel. 501/226-0348, www.raggamuffin-tours.com) in any of the water sports listed above, their unique trips cover enough activities that a separate listing is necessary. They are also distinctive for their trio of beautiful, Belizean-built boats designed especially to access shallow snorkeling spots. Raggamuffin provides a range of creative trips that, in addition to world-class snorkeling or fishing, also offer fresh food and overnight sailing trips that will have you camping out in style on any number of deserted cayes. This is one of the only outfits that *sails* to Hol Chan (full-day trip for the same price as motorized trips), and also offers sunset cruises and island-hopping adventures, including a three-day expedition to Placencia, where you'll be dropped off to continue your travels (US$250 pp includes all gear, food, snorkeling, and fishing for three days).

Massage and Bodywork

Check out the **Lotus House** (tel. 501/226-0273) on Front Street, just past Raggamuffin, for everything from traditional massage to fresh-fruit facials, Henna body tattoos, and tarot readings. Or try the **Transcendance Healing Center** (tel. 501/603-1976), also with a variety of energy work and treatments for very reasonable rates. There is no regular yoga on the island, but it's worth asking Cindy at Cindy's Café if there are any sessions you can join during your stay.

NIGHTLIFE AND ENTERTAINMENT

The biggest show in town is definitely the daily joining of sun and western horizon. **Lazy Lizard Bar** at the split has both the daytime sunbathing and sunset spot markets pretty well cornered. You can also find other, less crowded spots to watch the sunset by walking down the west side of the island and searching for an appropriate cocktail spot.

Popeye's has bands once in a while, as does **Oceanside,** which is definitely a regular hotspot (dart boards as well). For the late-night dancehall scene, just follow the crowds at midnight on their way to the disco near the northwest side of town.

Do not leave the island without enjoying a beverage in **The I & I Bar,** a three-story Tower of Reggae located in the middle of the island. We could try to explain the swing-seats and Monkey Walk, but you're better off just going yourself. **Herbal Tribe,** up Front Street, is developing quite the rootsy nighttime scene as well.

ISLAND ART AND SHOPPING

You'll find a sprinkling of small shops on and around Front Street. Several sell T-shirts, photos, books, shells, suntan lotion, maps, and typical Belizean souvenirs. There are also a handful of more interesting vendors of local art, including a pair located in the same building, near the

Water Taxi office: **Caribbean Colors Art Gallery** (tel. 501/206-0206) and **Tres Angelitas** both offer original jewelry, paintings, perfumes, and aromatherapy supplies.

Captain Chocolate's wife, Annie Seashore, runs **Chocolate's Gift Shop** (really more of a boutique) and sells a variety of dresses, skirts, shirts, and sarongs acquired during Annie's yearly trips to Indonesia. Colorful, high-quality Guatemalan bags, place mats, belts, and other goodies are also found here. Open daily.

If you forget your camera, James Beveridge (of Sea-ing Is Belizing, tel. 501/220-4079) is an excellent photographer of underwater marine life, terrestrial wildlife, and people. He sells slides and prints of his work. There's also the **One Love** shop at Rasta Pasta.

ACCOMMODATIONS

Remember, prices are sometimes negotiable depending on the time of the year, the number of tourists on the island, and how persuasive you are. You're never too far from the sea on Caulker, and the farther you get from the main part of town, the more exclusive your chunk of oceanfront property becomes. In town, "beaches" are often little more than sandy sidewalks for foot traffic and golf carts. During high season, most rooms are taken as soon as the tourists from Belize City arrive on the water taxi. Definitely make reservations at peak times.

Under US$25

Keep in mind that the law does not allow camping on public or private property without permission. The only "official" camping is at Vega Inn and Gardens (see listing under US$25–50) and, as at many places in Belize, the price to pitch a tent is almost as much as a cheap room.

Tina's Backpacker's Hostel (rastatin-abz@btl.net) is a converted private home, located to your right as you walk off the town dock. Tina, a well-traveled native islander, offers dorm-style rooms (US$10), plus a few nicer private rooms (US$20–30), all with shared bath, kitchen, and a relaxed community atmosphere.

one of Caye Caulker's dozens of beachfront budget hostels

Hang out on her funky little dock or garden benches and hammocks. The rooms are small, but clean and colorful. Tina's a dive master and may be starting a tour company as well.

Edith's Hotel (tel. 501/206-0069), with small and tidy rooms, is a hallmark on the center street of the island. Rooms come with hot/cold water, private baths, and ceiling fans for US$25; shared bath, US$18. **Daisy's Hotel** (tel. 501/226-0150, US$18) is another oldie. Run by a friendly family of many daughters, Daisy's is on Front Street, just inland from Lena's, and has 10 simple wooden rooms with fans and hot water in shared baths. **Lena's Guest House** (tel. 501/226-0106) has 13 oceanside rooms in an old building. There's nothing special here—US$25 for shared baths, US$30 with private baths.

Mira Mar Hotel (tel. 501/206-0357) is a two-story row of 19 bare-bones rooms a couple of blocks north of the public pier on Front Street; US$15 s/d for shared bath, US$20 for private bath. Up the road, **Romie and Jim's Inn** (tel. 501/601-3711) have a handful of clean but somewhat closed-in rooms, as well as a famous café and barbecue; US$20 with shared bath, US$25 private.

The six wood cabins at **Mara's Place** (up by the split, tel. 501/206-0056, from US$27) are a great value, if a bit small, with private hot-water baths and cable TV. Each unit has a small porch with hammocks. The property has a private dock with lounge chairs for guests to use. **M & N Apartments** (tel. 501/226-0229, US$30) is on the corner of the second cross street south of the split; rooms come with hot/cold water and are simply furnished.

Moving to the quieter, south end of town (walk along the beach toward the airstrip), you'll find **Tom's Hotel** (tel. 501/226-0102, toms@btl.net), popular with the young crowd and backpackers. There are lots of options—32 rooms, plus a few simple bungalows, from US$15–23 with shared bath, US$35 private bath. Tom's is very well-kept and clean, with hot/cold water, fans, louvered windows, tile floors, and a sea view.

Continuing down the beach, just past the Anchorage, look for **Lorraine's Guesthouse** (tel. 501/206-0162, US$18), with seven simple yellow casitas, three of them on stilts. A nice dock is available for sunbathing, and chairs and hammocks are on the beach. Each casita has a private bath, hot/cold water, and two beds.

Next door, **Ignacio's Cabins** (tel. 501/610-2200) has 19 purple clapboard huts on stilts surrounded by a scattering of palms, sea grapes, and cassarina trees. Each cabin comes with a private, cold-water bath, is very small, and may not be everyone's cup of tea—but they have lots of island character. Back-row cabins are US$13, front-row US$18.

US$25–50

The new, clean building on your right as you get off of the water taxi is **Trends Beachfront Hotel** (tel. 501/226-0094 or 226-0307, trends-bze@btl.net, US$40) with seven rooms, comfortable queen-sized beds, refrigerator, fans, and private baths. They've also got a building a block

and a half away with similar rooms, plus five simpler ones for US$20 with a private bath.

Two stories high, the brightly colored **Rainbow Hotel** (tel. 501/226-0123, rainbowhotel@btl.net, US$30/35 s/d fan, US$45/50 s/d a/c) has 17 clean, motel-style stucco rooms with h/c water, private baths, TV, tile floors; there are also two suites. The Rainbow Bar and Grill is across the street at the water's edge.

Ramon Reyes has one of the more popular spots on Caye Caulker and with good reason: **Tropical Paradise Hotel** (tel. 501/226-0124 or 226-0063, US$30–50) offers a wide selection of wooden cabanas with private ceiling fans, baths, h/c water, some with a/c. Check rooms before booking, as some are better-kept than others—the deluxe suites (US$70) are very nice with two double beds, a/c, TV, and private baths. There's a great on-site restaurant and the staff will help you plan your trips.

Morning Star Guest House (tel. 501/226-0347, www.jaguarmorningstar.com) is an excellent bargain, with three modern top-floor rooms (in the big white building with the mural on it) with private bath, fridge and coffee maker and TV. There's a diverse garden and courtyard (the owners planted over 100 fruit trees and other plants since Hurricane Keith wiped out most of the island's vegetation). US$35 for the top-floor rooms, US$38 for the ground-level casita, and only a one-minute walk to the water.

The **Tree Tops Hotel** (tel. 501/226-0240, www.treetopsbelize.com) is tucked back from the water between Tom's and Sea Beezzz, and is a luxurious little gem in a tall white building. The husband-and-wife team (Terry is English and Doris is German) have created beautifully decorated rooms with atmosphere—including two new suites (the Sunrise and Sunset) that have beautiful private balconies, TV, fridge, and h/c water bathrooms (US$80). Two more rooms share a bath and all have TV, fan, and fridge (about US$35). A room with private bath and sea view goes for US$42.

The **Seaview Hotel** (tel. 501/226-0205, seaviewcc@btl.net, US$45 plus tax) is a great deal, with four pretty and well-equipped rooms. Simple touches like a table and chairs and a fridge make it homey, and the Guatamalan rugs make it colorful. The veranda is less than 20 feet from the water.

Open November–April only, the **Sea Beezzz Hotel** (tel. 501/226-0176, US$45 plus tax) has six basic rooms run by a commercial fisherman from Montauk, NY. The rooms are nicely furnished with private bath. **Costa Maya Beach** (tel. 501/226-0462, US$40) can be reached through Tsunami Adventures and offers four nicely stocked cabanas (private bath, TV, veranda, h/c water, fridge, coffee maker) located up toward the split.

De Real Macaw (tel. 501/226-0459, www.de-realmacaw.com) has seven different units with private bath, mini-kitchens, TV, and quality beds, from US$45 to US$110 for a two-bedroom apartment; pet friendly. Nice views of the ocean from the various verandas.

The "naturally exclusive" **Vega Inn and Gardens** (tel. 501/226-0142, www.vega.com.bz) offers simple rooms in an old two-story building on the sand. Owned by the Vega family, longtime island residents, the hotel has a warm and friendly atmosphere. This is a family affair and they're a font of information about the island—past and present. Rooms with shared bath US$33, nicer rooms US$65, camping US$10 pp per night.

US$50–100

The **Anchorage Hotel** (tel. 501/226-0304, anchorage@btl.net, www.gocayecaulker.com, US$65) has 18 comfortable rooms in a modern cement building, all with mini-refrigerators, fans, and excellent cross-ventilation. Private bathrooms have tubs and hot water, and ocean-facing balconies are breezy and perfect for sunrises. **Popeye's** (tel. 501/226-0032, www.popeyesbeachresort.com) is now touting itself as a "beach resort" with four cabanas and four rooms, US$65 each.

The southernmost beachfront option is a good one: The five cabins at **Shirley's Guest House** (tel. 501/226-0145 or 600-0069, www.shirleysguesthouse.com) are built with beautiful tropical woods. There is a variety of rooms with a range of amenities; check website for rates.

Chocolate (tel. 501/226-0151, chocolate @btl.net, US$70) rents one beautifully furnished

room for non-smokers. You'll have h/c water, private bath, fan, cross-ventilation, a porch with a swing, a coffee maker, bedpost lights, tile floors—even terry cloth robes.

The Lazy Iguana B&B (tel. 501/226-0350, www.lazyiguana.net, US$95) is a four-story private home with four lovely, spacious rooms, all with private baths, hot water, and a/c. The top floor has a deck for lounging and a 360-degree view of the island. Rates include a massive breakfast in the owners' kitchen, with views of water to the east and west.

US$100–150

This price range is relatively new to the island, and continues to grow. There are more apartment rentals than there is room in this section—check the main Caye Caulker websites to reserve one for you and your family.

Just up from the main dock, you'll see some colorful apartment buildings for rent for US$100 and up. These are **Dianne's Beach House** (tel. 501/610-1956, www.staycayecaulker.com) and **Auxillou Suites** (tel. 501/226-0370, www.auxilloubeachsuites.com). To stay in someone's empty vacation home, sometimes for very reasonable rates, check out **Caye Caulker Rentals** (www.cayecaulker.org/cayecaulkerrentals).

The **Iguana Reef Inn** (tel. 501/226-0213, www.iguanareefinn.com) continues to raise the bar on the island with its 12 upscale rooms built around a well-kept compound on the west side of the island—the only real "resort" presently on Caye Caulker. Located behind the soccer field, its rooms are spacious and colorful, some with high vaulted ceilings and all with comfortable touches like mini-fridge, porch, bathtubs, h/c water, and other modern conveniences. Suites for US$107–127, continental breakfast included. The bar and beach area face the sunset and are more private and quiet than those on the island's windward side.

Several new condo-style accommodations include **Caye Caulker Condos** (tel. 501/226-0072, www.cayecaulkercondos.com), seven fully furnished suites for US$100–120. The rooms are a bit tacky, but fully functional and the rooftop hangout is stunning.

FOOD

Caye Caulker is finally shedding its reputation for mediocre food; style and service are creeping in and you'll enjoy exploring all the new options.

Budget

As in the rest of Belize, the cheapest options are the Mexican influenced "fast-food" stands, found all over town. Or seek out **Ⓜ Glenda's** on the west side of the island—still as good as ever, serving inexpensive food and cheap lobster burritos. In the morning, try her homemade cinnamon rolls and fresh-squeezed orange juice—by the glass or in an at-home recycled bottle—the best two bucks you'll spend on the island. **Marin's Upstairs Diner,** down the street from the Tropical Paradise, has a good menu and always-fresh fish; **Syd's,** east of Glenda's, makes good burritos and has a great Saturday night barbecue.

Swim across the split and follow the signs for a cheap Belizean lunch (US$3.50) at **Miss Claudette's,** open noon–3 P.M.

Cafés

Ⓜ Cindy's Cafe (tel. 501/226-0093) specializes in organic and natural breads (homemade bagels on weekends), baked treats, vegetarian lunches including hummus and falafel, and, most importantly, fine, dark-roast Guatemalan coffee brewed to perfection (the best cup of coffee we found in Belize, a statement not made lightly). There's also a growing book-trading library. **Mary Jo's Deli** looks inviting, as does the menu of sandwiches, quiche (US$3), salads, and calzones (9 A.M.–3 P.M. Thurs.–Mon.).

Many agree **Cocoplum Gardens** (8 A.M.–sunset) is well worth the walk. It's located near the airstrip and serves all kinds of organic, whole, gourmet food, including a lobster pizza and great salads. There's a natural store and nursery too.

Local Favorites

Try **Herbal Tribe** for a good vibe, slow service, and decent local dishes—when they get to your table anyway. Open for three meals, and there's live drumming (sometimes) and an art gallery on premises. **Hannah's** (formerly Poorman's Grill, renamed for a new daughter) is right on Front Street and has reasonable prices and a nice deck for breakfast, lunch, or dinner, although barbecue is their specialty.

Popeye's (tel. 501/226-0032) has a full dinner menu (chicken curry US$10), but specializes in pizza (US$17.50 for a large supreme). Delivery's available 4 P.M.–9 P.M.

And then there's the ever-wandering **Wish-Willy's Bar and Grill,** where you get both good food and friendly conversation (currently in a ramshackle setup on the west side). The selections are good—fresh seafood, tropical drinks—and vegetarians say thumbs up. **Chan's Garden,** on Back Street across from Lucy's Hotel, serves Chinese food and decent T-bone steaks, with some of the fastest service on the island.

After migrating to various other locations in Belize, **Ⓜ Rasta Pasta** is finally home on the beach in Caye Caulker, just a few hundred yards north of the town dock. Hopefully it will stick around, because they offer some of the best meals on the island with excellent, smiley service. From breakfast (real coffee) to their massive burritos (US$7), to happy hour (4 P.M.–7 P.M.), to a great and varied dinner menu, it's hard to go wrong here.

At the **Sand Box** (7 A.M.–10 P.M.), right at the end of the town dock, you'll find a sand floor inside and a casual atmosphere with a lot of local color. Great breakfast, lots of seafood: fish with curry rice, conch ceviche (US$3), seafood salad (US$10), plus stuffed eggplant and mushrooms (US$4). Beer, liquor, soft drinks, and fresh juices (watermelon, orange, and pineapple) round out the menu.

Tropical Paradise Restaurant, at the south end of Front Street, has a varied and very reasonably priced menu, serving three meals a day. For dinner check out the jerk lobster (US$11) or barracuda steak (US$7).

Upscale

Ⓜ Don Corleone's Caribbean Trattoria (tel. 501/226-0025, (5 P.M.–9:30 P.M. Mon.–Sat.) will, indeed, make you a meal you can't refuse—pasta and seafood entrées start at US$10–15, plus an impressive wine list and nice ambience, right on Front Street across from the water. Reservations only necessary during the holidays. **Vespucci's Table** is cheaper than the other Italian joints on the island, but they have a much better breakfast reputation than dinner.

Habanero's (tel. 501/226-0487) offers a lavish "eclectic international" menu, served up by two internationally trained chefs who aren't afraid to experiment with the day's catch; come for cocktails at 4 P.M.; the restaurant is open 5 P.M.–10 P.M. Big, lavishly presented portions (on the pricier side of the island, entrees from US$16 or so, specials US$23). This is a lively spot with modern lounge music and flair bartending (don't ask—just come check it out).

INFORMATION

There is plenty of online research you can do while planning your trip. The official site of the Caye Caulker Belize Tourism Industry Association (CCBTIA) is **www.gocayecaulker.com.** Probably a bit more useful, and featuring a semi-active message board, **www.cayecaulker.org** is another good spot. Both of these sites have more comprehensive and updated listings of lodgings and current Caulker goings on. Another good directory with lots of photos is found at **www.cybercayecaulker.com.**

There is no general information booth on the island; just walk off the dock and start asking around.

SERVICES

Atlantic Bank (9 A.M.–1 P.M.) is on Back Street, half a block south of Chan's Mini Mart; no ATM yet, but they'll process a cash advance on your credit card. There are a couple of **laundry** places in town, just ask—also, a number of women will do it by hand out of their homes.

A municipal complex in the middle of town hosts the **library, health clinic,** and **post office** (9 A.M.–noon, 1–5 P.M. Mon.–Fri., closes a bit earlier on Friday). The mail goes out three times a week—Monday, Wednesday, and Friday. The clinic will help you with meds—*if* they have the supplies. For any serious emergency, your best bet is a plane or boat to the mainland.

Internet Access

At press time, the only two options were right across the street from each other on Front Street. **Caye Caulker Cyber Café** (7 A.M.–10 P.M. daily, US$6/hr) has more and better computers, plus a full coffee and wet bar. **Cayeboard Connection** has no bar but a decent book trade, and is open 8 A.M.–9 P.M. daily.

Travel Agencies

Treasured Travels (Front St. next to Vespucci's, tel. 501/610-1956, www.staycayecaulker.com) acts as a full-service travel agent, as does **Tsunami Adventures** (tel. 501/226-0462, www.tsunami-adventures.com), located up toward the split—they can book your dive trip as well. The town's two Internet cafés can arrange bus tickets to Guatemala and boat trips to Honduras.

Groceries

If you're lucky, you may run into some cute kids strolling the sandy lanes balancing pans of homemade sweet crusts and wheat bread on their heads. The banana bread is heavenly.

Look around and you'll find **Chan's Mini Mart** (across from the Atlantic Bank). They've got a decent selection of fruits, drinks, and snacks for cheap meals. And, if you want fresh fish or lobster, ask at the Lobstermen's Co-op Dock on the backside of the island what time the fishermen come in with their catch. This is always a good place to buy fresh fish.

GETTING AROUND

The navigable part of town—from the airstrip north to the split—is only a mile long and easily

The Northern Cayes

sunset at the split: Caye Caulker's main event of the day

© JOSHUA BERMAN

traversed on foot. Still, a bicycle makes things a lot easier, especially if staying in one of the more southern accommodations. Ask if your hotel provides one, or rent at **Mary Jo's** on Front Street (US$2/hr or US$35/wk). **Amigos Golf Cart Tour and Taxi** (located on the beach in front of the Rainbow Hotel, tel. 501/226-0123 or 603-6385) also rents bikes and, yes, golf carts (US$15/hr). A golf cart taxi could be very helpful when moving around the island with luggage. Taxi guy **George Delcid** (tel. 501/601-4330) is very responsive, friendly, and accommodating.

GETTING THERE AND AWAY
By Air
Maya Island Air and Tropic Air make regular flights to Caye Caulker, flying to and from Belize City's municipal and international airports as part of their San Pedro run. The airstrip on Caulker is pretty simple—you wait under a tree or on the veranda of the small building that serves all flights. Fares are about US$25 one-way

to the municipal airport (about 10 minutes), about US$43 to fly to the international airport.

By Boat
The vast majority of visitors prefer the short cruise from either Belize City or San Pedro. In Belize City, you'll find the Caye Caulker Water Taxi Terminal at the north end of the Swing Bridge, with boats leaving between 9 A.M. and 4:30 P.M. Boats depart Caye Caulker from the new municipal dock on the east side of the island; buy tickets at the office there first (tel. 501/226-0992). Departures run 6 A.M.–4 P.M., with a 5 P.M. run on weekends, and to San Pedro 7 A.M.–5:30 P.M. The trip costs US$9 one-way, US$15 round-trip.

No regularly scheduled trips are available between cayes other than Ambergris and Caye Caulker, but you can request a stop at St. George's Caye or Caye Chapel. Most boats are open-air; a light wrap or rain jacket is handy for windy trips. The boats are oftentimes packed to the point of being overloaded. They are supposed to have a limit, but it isn't always observed.

Turneffe Islands Atoll

The handful of islands that make up Turneffe Atoll are three upscale resorts and one field research station. This is a renowned diving and fishing destination, 25 miles east of Belize City. The islands are mostly small dots of sand, mangrove clusters, and swampy land, though **Blackbird Caye** and **Douglas Caye** are quite large. With the preponderance of mangroves and coconut palms, many cayes are home only to sea- and wading birds, ospreys, manatees, and crocodiles; a few support small colonies of fishermen and divers.

If you're looking to hook a bonefish or permit, miles of crystal flats are alive with the hard-fighting fish. Tarpon are abundant late March–June within the protected creeks and channels throughout the islands. Those who seek larger trophies will find a grand choice of marlin, sailfish, wahoo, groupers, blackfin tuna, and many more.

Turneffe is accessible by boat from Belize City or by a longer ride from Ambergris Caye and Caye Caulker. Some choose a vacation package on a live-aboard dive boat or at one of the accommodations listed later in this section.

DIVE SITES

Rendezvous Point

This is a popular first-dive for overnighters out of Ambergris Caye. It provides a great opportunity for divers who haven't been under in a while to get their feet wet again. The depth is about 40–50 feet and affords sufficient bottom time to get a good look at a wide variety of reef life. Angelfish, butterfly fish, parrot fish, yellowtails, and morays are represented well. This will whet appetites for the outstanding diving to come.

N The Elbow

Most divers have heard of the Elbow (just 10 minutes from Turneffe Island Lodge), a point of coral that juts out into the ocean. This now-famous dive site offers a steep, sloping drop-off covered with tube sponges and deep-water gorgonians, along with shoals of snappers (sometimes numbering in the hundreds) and other pelagic creatures. Predators such as bar jacks, wahoo, and permits cruise the reef, and the drop-off is impressive. Currents sweep the face of the wall most of the time and they typically run from the north. However, occasionally they reverse or cease all together.

Lefty's Ledge

A short distance farther up the eastern side of the atoll is another dive to excite even those with a lot of bottom time under their weight belts. Lefty's Ledge features dramatic spur-and-groove formations that create a wealth of habitats. Correspondingly, divers will see a head-turning display of undersea life, both reef and pelagic species. Jacks, mackerels, permits, and groupers are present in impressive numbers. Wrasses, rays, parrot fish, and butterfly fish are evident around the sandy canyons. Cleaning stations are also evident, where you'll see large predators allowing themselves to be groomed by small cleaner shrimp or fish. The dive begins at about 50 feet and the bottom slopes to about 100 feet before dropping off into the blue.

Gales Point

Another "don't-miss" dive, Gales Point is a short distance farther up the eastern side. Here the reef juts out into the current at a depth of about 45 feet, sloping to about 100 feet before the drop-off. Along the wall and the slope just above it are numerous ledges and cave-like formations. Rays and groupers are especially common here— some say this may be a grouper breeding area. Corals and sponges are everywhere in numerous varieties.

Sayonara

On the leeward, or eastern, side of the atoll, the wreck of the *Sayonara*, a tender sunk by Dave Bennett of Turneffe Islands Lodge, lies in about 30 feet of water. Close by is a sloping ledge with interesting tunnels and spur-and-groove

The Northern Cayes

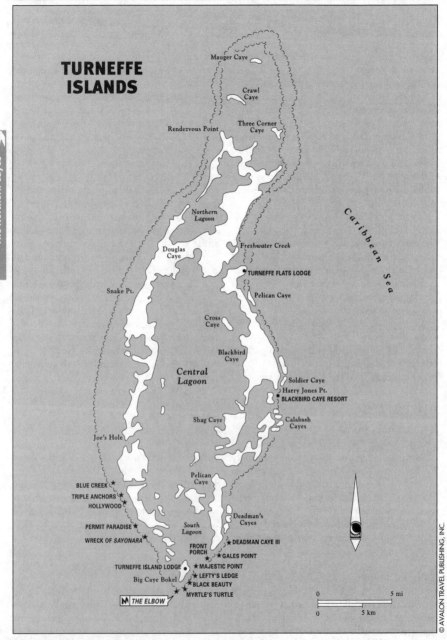

TURNEFFE ISLANDS

Mauger Caye

Crawl Caye

Three Corner Caye

Rendezvous Point

Northern Lagoon

Douglas Caye

Freshwater Creek

TURNEFFE FLATS LODGE

Snake Pt.

Pelican Caye

Cross Caye

Blackbird Caye

Central Lagoon

Soldier Caye

Harry Jones Pt.
BLACKBIRD CAYE RESORT

Shag Caye

Calabash Cayes

Joe's Hole

Caribbean Sea

Pelican Caye

BLUE CREEK

TRIPLE ANCHORS

HOLLYWOOD

PERMIT PARADISE

WRECK OF *SAYONARA*

South Lagoon

Deadman's Cayes

DEADMAN CAYE III

FRONT PORCH

GALES POINT

TURNEFFE ISLAND LODGE

MAJESTIC POINT

Big Caye Bokel

LEFTY'S LEDGE

BLACK BEAUTY

MYRTLE'S TURTLE

THE ELBOW

0   5 mi

0   5 km

© AVALON TRAVEL PUBLISHING, INC.

The Northern Cayes

formations. Healthy numbers of reef fish play among the coral, and some barracudas tag along. Large schools of permit are often drawn down by divers' bubbles. They give a marvelous three-dimensional quality to the dive as you see them spiraling down from the surface like a squadron of fighter planes.

Hollywood

A bit farther up the atoll, Hollywood offers divers a relatively shallow dive (30–40 feet) with moderate visibility, unless the currents have reversed. Here, you'll find lots of basket and tube sponges and lush coral growth. Many angelfish, parrot fish, grunts, and snappers swim here. Although not as dramatic as an eastern side dive, Hollywood has plenty to see.

ACCOMMODATIONS

While limited in number, the accommodations here have distinct appeals. The friendly **Turneffe Island Lodge** (US tel. 800/874-0118, Bel. tel. 501/220-4011 or 220-4142, turneffe@starband.net) accommodates up to 16 guests on Little Caye Bokel, 12 acres of beautiful palm-lined beachfront and mangroves. It's a popular location for divers, anglers, and those who just want to swing in a hammock under the palms.

At the southern tip of the atoll, the resort is a short distance north of its larger relative, Big Caye Bokel. This strategic location offers enthusiasts a wide range of underwater experiences—it's within minutes of nearly 200 dive sites. Shallow areas are perfect for photography or snorkeling; you can see nurse sharks, rays, reef fish, and dolphins in the flats a few hundred yards from the dock. All the dives mentioned earlier and many more lie within 15 minutes by boat. The dive operation is first rate, and advanced instruction and equipment rentals are available. This would be an excellent place to get that underwater photography certification. One diver we met on a 14-day visit had dived three different sites each day (never repeating one of them), and had half an hour of underwater video of dolphins.

Anglers have a choice of fishing for snappers, permit, jacks, mackerel, and billfish off the drop-offs. They can stalk the near-record numbers of snook, bonefish, and tarpon in the flats and mangroves. The lodge's fishing guide has an uncanny way of knowing where the fish will be.

The friendly ease about the lodge makes even shy guests feel at home. Rooms are next to the sea, have h/c water, private baths, and 24-hour electricity. The main lodge boasts a small bar with wooden deck overlooking the grounds, a spacious pine-paneled dining room that serves tasty meals in ample quantities, and a comfy lounge with TV, VCR, and ample reading material. The lodge also has a gift shop and evening activities so the guests won't get bored on their desert island. A one-week package includes meals, sports facilities, and transfers from Belize International Airport, with emphasis on either diving or fishing. A seven-night dive package costs US$1,800; many other packages are available.

On the eastern side of Turneffe Islands lies **Blackbird Caye Resort** (tel. 501/223-2772 or 220-9781, belizeus@bellsouth.net, www.blackbird.com, US$1,450 pp), 4,000 acres of a planned, environmentally responsible resort. At present, it offers 10 individual thatch cabanas, with hot-water showers, private baths, and double and queen beds, as well as a duplex and triplex featuring private rooms and a/c. A variety of seven-day fishing or diving packages are offered, including 3 dives a day, all meals, lodging, and airport transfers.

The **Blackbird-Oceanic Society Field Station** (US tel. 800/326-7491, fax 415/474-3395, office@oceanic-society.org, www.oceanic-society.org) is a modern research center created to study dolphins. A resident researcher takes groups to assist in counting and observing dolphin behavior in their natural habitat and sometimes to swim with them. Plan on a 90-minute boat ride from Belize City. The reef is a stone's throw from the resort beach; prepare to snorkel in an untouched area. Packages begin with your pickup at the Belize International Airport and include all meals; no alcoholic drinks are available on the island—feel free to bring your own.

For vacationing folks who want to concentrate on just a few things—fishing, fishing, and fishing—**Turneffe Flats** (US tel. 605/578-1304 or 800/815-1304, Bel. tel. 501/220-4046, vacation@tflats.com, www.tflats.com) is the place to go. Flats fishing for bonefish, tarpon, snook, and permit have put the resort on the map with fly fishers. A fleet of boats and guides is available, or anglers can wade. Larger boats venture out for reef fish, including snappers, wahoo, and groupers. Blue-water fishing for tuna and billfish is also available.

Guests who want to dive, or mix diving with fishing, will have ample opportunity to indulge. Seven-day dive packages include lodging, all meals, three dives per day, and a trip to Lighthouse Reef; or you can mix fishing and diving (rates start around US$1,300). The resort features tidy raised wooden structures along the beach with h/c water and private bath. Meals are served on a pleasant breezy deck just off the lodge building.

Lighthouse Reef Atoll

The most easterly of Belize's three atolls, Lighthouse Reef lies 50 miles southeast of Belize City. The 30-mile-long, eight-mile-wide lagoon is the location of the Blue Hole, a dive spot that was made famous by Jacques Cousteau and that is a favorite destination of dive boats from Belize City, Ambergris Caye, and Caye Caulker. The best dive spots, however, are along the walls of Half Moon Caye and Long Caye, where the diving rivals that of any in the world.

Think of the atoll as a large spatula with a short handle and a long blade. At the northern tip of the spatula blade, **Sandbore Caye** is home to a rusty lighthouse and a few fishing shacks. It is also the favorite anchorage of several of the dive boats that do overnight stops, including *Reef Roamer II.*

Big Northern Caye, across a narrow strait, is the location of Lighthouse Reef Resort. A landing strip just behind the resort is a convenient means of entry for resort guests and divers who wish to make only a day trip without the long watercrossing going and coming, which eats up most of the day. Here are long stretches of beach to walk, beautiful vistas, and large areas of mangroves and lagoons, home to snowy egrets and crocodiles.

Halfway down the spatula-shaped atoll, about where the blade meets the handle, lies the magnificent Blue Hole, a formation best appreciated from the air, but also impressive from the bridge of a boat.

At the elbow of the handle, and looking like some kind of Gilligan's Island, is **Half Moon**

Caye with its lighthouse, bird sanctuary, shipwrecks, and incredible diving offshore. Finally, on the imaginary handle we come upon **Long Caye,** a lonely outpost with a small dock, large palms, and glassy water.

Some anglers and beach bums do come to Lighthouse, but the lure of diving is what attracts most visitors. And at Lighthouse Reef, they are not disappointed.

DIVE SITES
Blue Hole

If flying over the offshore coast, you'll easily recognize this large circular formation with its magnificent blue-to-black hues surrounded by neon blue water. Though there are other, smaller, blue holes around Ambergris Caye, Caye Caulker, and elsewhere, this is the Blue Hole to beat them all. The submerged shaft is a karst-eroded sinkhole with depths that exceed 400 feet. In the early 1970s, Jacques Cousteau and his crew explored the tunnels, caverns, and the listing stalactites that were angled by past earthquakes. This twilight world has suspended sediment and little fish life.

Most dive groups descend to a depth of about 135 feet. Technically, this is not a dive for novices or even intermediate divers, though thousands have done it. It requires a rapid descent, a very short period at depth, and a careful ascent. For a group of 10 or more, at least three dive masters should be present. Critics write it off as a "hyped-up macho dive."

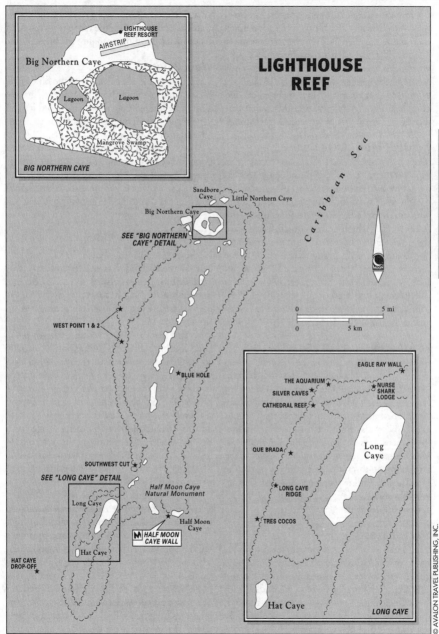

The Northern Cayes

BIG NORTHERN CAYE

LIGHTHOUSE REEF RESORT

AIRSTRIP

Big Northern Caye

Lagoon

Lagoon

Mangrove Swamp

LIGHTHOUSE REEF

Sandbore Caye

Little Northern Caye

Big Northern Caye

SEE "BIG NORTHERN CAYE" DETAIL

Caribbean Sea

0   5 mi
0   5 km

WEST POINT 1 & 2

BLUE HOLE

EAGLE RAY WALL

THE AQUARIUM

SILVER CAVES

CATHEDRAL REEF

NURSE SHARK LODGE

QUE BRADA

Long Caye

SOUTHWEST CUT

SEE "LONG CAYE" DETAIL

LONG CAYE RIDGE

TRES COCOS

Long Caye

Half Moon Caye Natural Monument

Hat Caye

HALF MOON CAYE WALL

Half Moon Caye

HAT CAYE DROP-OFF

Hat Caye

LONG CAYE

© AVALON TRAVEL PUBLISHING, INC.

From the standpoint of undersea life, the lip of the crater, down to about 60–80 feet, is a much more interesting dive. Be prepared for some of the largest midnight parrot fish you will see anywhere. Stingrays are also to be found in sandy areas, as are feather duster worms. Angelfish, butterfly fish, and small reef fish cluster around coral heads and outcroppings. Occasional barracudas and small groupers guard their territories.

Half Moon Caye Wall

They just don't come much better than this. Here on the eastern side of the atoll, the reef has a shallow shelf in about 15 feet of water where garden eels are plentiful. The sandy area broken with corals extends downward till you run into the reef wall, which rises some 20 feet toward the surface. Most boats anchor in the sandy area above the reef wall. Numerous fissures in the reef crest form canyons or tunnels leading out to the vertical face. In this area sandy shelves and valleys frequently harbor nurse sharks and gigantic stingrays. Divers here are sure to return with a wealth of wonderful pictures.

Tres Cocos

On the western wall, "Three Coconuts" refers to trees on nearby Long Caye. The sandy bottom slopes from about 30 feet to about 40 feet deep before it plunges downward. Overhangs here are common features, and sponges and soft corals adorn the walls. Another fish-lover's paradise, Tres Cocos does not have the outstanding coral formations you'll see at several other dives in the area, but who cares; there's a rainbow of marine life all about. Turtles, morays, jacks, coral, shrimp, cowfish, rays, and angelfish are among the actors on this colorful stage.

Silver Caves

The shoals of silversides (small gleaming minnows) that gave this western atoll site its name are gone. But, Silver Caves is still impressive and enjoyable. The coral formations are riddled with large crevices and caves that cut clear through the reef. As you enter the water above the sandy slope where most boats anchor, you'll be in about 30 feet of water and surrounded by friendly yellowtail snappers. Once again you'll see the downwardly sloping bottom, the rising reef crest, and the stomach-flipping drop into the blue.

West Point

Farther north and about even with the Blue Hole, West Point is well worth a dive. Visibility may be a bit more limited than down south, but it's still very acceptable. The reef face here is stepped. The first drop plunges from about 30 feet to well over 100 feet deep. Another coral and sand slope at that depth extends a short distance before dropping vertically into very deep water. The first and shallow wall has pronounced overhangs and lush coral and sponge growth.

HALF MOON CAYE

Dedicated as a monument in 1982, this crescent-shaped island was the first reserve created within the new efforts to protect Belize's natural beauty. Half Moon Caye, at the southeast corner of Lighthouse Reef, measures 45 square acres.

As you approach Half Moon Caye you'll believe you have arrived at some South Sea paradise. Offshore, boaters use the rusted hull of a wreck, the *Elksund,* as a landmark in these waters. Its dark hulk looms over the surreal blue and black of the reef world. The caye, eight feet above sea level, was formed by the accretion of coral bits, shells, and calcareous algae. It's divided into two ecosystems: The section on the western side has dense vegetation with rich fertile soil, while the eastern section primarily supports coconut palms and little other vegetation.

Besides boasting offshore waters that are among the clearest in Belize, the caye's beaches are wonderful. You must climb the eight-foot-high central ridge that divides the island and gaze south before you see the striking half-moon beach with its unrelenting surf erupting against limestone rocks.

Half Moon Caye's first lighthouse, built in 1820, sits on the eastern side of the caye. Another was built in 1848 and modernized and enlarged in 1931; today the lighthouse has entered the age of high technology with solar power.

The Tower

Everyone should go to the observation tower, provided by the Audubon Society in the ziricote forest, and climb above the forest canopy for an unbelievable view. Every tree is covered with perched booby birds in some stage of growth. In the right season you'll have a close-up view of nests where feathered parents tend their hatchlings. The air is filled with boobies coming and going, attempting to make their usually clumsy landings (those webbed feet weren't designed for landing in trees). Visitors also have a wonderful opportunity to see the other myriad inhabitants of the caye. Magnificent thieving frigates swoop by while iguanas crawl around in the branches, both always mindful of an opportunity to swipe a few eggs left unguarded.

Getting There

Only chartered or privately owned boats and seaplanes travel to Half Moon Caye Monument; no regular public transportation is available, although many resort guests fly. An option would be to take an inexpensive water taxi from Belize City to Ambergris or Caye Caulker and take one of the *Reef Seekers* out to Half Moon Caye (US$40 one-way, US$80 round-trip) the next day. Or, you could check with Belize Audubon Society in Belize City for other suggestions.

ACCOMMODATIONS

Lighthouse Reef Resort

Camping is no longer an option, but if you've got the cash, you can stay on Northern Two Caye at Lighthouse Reef Resort (US tel. 800/423-3114, Bel. tel. 501/223-1205, donna@scuba-dive-belize.com, from US$1,695). The island covers 1,200 acres, though almost half is mangrove lagoon with resident bonefish, crocodiles, and bird life. Sandbore Caye lies a short distance away. Seven-day packages are all-inclusive and offer different activities.

On shore, the resort offers 16 acres of tropical beauty, and nature has provided long, wonderful, alluring beaches, swaying palms, and a variety of bird and reptilian life. Accommodations are in elegant villas or duplex cabana-like rooms. Diving, snorkeling, and fishing (bonefishing and deep-sea game fishing) are unsurpassed. Divers must have certification cards with them and should bring their own gear, as rental equipment is limited. Slide processing is available.

Other Northern Cayes

CAYE CHAPEL

Just one-by-three-miles long, Caye Chapel is about 15 miles and 25 minutes by boat from Belize City. The caye is owned by a wealthy Kentuckian who is trying to attract corporate America to his 18-hole golf course and retreat.

Some people have criticized the development and management of the caye, citing environmental damage from dredging and fertilizer run-off. The resort claims otherwise, presenting a list of environmental accomplishments. If you've got the cash (lots of it—a single round costs several hundred dollars), swing by for a round and take a look yourself (tel. 501/226-8250, bzgolf@yahoo.com).

ST. GEORGE'S CAYE

This small caye, nine miles from Belize City, is shaped something like a boomerang, with its open ends facing the mainland. The caye is steeped in history and was the first capital of the British settlement (1650–1784). It was also the scene of the great sea battle between Spaniards and British settlers. Today, the small cemetery gives evidence of St. George's heroic past.

St. George's Caye is far from commercialized—on the contrary, it's very quiet, with mostly residential homes and their docks. There are several upscale accommodations with full-service dive shops here, plus the vacation homes of quite a few of Belize's elite. Check **St. George's Island Lodge and Cottages** (tel.

THE GRAY LADY

In all good myths and legends, the details are often sketchy, but facts are usually delicious. In the legend of the Gray Lady, it is said that Henry Morgan often roamed the waters of the Caribbean, frequently off the coast of Belize City. In his wanderings, Henry brought his fair lady with him, a very independent miss. It's easy to imagine that lovers occasionally get testy living in such close quarters aboard a caravel. And though Henry and his lady usually kissed and made up, one lightning-slashed night, just off the coast of St. George's Caye, they were unable to settle a nasty argument—something to do with the seaman standing watch the night before? He was the captain after all; his word was law! The lady ended up walking the plank into the stormy sea, gray gossamer gown whipping around her legs in the angry wind. Since that fateful night, the lady in gray has been roaming the small caye of St. George trying to find her blackguard lover. Don't scoff; some islanders will speak no ill of the Gray Lady, and on stormy nights they stay safely behind closed doors.

501/220-4444, fred@gooddiving.com, www .gooddiving.com).

THE BLUEFIELD RANGE

Scattered along the coast is a constellation of small cayes, some accessible by tourists, others only by drug traffickers. Seeking out accommodations on any of these islands is guaranteed to get you a unique Belize experience, as you'll be well away from the crowds of the more standard island destinations.

The Bluefield Range is a group of cayes a short distance south of Belize City. On one of the islands, 21 miles south of the city, is **Ricardo's Beach Huts and Lobster Camp** (tel. 501/227-8469 or 203-4970), the ultimate in funky. At last check, the accommodations were quite rustic and reasonably priced. Expect camp-out conditions: outhouse, bucket shower, bugs. Bring mosquito coils, repellent, and a mosquito-net bed/tent. On the upside, this is one of the few

chances to experience outer-island living just as it has been for the people who spend their lives fishing these waters. Ricardo's is "bloody ethnic with some really genuine people running it," observed a recent visitor.

ENGLISH CAYE

Though this is just a small collection of palm trees, sand, and coral, an important lighthouse sits here at the entrance to the Belize City harbor from the Caribbean Sea. Large ships stop at English Caye to pick up one of the two pilots who navigate the 10 miles in and out of the busy harbor. Overnights are not allowed here, but it's a pleasant day-trip location.

GOFF'S CAYE

Near English Caye, Goff's Caye is a favorite little island stop for picnics and day trips out of Caye Caulker and Belize City, thanks to a beautiful sandy beach and promising snorkeling areas. Sailboats often stop overnight; camping can be arranged from Caye Caulker by talking with any reputable guide. Bring your own tent and supplies. Goff's is a protected caye, so note the rules posted by the pier. Goff's has seen a major impact by the cruise ship industry, which sometimes sends thousands of people per week to snorkel around and party on the tiny piece of sand.

SPANISH LOOKOUT CAYE

This is a 187-acre mangrove island, located at the southern tip of The Drowned Cayes, which lie 10 miles east of Belize City. If you're not researching manatees with Earthwatch, you're most likely coming here to stay at **Spanish Bay Resort** (tel. 501/223-4526, spanishbay@belizediving .com). When you approach the resort from the sea on a sunny day, the simple white cabanas built over the blue-green water are quite spectacular. Five cabanas with 10 rooms, hot showers, and private baths are connected to the island by a dock. The resort offers popular three-night packages that include all meals and transfer to the island.

Diving is one of the favorite activities here. Manatees and dolphins are regularly seen foraging near the island. Juvenile reef fish, seahorses, lobster, and mollusks live among the red mangrove roots and seagrass beds. Tarpon and barracuda often come into the bay to feed on the abundant silversides. The resort is only one mile west of the main Barrier Reef and about eight miles west of central Turneffe Island.

Belmopan Area
and the Hummingbird Highway

This chunk of central Belize, comprised of the unpretentious capital of the country as well as one of the region's most stunning roads, the Hummingbird Highway, encompasses several distinct ecosystems: Pine savannah meets the Maya Mountains, and a massive underground cave system underlies it all. The area is drained by the Sibun and Caves Branch Rivers, which empty out into a large, lowland marshy region; opportunities to hike and float through it all abound.

PLANNING YOUR TIME

Some people spend their entire vacations (or at least the inland portion of them) in one of the adventure lodges of the region. Most, however, quickly pass through. The city of Bel-mopan certainly doesn't require much of your time, but the rest of the region may warrant a day or two. As you drive west on the Western Highway, save at least an hour for the Belize Zoo, and another hour for the hike in Guanacaste National Park. If you have the time, it is highly recommended to spend at least a full day visiting the other national parks along the Hummingbird Highway, and you might even choose to spend a rustic evening in one of the towns you'll be driving through as well. You may wish to spend a night or two at the ultra-tranquil Monkey Bay Wildlife Sanctuary, in a simple room or campground, studying in their library loft at night; many choose this location over Belize City as the first or final night of their trip.

© DANIELLE VAUGHN

Must-Sees

Look for **M** to find the sights and activities you can't miss and **M** for the best dining and lodging.

© DANIELLE VAUGHN

There are hundreds of deep, barely explored caves in Belize.

M Market Square: Take a stroll through Belmopan's small, bustling outdoor commercial section, then walk over to the plaza by the government buildings (page 103).

M Banana Bank Lodge: Go horseback riding at this famous riverside ranch—or cave tubing, jungle trekking, and rappelling at nearby Ian Anderson's Caves Branch or Jaguar Paw Resorts (page 105).

M Roaring River Golf Course: Shoot a leisurely nine holes at this relaxed set of links, just west of Belmopan (page 107).

M The Belize Zoo: This famous, lush home for animal ex-movie stars and more is an easy stopover as you travel between Belize City and points south and west (page 108).

M Blue Hole National Park: Get out the hiking boots, binoculars, and a bathing suit for a visit to this park and St. Herman's Cave, halfway down the Hummingbird Highway (page 111).

The Belize Zoo M

Banana Bank Lodge M

Market Square M Belmopan ⊛

M Roaring River Golf Course

M Blue Hole National Park

BELMOPAN AREA AND THE HUMMINGBIRD HIGHWAY

M Belmopan Area

BELMOPAN AREA AND THE HUMMINGBIRD HIGHWAY

Belmopan Area

BELIZE
CAYO

To Belize City

Belize River

River

M *THE BELIZE ZOO*

La Democracia

MANATEE JUNCTION

COASTAL RD.

M *BANANA BANK LODGE*

Belize

CHEERS

Monkey Bay Wildlife Sanctuary

AMIGO'S

JB'S

Sibun River

Guanacaste National Park

WESTERN HWY.

Roaring Creek

M *MARKET SQUARE*

BEAVER DAM

Belmopan

To San Ignacio

M *ROARING RIVER GOLF COURSE*

Armenia

IAN ANDERSON'S CAVES BRANCH

M *BLUE HOLE NATIONAL PARK*

JAGUAR PAW RESORT

HUMMINGBIRD

BLUE HOLE NATIONAL PARK VISITOR CENTER

HWY.

BLUE HOLE

Caves Branch

ST. HERMAN'S CAVE

Manatee Forest Reserve

BELIZE
STANN CREEK

OVER-THE-TOP

St. Margaret's

To Dangriga

MooN

Sibun Forest Reserve

CAYO
STANN CREEK

0   2 mi

0   2 km

© AVALON TRAVEL PUBLISHING, INC.

Belmopan

The majority of travelers see only Belmopan's bus terminal and the small open air market right next door, which many browse as they wait for their next ride. If you've got time, jog across the market to take a peek at the government buildings (only a couple hundred yards away)—they are incredibly gray, squat, and a bit post-apocalyptic, especially since efforts to keep their exteriors clean were abandoned. Their intentionally Maya-influenced arrangement—built around a central plaza—gives the scene just enough strange irony to make it worth the visit.

Belmopan has been the capital of the country since 1961, when it was built far away from the coast to keep it safe from storm damage. After Hurricane Hattie destroyed vast quantities of government documents (and buildings) in Belize City, Belmopan was built with the expectation that large numbers of the population of Belize City would move with the government center. They didn't. Industry stayed behind, and so did most jobs. Today, the masses are still in Belize City, which remains the cultural and industrial hub of the country. Some capital employees continue to commute the 50 miles back and forth each day. However, Belmopan was designed for growth and continues to expand, with the population approaching 9,000 souls. Today, the feel inside the city grid (within Ring Road) has been compared to a lower-middle class Los Angeles suburb, with rows of small cement homes and chain link fencing.

The long-promised museum has finally been built (it's the plain, gray box near the water tower), but there's nothing in it. Keep an eye on it. The town does have a large complex of sporting fields that includes basketball, volleyball, and tennis courts, as well as lots of space for spur-of-the-moment gatherings. Many come to Belmopan to do research in the **Belize Archives Department** (tel. 501/822-2097), a closed-stacks library popular with both local students and foreign researchers.

Belmopan is also home to the government's **Institute of Archaeology** (IOA, tel. 501/822-2106 or 822-2227), responsible for monitoring all ongoing archaeological projects in Belize and issuing permits for site work. The Institute of Archaeology also manages all archaeological parks and reserves, including the visitors centers and a staff of over 50 park wardens.

ORIENTATION

Belmopan is just east of the Hummingbird Highway (and just south of the Western Highway), and is usually accessed by Constitution Drive, which leads straight into the center from a roundabout. Banks, buses, market, and government buildings are tightly clustered within easy walking distance of each other. Turning right on Bliss Parade from Constitution Drive, you'll find the Belmopan Hotel on your right, and the Novelo's bus station and the market on your left. Bliss Parade joins Ring Road, which loops around the central town district. Ring Road passes various government buildings and embassies on the left before meeting back up with Constitution Drive.

N MARKET SQUARE

This is where the action is for the locals, the lines of stalls alive with the commerce and gossip of the area. Hang out here for a little while and you are sure to see a parade of local farmers, government workers, and colorful characters going about business. Try a tasty *tamale* or plate of *garnaches* (crispy tortillas topped with tomato, cabbage, cheese, and hot sauce) for next to nothing. Bananas, oranges, mangoes, tomatoes, chilies, and carrots are cheap, too; stock up before heading deeper into Belize.

ENTERTAINMENT AND NIGHTLIFE

Despite Belmopan's reputation for being a "dead" town, weekends can be quite alive in the capital city. Thursdays start with karaoke at the Bull Frog, but turn into a rockin' dance party around

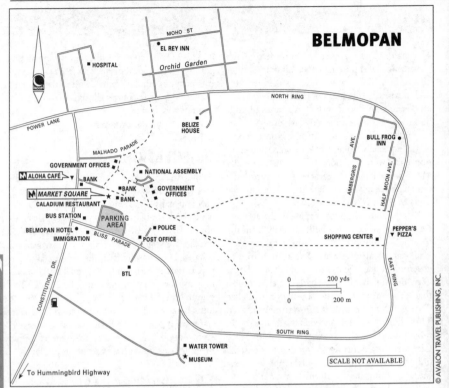

11 P.M. when the place gets packed. The rest of the weekend is ruled by **Tropical Delites,** better-known by its old name, **Roundabout,** located on the northeast corner of the traffic circle on the Hummingbird Highway. For a mellow, unpretentious bar, be sure to hit **La Cabaña,** in the western part of town by Las Flores, with cheap bar food and a friendly vibe.

SHOPPING

Besides the market, you'll find a few handy stores in Belmopan. **Angelus Press** has a good office supply and book store right by the bus station. **The Art Box** is on the Hummingbird Highway and has a unique selection of woodwork, watercolors, and picture frames, in addition to the standard gift shop fare (and Christian books and CDs).

ACCOMMODATIONS

It's slim pickings in Belmopan, especially for budget travelers; then again, if you're staying in Belmopan, you're probably a business person, diplomat, or development worker—or just lost. The least offensive of the offerings, and the most reasonably priced, is **El Rey Inn** (23 Moho St., tel. 501/822-3438, hibiscus@btl.net, US$20/25 s/d), with 11 tidy, austere rooms with private bath, h/c water, and fans.

If you need your air conditioning and television, the **Bull Frog Inn** (25 Half Moon Ave., tel. 501/822-2111, bullfrog@btl.net, www.bull-froginn.com, US$50–75) has 25 rooms that could be mistaken for any basic roadside hotel in the States. The on-site restaurant serves good food and the bar turns into an all-night disco on Thursdays.

Convenient to Market Square, government buildings, and the bus station, the contemporary **Belmopan Hotel** (tel. 501/822-2130, gsosa@btl.net, US$50/60 s/d) offers meeting rooms, a dismal swimming pool, restaurant, group facilities, and a communications center. The 20 well-worn rooms have a/c, fans, and cable TV. Peeling paint and dark hallways, but eager-to-please staff. The restaurant serves three meals daily; grilled lobster, seafood, and T-bone steak head the menu.

FOOD

The cheapest meals are had at the rows of market stalls and small restaurants that surround the bus terminal; if you have the time, walk across Constitution Drive to the **⋈ Aloha Cafe** (located to the right of the Scotia Bank) for a meal, or at least a milkshake; the owners have done a great job creating a unique and comfortable atmosphere here. **Pepper's Pizza** (tel. 501/822-0666) delivers free anywhere in town. It's decent 'za, but beware the buffalo wings.

The open-air restaurant and bar at the **Bull Frog Inn** have a solid reputation among even the elite of Belmopan, and this is one of the most popular spots in town to dine. The fish fillet,

chicken, and burgers are all good here, and moderately priced (entrees from US$10, much cheaper lunches). The inn serves fresh orange, lime, and grapefruit juice.

The Oasis is a new place across the Hummingbird Highway, on the river, that has gotten excellent reviews.

Getting There

By bus, it's damn near impossible *not* to visit Belmopan, as every bus traveling between Belize City and points west and south—even the expresses—pulls into the main terminal for anywhere from five to thirty minutes.

Near Belmopan

⋈ BANANA BANK LODGE

When they first arrived in Belize nearly 30 years ago, Montana cowboy John Carr and his wife, Carolyn, ran **Banana Bank Lodge and Jungle Equestrian Adventure** (tel. 501/820-2020, bbl@starband.net, www.bananabank.com) as a working cattle ranch. Today, most of the pastures have been converted to fields for growing corn and beans (or allowed to turn back to jungle), and the ranch now hosts their lodge. Although the place has electricity and a phone, it retains the ambience of the tropical ranch it used to be.

Rooms, suites, and cabanas are fanciful, no two are alike, and most have beautifully funky

bathtubs. The food is great, served family-style. Five cabanas each sleep up to six people, and five more rooms in the main house, three with shared bathroom, accommodate guests. One of the rooms with private bath is furnished with a waterbed. There are a couple of new poolside rooms as well (underneath the geodesic dome), and Internet access. Breakfast is included in the room rate. Lunch is US$10, dinner US$15.

Half of the 4,000-acre ranch is covered in jungle, and within its borders guests will discover not only a wide variety of wildlife but a respectably sized Maya ruin. Scattered around the property are many more small archaeological "house mounds." The ranch's lagoon, hand-dug centuries ago, today harbors several

Morelet's crocodiles and a bevy of frogs, happily croaking away.

With more than 130 saddle horses (always increasing, as John can't pass up buying a good animal), Banana Bank features horseback riding, but is also a place to bird-watch, fish, hike, or take a boat trip down the Belize River with plenty of time left for a cooling swim—in the river or the on-site swimming pool. A lazy ride via horse-drawn buggy into the surrounding countryside is another treat, as is nighttime stargazing through a massive 14" telescope.

There is also a zoo of sorts, which includes an aviary, a resident jaguar, and a couple of monkeys; most of the animals were given to the Carrs to care for. (Some were orphaned and others were pets who had outworn their welcome and could not live on their own in the wild.) The Carrs actively involve the local communities of Belizeans in their operation, and even host a soccer team. Carolyn is considered one of the country's premier artists, and if you admire her on-site studio and gallery, be sure to seek out her paintings in the House of Culture in Belize City.

Banana Bank feels isolated, but is easily accessed, located right across the Belize River, a mile or so north of the Western Highway as it passes Belmopan at Mile 47. Park your vehicle to the right under the trees, ring the gong, and amble down to the dock—shortly, someone will pull a boat along the rope stretched from bank to bank to fetch you. If you miss the first turnoff road, there's another past Roaring Creek Village at Mile 56, on the right. The sign says to take the road to the ferry, cross the river, and proceed to the ranch—a total of four miles.

GUANACASTE NATIONAL PARK

Located right at the "T" junction where the Hummingbird Highway heads south from the Western Highway, 50-acre Guanacaste National Park packs a lot within its small area. Managed by the **Belize Audubon Society, MacArthur Foundation, World Wildlife Fund,** and the government, the park gets its name from the massive guanacaste, or *tubroos,* tree near the southwestern edge of the property. Ceiba, co-

hune palms, mammee apple, mahogany, quam-wood, and other trees also populate the forest. Agouti, armadillo, coati, deer, iguana, jaguarundi, and kinkajou have all been observed in the park, along with more than 100 species of birds. Among the rarer finds are resident blue-crowned mot-mots.

There are about two miles of very easy trail to explore; feel free to bring a swimsuit and take a dip at the quiet spot where the Belize River and Roaring Creek meet. Picnic tables, benches, restrooms, and trash cans have slowly been added to the site, mostly with the help of Peace Corps Volunteers.

The park was originally the home of the former British city planner who was commissioned to relocate the capital to Belmopan after Hurricane Hattie heavily damaged Belize City in 1961. It's said that he chose the spot because of the proximity to the spectacular old guanacaste tree. The official decided almost immediately that the meadow should be set aside as a government reserve for future generations to enjoy. The huge tree, well over 100 years old, is more than 25 feet in diameter and host to more than 35 species of exotic flora, including orchids, bromeliads, ferns, philodendrons, and cacti, along with a large termite nest and myriad birds twittering and fluttering in the branches—a tree of life! When rivers were the main method of transport, travelers stopped here to spend the night under the protection of its wide-spreading branches. The only thing that saved the tree from loggers was its crooked trunk.

As you enter the park, walk across the grassy field; go left to get to the trail that brings you to the guanacaste. Beyond the tree, there's a looter's trench—someone long ago thought there was treasure buried here. The trench graphically demonstrates how a looter excavates and works a would-be treasure site (including Maya structures). Farther on, the path meets the shore of Roaring Creek, the westernmost boundary of the park. This is a wonderful and easy trail; you may or may not see another hiker, but you'll certainly see birds, delicate ferns, flowers, and long parades of wiwi ants.

Another option from the park entrance is to

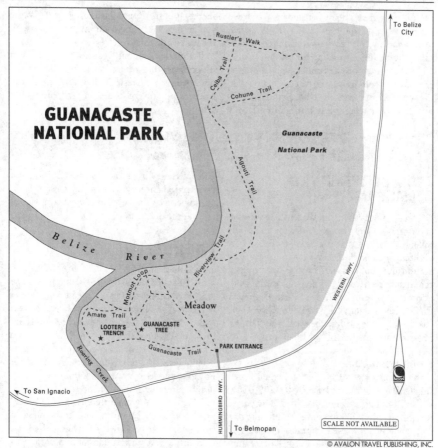

GUANACASTE
NATIONAL PARK

© AVALON TRAVEL PUBLISHING, INC.

cross the meadow and veer to the right. Here you'll find the steps that lead down to the Belize River. Along the shore, nature quietly continues its pattern of creation and subsistence. The *amate* fig grows profusely on the water's edge and provides an important part of the howler monkey's diet. In the center of this scheme is the tuba fish, which eats the figs that fall into the water, dispersing the seeds up and down the river—starting more *amate* fig trees. And so it goes—on and on. At dusk on a quiet evening, howler monkeys roar the news that they're having dinner—keep your distance, world! Park hours are 8 A.M.–4:30 P.M.; entrance US$2.50 pp, tours are self-guided.

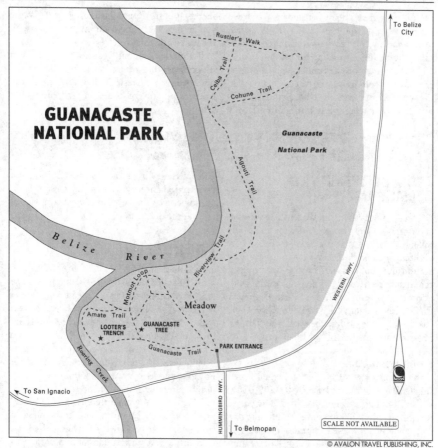 ROARING RIVER GOLF COURSE

An unpretentious, executive-type nine-holer (1,909 yards, par 32), Roaring River Golf Course (Mile 50 1/4 Western Highway, tel. 501/614-2031, martin@btl.net) is the only mainland course currently in operation. (On Caye Chapel, there's an upscale 18 holes.) The feel of the course, clubhouse, and equipment is perfectly Belizean: a bit rough around the edges but in a natural, comfortable way. A round is only US$15 per person, plus US$5 to rent clubs and pull carts. The course is well maintained, with a level layout, but with interesting landscaping dividing the fairways; greens boast Bermuda grass, grown from seed, and Paul, the South African owner, notes that his course uses very limited chemicals—"just a bit of spraying for the ants."

After sweating out a round, dip in one of the cool, shady pools of the river that runs through it; the water is fresh from the Thousand Foot Falls just upstream. Plant your non-golfing family members in the Roaring River for the day while you hit those links and confront the crocodiles in the water hazards.

If coming from San Ignacio, you can warm up on a **driving range** in Georgeville, on the north side of the Western Highway. There's also a new miniature golf course in San Pedro.

Along the Western Highway

FROM BELIZE CITY TO BELMOPAN

As you head west along the Western Highway, savanna and scraggly pines border the road. The milepost markers that run between Belize City and San Ignacio will help you find your way around the countryside. If you're driving, you can match the markers as you go by setting your odometer to zero as you turn onto Cemetery Road at the western edge of Belize City. You'll pass two service stations between the Western Highway and the turnoff for Belmopan.

Freetown Sibun

Three miles south of Hattieville, you'll find a small village (community tel. 501/209-6006) with a population of less than 100. The village was founded by runaway slaves back in the day, and its population used to peak around 2,000 during big logging runs. Today, you'll find campsites, canoe rentals, and hiking trails. Taxis are plentiful from the roundabout in Hattieville.

Manatee Junction

Driving west, note the junction with **Manatee Road** on your left at about Mile 29. (Look for the **Midway Resting Place,** a service station and motel of sorts on the southeast corner; its tall Texaco sign makes an especially good landmark at night, when the sign glows with bright colors.) This improved dirt road is the shortcut to Gales Point, Dangriga, and the Southern Highway. It's always a good idea to top off your tank, stock up on cold drinks, and ask for current road conditions here. Heavy rains can cause washouts on

a lot of these "highways." This is a drive best done in daylight because of the picturesque views of jungle, Maya villages, and the Maya Mountains in the distance.

⋈ THE BELIZE ZOO

Established in 1983, The Belize Zoo (tel. 501/220-8004, fax 501/220-8010, info@belizezoo .org, www.belizezoo.org) is settled upon 29 acres of tropical savanna and exhibits over 125 animals, all native to Belize. The zoo keeps only animals that were either orphaned, injured and rehabilitated, born in the zoo, or received as gifts from other zoos. The environment is as natural as possible, and each animal lives in its own shady jungle compound; there are no steel bars here.

The zoo is conveniently located at Mile 29 on the Western Highway, and is included in many day tours from Belize City and often as a stop during your airport transfer to or from your lodge in the western and southern parts of Belize. The independent traveler need simply jump off the bus and walk in.

History

Zoo Director Sharon Matola's accidental career began when, as a former lion tamer, she agreed to manage a backyard collection of local animals for a nature film company next door. However, after she had worked only five months on the project, funds were severely reduced, and it became evident that the group of animal "film stars" would have to be disbanded.

Sharon says that not only had these wild cats, birds, anteaters, and snakes become her friends and companions, but semi-tame animals, dependent on people for care, could not just be released back into the wild. As an alternative, she thought, "This country has never had a zoo. Perhaps if I offered the chance for Belizeans to see these unique animals, their existence here could be permanently established."

And so a zoo was born. From the very beginning, the amount of local interest shown in the zoo was incredible. The majority of the people in Belize live in urban areas, and their knowledge of the local fauna is minimal. The Belize Zoo offers Belizeans and tourists alike the opportunity to see the native animals of Belize.

School Programs and Wildlife Awareness

The Belize Zoo's modest beginnings hinged on the simple idea that children deserved the chance to grow up knowing animals, especially those living in the thick forests not too many miles from their city homes. The Belize Zoo receives over 10,000 schoolchildren every year as part of the progressive education programs, and popular zoo events include April the Tapir's birthday party; summer camps; Science Fair; Teacher Training; and Student Career Training.

The Belize Zoo is becoming increasingly well-known throughout the world. The unique educational programs and the conservation efforts of the zoo have consistently made international environmental news. Funds are always needed to support "dream projects" for the future: a reptile exhibit; a butterfly flight room; and, with the promise of help from the Monterey Bay Aquarium, a new "water world" exhibit. When visiting the zoo, ask about becoming a member in order to support these efforts.

The Belize Tropical Education Center

Across the street from the zoo, the Tropical Education Center (tel. 501/220-8003, tec@belize-zoo.org) was created to promote environmental education and scientific research. Meetings are held here for zoological news, reports, and educational seminars attended and given by people involved in zoology from around the world. The Center is equipped with a classroom, a library,

kitchen and dining area, and dormitories that can accommodate as many as 30 people (rates from US$15 pp). Great nature trails weave through the 84-acre site, and bird-watchers can avail themselves of a bird-viewing deck. Also available are canoe trips, nocturnal zoo tours, and natural history lectures.

MONKEY BAY WILDLIFE SANCTUARY

The 3,300-acre wildlands of Monkey Bay (tel. 501/820-3032, mbay@btl.net, www.monkey-baybelize.org) serve as the natural home to nearly all the animals represented at the Belize Zoo, just a mile east on the Western Highway. Although many may argue that the stress here is on the wildlife , others would say Monkey Bay is more about the word "sanctuary." This is a fantastic retreat—for student groups, families, naturalists, and paddlers. Some travelers find themselves so intrigued by the goings-on at this environmental education center and tropical watershed research station that they opt to stay in one of Monkey Bay's primitively rustic rooms longer than they had planned. The simple, wooden rooms in the main building include a mosquito net, use of shared bath, and are centered around a large, common, barnlike library and study space (over 500 titles available for reference, lots of local information). There are also bunks and a campground in a grove of pine trees. Fresh-prepared meals are available, plus a range of learning and adventure activities throughout Belize.

Monkey Bay offers various cultural learning programs that include homestays with both Maya and Garinagu communities; they also have a curriculum of tropical watershed ecology field courses. Groups and individuals are welcome for internships and volunteer programs as well. Homestays have a community service component.

Monkey Bay Wildlife Sanctuary consists of tropical forest, riparian, and savanna habitats, stretching from the Western Highway down to the Sibun River that flows from the Maya Mountains through the coastal savanna on its path to the Caribbean Sea. The area is home to exotic mammal species, including tapir, puma, jaguar,

Belmopan Area

© DANIELLE VAUGHN

the lodge at Monkey Bay: hostel, library, hangout, wildlife sanctuary HQ

and Morelet's crocodile. Over 250 species of birds have been recorded. The sanctuary borders the Sibun River biological corridor and has documented remains of ancient Maya settlements and ceremonial caves. A newly built trail system carries you through it all; you can hike, rent a canoe, or hire a caving guide—this is serious spelunking country as well. One option is a three-night camping expedition, where you'll hike to Five Blues Lake National Park.

You'll find two miles of trails, a 20-acre arboretum, and good swimming at nearby Sibun River. With the declaration by the Belize government in 1992 of the 2,250-acre **Monkey Bay Nature Reserve** across the river, there now exists a wildlands corridor between the **Manatee Forest Reserve** to the south and the sanctuary.

PIT STOPS

There are a few notable restaurant-bars clustered around Mile 31, right around where you first see the sleeping Maya giant in hills to the south. You'll first come to **Cheers** (tel. 501/614-9311, 6 A.M.–8:30 P.M. daily), with its interesting collection of orchids, license plates, and T-shirts.

Amigos is another good screened-in bar and restaurant.

J.B.'s Watering Hole

At around Mile 32, legendary J.B.'s Watering Hole (tel. 501/820-2071, neesemgm@btl.net) presents the traveler with an opportunity to slake a thirst and chew the fat with locals and other travelers. This "watering hole" in the middle of nowhere has been around for years. A former favorite of British forces (now gone), it's one of the few such places worth stopping at between Belize City and San Ignacio. Locals say Harrison Ford was a regular during the filming of *Mosquito Coast*. Originally run by J.B., it's long been under new management. It's a good stop for a burger or stewed chicken and a Belikin. Lift one to J.B.'s memory and the fair ladies who run it still; you'll be in good company.

For those who've had too many or for those who want an inexpensive base for further exploration of the area, J.B.'s now offers one- or two-bedroom accommodations with hot water and private baths for US$30. In one, known as the "jungle hut," furniture is made from local wood.

Along the Hummingbird Highway

This famous stretch of road was only paved a few years ago and boasts some of the most scenic driving in Belize. The highway passes through towering hills and lush broadleaf jungle as you cross the Caves Branch Bridge and enter the Valley of Caves. After another 20 miles, you'll climb into the Maya Mountains, pass the access road to Five Blues Lake National Park, experience the Over the Top pass, and then descend toward the sea. The junction with the Southern Highway is 20 miles farther—Dangriga is 25. You'll pass through citrus orchards, sleepy villages perched on the banks of rocky streams, craggy cliffs and gorges crusted with deep green beards of heavy jungle, and tracts of thick cohune forest. All will beckon you to stop, explore, and linger a bit longer.

◪ BLUE HOLE NATIONAL PARK

Covering 575 acres, Blue Hole National Park encompasses this water-filled sink, St. Herman's Cave, and the surrounding jungle. (Belize's other Blue Hole lies in the ocean at Lighthouse Reef.) Rich in wildlife, Blue Hole National Park harbors the jaguar, ocelot, tapir, peccary, tamandua, boa constrictor, fer-de-lance, toucan, crested guan, blue-crowned mot-mot, and red-legged honeycreeper. At about Mile 12.5 past Belmopan is a sign for St. Herman's Cave; ignore it and continue to the main park entrance about a mile down the road. You'll find a parking area and changing room for a dip in the deep blue waters of the Blue Hole.

The pool of the **Blue Hole** is an oblong collapsed karst sinkhole 300 feet across in some places and about 100 feet deep. Water destined for the nearby Sibun River surfaces briefly here only to disappear once more beneath the ground. Steps lead down to the swimming area, a pool 25 feet deep or so.

St. Herman's Cave is not as convenient to access. As you face the Blue Hole, the trail to St. Herman's Cave lies to the right and requires a hike of a little more than a mile and a half over rugged ground. The trail begins by the changing room. A flashlight and rugged shoes are necessities, and a light windbreaker or sweater is a wise choice for extended stays if you visit in the winter season. The nearest of the three entrances to the cave is a huge sinkhole measuring nearly 200 feet across, funneling down to about 65 feet at the cave's lip. Concrete steps laid over the Maya originals aid explorers who wish to descend. The cave doesn't offer the advanced spelunker a real challenge, but neophytes will safely explore it to a distance of about a mile. Pottery, spears, and the remains of torches have been found in many caves in the area. The pottery was used to collect the clear water of cave drippings, called *Zuh uy Ha* by the Maya.

The entire area is a labyrinth of caves where the ancient Maya once lived and roamed; some of the chambers still show signs of rituals long past. A variety of caves lie in the hilly limestone nearby and include **Mountain Cow** and **Petroglyph Caves.** The caves include cathedral-like ceilings hundreds of feet high as well as narrow, cramped passageways. Some have crystal-coated stalactites and stalagmites; others have underground streams that at times seem to speak in murmured voices. And while you won't likely find any Maya living in the caves, you will find a number of harmless bats. Remember: Bring a flashlight, extra batteries, and sturdy walking shoes. The surrounding lush jungle is thick with tropical plants, delicate ferns, bromeliads, and orchids.

It's best to visit most caves with a guide, and at the least, don't visit the park unless the wardens are there (8:30 A.M.–4:30 P.M.). The entrance fee is US$5 per person. Make sure to lock your car, and don't leave valuables in view.

ADVENTURE TRIPS AND ACCOMMODATIONS
Villages and Budget Accommodations

"Bed-and-breakfast" homestay options are available in several villages up and down the

Belmopan Area

Hummingbird Highway. **Armenia** is a quiet town, eight miles south of Belmopan, with a Maya and Latino population and shops, restaurants, bunk accommodations, and cabanas. **St. Margaret's,** at Mile 32, is the entrance to Five Blues Lake National Park and has some of the same services as Armenia, including accommodations. At Mile 40, in the village of **Ringtail,** look for **Primitas Farm Bed & Breakfast.** Just get off the bus in any of these towns and ask around. Cultural immersion adventures await.

Ian Anderson's Caves Branch Adventure Company and Jungle Lodge

Neither a "sightseeing" business nor a "resort," Ian Anderson's Caves Branch Adventure Company and Jungle Lodge (Mile 41 1/2 Hummingbird Hwy., via radio phone tel. 501/822-2800, fax 888/265-4579, info@cavesbranch.com, www .cavesbranch.com) offers expeditions that can be strenuous and exciting. This is a hub for social, active trippers; as Ian said a few years ago, "We're certainly not for everyone—thank God!"

The lodge is located on the bank of the Caves Branch River, under a 100-foot jungle canopy. All the guests come together in the open dining room for family-style meals (breakfast and lunch US$12, dinner US$17). Lodging rates are US$5 for the beautiful riverside tent sites (bring your own gear); US$15 for the fine-screened thatched co-ed dormitory with eight bunk beds, linen provided; and US$80–130 for beautifully simple jungle cabanas and suites. The screened accommodations are open to the sights and sounds of the surrounding wildness, many are shared bath, and privacy is limited. The main building has electricity, but accommodation lighting is by the glow of kerosene lamps—and yes, flush toilets and hot and cold water are available throughout (actually, the warm "jungle shower" is the highlight of many a guest's stay).

On the 58,000 acres of this private estate are 68 known caves, and Ian has discovered and explored them all, developing a variety of trips around many of them. The longest and deepest of these Maya ceremonial caves extends seven miles. Pristine dry caves glisten with crystal formations. Some caves still have pottery shards,

rappelling the "Black Hole Drop" sinkhole in Caves Branch

© DANIELLE VAUGHN

skeletal remains, and footprints coated with an icing of rock crystals. Ian offers one- to seven-day expeditions, including tubing trips through river caves. Ask about all the different packages, and about joining one of the "Bad-Ass" scouting expeditions, when the Caves Branch guides take off in search of new trips to offer their guests, usually in the low season. All expedition guides have received intensive training in cave and wilderness rescue/evacuation and first aid.

Access to Ian Anderson's Caves Branch is located on the Hummingbird Highway between the Blue Hole National Park Visitor Center and the parking lot for the Blue Hole itself; turn left (if headed south) and continue to the end of the mile-long dirt road. If traveling by bus, you'll have to hike in from here if you haven't arranged to be picked up by lodge staff.

Jaguar Paw Jungle Resort

Jaguar Paw (US tel. 888/77-JUNGLE, Bel. tel. 501/820-2023, cyoung@btl.net, www.jaguarpaw .com, US$170 s/d) is located on a 215-acre na-

CAVING PRECAUTIONS

When caving, go with a guide! Local guides know the mazelike caves like you know your way around your kitchen. Dangers while caving include getting lost, injured, or drowning in a flash flood. What might seem like a minor rain can create instant rises in water levels that can easily sweep you away, resulting in injury and, more likely, drowning. These caves are also dark—once past the entrance, all natural light disappears, making it necessary to wear headlamps and carry spare flashlights and batteries. With such limited vision, it is easy to hit stalactites and whack your head on sloping and shallow ceilings, so wear a hard hat. Twisting, turning corridors make it very easy to lose your sense of direction. Finally, respect life in the cave—don't use forming stalactites as handholds, because body oils destroy years of growth. Never disturb or remove anything.

ture reserve in the middle of cave country. It's accessed from the Western Highway, east of Belmopan, at the end of a 15-mile gravel road to the south. Jaguar Paw is steps away from the Caves Branch River and its innumerable shoreline caves. Perch yourself on an inner tube and let the river pull you in and out of water-filled black caverns; go on an all-day jungle walk with friendly guides and learn about medicinal plants, blossoms, and jungle creatures; walk through dry caves with bats by the hundreds zooming all around you. Put on your boots and go rock climbing. Or, just kick back at the pool or catch the latest game on satellite TV at the bar.

Cy and Donna Young have spent years creating a bit of high-tech beauty in their isolated piece of Eden. Sixteen rooms have electricity, hot showers, and air-conditioning. Art from around the globe is displayed on tables and decorates the walls, and handmade quilts and sheets by the Mennonites keep you warm on cooler nights; these personal touches add to guests' contentment.

The lobby, dining room, and bar are in a cement building styled as a Maya ruin. On one inside wall is a reproduction of the Bonompak murals, famous Maya murals in Mexico. The dining room is comfortable and an elegant menu is offered by friendly staff. Try the seafood pasta with fresh fettuccine in a delicious Alfredo sauce. For breakfast, the French toast with zesty spices is a favorite. Meals are tasty, although it may not be enough food for some big appetites. Dinner runs about US$15–20.

Check out the building by the river with small kitchen/bar, gift shop, changing rooms, and six toilets. This structure will hold 125 people, enough for a nice-sized party. To get there from the Western Highway, turn left at Mile 37 and follow the road seven miles; the signs are pretty good—otherwise, every time you come to a junction, keep to the right.

FIVE BLUES LAKE NATIONAL PARK

Located on the Hummingbird Highway at Mile 32, the park (info@fiveblues.org, www.five-blues.org, US$2–4) can be reached by taking a local bus from the terminal in Belmopan to St. Margaret's Village. Within the village, the park office is on the way to the park. The local rangers are both knowledgeable and willing to help with any questions that you may have. From the park office, a four-kilometer road leads to the park. This road may be hiked, or the rangers will be more than willing to provide transportation.

Within Five Blues Lake National Park, several Maya sites are accessible to visitors. Within the Duende Caves, ceremonial pottery can still be found. While some of the more significant sites are heavily regulated by the Belizean Institute of Archaeology, Five Blues Lake provides ample opportunity for visitors to witness Maya writings and pottery.

Entrance fees go toward supporting the park and can be paid to the ranger on duty. At the park's entrance, a visitors center with maps of the trails is available, along with picnic tables. In addition, bathroom facilities are available behind the visitors center. From the visitors center, you may take any of the park's trails, or go directly to the lake. Be sure to explore St. Margaret's Village and ask about camping and homestay accommodations.

Cayo and the Mountain Pine Ridge

Of Belize's western highlands, John Lloyd Stephens wrote in his famous travelogue that between the coast "and the inhabited part of Central America is a wilderness, unbroken even by an Indian path. There is no communication with the interior except by the Golfo Dolce or the Balize River; and, from the want of roads, a residence there is more confining than living on an island."

This was the 19th century, well before the construction of the Western Highway that now zips travelers from Belize City to the Guatemalan border in under two hours. Still, there remains a remote feeling to the largest and most temperate of Belize's six districts that many intrepid travelers find quite attractive. And, as you move away from the small number of roads in Belize's western core, Stephens' words are as true as ever—it really is a jungle out there. So put away that mask and snorkel and catch a fire in Cayo!

© JOSHUA BERMAN

The Cayo District's broad eastern edge is home to Belmopan, Belize's tiny capital; its western side comprises Belize's steep, remote interior, which runs into Guatemala's massive Petén forests. This area is serviced by the small city of San Ignacio, a cool town in every sense of the word. Cayo's own version of Belize's tourism boom is based on a long and varied menu of activities, trips, and tours—and a unique selection of accommodations to house so many weary explorers. Different types of travelers enjoy all the different accommodations, from the remote upscale jungle lodges of the region to the burgeoning budget scene in San Ignacio. The area offers an extensive and varied selection of mountain cabanas, jungle lodges, and river resorts, any one of which can serve to feed and shelter the active traveler in between caving, biking, and paddling expeditions. Accommodations range from backcountry campgrounds and elvish tree houses to luxuriously exclusive hideaways.

Cayo boasts a rich mixture of people, places, and creatures. Maya, Mennonites, mestizos, Anglos, Creoles, Guatemalans, and Chinese all commingle in government, commerce, agriculture, and tourism. The Maya Mountains, Vaca Plateau, and Mountain Pine Ridge are important geological features and several major rivers drain the highlands, including the Branch, Macal, Mopan, and Sibun. Savanna, broadleaf jungle, and pinelands form a patchwork of habitats for a wide diversity of flora and fauna.

At one time, the majority of the people in Cayo were mestizos. In those days, this bustling area depended mostly on the forests, especially at the port of San Ignacio, where logs and *chicle* were sent down the river to the sea, then shipped across the world's oceans. Access to the area around San Ignacio, bordered on two sides by rivers, was limited to river traffic. Thus arose the name, Cayo, or "island" in Spanish (San Ignacio Town used to be called "Cayo," and many locals still call it that). Today, while many residents are descendants of the original settlers, a great many are refugees from unsettled areas in Guatemala and El Salvador. Cayo District still relies on its natural resources, producing some lumber, but also dealing in new agricultural ventures (citrus, peanuts, and cattle) and, of course, serving as a booming tourist center.

PLANNING YOUR TIME

Budget travelers may see their dollar go a bit farther in Cayo than in other parts of Belize, enticing them to stick around longer than they'd planned—and they won't be disappointed. Days fly by differently up here than they do at the beach—maybe because of how busy most Cayo visitors find themselves, signing up for a new activity every day. But there's no rush, and you can easily bop around the area for weeks without getting weary (unless you're the kind of person who gets bored by too many trees and spectacular waterfalls).

But alas, most travelers are on tight schedules, and must be efficient with their allotted Cayo days. In that case, begin in San Ignacio—strike up a friendship with fellow guests at your hotel, enjoy the narrow streets and cafés with them, and then set off early in the morning for a local tour with a packed lunch and plenty of water. Save one day for caving, one for canoeing, one for Maya ruins, and one for a nature hike—how many's that? Add one or two more days to rest and recuperate before heading back to the Caribbean. If you can't spare a week, Cayo offers several time-saving combinations of the aforementioned activities—Actun Tunichil Muknal, for instance, is a hiking, swimming, caving, and archaeology trip all wrapped in one. And even if you've only got a day or two, San Ignacio is close enough to the coast and worth a trip; the forest runs right up to the city limits, where you'll find several trails and a decent archaeological site.

SPORTS AND RECREATION

Cayo District is home to a beautiful lattice of trails, from short **nature walks** and **medicine trails** to a range of **hiking trips** through the surrounding hills. **Mountain biking** the Cayo District is fun, beautiful, and a great way to burn off a few Belikins. Routes abound—take the dirt roads around San Ignacio and Bullet Tree, or head up into the Mountain Pine Ridge area;

Must-Sees

Look for **M** to find the sights and activities you can't miss and **N** for the best dining and lodging.

M Medicinal Jungle Trail and Iguana Exhibit: A wonderfully pleasant and informative guided walk, less than an hour long and a short walk from downtown San Ignacio (page 121).

M Cahal Pech Archaeological Site: Unique for both its archaeological intrigue and location within the city limits of San Ignacio, your walk up the hill will be well worth it (page 122).

M Actun Tunichil Muknal: Spelunk it in any of Cayo's fascinating caves, especially this one—the "Cave of the Crystal Maiden" is the wettest, dirtiest, most adventurous underground trip available. More caving action is available at Barton Creek, Río Frio, and Chechem Ha Caves (page 131).

M Thousand Foot Falls: The trip to Central America's highest waterfall is well worth enduring the rough access road. You can't swim here, but the vista of the falls from the lookout on the canyon's edge is stunning (page 138).

M Caracol Archaeological Site: One of the more difficult major ruins to access in Belize (you'll en-

© JOSHUA BERMAN

the recently excavated Canaa Temple at Caracol

dure a bumpy, multi-hour ride along the Mountain Pine Ridge), Caracol is rife with discovery, beauty, and long, peaceful views of the countryside from atop its newly excavated temples (page 141).

M Temple IV: It's definitely worth spending a day or two in Guatemala to explore the ruins at the famous ancient Maya city of **Tikal.** The view from the top of this, the tallest surviving Maya structure, is stunning (page 155).

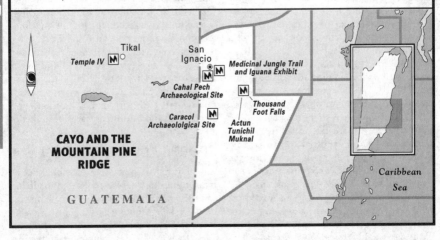

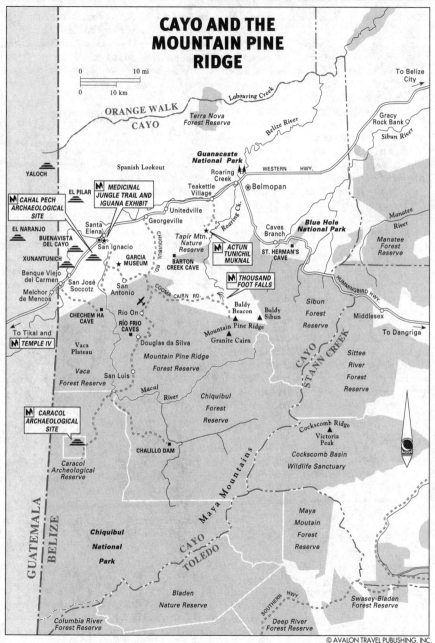

CAYO AND THE MOUNTAIN PINE RIDGE

0   10 mi
0   10 km

To Belize City

ORANGE WALK
CAYO

Labouring Creek

Terra Nova Forest Reserve

Belize River

Gracy Rock Bank

Sibun River

Guanacaste National Park

Spanish Lookout

Roaring Creek

WESTERN   HWY.

Teakettle Village

Belmopan

YALOCH

EL PILAR

MEDICINAL JUNGLE TRAIL AND IGUANA EXHIBIT

Unitedville

Georgeville

Roaring Ck.

Caves Branch

Blue Hole National Park

Manatee River

CAHAL PECH ARCHAEOLOGICAL SITE

Santa Elena

EL NARANJO

BUENAVISTA DEL CAYO

San Ignacio

Tapir Mtn. Nature Reserve

ACTUN TUNICHIL MUKNAL

ST. HERMAN'S CAVE

Manatee Forest Reserve

XUNANTUNICH

GARCIA MUSEUM

BARTON CREEK CAVE

Benque Viejo del Carmen

San José Soccotz

THOUSAND FOOT FALLS

HUMMINGBIRD HWY.

Melchor de Mencos

San Antonio

Río On

Baldy Beacon

Baldy Sibun

Sibun Forest Reserve

Middlesex

CHECHEM HA CAVE

RÍO FRIO CAVES

Mountain Pine Ridge

Granite Cairn

To Dangriga

To Tikal and
TEMPLE IV

Douglas da Silva

Mountain Pine Ridge Forest Reserve

Sittee River Forest Reserve

Vaca Plateau

Vaca Forest Reserve

San Luis

Macal

River

Chiquibul Forest Reserve

CARACOL ARCHAEOLOGICAL SITE

CHALILLO DAM

Cockscomb Ridge

Victoria Peak

Cockscomb Basin Wildlife Sanctuary

Caracol Archeological Reserve

GUATEMALA

BELIZE

CAYO
STANN CREEK

CAYO
TOLEDO

Maya Mountains

Chiquibul National Park

Maya Mouatain Forest Reserve

Bladen Nature Reserve

SOUTHERN HWY.

Swasey-Bladen Forest Reserve

Columbia River Forest Reserve

Deep River Forest Reserve

COOMA   CAIRN   RD.

CHIQUIBUL   RD.

Cayo & Mount. Pine Ridge

© AVALON TRAVEL PUBLISHING, INC.

swimming holes and waterfalls abound as destinations.

Equestrians will find **horseback riding** services at a number of resorts and tour operators in and outside San Ignacio. The archaeological sites of Cahal Pech, Caracol, El Pilar, and Xunantunich are within easy driving (or even walking, horseback riding, and biking) distance of the town. Countless other mounds and ruins are scattered throughout the surrounding jungle—and of course, Caracol, the granddaddy of Belizean archaeological sites, is only a two-hour drive into the hills.

Many Cayo resorts offer excellent guided **cave trips** of varying levels of difficulty, for everyone from the beginning spelunker to the professional speleologist; day and overnight trips are available. Ask about the varied experiences to be had in Handprint Cave, Yaxsahau (Cave of the Ceiba Tree Lord), Actun Tunichil Muknal, Barton Creek Cave, Chechem Ha Cave, or any of the most recently discovered ones that are as yet unnamed.

A wise man once said, "The only way to float is downstream." **Canoeing, kayaking,** and **tubing** are all popular ways to enjoy the Macal and Mopan Rivers. Actually, one popular trip is to paddle *up* the Macal River from downtown San Ignacio, making your way to the Ix Chel Medicine Trail or Belize Botanic Garden.

SHOPPING

Much of Belizean craftwork originates here in Cayo and is available for sale at a few roadside gift shops, galleries, and workshops. The most extensive is **Caesar's Place,** a friendly shop at Mile 60 on the Western Highway. Some of the country's most famous slate carvers are in the area, as is **Octavio Sixto** in Benque Viejo, with his detailed miniature replicas of Belizean shacks and landmark buildings. There is always a row of Belizean and Guatemalan craft stalls by the Xunantunich Ferry and a number of cramped and brimming gift shops in downtown San Ignacio. The Magana family has two shops, **Magana Zactunich Art Gallery,** south of Cristo Rey Village, and **Magana's Art Center,** at the east edge of

San José Succotz. Both sell small ceramics, slate carvings, and other crafts. On the north edge of San Antonio, the Garcia sisters run their **Tanah Mayan Art Museum** and store. In Benque Viejo, **Galeria del Arte de Gucumaz** has a choice of Belizean and Guatemalan crafts at reasonable prices.

CAYO GUIDES AND TOUR OPERATORS

At last count, there were 150 (and growing) licensed tour guides in the Cayo District, Belize's largest chapter of the Tour Guide Association. Most work either directly for one of the area jungle lodges, or for one of the tour operators listed below, and a few are independently famous and run their own trips. Probably the easiest and most common way that independent travelers find guides is to use a third party booking agent like **Eva's Restaurant** or the **Green Dragon Internet Café.** Both establishments have networks

view of the upper Macal gorge from the Vaca Plateau

of respected guides and tour operators that cover the full spectrum of area activities—this system usually costs no extra to the tourist and it discourages guides from stalking customers in the streets. Or to book a trip on your own, just walk into any tour operator office—most are on Burns Avenue, or in a row of shacks on the road toward the Wooden Bridge.

In addition to the Actun Tunichil Muknal cave trip, **Pacz Tours** (tel. 501/824-2477 or 600-7419, pacztours@btl.net, www.pacztours.com) offers a number of expeditions, including overnight camping options involving some combination of river running, waterfall quests, ruins, caves, and rappelling. As for their professionalism and gear, well, put it this way: when *National Geographic* or *Discovery Channel* comes to Belize, they call Pacz. You could also contact **Cayo Gial Tours** through the San Ignacio Resort Hotel.

Mayawalk Adventures (tel. 501/824-3070, mayawalk@btl.net) maintains an open-air shop and bar at 19 Burns Avenue, right across from Eva's, and will take you to Actun Tunichil Muknal and beyond; they have an impressive fleet of vans and canoes. **River Rat** (tel. 501/601-4599 or 609-6636, info@riverratbelize.com) specializes in kayak expeditions and overnight float trips;

ask around for "Gonzo" in the Green Dragon or Eva's.

Be sure to walk the row of tour operator shacks near the open market—they are all small, Belizean-owned operations, and may be cheaper if you are booking yourself independently. Among these, **David's Tours** (tel. 501/824-3674) is one of the old standbys, offering volumes of local knowledge and the full range of tours. Also check **Maya Mystic** (tel. 501/804-0055), open seven days; ask about the "Monkey Tail" overnight camping trip. **Green Valley** (tel. 501/601-4740) also has an overnight trip, plus the basic menu.

Tony's Guided Tours (tel. 501/824-3292) is probably the most economical, independent trip on the river at US$17.50 per person. For the more adventurous, Tony also offers a five-day canoe/camp trip to Belize City (US$65 pp, per day, all-inclusive). He provides everything except your personal effects.

Amigos Belize (tel. 501/603-9436, www.amigosbelize.com), located on the Santa Elena side of the Hawksworth Bridge, specializes in day and overnight canoe trips on the Macal River, as well as overnights to their private paradise on Turneffe Island, with camping and a couple of cabanas.

San Ignacio

There is something indescribably alluring about the capital of Belize's western district. Maybe it's some remnant Maya magic, drifting downhill from the ruins of Cahal Pech, or maybe it's the soft mist itself, quieting the village on rainy-season mornings and blanketing the floodplains to the east. Maybe it's the raw vitality of the surrounding wilderness that bumps right up against the town and breathes so much healthy energy through San Ignacio's streets—or maybe it's what happens when all of these factors combine with a kind, good-hearted, diverse community of people. Belizeans of all creeds and colors happily reside in San Ignacio, as do an increasing number of both transient and transplanted foreigners. Roots, culture, and music is in the air, and there is as much Rasta flavor in

Cayo as there is Creole, Guatemalan, Garinagu, and Gringo.

There is budget lodging galore in San Ignacio, as well as a broad range of food—from rice-n-beans to curried lamb, from veggie burgers to pork ribs. And, of course, there is more to do than anyone—even permanent residents—has time for, with all manner of active expeditions leaving from Burns Avenue each and every morning.

ORIENTATION

Visitors to San Ignacio from the east first pass through its sister city of Santa Elena, turning right at the Social Security building and continuing across the **Wooden Bridge,** a low-resting affair that places you on the San Ignacio side of

SAN IGNACIO

To Branch Mouth

MIDAS RESORT

HODE'S

CEMETERY

CEMETERY ST.

BURNS AVE.

WEST ST.

SAVANNAH ST.

1ST ST.

BLANCANEAUX ST.

2ND ST.

SIMPSON ST.

YOLI'S PIZZA

CELINA'S SUPER STORE

BROASTER'S SPORTS STADIUM

WOODEN BRIDGE

NOVELO'S BUS TERMINAL

SEE "SAN IGNACIO DOWNTOWN" MAP

SNOOTY FOX

MOON

BACK ST.

SURVEY ST.

SPORTS GROUND

HOSPITAL

MAYA ST.

LEBANON ST.

SAVANNAH ST.

KING ST.

GEORGE PRICE AVE.

WESTERN HWY.

To Bullet Tree Falls and El Pilar

WAIGHT ST.

CHURCH ST.

FAR WEST ST.

WEST ST.

MISSIAH ST.

HAWKSWORTH BRIDGE

To Safe Tours, Belize City, Cristo Rey, and Mountain Pine Ridge

SCHOOL

CHURCH

VICTORIA ST.

AMIGOS BELIZE

Santa Elena

BACK ST.

SURVEY ST.

OLD BENQUE RD.

Eastern Branch Belize (Macal) River

To Sanny's Grill and Eva's

APOLLO ST.

SAN IGNACIO HOTEL

MEDICINAL JUNGLE TRAIL AND IGUANA EXHIBIT

CARMELITA ST.

PIACHE HOTEL

BUENA VISTA RD.

LISSE'S GUEST HOUSE

CARMELITA ST.

SCALE NOT AVAILABLE

To Benque Viejo del Carmen and Guatemala

WINDY HILL RESORT

TEXACO

VICTOR GALVEZ STADIUM

ROSE'S GUESTHOUSE

CAHAL PECH VILLAGE RESORT

CAHAL PECH DISCO

CAHAL PECH ARCHAEOLOGICAL SITE

© AVALON TRAVEL PUBLISHING, INC.

Cayo & Mount. Pine Ridge

© JOSHUA BERMAN

The Hawksworth Bridge spans the Macal River and connects Santa Elena to San Ignacio.

the Macal River, close to the open market grounds. From there, turning left will bring you directly into "downtown" San Ignacio, marked by a five-pronged intersection that is nearly always abuzz with activity. **Burns Avenue** crosses here, and is the main drag for locals and tourists alike. The Novelo's bus station is located about three blocks up Burns Avenue from the big intersection. Within two or three blocks in any direction from that intersection, you'll find most of San Ignacio's budget accommodations, restaurants, Internet cafés, and tour operators.

The town's three banks are on the block of Burns Avenue that stems east (toward the river) from the big intersection, and at the end of that block you'll find a tiny traffic circle in front of the Police Station which guards the western abutment of the **Hawksworth Bridge.** Only eastbound traffic is allowed on the one-lane bridge between Santa Elena and San Ignacio. It is the only suspension bridge in Belize and in its two-way past, whoever reached the center of the bridge first had the right of way, and the other vehicle had to back off; occasionally the local gendarme had to come along and measure car

distances to settle drivers' arguments. Old-timers say the water rose as high as this bridge during Hurricane Hattie. Any of the roads that lead uphill from downtown San Ignacio will eventually place you back on the Western Highway heading toward Benque.

SIGHTS

Even if you arrive late in the afternoon, there is still time to enjoy a tour of the Cahal Pech ruins or a short nature hike on the banks of the Macal River (only three blocks from the city center).

▶ Medicinal Jungle Trail and Iguana Exhibit

This interpretive herb trail and iguana breeding project (the full name is the Green Iguana Conservation Project) is accessed through the San Ignacio Resort Hotel (tel. 501/824-2034), on 14 lush riverside acres. Tours of the herb trail or the iguana project are available for less than US$6 a person; plan on forty-five minutes for either talk. With the money earned from curious tourists, the hotel owners are able to keep the

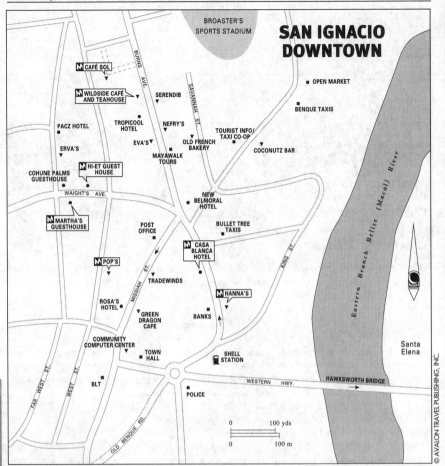

trail maintained and the iguana project going—and to prevent the heavily vegetated riverbank from being developed (crucial to the cleanliness of the local water supply). To date, 175 species of birds have been observed here (including a rare family pair of black hawk eagles), plus a number of mammals.

When the iguana population was on a noticeable downward cycle, the folks at the San Ignacio Resort Hotel created this successful breeding and release project. Groups go on hunts, capture the females, and highjack the eggs, which they raise in a predator-free, food-rich environ-

ment before releasing them back into the wild. The program has also trained former iguana hunters to become iguana guides, a far more profitable and sustainable endeavor, and hosts many school groups, featuring the Iguana Kids Club and Adopt an Iguana Program.

Cahal Pech Archaeological Site
The ruins of Cahal Pech ("Place of the Ticks") still have a covering of jungle around them. A steep 10-minute walk from downtown San Ignacio, Cahal Pech is a great, tree-shaded destination, with amazing views of the valley to the

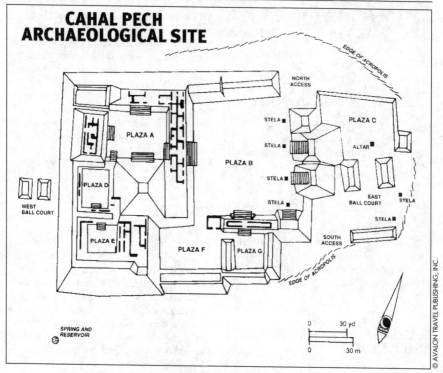

CAHAL PECH ARCHAEOLOGICAL SITE

EDGE OF ACROPOLIS

NORTH ACCESS

PLAZA A

PLAZA B

PLAZA C

STELA

STELA

STELA

ALTAR

PLAZA D

WEST BALL COURT

STELA

STELA

EAST BALL COURT

STELA

STELA

PLAZA E

PLAZA F

PLAZA G

SOUTH ACCESS

EDGE OF ACROPOLIS

SPRING AND RESERVOIR

0   30 yd
0   30 m

© AVALON TRAVEL PUBLISHING, INC.

north. Cahal Pech was discovered in the early 1950s, but scientific research did not begin until 1988, when a team from San Diego State University's Department of Anthropology began work. Thirty-four structures were compacted into a three-acre area. Excavation is ongoing and visitors are welcome. You'll pay a small fee at Cahal Pech Visitor Center (tel. 501/824-4236, 6 A.M.–6 P.M. daily), which also gives you access to a small museum of artifacts found at the site. Nearby **Tipu** was an important Maya-Christian town during the early years of colonization. Tipu was as far as the Spanish were able to penetrate in the 16th century.

RECREATION

Book your horseback riding trip at **Easy Rider** (tel. 501/824-3310), an independent operator who charges reasonable rates and gives

good service, based out of an office in San Ignacio next door to Eva's; novices welcome. **Mountain Rider** is a small, no-frills, family-run operation just past the village of San Antonio, driving toward the Mountain Pine Ridge; look for their sign and stop in to find out more details. Also check Mountain Equestrian Trails, with one of the biggest trail systems in the Pine Ridge.

Rental bicycles can be found at the Tropicool Hotel in San Ignacio, plus a few other places. Top-notch mountain bike tours are offered at Chaa Creek; very skilled and experienced guides take riders on some reportedly kick-ass single track. Canoe up the Macal River to visit Chaa Creek and the Botanic Gardens at duPlooy's; rent a boat and/or guide from Amigos Belize or Cayo Gial (usually about US$25–30 pp; see section on area tour operators earlier in this chapter).

CANOE RACES

One of the world's longest canoe races, taking five days for several hundred canoes to paddle the 180-mile length of the Belize River from the Cayo highlands to the Caribbean Sea, is **La Ruta Maya Belize River Challenge.** The race is held during the first week of March, timed to coincide with Baron Bliss Day celebrations. Increasingly popular since its inception in 1998, La Ruta Maya has a number of different divisions and offers more than US$15,000 in prize money.

The **Belize Extreme Canoe Adventure Race** (inquiries@bighjuices.com) is held sometime in September, when participants paddle nonstop for 19–24 hours.

The races feature special divisions, such as "Master's" (over 40), women's, mixed gender, and amateur. They are part athletic event, part tourism draw, and part *fiesta.* The competitive feeling among the tiny Belizean population makes it a lot of fun.

MASSAGE, BODYWORK, AND HEALING

The famous Dr. Rosita Arvigo runs her **Ix Chel Wellness Center** on Buena Vista Road (tel. 501/602-1179 or 820-4031), open a few days a week between December and May only; consults and treatment in herbology, massage therapy, and "Maya Mother Massage." Rosita and her husband, Greg Shropshire, have been practicing the ancient Maya art of healing for some years. Both are graduates of Chicago National College of Naprapathy; Rosita is a professor of botanical studies and has been a practicing herbalist for more than 20 years. She was also an apprentice of the late Don Eligio Panti, a Maya bush doctor who lived to be 103 years old. Rosita has written several books about her experience with Don Eligio, who spent much of his life healing people using only the ancient Maya method plus added techniques learned from a Carib Indian during the *chicle* days of the 1930s.

A well-known Maya healer in the Bullet Tree Falls area is **Miss Beatrice;** contact her through the Cohune Palms Guest House.

Eva's **Massage Therapy** (tel. 501/824-3423, ebuhler@btl.net) is located just down from the Texaco Station on the western highway exiting town toward Benque. **Juanita** gives reasonably priced facials and massages in her shop (tel. 501/824-2508) on the third floor of the Burns Avenue Shopping Mall. Out of town, there are two full-service, upscale spas: one at Chaa Creek, the other at Blancaneaux. Lastly, **Susan Hirsch** offers physiotherapy, acupuncture-massage, and reiki at the Janus Foundation (Mile 4.5 Pine Ridge Rd., tel. 501/820-4004, s.hirsch@janus-foundation.org).

NIGHTLIFE

If you have the energy after a day out on the river or hiking the jungles, you have several good choices for a quiet drink or, on weekends, a decent nightlife. Just follow the masses as they trek between bars and discos. Many start the night at **Coconutz,** then work their way up to the dancing at **Legends 2000** or the massive **Cahal Pech Entertainment Center,** perched above the town next to the Maya ruins. This is a fine place to meet fellow travelers and mix with the locals. There are still occasional concerts and dances at the **Blue Angel** in the center; across town, **Hode's** can get going as well. Stroll across the Hawksworth Bridge to survey the scene at **Coconutz Too** and **Déjà vu Night Club,** just don't stumble down the river embankment on your way out.

For live music, **Lisse's Guest House,** located on the hill leading up out of town (toward Benque), is known for hosting some of the area's finest local musicians. **Caesar's Place,** 10 minutes east of San Ignacio, can be a happening outdoor café on weekends, depending on who drops in for the jam session. If you know how to pluck, strum, or fiddle, drop by and join in. Occasionally, the **Riverside River Lodge** in Bullet Tree hosts concerts and festivals.

Got no dancing skills? Show up Wednesday nights at the San Ignacio Resort Hotel for **Latin dance lessons,** but be sure to check that the classes are still going on; only US$5 for basic bachatta, merengue, and salsa steps.

ACCOMMODATIONS

Choices abound for such a small town, many of them pretty cheap, although quality isn't always the highest. Luckily this isn't an area where you'll want to hang out in your room all day anyway.

Camping

Cosmos Camping (15 Branch Mouth Rd., tel. 501/824-2116, cosmoscamping@btl.net, US$3.50 pp) is a 15-minute walk from town, just past Midas Resort, and has pretty grounds, lots of big trees, and mowed lawns where you can pitch a tent. It's on the Mopan River and has shared bath and showers. A few decrepit cabanas rent for a couple dollars more.

Campers are also welcome at **Midas Resort** (tel. 501/824-3845, US$7). Also up the Branch Mouth Road, **Smith's Family Farm** (tel. 501/824-3632) offers secluded camping, lovely cabanas, home-cooked meals, vegetarian specials, and tours. **Inglewood** (tel. 501/824-3555, www.inglewoodcampinggrounds.com) offers full hookups for RVs on the side of the highway a couple miles west of town. Following the same road, you'll find campgrounds at **Clarissa Falls** and **Trek Stop** as well (see listing in the Along the Western Highway section later in this chapter). You may also want to consider the options down the Hydro Road.

Under US$25

The **N Hi-Et Guest House** (tel. 501/824-2828) is an excellent budget option, built right into the owner's large home. The five rooms with shared baths and cold water are clean and comfortable with hardwood floors; US$10/13 s/d. The five rooms with private bath in the next building are a big step up in quality and not much in price—tiled floors, well-kept, balconies, US$18 s/d. Around the corner, the **Tropicool Hotel** (30A Burns Ave., tel. 501/824-3052) has 10 simple, clean rooms with shared bath for US$10/12.50 s/d, or very nicely kept and furnished cabins with private bath, TV, and fan for US$25 a couple.

Very reasonable, friendly lodging can be found at **J & R's Guest House** (20 Far West St., tel. 501/824-2502, jrguesthouse@yahoo.com, from US$7.50). In the center of town on Far West Street, **Pacz Guest House** (tel. 501/824-4538, pacz@btl.net) is a small hostelry with five clean, simple rooms; US$12.50/20 s/d for shared bath, a bit more for private bath. Free tea or coffee is available in the morning, and there's a nice common space around a television. They also offer lots of exciting tours. The **New Belmoral Hotel** (tel. 501/804-3502, US$15/18 s/d), right smack in the middle of town, has 11 cheap rooms with private bath, old TVs, and fans. Run by a warm, friendly family, the only drawback is mismatched linoleum and the concrete rooms feel a bit close. **Rosa's Hotel** (tel. 501/804-2265, rosashotel @yahoo.com, from US$20/23 s/d) has a selection of rooms with private bath and fan or a/c; rooms range from small and stuffy to high and airy—check out a few before deciding.

The classiest budget hotel has to be the **N Casa Blanca Hotel** (tel. 501/824-2080), winner of the 2003 Best Small Hotel in Belize award, with eight immaculate, cozy rooms for US$22/27 s/d, private bath, h/c water, TV, beautiful common living room, kitchen, balcony, and rooftop; located on Burns Avenue near the banks.

US$25–50

N Martha's Guesthouse (10 West St., tel. 501/824-3647, www.marthasbelize.com, US$45 d) continues to offer an atmosphere of simultaneous privacy and conviviality in a homey

Cayo & Mount. Pine Ridge

EXPLORE YOUR LODGING OPTIONS

Be sure to fully review all the accommodations listed throughout the Near San Ignacio section before booking. Most of these jungle lodges, river retreats, and campgrounds are tucked into the bush just enough to feel remote, but in reality, they are only a few miles from San Ignacio Town. Just like the many beach resorts along Belize's coastline and islands, Cayo's varying accommodations offer different personalities, depending on each owner's personal visions and ideals.

setting, with an abundance of common lounging areas for guests to mingle if they so desire. The rooms are classy, with hardwood floors and furniture, private bath, fans, hot water, and cable television. Laundry services are available. There's an excellent restaurant downstairs, and the location is central.

The **Aguada Hotel** (tel. 501/804-3609, aguada@btl.net, www.aguadahotel.com, US$30) is on the edge of Santa Elena, a five-minute cab ride from downtown San Ignacio, and offers a quiet night's sleep in its 20 simple, colorful rooms with hot-water private baths and a/c. There's also a pool, email, and laundry services, and a restaurant serves breakfast, lunch, and dinner. This is a great spot for groups.

About a quarter-mile out of town at Branch Mouth Road, check out **Midas Resort** (tel. 501/824-3845), a small, family-run lodging. You'll find seven cottages with thatch roofs, situated on five acres along the banks of the Macal River (down a 300-yard path from the cottages). All cabins offer private bathrooms. No electricity is available yet, but oil lamps and hot water are provided. Campers are welcome. A restaurant serves breakfast and lunch, and a small gift shop in the reception area has a few knickknacks. Credit cards are OK.

US$50–100

Talk about a vista! **Cahal Pech Village** (tel. 501/824-3740, www.cahalpech.com) offers a variety of rooms and cabins spread out on spacious grounds with stunning views of San Ignacio and the valley below. The 15 rooms have private bath, a/c, and cable TV (US$65); thatch and wood cabanas with private bath, h/c water, TV, and porch go for less than US$55; suites and apartments are available too. A restaurant, bar, and gift shop round out the resort.

Located one mile west of San Ignacio, the **Log Cab-Inn** (tel. 501/824-3367, logcabins@btl.net, www.logcabinns-belize.com, US$55/65 s/d) is run by super-friendly people, and is a full-service resort with 12 rustic yet comfortable mahogany cabins. The resort's facilities include a dining room, bar, hilltop deck, and a swimming pool. The restaurant is constructed from a mix of wood—cedar, cabbage bark, ziricote, and mahogany. Breakfast is a filling meal of eggs, fry jacks, sausage, fruit, and all-you-can-drink fresh-squeezed OJ for US$6. Lunch and dinner will cost about US$6–10. Very reasonable meal plan options are available.

Fit for royalty, **San Ignacio Resort Hotel** (tel. 501/824-2034, 824-2125, or 800/822-3274, sanighot@btl.net, www.sanignaciobelize.com) is rightly proud of hosting Her Majesty Queen Elizabeth in 1994. Perched above the lush Macal River Valley, the resort offers incredible views of rainforest and wildlife from each of its 24 deluxe air-conditioned rooms, some with their own secluded balcony; the rooms are up to par with any state-side standard hotel, with private tiled baths, cable TV, and telephone (US$84/110 s/d). There are a few economy rooms without a/c or TV for US$45/50 s/d. The hotel also hosts the Stork Club Bar & Grill, Running W Steakhouse & Restaurant, a jungle-view patio deck and swimming pool, basketball court, disco, gift shop, sightseeing tours, and convention facilities. As an added touch, it has 14 acres of forest along the river with marked trails and a swimming beach. Bird-watching tours are available with the on-site guide who will also show you the **Green Iguana Conservation Project** and the **Medicinal Jungle Trail,** located on the hotel's grounds.

Over US$100

Windy Hill Resort (tel. 501/824-2017, fax 501/824-3080, windyhill@btl.net, www.windyhillresort.com) sits on a rise just west of San Ignacio. You'll find upscale rustic charm with thatch-roof cottages, green grass, private baths, h/c water, ceiling fans, 24-hour electricity, a swimming pool, and a recreation hut complete with TV, hammocks, bar, table tennis, and billiards. Windy Hill specializes in all kinds of tours and mulit-day packages with meal plans. Guests enjoy the friendly efficiency with which the place is run and the variety of activities: canoeing, caving, horseback riding, nature tours, and hiking trails. Ask about escorted tours to Guatemala and archaeological sites in the area. Meals are served in a casual, thatch-roof dining room.

FOOD

Fast and Cheap

San Ignacio has a higher than average amount of cheap Mexican fast-food places, and a few *pupuserias* to boot. Check out the ones in the basement of the Burns Avenue Mall, or across from the Belize Bank. The **Old French Bakery** (7 A.M.–9 P.M. Mon.–Sat.) is also on the bottom floor of the mall and serves delicious breads and pastries. The tiny **coffee shop** connected to the Serendib Restaurant sells ice cream as well as meat pies and generous vegetable patties, a perfect meal on the go.

The best **barbecue** chefs set up in Santa Elena, just over the Hawksworth Bridge, and they cater especially to weekend party crowds, offering greasy mounds of meat, rice, and beans used by many a customer to soak up all that beer sloshing around in his stomach.

Low-Key Belizean

Some have called **Erva's** (4 Far West St., tel. 501/824-2821) the best Belizean food in Belize—a bold statement indeed; try for yourself. It is a cozy, quality, family-run restaurant that often caters to groups. **M Pop's** may be the closest Belize comes to a small-town, cramped American diner with booths, bottomless cups of coffee, and customers watching CNN and talking religion and politics—except Pop's is owned by a 100-percent Belizean Hemingway lookalike (6:30 A.M.–2 P.M. daily). Located just south around the corner from the 5-way intersection; ask anyone nearby for directions.

Eva's Restaurant and Bar (22 Burns Ave., tel. 501/824-2267) is not only a tourist and activity center, it's also the place for basic dishes like stew chicken, burgers, pork chops, burritos, and a lot more (meals around US$5). Box lunches are available, as is fresh-squeezed OJ. Check out the patio through the back door; there's Internet access too. **Nefry's,** across from Eva's, offers linen-clad, candle-lit tables that make you expect a more expensive menu. Fine Belizean fare (entrees around US$5–7) with a dash of Middle East (lamb kabobs and couscous for US$8). It's open 6 A.M.–10 P.M., seven days a

week. Nefry's specializes in feeding hearty breakfasts to tourists about to head off for their daily Cayo adventure.

For ambience, you'll want to try **Sanny's Grill,** a bit out of the way (located toward the western exit to Benque, just down from the Texaco Station), but well worth it for the fine menu and nice lighting and music. In addition to steaks, pork chops, and seafood entrees from US$10, the **Running W Steakhouse and Restaurant** (in the San Ignacio Resort Hotel, tel. 501/824-2125) also serves up an open-air dining patio above the Macal River; Belizean classic plates from US$4, featuring meat from their own ranch.

International

M Hanna's offers all basic Belizean food, but it's also got a huge, cosmopolitan menu that includes Asian, Indian, and vegetarian dishes (and an ample wine list), all prepared with organic food and meat raised by the owner himself, a transplanted Zimbabwean; open for all three meals, and very popular with tourists. Same goes for **M Café Sol,** a comfortable, colorful place around the corner from the Novelo's station— you can't go wrong with anything on the menu here, which includes wraps, soy burgers, pastas, and salads. Entrees at both places are in the US$5–12 range.

Near the Venus Hotel, you'll find the **Serendib Restaurant,** owned by a Sri Lankan and, along with good hamburgers and chow mein, serving excellent curries and dahl. Reasonably priced, a broiled lobster dinner or San Ignacio Giant Steak will set you back only about US$12. Across the street, the **M Wildside Café and Teahouse** offers Belizean Ital (vegetarian) cuisine and a menu of herbal teas exclusively from the surrounding forests; there's an art cooperative on site as well. Open from 7 A.M., meals about US$5 and delicious.

Maxim's Chinese Restaurant (23 Far West St.) has a good reputation among the locals. A family-run café, it serves mainly lunch and dinner. Prices are moderate; you won't pay much over US$10 for the best meal in the house and a beer.

Martha's Kitchen has some of the best pizza in Cayo, plus a full menu like stir-fried vegetables (about US$6), T-bone steak with gravy and fries, (US$8), or a simple club sandwich (US$4). Visitors also give high praise to **Yoli's Pizza.**

TOURIST INFORMATION

There is an official tourist information post at the Cahal Pech Visitor Center (tel. 501/824-4236), and the BTIA, offering brochures of local resorts, taxi charters, and a town map, has a stand near the Savannah Taxi Co-op downtown. However, you'll find out much more by reading the posters and advertisements at Eva's Restaurant—it's like reading a four-walled catalog for the area's activities and accommodations. Many travelers make Eva's their first stop in town, as it's a gathering spot not only for knowledgeable wanderers but also for the folks who run the cottages and tours. Owner Bob Jones is a walking database of information for just about anything that's happening in San Ignacio and along the river (and he will patiently explain it all to you). Information and tour booking is available in many other restaurants, hotel front desks, and Internet places in San Ignacio as well, notably the Green Dragon.

SERVICES

Atlantic Bank, Scotia Bank, and **Belize Bank** are all on Burns, just past the Hawksworth Bridge as you come into town. Martha's Guesthouse offers daily **laundry** service 7 A.M.–8 P.M., as does a launderette tucked into a DVD rental place in the same building as Coconutz (US$5 for wash, dry, and fold). Across from the bus station, **Celina's Super Store** (43 Burns Ave., tel. 501/824-2247) is the largest, most well-equipped supermarket in town, but there are many others scattered around as well. The **Green Dragon** has all your favorite imported natural products, plus a current selection of reading and reference material. **Angelus Press,** on the top floor of the Burns Avenue Mall, also has some books, in addition to copy machines and office supplies. **Belicolor,** next to the post office, develops film, sells many camera batteries, and has some camera equipment.

For travel arrangements, **Exodus International** (tel. 501/824-4400, exodus@btl.net) is located at the beginning of Burns Avenue (near the bridge).

Internet Access

The abundance of top-notch, modern Internet options in San Ignacio is impressive—and they're all located within a block of each other. For the most *tranquilo,* best-smelling, overall vibe, start with the **Green Dragon,** which has espresso, high-speed satellite, and a number of laptop docks; the outdoor patio is quite pleasant (and wired). This is also a health food store, book store, and real estate office (tel. 501/824-4782, www.greendragonbelize.com).

Tradewinds has the most generous hours (7 A.M.–11 P.M., closed Sun.) and big, comfy chairs. The **Community Computer Center,** up the block from both, is cheapest by far and has the most machines. The newest is **Cafe Cayo,** located on Burns Avenue next to the Belize Bank, where monitors are arranged to give you privacy. You can also just hang out in the TV lounge and enjoy a cappuccino. Cafe Cayo has an Italian menu and is open late.

GETTING AROUND

Downtown San Ignacio is tiny and entirely walkable. The hill to Cahal Pech isn't far, but quite a workout. Taxis there or anywhere else within the city limits cost less than US$3 pp. Cheap *colectivo* taxis run from San Ignacio in all directions throughout the day, making it easy to get to towns and destinations in the immediate vicinity (including Bullet Tree, Succotz, and Benque). In addition to the main buses running back and forth on the Western Highway, village buses come into Market Square from most surrounding towns, returning to the hills in the afternoons. To the south, buses only run as far as the village of San Antonio—perhaps someone will think to start public transportation to Caracol once the road is improved.

Car Rentals

Anyone wishing to travel independently to the Mountain Pine Ridge, Caracol, the Hydro Road, or El Pilar, may consider renting a car—either in

Belize City or at one of the few places in San Ignacio and Santa Elena. It's not cheap, but the only other way to get to these places is either by chartered taxi or jungle lodge shuttle, so it may be well worth your while, especially if you have a group.

At the top of the Old Benque Road at the western edge of San Ignacio, you'll find **Cayo Rentals** (tel. 501/824-2153, abscomputer@btl .net), with a handful of newish vehicles for rent in the Texaco Station parking lot; US$75 per 24 hours, *including* taxes and insurance (cheaper than any place in Belize City). Across the bridge in Santa Elena, **Safe Tours Belize** (tel. 501/824-4262 or 614-4476, dcpil@yahoo.com, www.safe-toursbelize.com) has a small fleet of Isuzu Troopers and 15-passenger vans.

GETTING THERE AND AWAY

All the resorts can arrange for a transfer from the international airport in Belize City, from US$125. Shared shuttle to the Caye Caulker Water Taxi Terminal can be arranged at a number of tour operators as well for not much more than an express bus ticket if you have enough people.

By Bus
Novelo's runs through the middle of town, stopping at the station on Burns Avenue as part of the daily Belize City–Benque route. Expect only limited service on Sunday. Expresses take about two hours between Belize City and San Ignacio, including the quick stop in Belmopan. Regular buses leave every hour, and there are a handful of daily expresses between 7 A.M. and 7 P.M. Check on the express departure times the day before your journey, as the schedule changes from time to time.

To Guatemala or Mexico
The Mexican bus lines Linea Dorada and San Juan both travel through Belize between Guatemala and Chetumal, with a stop at Amigos Belize Tour Company (tel. 501/603-9436, www.amigosbelize.com), located at the Santa Elena end of the Hawksworth Bridge, where you can buy bus tickets to anywhere in Mexico.

East of San Ignacio

The stretch of Western Highway between Guanacaste National Park (where the Hummingbird Highway heads south) and Santa Elena has a number of notable destinations and lodgings.

TEAKETTLE AREA

Only a few miles west of the Hummingbird Highway junction, the roadside village of Teakettle greets you with a jarring series of speed bumps. Turning left at the Pook's Hill sign carries you past cornfields grown atop ancient Maya residential mounds, all the while skirting a massive chunk of seriously beautiful bush that comprises the following areas.

Tapir Mountain Nature Reserve
Covering 6,741 acres, Tapir Mountain is one of the newest jewels in the country's crown of natural treasures. The deep, steamy jungle is ripe with an abundance of plant life. Every wild thing native to the region roams its forests, from toucans to tapirs, coatis to kinkajous.

At present, the reserve is off-limits to all but scientific expeditions. However, you can see a piece of it by going on the Actun Tunichil Muknal trip.

Pook's Hill Lodge
Once you arrive at the remote clearing that is Pook's Hill Lodge (tel. 501/820-2017, pooks-hill@btl.net, www.pookshillbelize.com, US$104/148 s/d), you'll have a hard time believing that you are only 12 miles from Belmopan and 21 miles from San Ignacio, so dense and peaceful is the forest around you. Towering hardwoods, flowering bromeliads, and exotic birds hem in the accommodations, which are built around a small Maya residential ruin. Pook's Hill is a 300-acre private nature reserve, bordered by the Tapir Mountain Nature Reserve and the Roaring River,

© JOSHUA BERMAN

a relic of the old days

and offering active travelers 10 thatch-roof, mid-scale cabanas from which to base their Cayo explorations. The cottages have private baths, electricity, and comfortable furnishings. The lounge/bar area overlooks a grassy knoll that gently slopes toward the creek; be sure to take advantage of one of the many natural history books in the bookcase. The dining room is downstairs from the lounge, and good, filling meals are served family-style. They accommodate vegetarian or other preferences when given advance notice.

To get there, call for a free transfer from Belmopan; if driving, look for the hand-painted sign at Teakettle Village (around Mile 52.5), turn left onto the road, and follow the signs that lead the way. After four miles, turn right—the property begins less than a mile down the road. Another three-quarters of a mile through a tunnel of broadleaf will take you to the lodge.

Warrie Head Ranch and Lodge

Just a couple miles west of Teakettle Village, Warrie Head (contact Belize Global Travel Services in Belize City, tel. 501/227-7185 ext. 240, bzadventur@btl.net, US$80) is a 137-acre former logging camp and banana plantation that now serves antique-loving Cayo visitors looking for easily accessible accommodations. The ranch house is a bit reminiscent of visiting one's grandmother—rooms are decorated with antique Belizean colonial furniture, comfortable patterned bedspreads, and extra touches like pretty lamps and pictures that make these feel more like home bedrooms than hotel rooms (some are nicer than others).

The lodge is close to the main highway (and the treasures of San Ignacio and the surrounding areas), yet far enough away that you forget about the outside world. A stroll down a grassy hillside brings you to bubbling cascades and waterfalls where the Belize River and Warrie Head Creek meet, a walking trail, and a spring-fed pool that's perfect for swimming (when there's water). There are also orchid trails, lots of birds, and 40 varieties of fruit trees. Miss Lydia runs the dining room and serves delicious food with a smile. Owners Bia and Johnny Searle offer river trips, excursions to the popular sights in the country, and horseback riding. If you have the chance, take the time to talk to Bia. She was born and raised in Belize and can tell you about Belize, past and present. She has wonderful stories about growing up with a Creole

Massive cohune palms dominate the forest at Pook's Hill.

nanny who became her surrogate mother and grandmother to her children for many years before her death.

Continuing West

Probably the best and most complete gift shop in the country, **Caesar's Place** (tel. 501/824-2341, fax 501/824-3449, info@blackrocklodge.com) is also a restaurant, bar, lodging, and, once a month, a jazz club. Located at Mile 60, about 10 miles west of San Ignacio, the shop (8 A.M.–5:30 P.M. daily) is a borderline museum, with all conceivable Belizean crafts in addition to Indonesian wood carvings, Dominican paintings, Guatemalan masks, Nicaraguan soapstone statues, and Haitian woodwork (plus amazing carvings and sculptures from the on-site woodshop). Check your email here, browse the shop, then enjoy a glass of wine or meal in the shaded café; the food is fantastic (US$7 breakfast and lunch, more for dinner, from 6:30 A.M. daily). Caesar's six clean

garden rooms, each with private bath, h/c water, tile floors, and ceiling fans, go for US$50, camping US$5 per person; full RV hookups can be negotiated too. This is also the home office of the **Black Rock River Lodge**.

Mennonite Country

Follow the sign to **Spanish Lookout Village**. It's always a surprise in the tropics—the landscape suddenly changes from ragged forest covered with vines, creepers, and delicate ferns to neat barns and rolling green countryside. This is one of the Mennonite communities whose founders brought a small bit of Europe with them and, over the years, developed a fine agricultural industry that supplies a large part of the milk, cheese, and chicken for the country.

ⓜ ACTUN TUNICHIL MUKNAL

This is the acclaimed "Cave of the Crystal Maiden," featured in *National Geographic Magazine* and quickly becoming Belize's most popular underground experience. This cave is for fit and active people who do not mind getting wet and muddy—and who are able to tread lightly! After the initial 45-minute hike to the entrance (with three river fords) and a swim into the cave's innards, you will be asked to remove your shoes upon climbing up the limestone into the main cathedral-like chambers. The rooms are littered with delicate Maya pottery and the crystallized remains of 14 humans. There are no pathways, fences, glass, or other partitions separating the visitor from the artifacts. Nor are there any installed lights. The only infrastructure is a rickety ladder leading up to the chamber of the Crystal Maiden herself, a full female skeleton that sparkles with calcite under your headlamp's glare, more-so during the drier months.

Please be careful—the fact that tourists are allowed to walk here at all is as astonishing as the sights themselves (at the time of this writing, somebody had already trod on and broken one of the skulls). Only two tour companies are licensed to take guests here: **Pacz Tours** and **Mayawalk**, both based in downtown San Ignacio.

North of San Ignacio

BULLET TREE FALLS

This old, lazy village lies less than three miles out of San Ignacio on the road to El Pilar. Bullet Tree's ultra-mellow riverbank mood, combined with cheap and easy access to the relative bustle of San Ignacio, make it a pleasant mid-range alternative to the usual Cayo fare of jungle lodges and backpacker camps. There are now five clusters of riverside cabins, each on their own hammock-equipped compound of *palapa* shades and broadleaf riparian jungle. There are also a few famed healers in town and a nearby medicine trail, to which you can walk with a guide and then float back down the Mopan River (just don't miss your hotel's dock or you'll end up in Belize City). Of course, Bullet Tree overnighters still have access to the full range of Cayo area activities, right down the road and easily accessed by *colectivo* taxis (US$1 a person, or US$5 for a private cab).

Some come to Bullet Tree specifically for the services of local Maya healer **Miss Beatrice,** who offers very reasonably priced consults for various health and spirit problems.

EL PILAR ARCHAEOLOGICAL SITE

Seven miles north of Bullet Tree Falls, these jungle-choked Maya ruins are only visited by a handful of curious tourists a day; its rough approach road plus the lack of attention paid to it by most tour operators help make El Pilar the excellent, uncrowded day trip that it is. Two groupings of temple mounds, courtyards, and ball courts overlook a forested valley. Aqueducts and a causeway lead toward Guatemala, just 500 meters away. There have been some minor excavations here, including those of illegal looters, but it is very overgrown, so the ruins retain an intriguing air of mystery. Many trees shade the site: allspice, gumbo-limbo, ramon, cohune palm, and locust. It's a beautiful hiking area and wildlife experience as well.

Even if you book your El Pilar trip in San Ignacio, be sure to start your quest with a visit to the **Amigos de El Pilar** visitors center (9 A.M.–5 P.M. daily) and **Be Pukte Cultural Center** in Bullet Tree Falls. Here you'll find a scale model of the ruins, some helpful booklets and maps, and guide and taxi arrangements (about US$25 for a taxi to drive a group out and wait a few hours before taking them back). Or, you can rent a mountain bike at Cohune Palms and make a workout of it—the road's so bad, you'll probably beat the cab anyway. There's also a surprisingly wide selection of booklets and information available at the gift shop in the San Ignacio Resort Hotel.

Accommodations

Rolling into town, you'll pass the soccer field on your right, then come to a fork in the road; this is the bus stop—fork left to cross the bridge and reach the turnoff for El Pilar, right to check in at one of three accommodations. **Co-hune Palms** (tel. 501/609-2738, www.cohunepalms.com) offers a handful of thatch, bamboo, and wooden structures around a hang area and kitchen, all enveloped in a truly wild environment and perched atop a steep bank of the Mopan. Rooms with shared bath and hot shower start at US$18/30 s/d, or try a fancier version with private bath for US$50 a couple. Reserve one of the huts with a "hammock bed" for a *real* swingin' night, baby. Owners Bevin and Mike are a wealth of Bullet Tree knowledge, and they'll help you plan your time, get to and from San Ignacio, and rent you tubes and bicycles with which to explore their backyard. Contact them at the number above or at their Cohune Palms Guest House in San Ignacio. Cooking in the communal kitchen can be a pleasant, homey relief after wining and dining through the rest of Belize, but they'll probably be serving meals to guests by the time you read this (check first).

Just up river, the **Parrot's Nest** (tel. 501/289-4058, www.parrot-nest.com) has fantastic on-site bird-watching in the trees and lawn that surround six simple, cozy cabins, including two "tree houses" on stilts under the limbs of a gigantic guanacaste tree. Each cabin has 24-hour electricity, a linoleum floor, and a simple single or double bed, with the breeze providing "natural" air-conditioning with the help of fans (US$40–45 per cabin, dinner and breakfast included, shared bath, hot water; US$50 private bath).

The first place you see after turning at the bus stop, **Iguana Junction** (tel. 501/820-4021), has eight straightforward rooms and cabins, US$30 s/d shared, US$40 s/d private bath and hot water, meals available. The **Riverside River Lodge** (tel. 501/820-4007), across the bridge, is the only place in town to party it up to loud music, and sometimes live shows, but you probably wouldn't get much of a quiet sleep in their adjoining lodge (only if there's a party though, ask about rooms, US$65).

Upstream, you'll find the peaceful **Paslow Falls Cottage** (tel. 501/609-5212, marlonwaight@hotmail.com, US$25/30 s/d), with direct access to the medicine trail, with guide Don Beto, a local bush doctor.

South of San Ignacio: The Mountain Pine Ridge

A great many of Cayo's natural treasures are found within this vast crinkle of mountains, as are some of the region's most charming accommodations. Despite bark beetle damage to vast tracts of pine trees in the Mountain Pine Ridge Forest Reserve, its waterfalls, swimming holes, and vistas are still very much worth enduring the rutted-out roads, and you'll see the pine forests regenerating. Points of interest, parks, and accommodations are presented in this section in the order they are found as one travels south from San Ignacio (along the two roads that access the Pine Ridge); many resorts are destinations in their own right—travelers come to enjoy the waterfalls at Five Sisters, or the restaurant at Blancaneaux, just as they would seek out the area's Maya ruins and fascinating caves.

THE CRYSTAL REY ROAD

Heading south from Santa Elena, this road winds through the villages of Cristo Rey and San Antonio before joining the Chiquibul Road on the Mountain Pine Ridge. It is slightly shorter and usually provides better maintained access to most of the Pine Ridge's attractions than the Chiquibul Road, and it offers a handful of interesting stops along the way. Village buses that travel the road leave the center of San Ignacio daily, and shared taxis should be available for reasonable rates as well. Most tour operators who travel this road will stop at any of the following places, depending on group size and desires.

Maya Mountain Lodge and Tours

Only one mile south of the Western Highway, Maya Mountain Lodge (tel. 501/824-2164, www.mayamountain.com) feels remote enough to warrant a listing outside of town. This is a moderately priced jungle hideaway operated for the last 22 years by Suzi and Bart Mickler. The lodge is only a short distance off the Western Highway, yet miles from the rest of the world. A meandering trail through the gardens has signs identifying a variety of plants, trees, and birds. Accommodations range from six primitive rooms (US$49 fan, US$69 a/c) to quaint cottages with extra bunks and wood furniture (US$99). The Micklers take pride in the friendliness and efficiency of their staff—and in their restaurant. They claim to serve "gourmet in the jungle," featuring homemade breads and buckets of fresh-squeezed orange juice (their Ba'hai Faith prevents them from selling liquor for profit, but you are welcome to bring your own). Breakfast and lunch cost US$8, and dinner is US$16. Ask about workshops on biodiversity and multiculturalism. This is a great place for families, with discounted (or free) rooms and tours for children.

Cayo & Mount. Pine Ridge

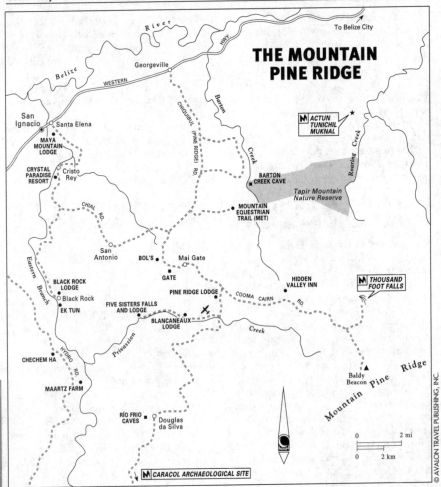

Crystal Paradise Resort

Owned and operated by the Tut family, Crystal Paradise (tel. 501/820-4014 or 824-2772, cparadise@btl.net, www.crystalparadise.com, US$55/75 to US$95/125 s/d) is a wonderful retreat overlooking the Macal River. Before the advent of tourism, the Tut family (Victor and Teresa and their 10 children) grew fruits and vegetables and then transported them by canoe to the town market in San Ignacio. These days, Victor still grows fruits and vegetables and is working on a future addition to Crystal Paradise Resort, a jungle campground facility. The sons, who are avid bird-watchers and nature-lovers, maintain the beautiful grounds, and serve as your guides on a variety of tours including hiking, biking, horseback riding, kayaking, and bird-watching. Teresa and daughters keep the guest rooms clean and comfortable and also cook up the best in traditional Belizean and international cuisine. Accommodations come in several styles on the property. If you're lucky, you may get one of the simple thatched cabanas near the wide, open dining *palapa* that overlooks the river. These have compelling views of the Macal Valley and have cement walls, tiled floors, h/c showers, and shaded verandas for relaxing (US$125). Others are clean and comfortable but more of a clapboard style; all offer ceiling fans and electricity. The Tuts also own other property nearby that's great for bird-watching and nature walks, and they offer tours around the countryside. Rates include breakfast and dinner.

Slate Carving Art Galleries

About six miles south, look for the **Sak Tunich Art Gallery,** home of the Magana brothers, Jose and Javier. This indoor-outdoor display is built into the hillside on your left and is worth a look for anyone interested in Maya crafts. A couple miles further, you'll find more at **The Garcia Sisters'** (tel. 501/820-4023, artistmai1981@btl.net); these six siblings made a nationwide name for themselves when, in 1981, they turned to their innate Maya heritage and began re-creating slate carvings reminiscent of their ancestors at Caracol. Their Maya art gallery, shop, and museum are called the **Tanah Mayan Art Museum,** located on the Crystal Rey Road, just outside of San Antonio. The Tanah Museum is a one-room affair, built in the old Maya way with limestone and clay walls; the floor is a parquet of logs and limestone, and the roof is typical thatch of bay and palm leaves, picked and placed on the nights of the full moon to give them a longer life. The sisters, nieces of the famed healer Don Eligio Panti, are charming and determined ambassadors of San Antonio village, as well as clever artists who make hand-drawn art cards depicting the wildlife of Belize, Belizean dolls, native jewelry, and medicinal herbs. Ask about the Itzamna Society, a community-based NGO of which Maria is the Chairperson and which works to protect the forest and community.

Noj Kaax Meen Elijio Panti National Park

This new 13,000-acre reserve of mountains surrounding the village of San Antonio is a community-based effort to preserve the forest and honor the wildlife and spirits that reside there. The visitors center is located three miles outside of town, but the contact is María Garcia (tel. 501/820-4023, artistmai1981@btl.net). Ask around town regarding guides to take you to the trails, waterfalls, and peaks. The park is also reportedly an experiment in people power and agroforestry, augmenting the unreliable tourism dollar with cooperative production of cacao, *xate,* and hardwood cooperatives.

Village of San Antonio

With a population of 2,350 Maya descendants, mostly milpa farmers and, increasingly, employees at nearby lodges, San Antonio has the potential to serve as a low-key gateway to the surrounding wilderness. There are horse and hiking trails nearby, as well as several caves, waterfalls, and ruins. Ask at the small **Eligio Panti Museum** about available guesthouse lodging, camping, and guided tours in the area. Continuing beyond San Antonio, you'll find **Mountain Rider,** a small horseback riding operation.

THE CHIQUIBUL (OR PINE RIDGE) ROAD

The Chiquibul Road begins at Mile 63 on the Western Highway (at Georgeville) and heads south over the Mountain Pine Ridge to end, 30-something miles after it began, at Caracol. You'll pass through tropical foothills, citrus farms, and cattle ranches before the terrain rises, gradually changing to sand, rocky soil, red clay, then, finally, groves of sweet-smelling pines. Creases of land within narrow river valleys are rich with stands of hardwood trees, many covered with orchids and bromeliads. Here and there small clearings have been carved out of the jungle by *milperos* (slash-and-burn farmers), and picturesque clusters of thatch huts surrounded by banana and cohune palms suggest the daily struggles of the campesino. The road is notorious for becoming a slushy mud bed after long rains; recent improvements for dam workers (the Chalillo site) and a grant to improve the final stretch to Caracol should make things better.

Cayo & Mount. Pine Ridge

Janus Restaurant

Four and a half miles from the highway, you'll find a driveway leading up to the beautifully landscaped grounds of the **Janus Foundation** (tel. 501/820-4004, www.janusfoundation.org), a 2,500-acre private reserve that has only recently turned to tourism to help sustain all its projects, research, and vocational training that in the past have been funded by donations from Europe. The Janus Restaurant (9 A.M.–7 P.M. daily) serves hearty meals consisting of organic vegetables grown on-site, bread from their bakery, meat from their own livestock, and homemade ice cream.

Slate Creek Preserve

A group of local private landowners and lodge operators have set aside 3,000 acres as a private preserve. The purpose of the preserve is to protect the watershed, plants, and animals of a valley called the Vega, one of several valleys in the area. The unique ecosystem of limestone karst, which borders the Mountain Pine Ridge Forest Reserve, teems with life. Mahogany, santa maria, ceiba, cedar, and cohune palms tower above. Orchids, ferns, and bromeliads are common. Birds such as the aracari, emerald toucanet, keel-billed toucan, keel-billed motmot, king vulture, and various parrots and hummingbirds are to be found here. Puma, ocelot, coati, paca, and anteater roam the forests.

Mountain Equestrian Trails (MET)

There is no better way to explore the Slate Creek Preserve than on one of the Bevis family's steeds, returning each afternoon to rest up in one of their lovely jungle cabanas (US tel. 800/838-3918, Bel. tel. 501/820-4041 or 600-1297, met-belize@hotmail.com, www.metbelize.com, from US$100/120 s/d). Visitors have a choice of gentle or spirited horses to carry them over the 60 miles of trails that wander through the surrounding forest. Trips are designed to suit every taste, with mountain trails that wander past magnificent waterfalls, swimming holes, pine forests, Maya caves, exotic butterflies, and more than 150 species of orchids. The equestrian trails are only a few miles from Río Frio Caves and Thou-

sand Foot Falls, where the water drops 1,600 feet into the jungle below. Programs are designed for both beginners and experienced riders—children at least age 10 with previous riding experience are welcome. Guests will find 10 lovely, spacious cabanas of thatch, stucco, and exotic wood interiors with private bathrooms and h/c water (no electricity—yet). Meals are served in the cozy cantina/restaurant, which serves a variety of excellent food (breakfast US$7, lunch US$10, dinner US$18, plus tax). No matter that the small cantina is a 20-minute drive from San Ignacio; it still attracts visitors and locals from all around for drinks, dinner, and good conversation. All-inclusive, multi-day packages available, riding fees extra. Riders are required to carry personal liability insurance to cover themselves while touring. **Chiclero Trails Campsite** offer safari-style tents located under the rainforest canopy, with beds, mattresses, linens, private covered deck, and close access to restrooms and showers, US$20 pp per night. Meals for groups are served in an insulated tent in the camp.

Green Hills Butterfly Ranch and Botanical Collections

Located at Mile 8, this outstanding butterfly breeding, education, and interpretive center is run by Jan Meerman and Tineke Boomsma (meerman@btl.net). Displays include all stages of the life cycle of a butterfly (egg-caterpillar-pupa-butterfly), and visitors can watch them all. Between 25 and 30 different species are raised at the center, including the tiny glasswing, the banana owl—the largest butterfly in Belize—and of course the magnificent blue morpho. Arrive early enough in the morning and watch a butterfly emerge from a pupa right before your eyes—a grand experience. Jan's newest guidebook on butterflies in Belize, *Lepidoptera of Belize*, should be available soon. Tineke, also involved in research, spends many hours each day feeding and caring for these wondrous miracles of life. Both Tineke and Meerman have spent years studying butterflies, nourishing the plants they eat, and watching the interaction of different species of butterflies. Tours of the center take about an hour and give you a chance to see and learn about these beautiful fluttering creatures. The tour through the flight rooms (2,700 sq. ft.), brings you up close to hundreds of flitting butterflies of all colors. Open 8 A.M.–4 P.M. daily. Last tour begins at 3:30 P.M. Entrance fee for guided tour, US$4 pp, minimum of two people. Group rates available.

Barton Creek Cave

This is a cathedral-like wet cave, once used for ceremonial purposes and human sacrifices by the Maya, now ragingly popular among Cayo visitors who fancy floating through the tall, quiet cavern. The experience is impressive and available to anybody physically able enough to step into a canoe. Contemplate the quiet as your guide slowly paddles you deeper into the earth, the watery sound of his paddle echoing on the limestone. The cave was re-discovered in 1970 by a pair of Peace Corps Volunteers who found that the cave had already been extensively looted. Archaeologists didn't study the cave until 1998; they found large ceramics on high ledges, plus evidence of 20 human remains, including a necklace made of finger bones. The cave is at least seven miles deep, but tours only go in about a mile or so before turning around.

Barton Creek is protected and managed by government archaeologists, and is accessed by turning off the Chiquibul Road around Mile 4, then driving 20–30 minutes on a bumpy road through orange groves and a small Mennonite settlement (you'll need to have someone who knows the way with you, as there are many roads and no signs). The visitors center charges US$5 pp, then you'll have to rent canoes (US$7.50 per boat), lights, and a guide, all available at **Mike's Place,** right there at the cave's entrance. Most visitors, however, arrive as part of a pre-paid tour and won't need to worry about such details.

THE MOUNTAIN PINE RIDGE FOREST RESERVE

After steadily ascending along the Chiquibul (Pine Ridge) Road for 21 miles, a gate across the road marks your entrance to Belize's largest and oldest protected area, established in 1944. The 300-square-mile area (126,825 acres) features

Caribbean Pine and bracken ferns instead of the typical tropical vegetation found in the rest of Belize. It also features a massive granite uplifting; the exposed rocks are some of the oldest formations in the Americas (they also make for incredible swimming holes and waterfalls). In fact, some geologists think that the Mountain Pine Ridge (whose highest point is 3,336 feet above sea level at Baldy Beacon) was one of the only exposed islands when the rest of Central America was underwater.

Cycles of Disaster

Shortly after its creation, the Pine Ridge experienced a huge forest fire which, combined with the cycles of logging, left an unnaturally uniform population of trees, making the forest further susceptible to disease and insects. Most recently, a three-year drought helped establish a disastrous infestation of the southern pine bark beetle *(Dendroctonus frontalis),* a destructive bug that has devastated many other forests in Central and North America.

The beetle establishes itself under the bark, where it eats, mates, and lays eggs. It spreads by jumping from tree to tree; the only way to stop it is by clear-cutting massive buffer zones around the affected areas as large as 240 feet wide (similar to how forest fires are fought). This was how the battle was played out when government foresters and the two local timber concessions went to war against the beetle in 2000—cutting, burning, cleaning, and cutting some more. Their efforts were too little too late, and only a small section of the forest was saved (look across the creek from either Blancaneaux or Five Sisters to see some of the surviving forest patches). The beetles spread faster than the pine cones could mature, effectively interrupting their reproductive cycle.

Today, the forest is coming back wonderfully—thanks to both naturally rich seed sets, and a massive replanting campaign (24 million seedlings are required for reforestation of 70,000 acres over four years). It will be another 15–20 years before the new generation of pines fully matures, however. Check out www.reforestbelize.com for an update and to find out how you can help.

Cayo's famous pine trees are already regenerating after the bark beetle catastrophe in 2000.

Visiting the Reserve

Most tour operators offer day trips to the Pine Ridge's attractions, listed in this section, and often combined with a trip to Caracol Ruins. There are way more sights than can be fit into a day, but there are a number of lodges that can put you right in the thick of it all.

The forestry station at Douglas De Silva Reserve (formerly called Augustine) used to be a small village of loggers and forestry workers, before the pine beetle and massive layoffs. You can now camp on the mowed grounds of the old school, but the black flies can be pretty horrendous here. Those interested in camping must get permission from the forest guard at the entrance.

Hidden Valley Inn

Situated on 7,200 acres of private property in the heart of the Mountain Pine Ridge Forest Reserve, Hidden Valley Inn (tel. 501/822-3320, reservations@hiddenvalleyinn.com, about US$150) is a quiet paradise for hikers and bird-watchers who will have a blast exploring the re-sort's 90-plus miles of walking trails and old logging roads—and then cozying up in front of their cottage's fireplace, listening to the birdsong outside (especially nice during the cool, misty, rainy season). The property encompasses lush broadleaf forest and pine tree habitat, and the two diverse ecosystems are divided by a geological fault line, which marks the edge of a towering 1,000-foot escarpment. Numerous watercourses spring from the mountain and then cascade down the steep slopes, often into deep, inviting pools; Hidden Valley's trail system runs through it all. The active trekker can spend days exploring, and the staff at the Inn can assist with vehicle shuttles. Bird-watchers, be prepared to check off Orange Breasted Falcons, King Vultures, Stygian Owl, Azure Crowned Hummingbirds, Green Jays, Golden Hooded Tanagers. Picnic lunches are provided for the myriad day trips available.

The Inn itself is comprised of a main house built of local hardwoods that feels more like a comfy ski lodge than a tropical resort, with several spacious common rooms including a fireside lounge, card room, TV room, library, and the restaurant, where creative dinners are served in candlelit splendor. The 12 cottages have *saltillo* tile floors, vaulted ceilings, cypress-paneled walls, fireplaces, ceiling fans, screened louvered windows, comfy beds, and private baths with h/c water. Ask about special packages. Hidden Valley Inn is located three miles in from the Mile 14 turnoff onto Cooma Cairn Road—just follow the signs.

Thousand Foot Falls

Occasionally referred to as "Hidden Valley Falls," this torrent of Roaring Creek is probably a good deal taller than a thousand feet and is considered the highest waterfall in all of Central America. The turnoff to the falls is located only a couple of miles beyond the Forest Reserve gate and is well-signed. From the turnoff, the road continues down for about four miles and brings you to the falls and a picnic area. View the falls from across the gorge and through breaks in the mist; US$2 pp. A small store and picnic tables can be found at the viewpoint, open 7 A.M.–5 P.M. daily.

© JOSHUA BERMAN

Cayo & Mount. Pine Ridge

Morning mist clears just enough for a glimpse of the Thousand Foot Falls, actually 1,600 feet high.

surrounded by scores of pine tree seedlings that are getting along just fine. Screened-in, creek-side lounge areas offer shade and a babbling brook, great after that bumpy, 32-mile trip back from Caracol—and before your walk down to the Pine Ridge Lodge's 85-foot waterfall. US$79 per couple, rate includes continental breakfast (freshly baked rolls, local honey, coffee, and fresh fruit); lunch US$7, dinner US$17.50. Catering to vegetarians is a specialty. The lodge is only seven miles north of Río On Pools; ask about tours and transfers.

Blancaneaux Lodge

Francis Ford Coppola first came to Belize just after the country gained independence in 1981; he tried and failed to persuade the new government to apply for a satellite license in order to become a hub of world communications. He did, however, succeed in finding an abandoned lodge on a pine-carpeted bluff overlooking the rocks and falls of Privassion Creek. Blancaneaux served as a private retreat for the film producer until 1993 when he "tricked it open" by flying a group of family and friends down for his 54th birthday.

Blancaneaux Lodge (tel. 501/824-4912, info@blancaneaux.com, www.blancaneaux.com) remains one of Belize's premier resorts, featuring the design and décor of the Coppolas and Mexican arcitect Manolo Mestre. Tropical splashes of color, dark hardwoods, Central American lines, and soaring thatch ceilings mark Blancaneaux's 10 cabanas and seven luxurious villas (US$200–400 a couple, plus tax and service). New additions include a hot pool above the river and a spa built in an Indonesian rice house with Thai massage therapists.

An on-site hydroelectric dam powers the entire operation, and an organic herb and vegetable garden supplies much of the restaurant's needs. The lodge is located at Mile 14.5 and has its own airstrip, which many guests prefer to the 2.5-hour drive from Belize City.

Blancaneux's **Ristorante Montagna** offers an exquisite Italian-centric menu, with a range of salads, pastas (US$14), sandwiches, delicious pizzas from one of the country's only wood-burning

Pine Ridge Lodge

Five miles beyond the Forest Reserve gate, you'll find yet another unique hillside lodging with its own primitively comfortable personality. On the banks of the Little Vaqueros Creek, the Pine Ridge Lodge (US tel. 800/316-0706, local radio tel. 501/606-4557, PRLodge@mindspring.com, www.pineridgelodge.com) offers six rooms in their "forestview, mayan, and riverview cottages," all with private bathroom, hot water, porch, and appealing décor and furnishings. There's no electricity, just quaint kerosene lanterns for reading at night. True, the beetle blight left the place with a depressing collection of pine stumps, but owners Vicki and Gary Seewald have done a superhuman job at restoring the grounds—they've planted bright and beautiful gardens that feature a growing collection of orchids and other epiphytes, all pizza ovens (US$15), and, of course, a selection of wines from Coppola's Napa Valley vineyards—smooth, but costly.

Five Sisters Lodge

The Five Sisters Lodge (tel. 501/820-4005, fivesisterslodge@direcway.com, www.fivesisterslodge.com), high above the inviting Privassion Creek, has been a destination since 1991. Inspired by the natural beauty of his property, Belizean Carlos Popper set off to design his lodge with one clear objective: To provide sustainable architecture in harmony with the natural world around it. Considering the location above the famous falls (from which the lodge gets its name),

prices are very reasonable: A standard room with private bath, h/c water, and varying views is US$105 a couple, including continental breakfast; luxury rooms—with nicer views and hardwood floors—are just a few dollars more. All perched on the top of the steep canyon, accommodations range from simple boxy rooms to beautifully thatched cabanas overlooking the river—14 units in all. The honeymoon suite has brightly colored bedspreads, mosquito netting, and complete privacy. The dining room serves Belizean and Mexican dishes. Restaurant prices are US$6 breakfast and lunch, US$17.50 dinner, and packages for longer stays are offered. Even if you don't stay here, come by, have a beer on the

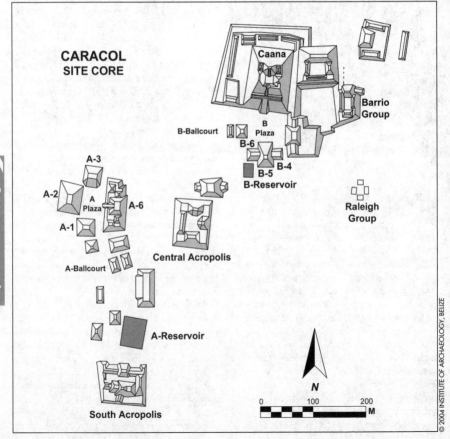

CARACOL SITE CORE

Caana

Barrio Group

B-Ballcourt

B Plaza

B-6

A-3

B-5 · B-4

B-Reservoir

A-2

A Plaza

A-6

Raleigh Group

A-1

Central Acropolis

A-Ballcourt

A-Reservoir

N

South Acropolis

0   100   200
M

outdoor deck, and enjoy the commanding view above the river. The hearty can walk the 300 steps down to the river and quench their thirst at the small island bar. If you have a few too many down there, not to worry—the motorized funicular will carry you back up the hill—at least between 8 A.M. and 4 P.M.

Río On Pools and Río Frio Cave

Most Caracol packages try to squeeze in an afternoon stopover at these lovely sites. Continuing south toward Augustine, you will cross the Río On. It's well worth the climb over an assortment of worn boulders and rocks to a delightful site with waterfalls and several warm-water pools; don't forget your camera. There's a parking area just off the road. Turn right at Douglas De Silva Ranger Station (the western division of the Forestry Department) and continue for about five miles to reach Río Frio Cave. Follow the signs to the parking lot. From here, visitors have a choice of exploring nature trails (note the purple ground orchids growing along the paths) and two small caves on the road or continuing to the largest and most well-known river cave in Belize, the Río Frio, with an enormous arched entryway into the half-mile-long cave. Filtered light highlights ferns, mosses, stalactites, and geometric patterns of striations on rocks. Each step stirs up the musty smells of the damp rocky cave. Watch where you walk; sinkholes are scattered here and there, and a narrow stream flows along the gravel riverbed.

ⓜ CARACOL ARCHAEOLOGICAL SITE

One of the largest sites in Belize, archaeologists Diane and Arlen Chase believe that Caracol is the Maya city-state that toppled mighty Tikal, just to the northwest, effectively shutting it down for 130 years. Located within the **Chiquibul Forest Reserve,** Caracol is *out there,* offering both natural wonders and Maya mystery. To date, only a small percentage of the 177 square kilometers that make up the site has even been mapped, identifying only 5,000 of the estimated 36,000 structures lying beneath the forest canopy.

© JOSHUA BERMAN

the view from Caracol's Canaa Temple, "Sky Place," tallest man-made structure in Belize

DAMMED IF THEY DO . . .

The most controversial and high-profile environmental issue in Belize in recent years is no doubt the Chalillo Dam (chah-LEE-yo), a holding reservoir project currently being laid across an upper tributary of the Macal River.

"Surreal" is the word used by geologist Brian Holland to describe the double-talk, deception, and denial by proponents of the Chalillo Dam. The project, which has received international media attention, has proceeded even as court challenges regarding its legality continue to be played out and initial phases of construction reveal enormous technical concerns.

As the issue went to another round of the London-based Privy Council, the Canadian company who carried out the environmental impact statement was found to have concealed a key document damning the dam. The report, written by a geologist commissioned by Fortis, Inc., the Canadian underwriters of the dam and the majority shareholder of Belize's electric company (BEL), concluded that 1) the bedrock at the dam site was incorrectly stated to be of granite when in fact it is made of soft sandstones and weak shales, 2) Fortis engineers digitally altered a map to remove the Cumacairn fault line that runs through the dam site, and 3) there is potential for the proposed dam reservoir to "leak like a sieve" because of limestone caves upstream.

Of course, Chalillo opponents are also worried about the ecological and cultural impacts of the dam—threats to endangered species like the scarlet macaw and tapir, and flooding of unique habitat which also contains at least seven unstudied Maya ruins. There's also the increasingly expensive construction costs and doubts as to whether the projected 5.3 megawatts will even decrease the cost of power for Belizeans, as promised.

But Holland says that the important thing to look at now is not the birds or the economics, but basic geology and a bit of history: "People need to think about the Teton Dam," he says, referring to the last dam ever constructed in the United States—the one that catastrophically collapsed upon completion in June 1976, unleashing an 80-billion-gallon wall of water that resulted in 14 deaths and US$1 billion in damage.

Meanwhile, supporters of the dam accuse environmentalists of grasping for straws in a last-ditch effort to halt construction. Accusations fly, both sides call each other "liars and hypocrites," and still, the bulldozers drone on.

The centerpiece is no doubt the pyramid of **Canaa** which, at 136 feet above the plaza floor (roughly two meters higher than El Castillo at Xunantunich), is one of the tallest structures—modern or ancient—in Belize. Canaa was only completely unveiled of vegetation in 2003 by the Tourism Development Project (TDP), whose work is responsible for most of the structures you see. The vistas from the top of Canaa are extensive and memorable.

In addition to the aforementioned superlatives, Caracol, a Classic period site, is noted for its large masks and giant date glyphs on circular stone altars. There is also a fine display of the Maya's engineering skills, with extensive reservoirs, agricultural terraces, and several mysterious ramps. Caracol has been studied for over 20 years

by archaeologists the Chases and their assistants, student interns from Tulane University and University of Central Florida. According to John Morris, an archaeologist with Belize's Institute of Archaeology, a lifetime of exploration remains to be done within six to nine miles in every direction of the excavated part of Caracol. It's proving to have been a powerful site that controlled a very large area, with possibly over 100,000 inhabitants. The jungle you see now would have been totally absent in those days, the wood cleared to provide fuel and agricultural lands to support so many people.

Many carvings are dated A.D. 500–800, and ceramic evidence indicates that Caracol was settled about A.D. 300 and continued to flourish when other Maya sites were in decline. Carvings on the site also indicate that Caracol and Tikal engaged in ongoing conflicts, each defeating the other on various occasions. After the war in A.D. 562, Caracol flourished for more than a century in the mountains and valleys surrounding the site. A former archaeological commissioner named the site "Caracol" because of the winding logging road to reach it, although some contend it was because of all the snail shells found during initial excavations.

Visiting the Site

The small visitors center presents a scale model and interesting information based mostly on the work of the Chases over the last two decades. A new **Monument Museum** will allow tourists to view a range of artifacts and stelae from the site and will be based on the work of the TDP. There are no official guides on-site, as most groups arrive with their own. However, the caretakers know Caracol well and will be glad to walk you through and explain the site for a few dollars.

Most tours start with the Raleigh Group, move by the enormous ceiba trees, then circle through the archaeologists' camp and end with a bang by climbing Canaa. To prepare yourself—and to check on the latest discoveries and trail maps, click over to www.caracol.org.

Most tour operators offer Caracol day trips, often involving stops at various caves and swimming holes on the way back through the Mountain Pine Ridge. A few, like **Everald's Caracol Shuttle** (tel. 501/804-0090 or 603-5705, caracolshuttle@hotmail.com), specialize in it. The ride should take anywhere from two to three hours, depending on both the weather and the progress made by road improvement crews who hopefully will not run out of money before you read this. If driving, 4WD vehicles are a must; gas is not available along the 50-mile road, so carry ample fuel. Camping is not allowed in the area without permission from the Institute of Archaeology in Belmopan. The closest accommodations are those along the Pine Ridge Road.

West of San Ignacio

It is only about 11 miles to the border with Guatemala, but, in true Belizean fashion, the short distance—and the hills around it—is jam-packed with attractions and accommodations for all budgets and active tastes.

DOWN THE CHIAL ROAD

About five miles west of San Ignacio, look for a turnoff to the left onto a well-maintained dirt road; the Chial Road will carry you back to the banks of the Macal River and some of Belize's most acclaimed accommodations.

Just after the turnoff for Black Rock, you'll find the **Green Heaven Lodge** (tel. 501/820-4034, ghlodge@btl.net, www.ghlbelize.com, US$90 d). It has four simple cabins and a restaurant that serves tasty French dishes, including daily specials like chicken cordon bleu (US$10), and quiche lorraine (US$6). Other choices are stewed pork with curry with white and port wines and pine nuts for US$10, or shrimp spaghetti for US$9.

The Lodge at Chaa Creek (tel. 501/824-2037, reservations@chaacreek.com, www.chaacreek .com) is more than just one of the top-rated jungle lodges in Central America; this was one of the first cottage resorts of its kind in the Cayo District. Chaa Creek's 340 acres on the Macal River also host the **Blue Morpho Butterfly Breeding Center,** the **Chaa Creek Natural History Museum** (with exhibit areas that examine ecosystems, geology, and Maya culture in the Cayo area), and the **Ix Chel Farm and the Maya Medicine Trail.** Owners Mick and Lucy Fleming, an American wife–British husband team, are world travelers who came to visit Belize in the late 1970s, fell in love with the land, and never left. The 23 *palapa*-roof cottages have a medieval fairytale feeling. Individually designed and decorated, the cottages all have electricity, private bath with hot water, and are exquisitely furnished with Mexican-tile floors, rich Guatemalan fabrics, and works of art from around the world; two "treetop" cabins perch on the riverbank, their wide porches boasting whirlpool tubs and views of dozens of massive iguanas basking in the branches.

The Belizean chef prepares wonderful meals, with many of the ingredients coming from a local Maya farm (which guests can visit); breakfast US$10, packed lunch US$8, dinner US$26. The spa is set on a beautiful bluff above the lodge, with views of the hills across the river; one feels relaxed just walking into the open-air lounge area and listening to the music over a cup of tea; full and modern treatments available to guests and walk-ins alike. Contact the Chaa Creek front desk or their office in San Ignacio.

In addition to the standard retinue of day trips, Chaa Creek guests can choose from a number of on-site activities for no extra charge: daily pre-breakfast bird-watching walks, swimming in the Macal, hiking the trails, or venturing out in one of their canoes—San Ignacio is a two-hour float downstream, or you can paddle upstream to duPlooy's to tour the Botanic Garden (strong paddlers only). The newest addition is a fleet of high-end Specialized mountain bikes. Chaa Creek guides are available for all trips, including biking, and they undergo a truly impressive training retinue—including U.S. National Park Service Ranger and rescue training, plus bike training in the Grand Canyon and Utah slickrock country.

The **Camp at Chaa Creek** is a group of 10 canvas-roofed, stilted cabin-tents, in their own clearing near the river, about a 10-minute walk along the medicine trail from the activity of the main lodge. US$55 pp gets you a lantern-lit cabin with an almost-private porch, dinner and breakfast, and use of the shared bathroom and shower house. Meals are eaten communally under a thatch roof, with a bar available as well. And, of course, camp guests have access to all the main Chaa Creek facilities and activities.

Set on 90 lush acres of rolling countryside on the banks of the Macal River is **duPlooy's Cottage Resort** (tel. 501/824-3101, info@duplooys.com, www.duplooys.com). The duPlooys have planted their newly acquired acreage with thousands of trees, a fruit orchard, and the **Belize Botanic Garden.** Guests have a number of choices: the comfy Pink House's six rooms with two shared bathrooms (US$40/50 s/d); Jungle Lodge cabins (US$130) with screened porches, private bath, hot showers, and ceiling fans; or bungalows (US$165), accessed by a wooden catwalk and offering its own canopy tour on the steep river bank, plus king bed, refrigerator, coffeepot, bathtub, and hammocks on the deck. Other options are great for families and groups. Meal plans, pack lunches, and the dining room provide top-notch, cow-free sustenance—vegetarians welcome.

duPlooy's offers a sandy river beach with swimming, walks in the garden, horse trails, hiking, orchids, and bird-watching tours (300 species spotted in this area alone). There are various horseback riding options, including a ride through the woods to Cahal Pech Maya ruins, then into San Ignacio, where you can tie up in front of a restaurant and order a beer and burrito. Of course, the full retinue of local trips is available, including nearby caves, waterfalls, ruins, even Tikal in nearby Guatemala; or you can float in a tube or canoe downstream to other jungle resorts where you'll radio back to duPlooy's for a pickup.

Black Rock Belize Jungle River Lodge (tel. 501/824-2341, info@blackrocklodge.com, www.blackrocklodge.com) has fourteen cabins (US$65 shared bath, US$85 private bath), plus deluxe options for a bit more dough. Excellent food is served in an open-air dining pavilion. Though in a primitive setting of 250 jungle acres, Black Rock uses modern technology to provide solar electricity, solar hot water, and solar water pumps. Meals are US$8 full breakfast, US$9 lunch, US$16 dinner. **Ek Tun** (tel. 501/820-3002, info@ektunbelize.com, www.ektunbelize.com) is an upscale, isolated couple of cottages in the middle of 200 prime natural acres of the upper Macal River Valley. Excellent meals include Mexican specialties, lots of fresh fruit, spicy local dishes, and each day an elegant dessert. Most of the fruits and vegetables served are grown in the Ek Tun gardens. The intimate atmosphere makes Ek Tun a favorite for honeymooners; children under 12 stay for half price, packages available.

ALONG THE WESTERN HIGHWAY

Although the chief attraction on this stretch of road between San Ignacio and the Guatemalan border is the Xunantunich archaeological site, there are also a number of budget lodging and camping grounds that many backpackers use to rest up and explore the area between their Guatemalan and Caribbean adventures. Most of these places are close enough to San Ignacio that guests can easily pop into town for dinner and then back out to their tent or cabin in a bus or cheap taxi.

Clarissa Falls Resort (tel. 501/824-3916, clarifalls@btl.net, www.clarissafalls.com) is located at the end of a mile-long dirt road, accessed on the right at Mile 70.5 of the Western Highway. This is a laid-back, riverside affair where guests either camp in their own tents (US$7.50 pp), bunk up in the bamboo and thatch dormitory (US$15 pp), or stay in a more-upscale cottage with private bath (US$65 s/d). The shared toilet and shower building has hot and cold water and is cement-basic. The Mopan River is the main attraction here, as are the nature trails and hike to Xunantunich, the highest pyramid of which is visible from the cottages. The dining room serves good Mexican food, including a few specialties such as black mole soup and great, cheap Mexican-style tacos; around $6 for a meal like stuffed squash.

A bit more accessible is the ℕ **Trek Stop** (tel. 501/823-2265, susa@btl.net, www.thetrek-stop.com), a backpacker classic offering 10 cabins set in lushly planted gardens on 22 acres of second-growth tropical forest. There are also camping facilities (access to composting toilets and solar showers), a patio restaurant with inexpensive Belizean dishes, and walking access to the Xunantunich ruins. Rates are US$10 pp for the simple wood cabins with twin or double beds, electricity, porches, and shared bath. Inner tubes, inflatable kayaks, and mountain bikes are available for rent. Even if you're not spending the night here, come visit the **Tropical Wings Nature Center,** one of the best and most diverse butterfly ranches in the country.

© JOSHUA BERMAN

The spa at Chaa Creek looks over the Macal River Valley.

Be sure to leave time for a round on Belize's only **Disk Golf Course,** a nine-basket Frisbee golf game through the jungle, disks available, only US$2.50 pp. The course is a par 31 with narrow and challenging fairways that leave little room for error (wear long pants and closed footwear to retrieve those errant drives). There is a nice view (and sometimes breeze) from the Maya ruins atop hole six.

San José de Succotz

About 6.5 miles from San Ignacio, you'll find this hillside village on your left, above the Mopan River, right where the ferry to Xunantunich is located. In Succotz, the first language is Spanish and the most colorful time to visit is during one of their fiestas: March 19 (feast day of St. Joseph) and May 3 (feast day of the Holy Cross).

A stroll through the rough village streets is enjoyable if you're into observing village life. **Magana's Art Center** is the workshop of David Magana who works with the youth of the area, encouraging them to continue the arts and crafts of their ancestors. You'll find the results inside in the form of local wood carvings, baskets, jewelry, and stone (slate) carvings unique to Belize. There are a few taco stands in town, a restaurant called the **Red Jaguar,** and the **Succotz Learning Center,** a library and study hall of sorts with a few snacks and beverages for sale (ask for Tino Penado's house to find it); while you're there, note the charming, two-story blue house next door—perfect for guidebook writers on a deadline.

Mopan River Resort

This all-inclusive, upscale lodge (tel. 501/823-2047, www.mopanriverresort.com) is set on 10 beautiful acres across from the village of Benque del Viejo and is a fine option for travelers looking for comfort and easy access to Tikal and all the Cayo attractions. Packages (three-day minimum) run around US$200 per day and are truly all-inclusive: lodging, meals, alcohol, tours, and airport transfers; the daily rate drops the longer you stay. The nicely furnished cabanas are also equipped with TV/VCRs and a selection of movies is available in the gift shop. Buffet and family-style dinners are themed and breakfasts are cooked to your liking. Swimming in the river is not advised, but a lovely pool is provided for guests. Open November–April only, small weddings welcome—Pam, one of the owners, is a minister and can tie the knot for you in the riverside chapel.

Xunantunich

One of Belize's most impressive Maya ceremonial centers, Xunantunich rests atop a natural limestone ridge with a grand view of the entire Cayo District and Guatemala countryside. The local name for the site, Xunantunich (shoo-NAHN-tanich), or "stone lady," continues to be used, even after the ancients' own name for the site, "Ka-at Witz," or "Supernatural Mountain," was recently discovered, carved into a chunk of stone.

Xunantunich is believed to have been built

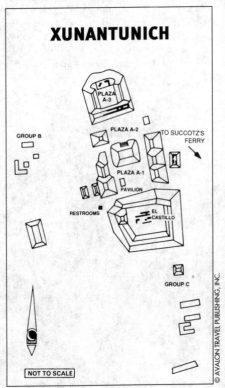

XUNANTUNICH

NOT TO SCALE

sometime around 400 B.C. and deserted around A.D. 1000; at its peak, some 7,000–10,000 Maya lived here. Though certainly not the biggest of Maya structures, at 135 feet high **El Castillo** is the second tallest pyramid in Belize (missing first place by one foot!). The eastern side of the structure displays an unusual stucco frieze (a reproduction), and you can see three carved stelae in the plaza. Xunantunich contains three ceremonial plazas surrounded by house mounds. It was rediscovered in 1894, but not studied until 1938 by archaeologist Sir J. Eric Thompson. As the first Maya ruin to be opened in the country, it has attracted the attention and exploration of many other archaeologists over the years.

In 1950, the University of Pennsylvania (noted for its years of outstanding work across the Guatemala border in Tikal) built a facility in Xunantunich for more study. In 1954, visitors were invited to explore the site after a road was opened and a small ferry built. In 1959, archaeologist Evan Mackie made news in the Maya world when he discovered evidence that part of Xunantunich had been destroyed by an earthquake in the Late Classic period. Some believe it was then that the people began to lose faith in their leaders—they saw the earthquake as an unearthly sign from the gods. But for whatever reason, Xunantunich ceased to be a religious center long before the end of the Classic period.

Located eight miles west of San Ignacio, the site is accessed by crossing the Mopan River on the Succotz Ferry, easily found at the end of a line of crafts vendors. The hand-cranked ferry shuttles you (and your vehicle, if you have one) across the river, after which you'll have about a mile's hike (or drive) up a hill to the site. The ferry, which operates 8 A.M.–3 P.M. daily, is free, but tipping the operator is a kind and much-appreciated gesture. Don't miss the 4 P.M. return ferry with the park rangers, or you'll be swimming.

Entrance to the site is US$2.50 pp; guides are available for US$20 per group and are

© JOSHUA BERMAN

Cayo & Mount. Pine Ridge

The Xunantunich pyramids look out over the Mopan River Valley and forests of the Guatemalan Peten.

© JOSHUA BERMAN

crossing the Mopan River on the road to Xunantunich

recommended—both to learn about what you're seeing and to support sustainable tourism, as all guides are local and very knowledgeable.

BENQUE VIEJO DEL CARMEN

After the ferry, the village of Succotz creeps over the hill and becomes Benque Viejo, the last town in Belize (the border is about one mile farther). This is a quiet little town with a peaceful atmosphere. Benque Viejo has been greatly influenced by the Spanish, both from its historical past when Spain ruled Guatemala and later when Spanish-speaking *chicleros* and loggers worked the forest. At one time, Benque Viejo ("Old Bank"—riverside logging camps were referred to as banks) was a logging camp. This was the gathering place for *chicle* workers, and logs were floated down the river from here for shipment to England.

The Latin influence persists with today's influx of Guatemalans. A group of foreign doctors who donate free medical assistance visit the Good Shepherd Clinic in Benque Viejo every year. People come from all over the district for this needed service; families even come from across the Guatemala border. Tourists generally do not choose to stay in the town of Benque, as so many options are available right up the road. There are a couple of dismal hotels however, and some decent Chinese restaurants, notably Allan's. You might find some Guatemalan crafts for sale if you walk around.

Getting There and Away

Buses between Belize City, Benque, and the Guatemala border run daily, starting at ungodly hours on both ends. Most bus service to and from San Ignacio also services Benque and the border. The most efficient way to travel to the border (or to any of the sites along the Western Highway mentioned earlier in this chapter) from San Ignacio is by *colectivo* taxis, which run in a constant and steady flow roughly 6 A.M.–7 P.M.; the ride should cost less than US$2, but you take the chance of sharing your cab with as many people as your driver can fit. By private taxi, expect to pay about US$10 per cab for the same trip.

SOUTH ON THE HYDRO ROAD

Chechem Ha Cave and the Vaca Plateau

Just before reaching the border station in Benque, a well-graded and maintained dirt road splits off to the left and heads south 11 miles, where it dead-ends at the Mollejon Dam. The country is sparsely populated broadleaf forest with a scattering of small farms, steep hills, waterfalls, caves, and two primitive accommodations from which to explore it all. Both are located on the Vaca Plateau, with accessible views of the ancient Macal River Valley. Both are also remote and very close to nature—if you can't go without modern amenities for a day or two, you'd better stay in town.

The road is equipped with mile markers on small white posts. A couple miles in, a right turn leads to the border village of Arenal. Nothing there but a few hundred tight-knit *milperos* scraping a life from the soils of the Mopan River Valley.

At Mile 8, you'll find a turnoff to the left for **Chechem Ha Farm** (tel. 501/820-4063), located another mile or so down a rutted road and belonging to the Morales family. The place is designed to give nature-loving tourists the chance to enjoy the Chechem Ha Spring, Chechem Ha Falls (a spectacular 175-ft. cascade with a treacherous trail down to its misty bottom), and the increasingly popular Chechem Ha Cave, a dry cave—except for the dripping water that creates all the formations over the years. The couple of cabins, made of clay, rock, wood, and thatch, are well-constructed and comfy looking; there is also a new bar, restaurant, and gift shop. US$41 pp gets you a night's stay and three meals; camping is US$5 pp, bring your own tent. Individual meals are available (US$5–10), as is an inexpensive transfer from Benque. Fireflies will light up the night and all manner of jungle birds will call from the trees. You'll eat under a thatch *palapa* and bathe in the nearby stream or under the waterfall below the lip of the plateau.

© JOSHUA BERMAN

You are viewing Belize's best ass.
Resides at Martz Farm.

one reason to visit Maartz Farm

Cayo & Mount. Pine Ridge

Loaded with Maya pottery, the ceremonial Chechem Ha Cave is protected by the government, which allows only guided tours and (of course) nothing can be removed. The pottery inside is estimated to be as old as 2,000 years. You can climb and explore various ledges and passageways, but the highlight is a deep ceremonial chamber in the heart of the hill. In some places, you need a rope to help you get around. While those of average physical abilities can enjoy Chechem Ha Cave, take care when moving amid the pottery.

Less than a mile beyond the Chechem Ha road, another left turn will carry you to **Martz Farm** (tel. 501/614-6462, martzfarm@hotmail.com, www.martzfarm.com), a wonderfully unique and relaxed homestead, built and maintained by the hardworking Martinez brothers, Jose and Lazaro (and their families). They've constructed a handful of tree houses and natural cabins, each apparently sprung from wild childhood fantasies. All are open to the forest air (mosquito nets provided), and one is even built over a private dip pool in the passing creek. Jose's German wife, Mirriam, cooks family-style meals over a traditional fire hearth in the dirt-floor kitchen, and farm animals wander the grounds with the guests. Prices run around US$15 per person per night, plus US$20 for three meals; free transfers from Benque, sometimes San Ignacio too. (Lazaro should be opening a campground up the road for US$5 pp, carry your own camping gear.) There are enough activities on Martz Farm and the adjacent **Da Silva Forest Reserve** to keep some guests happily occupied for weeks—hikes of all lengths, horseback rides, and waterfall crawls are all popular; guided trips available from around US$25/day, depending on the trip. Or just spend the day in your tree house communing with all the life humming around you.

Tikal, Guatemala

Tikal National Park is a wildlife preserve covering 25 square miles. The Tikal ruins are among the more outstanding in the Maya world. They have been excavated and restored extensively, but what you'll see is only a small part of what is still buried and unexplored in the rainforest.

As is the case with most Maya ceremonial centers, archaeologists are learning more and more about life in Tikal and its 3,000 structures (with 10,000 more foundations). They have mapped 250 stelae that the Maya left behind. In recent years, they have learned to decipher the Maya hieroglyphs, and about 80 percent of the Maya's written record has been translated.

Parque Nacional Tikal has been protected from loggers and *milperos* for more than three decades, so in addition to the cultural attraction, Tikal is a phenomenal nature and wildlife experience. You'll hear and, with luck (if you're up very early in the morning), see the howler monkeys that live in the treetops on the site. Hundreds of parrots will squawk at you as you wander through **Twin Complex Q and R**—this is their domain. And while wandering the **Great Plaza** and the **Lost City,** you'll see colorful toucans fly between ancient stone structures and tall vine-covered trees.

Throughout the site, you'll see several twin complexes with identical pyramids facing each other across a central plaza. No one knows why they were built this way. At Twin Complex Q and R, one pyramid has been excavated and restored, while its opposite is just as it was found—covered with vines and jungle growth. You'll see this sort of juxtaposition frequently throughout Tikal.

Tikal is huge, and a full explanation of the site is beyond the scope of this book; check out *Moon Handbooks Guatemala* or pick up a map and booklet at the visitors center and enjoy.

HISTORY
The Maya
The first Tikal Maya were farmers who, as far back as 750 B.C., chose the high ground that rose above the vast, steamy swamps of Petén for their settlement. The earliest evidence of their presence is some of the trash they left behind. Living on a major route between the lowlands and the cooler highlands, the Tikal villagers began a healthy trade in flint. The stone was plentiful here, and was prized for tools and weapons.

By 600 B.C., the Maya had begun their construction of Tikal ("The Place of Voices"). Over the next 1,500 years, they built their platformed city in layers, razing structures to gather material to build more.

By about 200 B.C., the Maya were building ceremonial structures. By 100 B.C., the great Acropolis was in place, and the Great Plaza was already as large as it would be hundreds of years later, when the population of Tikal reached its peak of about 55,000 people. From 50 B.C. to A.D. 250, the Maya created even more elaborate architecture on these early foundations. They also carved monuments, though they did not yet use hieroglyphics.

With the beginning of the Early Classic period in about A.D. 250, the Maya's monuments grew larger and became more formal and less ornate, but the plans for their temples changed little. They built the causeways to connect the parts of their city and carried on a thriving trade. Carvings on monuments and burial practices show a close relationship with Teotihuacán in Mexico. The monuments also describe Great-Jaguar-Paw and Smoking-Frog's conquest of nearby Uaxactún in A.D. 378. In 562, Lord Water of Caracol defeated Tikal in a great "ax war," and Tikal produced no monuments for 135 years. But in 682, Ah-Cacau took the throne and began to restore Tikal to its former glory. The great king was buried in the Temple of the Giant Jaguar.

Most of the construction at Tikal was in the Late Classic period, which began in A.D. 550 (shortly before Tikal's defeat by Caracol) and ended in A.D. 900 (when the entire society collapsed). In and around the ceremonial parts of the city lie 200 stone monuments in the form of stelae and altars. Archaeologists have pieced together Tikal's history from the carvings. The burials at Tikal also hold a clue to the structure of the society.

In the six square miles of Tikal that have been excavated, archaeologists have found hundreds of little buildings that they believe were domestic. Usually they're found in small clusters on elevated sites suitable for housing an extended family. Most people were buried beneath the floors of their houses. Their bones were smaller and weaker than the bones of the folks buried in the great tombs. The range of the housing construction, in size and quality, also suggests great variety in people's status and wealth.

But in A.D. 900, the entire society fell apart, not only at Tikal but throughout the Maya world. Post-Classic Maya continued to use the site for several centuries, and even moved several of the stelae around in an attempt to restore the city for their own purposes, but the jungle eventually reclaimed Tikal.

The Archaeologists

Hidden Tikal was mentioned in 18th-century Guatemala archives, but not until 1848 did the government mount an official expedition. The governor and commissioner of the Petén visited Tikal, and their report, along with an artist's drawings of the stelae and lintels, attracted attention in Europe, where the report was published. A Swiss doctor, Gustav Bernoulli, visited in 1877. He had some of the lintels removed (from Temples I and IV).

The first maps of Tikal were drawn by Alfred Percival Maudslay, who visited in 1881 and 1882 and whose workmen liberated the temples from the forest. He published his accounts along with the first photographs of the site. Teobert Maler continued in this vein; he visited in 1895 and 1904, mapping and photographing as he worked for the Peabody Museum of Harvard University. He wouldn't relinquish his site map, though, and the museum hired Mayanist Alfred Marston Tozzer and R. E. Merwin to finish the job.

Sylvanus G. Morley, for whom the Tikal museum is named and who was head of the Carnegie Institution's archaeology department, used Maudslay and the Peabody Museum's reports as a base, and devoted himself to recording the writing of the Maya. In 1956 the University of Pennsylvania launched the project to excavate Tikal and appointed Carnegie archaeologist Edwin Shook to lead the project. Since then, only part of the immense site has been excavated and restored.

VISITING THE RUINS
Entrance Fees and Hours

At the main gate to the park you'll pay a fee (Q50, about US$7). Do not lose your ticket! Continue north along the road until you reach the visitors center complex on your left; there's a museum, a few gift shops, a tour guide stand, an overpriced restaurant, and the famous white plaster scale model of the Tikal ruins. Beyond these buildings, on the right hand side, is a large parking lot (and former airstrip), where you'll find the park's three hotels and one campground.

The ruins proper—and the gorgeous trail network that runs through and around them—are officially open 6 A.M.–6 P.M. Depending on the time of year, these hours may interfere with visitors' plans to watch the sun rise or set from the top of Templo IV (due to dangerously slick limestone and degradation of the ruins, climbing to

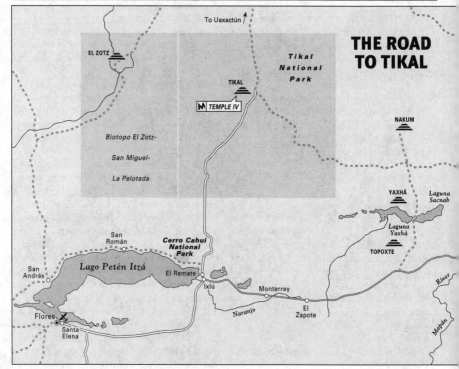

THE ROAD TO TIKAL

the top of the other structures that rise above the tree canopy is often prohibited). Some say you can talk with the ticket control officers to get special permission to enter early or stay late, but this could not be verified. A ticket purchased after 3 P.M. is valid for the next day; you'll need to show it to ticket control when you enter the following morning. If you overnighted in the park and need a new ticket, you can purchase it right there at ticket control.

Walking the Site

The ruins of Tikal encompass six square miles and are connected by a fantastic, although sometimes confusing, trail system. This means you'll be doing quite a bit of walking, nearly all of it on flat ground—except, of course, when climbing the pyramids themselves. Prepare as you would for a nature hike rather than a museum visit—comfortable walking shoes, a snack, more water than you think you'll need,

and a rain jacket during the wet season (and also for the monkeys who take great pleasure in urinating on hikers—seriously). There are a number of shelters in case it really starts coming down, and a few beverage stands, but no food is available.

If you plan on spending a few days exploring the ruins (most agree that you need at least two full days to take it all in), hiring one of Tikal's 50 or so guides on your first foray in will get you oriented for further solo trips into the park. Guides are readily available at the visitors center, speak many different languages, and cost about US$10 per person for a 3.5 hour tour (this is the *colectivo* rate, personal guides are a bit more). As long as you stay on the trails among the ruins and within earshot of other visitors and park guards, you shouldn't need to worry about getting lost, but be advised: Tikal is surrounded by a vast and wild jungle and there are no fences or markers to denote the boundary. It is not unheard of for dis-

© AVALON TRAVEL PUBLISHING, INC.

The Great Plaza

One mile from the museum, this plaza, considered the heart of ancient Tikal, is highly complex in design. The Great Plaza covers three acres; its plastered floor, now covered with grass, is made of four layers, the earliest laid in 150 B.C. and the latest in A.D. 700. Two great temples, I and II, face each other across the plaza, around which are scattered palaces, altars, a ball court, and 70 stelae—the memorial stones carved of limestone that tell of Maya life and conquest. Terraces and stairways lead up and down into a plethora of architecturally intense buildings. Most of these palaces were ceremonial centers, but a few are believed to have been apartments. If you climbed and poked around into every structure at the Great Plaza, it would take you at least an entire day.

Temple I

Because of its grace, form, and balance, this is probably the most photographed temple at Tikal. Also known as the **Temple of the Giant Jaguar** (named for a carving on one of its lintels), it rises 172 feet above the East Plaza behind it. Nine sloping terraces mark its sides, and its roof comb sits 145 feet above the Great Plaza floor. Atop the building platform is a three-room temple. Its central stair was used by workmen to haul building materials to the top of the temple. It's believed to have been built in about A.D. 700 for King Ah-Cacau, who brought Tikal out of its dark ages after its defeat by Caracol. His tomb was found inside during the restoration, and some of the grave goods, including 180 jade ornaments, pearls, and bone carvings, are on display in the museum/visitors center.

Temple II

Called the **Temple of the Masks** for the carvings on its lintel, this smaller structure faces Temple I across the Great Plaza. One of the few Maya temples ever dedicated to a woman, it was built for Ah-Cacau's queen, and is smaller and less steep than his. It stands about 125 feet above the Great Plaza, though if its roof comb were intact, the temple would have stood close to 140 feet. Like its counterpart across the way, it also has

tracted visitors to find some old trail leading away from the ruins (be especially careful around Complex P, as one can easily end up on the road to Uaxactun).

Additional Information and Tour Guides

Wandering the ruins on your own is an unforgettable and perfectly enjoyable experience. However, a deep, deep well of additional knowledge about Tikal—from the construction and politics of the great Maya city, to the extraordinary excavation efforts, to the fascinating natural world that engulfs today's Tikal—is readily available. Start with archaeologist William Coe's *Tikal: A Handbook of the Ancient Maya Ruins,* which has the best map of the site, and continue your reading with any of the scores of books and articles that have been published about Tikal.

Cayo & Mount Pine Ridge

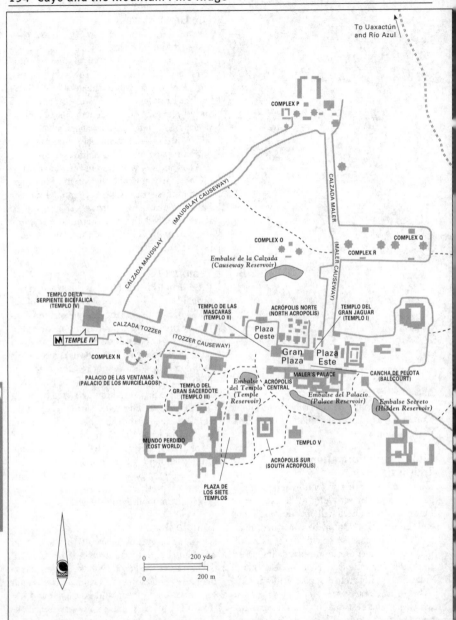

To Uaxactún
and Río Azul

COMPLEX P

CALZADA MALER

CALZADA MAUDSLAY
(MAUDSLAY CAUSEWAY)

COMPLEX O

COMPLEX Q

Embalse de la Calzada
(Causeway Reservoir)

COMPLEX R

(MALER CAUSEWAY)

TEMPLO DE LA
SERPIENTE BICEFÁLICA
(TEMPLO IV)

TEMPLO DE LAS
MASCARAS
(TEMPLO II)

ACRÓPOLIS NORTE
(NORTH ACROPOLIS)

TEMPLO DEL
GRAN JAGUAR
(TEMPLO I)

TEMPLE IV

CALZADA TOZZER

Plaza
Oeste

(TOZZER CAUSEWAY)

COMPLEX N

Gran
Plaza

Plaza
Este

PALACIO DE LAS VENTANAS
(PALACIO DE LOS MURCIÉLAGOS)

TEMPLO DEL
GRAN SACERDOTE
(TEMPLO III)

Embalse
del Templo
(Temple
Reservoir)

ACRÓPOLIS
CENTRAL

MALER'S PALACE

CANCHA DE PELOTA
(BALLCOURT)

Embalse del Palacio
(Palace Reservoir)

Embalse Secreto
(Hidden Reservoir)

MUNDO PERDIDO
(LOST WORLD)

TEMPLO V

ACRÓPOLIS SUR
(SOUTH ACROPOLIS)

PLAZA DE
LOS SIETE
TEMPLOS

0   200 yds

0   200 m

TIKAL

HOTEL TIKAL INN

JAGUAR INN

MUSEO TIKAL
(MUSEO SYLVANUS MORLEY)

HOTEL JUNGLE LODGE
(HOTEL POSADA DE LA SELVA)

CAMPING TIKAL

CAFÉ DEL
PARQUE

COMEDOR LA
JUNGLA TIKAL

Embalse Tikal
(Tikal Reservoir)

MUSEO DE LAS ESTELAS/
CENTRO DE VISITANTES
(VISITOR CENTER)

COMEDOR IMPERIO MAYA

To El Remate
and Flores

CALZADA MÉNDEZ

(MÉNDEZ CAUSEWAY)

TEMPLO DE LAS
INCRIPCIONES
(TEMPLO VI)

© AVALON TRAVEL PUBLISHING, INC.

three rooms at the crest. In front of Temple II lies a large block that archaeologists speculate served as a reviewing stand—priests standing on it could see the crowds in the plaza below and in turn they could be seen by all.

East Plaza

This immense plaza, east of the Great Plaza and backing up to the Temple of the Giant Jaguar, was once a formal plastered area covering 5.5 acres. Two of the city's causeways, **Mendez** and **Maler,** lead from here. This plaza is the site of the only known sweathouse at Tikal, and it's also the site of a ball court and what appears to be the marketplace. Trash and other evidence shows that the Maya continued to use the ball court after the collapse of Tikal in A.D. 900.

◪ Temple IV

It's another long walk, but follow your map and visit challenging Temple IV, the **Temple of the Double-Headed Serpent.** Facing east, it's a popular spot from which to watch the sunrise. The platform itself has not been excavated, and only those in good physical condition will want to climb the six ladders (sometimes all you can cling to are roots and branches) to the top. Yaxkin Caan Chac, the son and successor of Ah-Cacau, built Temple IV about 40 years after Temple I was built for his father. Today, Temple IV is the tallest surviving Maya structure from pre-Columbian history—212 feet from the base of its platform to the top. Not until the turn of the century, when elevators came along, were taller buildings constructed in this hemisphere. Temple IV also houses a three-room temple, with walls up to 40 feet thick. From the summit of Temple IV, the sight of the entire area is breathtaking. The jungle canopy itself rises 100 feet into the air, and the tops of the other white temples of Tikal rise above the tops of the trees.

Temple V

Though the climb to the top of Temple IV is strenuous, it pales in comparison with the ascent to the north-facing Temple V. Like Temple I, it was built about A.D. 700; it rises about 190 feet. After clambering through underbrush

SAFETY CONCERNS IN GUATEMALA

Guatemala has experienced considerably more political instability and domestic strife than its neighbor, Belize, in the last few decades; consequently, the country has, at times, been prone to bouts of desperation-fueled robberies and assaults. It is a rare traveler who has not heard stories about tourist-targeted crimes, especially in the Tikal area.

Rest assured: Although things are always apt to change, at the time of this writing, traveler security has never been better in Guatemala, thanks in large part to a new force of Tourist Police, called **Politur,** trained and assigned specifically to protect, inform, and aid visitors to the country's top destinations, including Tikal. There are about 425 officers in the country, with roughly 60 individuals assigned to both Tikal National Park and its approach road. Politur is made up of trained police officers, armed with pistols but still lacking in basic supplies, transportation, and English skills.

For timely, and no doubt conservative, security information as you depart for Guatemala, call the **State Department Travel Advisory Office** in Washington, D.C., 202/647-5225. Or for more detailed information, contact the **Guatemalan Embassy** in Washington, D.C., 202/745-4952.

to reach the top of the former stairway, hardy climbers have the option of hoisting themselves up through a hole in the roof comb that appears to have been dug sometime before archaeologists discovered Tikal. Some travelers have reported that the dark, forbidding interior of the roof comb contains ropes and ladders to gain access to the very top of Temple V, from which there is a remarkably focused view of the other temples of Tikal.

Hieroglyphs and Stelae

The earliest stela at Tikal, number 29, was probably carved in A.D. 292. The latest is number 11, carved in 869. In between, the stelae record the births and deaths of kings, the cycle of festivals and seasons, and sagas of war. Even a long pause in the production of stelae, beginning in 557 and ending in 692, has a story to tell. Mayanists have deduced (now that they have discovered how to read as much as 80 percent of Maya writing here and at other Maya sites) that Tikal lost a great battle with Caracol, and the hiatus coincides with Caracol's dominance of the region. The inscriptions of Tikal also show that a single dynasty ruled the kingdom from the Early Classic period until the society collapsed in A.D. 900. Yax-Moch-Xoc founded the line and ruled from about 219 to 238. Though he

was not the first leader to be memorialized at Tikal, he apparently was so magnificent that he was recognized as the founder of a dynasty—the inscriptions are the first in which the Maya recorded the concept of a founding ancestor. His descendants made up the royalty of Tikal. Among them were kings with nicknames like Great-Jaguar-Paw, Moon-Zero Bird (who took the throne in A.D. 320), and Curl-Snout (A.D. 379), all of whom followed the founder of the Tikal royal line, Yax-Moch-Xoc.

ACCOMMODATIONS AND FOOD

Accommodations within Tikal National Park obviously put you closest to the ruins, great for travelers who really want to focus on the pyramids and catch a sunrise or two. The majority of overnight Tikal visitors, however, book themselves in the island city of Flores or its sister town of Santa Elena, about an hour's drive southwest of the park; that's where you'll find the greatest quantity and widest range of lodging and restaurant options. Additionally, as security issues continue to improve and the number of visitors increase, the village of El Remate is an increasingly popular base camp; it is only 30 kilometers south of Tikal, boasts plentiful budget lodging and camping, and is a relaxed, lakeside destination in its own right.

At the Ruins

Hotel development in the park has been kept to a wonderfully *tranquilo* level, with only three hotels and one campground. This translates into a limited supply for a sometimes high demand, especially around Christmas, New Year's, and Easter, when reservations are recommended. Accommodations are very simple; most do not have 24-hour electricity or telephones (the latter means credit cards may not work). Each hotel has its own low-key dining room and shuttle services to Flores and the Belize border. Phone numbers listed here usually connect to a Santa Elena office.

The **Jaguar Inn** (tel. 502/926-0002, fax 502/926-2413, solis@quetzal.net) has dorm beds for about US$11, plus nicer lodge rooms with private bath and hot showers for US$30/48 s/d; camping (US$3.50) and mosquito-netted hammocks (US$6.50) also available. Electricity (private generator) is on until about 10 P.M.; candles are provided for later in the evening.

The **Jungle Lodge,** also called **Hotel Posada de la Selva** (tel. 502/476-8775, fax 502/476-0294 in Guatemala City, reservaciones@junglelodge.guate.com), offers rooms from US$26/31 to US$54/72 s/d. The 50 rooms have hot showers, ceiling fans and porches. A bit more upscale, the **Tikal Inn** (tel. 502/926-0065, US$81 per couple) has 17 bungalows and 11 rooms surrounding a pleasant swimming pool. Rates include breakfast and dinner. There is also a campground, run from an office in the visitors center, for about US$4 a person, with a central bathroom and shower house.

In addition to the hotel restaurants, there are three reasonably priced *comedores* near the visitors center. As for services, there is a post office in the visitors center. Internet is brand new in the park, with a satellite setup at Jaguar Inn with an Ethernet hookup and WiFi; more options are probably on the way.

El Remate

A village of about 300 families strung along the road to Tikal, El Remate is located on the east end of Lake Petén-Itza, 30 kilometers from both Flores and the park. Camping and budget accommodations are plentiful, as is transportation both north and south. Although El Remate serves most travelers as a convenient, relaxed base camp for their Tikal experience, this is also the gateway to the **Biotopo Cerro Cahuí,** a 650-hectare broadleaf forest preserve located a short walk along the road that breaks off to follow the north shore of the lake. The Biotopo boasts an excellent six-kilometer trail with the chance to see a few of the 300 bird species, 40 mammal species, 20 reptile and amphibian species, and 20 species of fish that have been identified here. There are also great views of the lake.

El Remate is located just a few minutes' drive north of the junction at Ixlu. There are basic services here, plus a nice row of craft huts along the west side of the road, featuring Guatemalan textiles, wood carvings, jade pieces, and more. Stop in for a cold Gallo at **La Canoa de San Pablo**—great coffee, too, to drink by candlelight as you strain your eyes to look at the crafts for sale.

There are plenty of new accommodations going up in El Remate, so be sure to poke around before making a decision. There are several campgrounds near the south end of town, including the longstanding backpacker-friendly **Camping y Hospedaje Sal Itzá,** set back from the road on the right, with thatched structures and mosquito-netted mattresses, or campsites for less than US$3 pp. There are a few funky places built into the hillside on the right as you continue into town, including the **Mirador del Duende** (The Dwarf's Lookout), with open bungalows for under US$5 pp. Camping is available, and there are great sunset lakeviews and a reasonable vegetarian restaurant. A bit farther north, on the left, the **Hotel Sun Breeze** is an excellent choice, with simple rooms with shared bath for US$5/7 s/d and a very friendly staff.

Just after the Hotel Sun Breeze, the road to Cerro Cahuí splits to the left to follow the lakeshore, while the main highway continues north; the Centro de Salud (Health Clinic) and police station are here on your right. At the road junction, you'll find the lost gringo himself in the **Casa de Don David**—El Remate's long-standing meeting place, homestyle restaurant, and mid-range hotel. Don David (tel. 502/306-2190, info@lacasadedondavid.com) charges US$16/20 s/d with cold water, US$20/26 with hot (or at least warm) showers. Great food, lots of tourist information, friendly and family-run. Located back toward the south a half mile or so, the **Mansione del Pajaro Serpiente** (tel. 502/702-9434) offers a group of hillside cottages with hot water and private bath from US$10–20 pp; there's a restaurant, and two swimming pools built into natural rock.

Don David's original project in Guatemala was a hippie campground on the north shore of the lake, 2.8 kilomters west of the Cerro Cahuí junction, which developed into a well-known hotel called **El Gringo Perdido** (tel. 502/334-2305 in Guatemala City); about US$15 pp, basic rooms with beach access and a restaurant. Ask around the junction in El Remate about transportation.

An upscale hotel, the **Westin Camino Real Tikal** (US tel. 800/937-8461, Guat. tel. 502/926-0204, caminor@infovia.com.gt), is about 40 minutes away from the Tikal site, in the village of San José Petén (4.5 kilometers west of the Cerro Cahuí junction). Spacious bungalows go for about US$120 (luxurious bathrooms, a/c, minibars, international telephone service, cable TV, and individual balconies overlooking the lake); the hotel is on a lovely site on 220 acres above Lake Petén-Itza. The hotel offers a wide selection of sporting options, including hiking, swimming, fishing, canoeing, bicycling, sailboarding, and sailing. In the main building, guests will find a full-service restaurant, swimming pool, snack bar, lounge, and lakeview bar open till midnight. Custom Tikal trips and transport are available as well.

Flores and Santa Elena

Flores, about an hour by road from Tikal (60 km), is historically the most popular overnight spot for Tikal visitors, especially since the airstrip was relocated to its sister city, Santa Elena.

In *Moon Handbooks Guatemala,* Wayne Bernhardson writes, "the island city of Flores has greater intrinsic charm than almost any other Guatemalan town—its irregular street pattern and narrow, circuitous alleyways give it a medieval feeling, and the many gingerbread porches and balconies add a touch of vernacular architectural distinction."

Flores and Santa Elena host the full gamut of services, transportation, and accommodations from roachy dives to the lap of luxury.

GETTING THERE AND AWAY
By Air

Many visitors opt to come by plane, and flights are available from Belize, Guatemala, and Mexico Cities. Flights from Belize's Philip Goldson International Airport are scheduled on Tropic Air (US$186 round-trip). The airport in Flores (tel. 502/926-0348) is newish and modern, much more so than the town it services.

By Ground

Most Belize tourists who sign up for a trip to Tikal will have all their transportation taken care of, either in a private shuttle from Belize City, San Ignacio, or directly from their resort or lodge. Independent (i.e., patient and tolerant) travelers should also have no problem piecing together their own route to the ruins, or to any of the nearby towns.

The road in Guatemala is terrible, and it will take about 1.5 hours to reach the entrance to Tikal National Park, after which the road is excellent for the final 30 miles to the site itself. There is no direct public transportation from the Belize border to Tikal (except in chartered taxis and mini-buses, a good option for groups). The only bus that runs from the border is a Guatemala public bus that goes to Flores. You can spend the night here and take the morning bus to Tikal (board in front of the San Juan Hotel). The border-to-Flores bus is usually very crowded with chickens and the works. Or get off at the crossroads in Ixlu, where another northbound bus can whisk you to El Remate or all the way to Tikal.

From Belize City

You can always go to Novelo's, catch a local bus to

the border, then walk across and go it alone from there, making all your own connections. If, however, you are less confident in your Spanish and would rather go direct for a few dollars more, there are at least four small, private tour companies, all based at their various kiosks in the Water Taxi Terminal by the Swing Bridge in Belize City, that offer direct bus service to Chetumal, Mexico and Flores and Tikal, Guatemala. They are: **S & L Travel and Tours** (tel. 501/227-7593 or 227-5145, sltravel@btl.net, www.sltravelbelize.com), **Mundo Maya Deli, Gifts, Travel & Tours** (tel. 501/223-1235, mundomayatravel@btl.net), **Kaisa International,** and **San Juan Tours.** Daily, direct service is available to both Flores (US$15) and Tikal (US$20). It takes about 4.5 hours to either one, although border hassles can increase that time significantly. From Flores it's another 8 hours or so to Guatemala City, 12 to Antigua.

From Cayo

Mexican bus lines Linea Dorada and San Juan both stop at **Amigos Belize** (tel. 501/603-9436, www.amigosbelize.com), a tour operator located at the Santa Elena end of the Hawksworth Bridge, where you can buy bus tickets to anywhere in Mexico.

THE BORDER AT MELCHOR

The western *frontera* into Guatemala is a quick 11 miles from San Ignacio, a trip made for less than US$2 pp in a *colectivo* taxi, less in a passing bus bound for Benque Viejo. A private taxi from San Ignacio should cost less than US$15 total. Inquire around San Ignacio, or in Eva's for times. Be prepared to pay your US$15 exit fee on the Belizean side (every cent of which goes to the private "Border Management" company, a point of contention for local tour providers and would-be Guatemala day trippers). You may also be asked to pay a US$4 "PACT" tax, which goes to Belize's protected area system; ironically, this is money well-spent, but not always collected. Expect the usual throng of money-changers to greet you on both sides of the border—they're fine to use, as long as you know what rate you should be getting—or you can use the official Casas de Cambio on either side.

If you're driving your own car, make sure you have all the necessary papers of ownership, which they *will* want to see. You are required by law to have your tires fumigated, for which the cost is a few Belizean dollars.

After clearing Guatemalan immigration and shaking off the sometimes aggressive *taxistas,* you'll find yourself on the edge of the Mopan River, across which begins the town of **Melchor de Mencos.** Before crossing the bridge, you'll find the **Río Mopan Lodge** (tel. 502/926-5126, info@tikaltravel.com) on your left, a nice riverside hotel and restaurant, whose proprietors (a Swiss–Spanish couple) are a wealth of information on remote ruins in the area; riverside rooms go for US$15 s/d with private bath. There are a number of other places in Melchor if you get stranded in town for some reason, or are embarking on your own jungle expedition to unexplored ruins.

Once across the border, it's pretty easy sailing, but keep a couple of things in mind. When passing military camps (and you will pass several on the way to Tikal), do not take *any* photos. If you're aiming your lens at the lovely river and the water happens to flow in front of the guard station, you can get into difficulties, no matter how innocent it seems to you. The Guatemala military is very touchy. Don't be surprised if you're stopped by the military and asked for your papers several times; keep your passport and visitor's permit handy, smile and answer all questions, and you'll soon be on your way.

Dangriga and the Southern Coast

Stann Creek District is unique for being the second-smallest and also one of the most diversely jam-packed of Belize's six districts. To visit the attractions of this area is to experience a microcosm of nearly everything Belize has to offer. Naturally and culturally diverse, Stann Creek contains a range of worlds: To the east, long stretches of beach are stepping stones to underwater worlds and hundreds of deserted islands. To the west, jungles, jaguars, monkeys, rivers, and ruins lie in the shadows of Belize's highest peaks. In Dangriga and the surrounding villages, the Garinagu (or Garifuna) people sur-

vive and thrive, continuing to confront the challenges inherent in maintaining such a close and unique culture. Spanish-speaking fishermen paddle through the cayes, diving for lobster and conch for days on end.

The economy is varied here as well, with tourism being just as important as the citrus, banana, and shrimp industries. According to the Belize Tourism Board, Stann Creek is the fastest-growing tourism region in the country, although only along the Placencia Peninsula is the rapid development at all apparent.

For the choosy traveler, there is plenty to

pick from. There are full-on tourist destinations like Placencia with its ramshackle village, strings of resorts, and post-hurricane optimism. Right up the coast, there are low-key, slack-paced towns like Hopkins and Sittee River; while Dangriga's roots throb in the streets, home to a third of Stann Creek District's 33,000 inhabitants. Any one of these areas can be used as a base to explore nearby cayes, coral, and the Cockscomb Basin.

PLANNING YOUR TIME

Want to plant yourself in the sand and have drinks brought to you for a week? Pick a resort, any resort—there is a wide range from which to choose. If you'd rather go deep, though, there is enough in this one district of Belize to entertain a curious traveler for weeks. Here's the ultimate Stann Creek tour for someone with an open mind and lots of vacation time: Start by turning off the Hummingbird Highway to visit **Five Blues Lake National Park,** camping and hiking for a few days. Continue with a week in **Dangriga, Hopkins,** and **Sittee River,** getting a feel for the Garinagu way of living; take a drumming lesson and sample some home-brewed bitters. Then turn back into the hills, trekking into **Mayflower National Park** for a couple of days before bouncing down the road to spend a night in **Maya Center.** Here you can shop for local crafts, converse with herbal healers, and arrange a **Maya Mountain** expedition across the **Cockscomb Basin Wildlife Sanctuary** with a local guide whose last gig was leading a *National Geographic* team in the same area.

Then triumphantly descend back to the shoreline and charter a sailboat to play pirate in the cayes; strand yourself for a week in **Glover's Atoll** and attempt to photograph a whale shark or manta ray. Finally, run your boat aground on the **Placencia Peninsula** and rent a cheap cabana in which to recuperate and process how much you just experienced in only one tiny slice of this incredible country.

Of course, if you've only got a week, simply pick and choose from the above list and plan according to your needs; day trips are available to nearly everywhere and you can't go wrong.

THE LAND AND PEOPLE

Stann Creek District begins just after the **Over the Top** pass on the Hummingbird Highway, the surrounding rainforest thick with broadleaf greens, delicate ferns, bromeliads, and orchids. As you approach Dangriga, the wilderness gives way to vast groves of citrus, and finally, the coastal plain and offshore world beyond.

Over the millennia, rivers and streams gushing from the Maya Mountains have deposited a rich layer of fertile soil, making the coastal and valley regions ideal farming areas. The banana industry, once vital in the area, was wiped out by a disease called "Panama Rot" many years back. However, with new technology, a strain of bananas has been developed that appears to be surviving and promises to grow into a profitable operation. Stann Creek's citrus industry produces Valencia oranges and grapefruit, which are then processed (on-site) into juice—one of Belize's most important exports. The business center of the citrus industry, Dangriga has rebounded with

CITRUS FARMS

Stann Creek offers excellent conditions for raising citrus fruit, first introduced into the country in the early 1920s. Nine hundred grafted trees were imported from Florida, and with a great deal of TLC, they won blue ribbons at agricultural shows in England in 1928–31. But as much as the Europeans were impressed with Belizean oranges, freight costs made shipping the whole fruit impossible and they had to be content with the juice.

Over the years, despite fluctuating prices and hurricanes that have flattened the trees, a combination of external events has given the Belizean citrus industry a big boost. In 1983, President Reagan removed taxes from Caribbean-grown citrus. Soon after, severe frosts damaged and limited fruit production in Florida and Texas, followed by a canker disease on Florida citrus that dealt another blow for the U.S. citrus industry. This enabled Belize to get a toehold in trading, and it has been climbing ever since.

Dangriga & Southern Coast

Must-Sees

Look for **M** to find the sights and activities you can't miss and **N** for the best dining and lodging.

M **Tobacco Caye:** Sitting right atop Belize's Barrier Reef, Tobacco Caye can be as much a social gathering of world travelers as it can an isolated, island experience, depending on the time of year (page 172).

M **Hopkins:** This village is on an ultra-tranquil stretch of beach and, along with nearby Sittee River Village, can serve as an uncrowded base for canoeing, diving, sailing, windsurfing, fishing, and other trips (page 177).

Tobacco Caye

M **Cockscomb Basin Wildlife Sanctuary:** Go for a nature hike and river float in this extensive reserve, famous for its multitude of birds, jaguar tracks, and other jungle critters. Stay overnight or do it as a day trip from anywhere in the area (page 181).

M **The Sidewalk Strip:** In Belize's most up-and-coming low-key tourist hang, **Placencia,** check

out the world's narrowest street—it's 4,071 feet long and 4 feet wide. Walking its length offers ample opportunities for shopping, eating, and getting a sense of village life (page 191).

M **Monkey River:** A pleasant half-day outing from Placencia, the boat trip up Monkey River to the village of the same name is excellent for bird-watching as well as seeing crocodiles and monkeys (page 200).

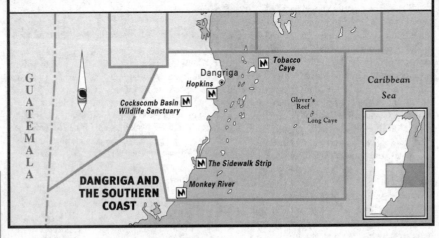

© JOSHUA BERMAN

Dangriga & Southern Coast

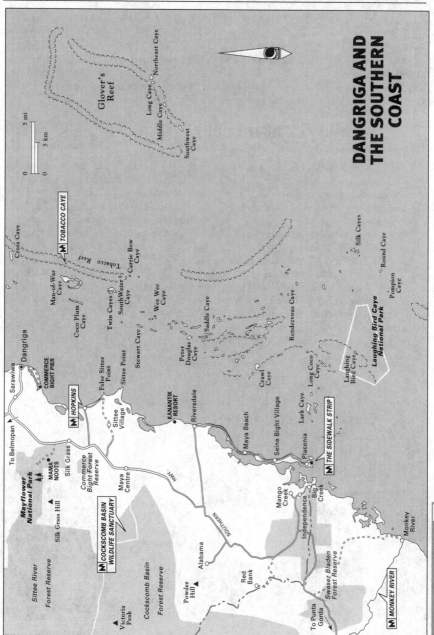

DANGRIGA AND THE SOUTHERN COAST

Glover's Reef
Northeast Cave
Long Cave
Middle Cave
Southwest Cave

5 mi
5 km
0

Cross Caye
TOBACCO CAYE
Tobacco Reef
Man-of-War Caye
Coco Plum Caye
Carrie Bow Caye
Twin Caves
SouthWater Caye
Wee Wee Caye
Saddle Caye
Stewart Caye
Peter Douglas Caye
Rendezvous Caye
Silk Cayes
Round Caye
Pompion Caye
Laughing Bird Caye National Park
Laughing Bird Cave
Crawl Caye
Long Coco Caye
Lark Cave

Dangriga
Sarawiwa
COMMERCE BIGHT PIER
To Belmopan
HOPKINS
False Sittee Point
Sittee Point
Sittee Village
KANANTIK RESORT
Riversdale
Maya Beach
Seine Bight Village
Placencia
THE SIDEWALK STRIP

Mayflower National Park
MAMA NOOTS
Silk Grass Hill
Silk Grass
Commerce Bight Forest Reserve
Maya Centre
COCKSCOMB BASIN WILDLIFE SANCTUARY
Sittee River Forest Reserve
Cockscomb Basin Forest Reserve
Victoria Peak
Powder Hill
Alabama
Red Bank
SOUTHERN HWY.
Mango Creek
Big Creek
Independence
Swasey Bladen Forest Reserve
To Punta Gorda
Monkey River
MONKEY RIVER

N
Dangriga & Southern Coast

© AVALON TRAVEL PUBLISHING, INC.

vigor since being wiped out by Hurricane Hattie in 1961.

The indigenous population of southern Belize dates back 3,600 years and the Mopan Maya are still well represented, especially in towns like Maya Center and other villages in these hills. The earliest white settlers were Puritans from the island of New Providence in the Bahamas. These simple-living people began a trading post (also known as a "stand," which over time deteriorated to "Stann"), and spread south into the Placencia area. The town's destiny was drastically altered when the first boats of Garinagu people reached the shore from Roatan.

Dangriga

"Mabuiga!" shouts the sign in the Garifuna tongue, welcoming you to this cultural hub and district capital. Built on the Caribbean shoreline and straddling North Stann Creek (or Gumagarugu River), Dangriga's primary boast is its status as the Garinagu people's original port of entry into Belize—and their modern day ethnic center as well. But although the majority of Dangriga's 11,000 or so inhabitants are Garinagu descendants of that much-celebrated 1823 landing, the rest are a typically rich mix of Chinese, Creoles, mestizos, and Maya, all of whom can be seen interacting on the town's main drag.

Aside from Dangriga's ideal location for accessing the surrounding mountains and seas—and the limited, but adequate tourist infrastructure available to do so—its chief attraction may just be its total lack of pretense. Dangriga (formerly known as Stann Creek Town) does not outwardly cater to its foreign visitors as does Placencia or San Pedro—there is simply too much else going on in this commercial center (like fishing, farming, and serving the influx of Stann Creek villagers who come weekly to stock up on supplies) for the people to need to put all their eggs in the tourism basket.

If poking around the casually bustling vibe of Dangriga (which, by the way, means something

Dangriga is an unassuming cultural and commercial hub, located where the Hummingbird Highway ends at the Caribbean Ocean.

© JOSHUA BERMAN

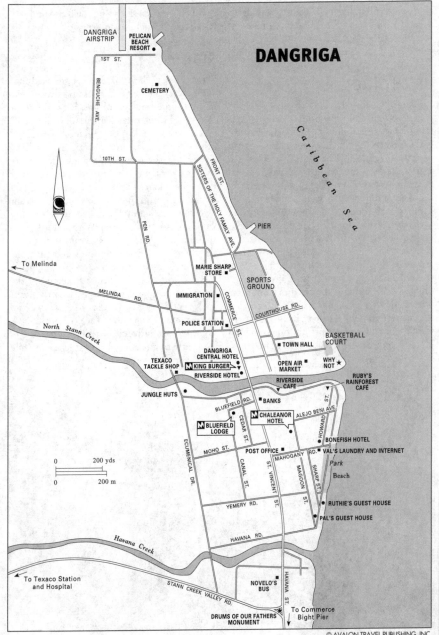

DANGRIGA

DANGRIGA AIRSTRIP

PELICAN BEACH RESORT

1ST ST.

BENGUCHE AVE.

CEMETERY

10TH ST.

FRONT ST.

SISTERS OF THE HOLY FAMILY AVE.

PIER

PEN RD.

To Melinda

MELINDA RD.

North Stann Creek

MARIE SHARP STORE

IMMIGRATION

COMMERCE ST.

SPORTS GROUND

COURTHOUSE RD.

POLICE STATION

Caribbean Sea

BASKETBALL COURT

TEXACO TACKLE SHOP

DANGRIGA CENTRAL HOTEL

TOWN HALL

KING BURGER

RIVERSIDE HOTEL

OPEN AIR MARKET

WHY NOT

RUBY'S RAINFOREST CAFE

JUNGLE HUTS

RIVERSIDE CAFE

BLUEFIELD RD.

BANKS

CEDAR ST.

CHALEANOR HOTEL

ALEJO BENI AVE.

HOWARD ST.

BLUEFIELD LODGE

MOHO ST.

POST OFFICE

MAHOGANY RD.

BONEFISH HOTEL

VAL'S LAUNDRY AND INTERNET

ECUMENICAL DR.

CANAL ST.

ST. VINCENT ST.

MAGOON ST.

SHARP ST.

Park

Beach

YEMERY RD.

RUTHIE'S GUEST HOUSE

PAL'S GUEST HOUSE

0   200 yds

0   200 m

To Texaco Station and Hospital

Havana Creek

HAVANA RD.

HAVANA ST.

STANN CREEK VALLEY RD.

NOVELO'S BUS

To Commerce Bight Pier

DRUMS OF OUR FATHERS MONUMENT

© AVALON TRAVEL PUBLISHING, INC.

Dangriga & Southern Coast

like "sweet, still waters" in Garifuna) sounds intriguing, you'd do well to stay a couple nights as you pass between surf and turf. And if it's culture you're looking for, just listen for the drumming.

ORIENTATION

Speaking of drums, that's exactly what will greet you as you pull into town: three massive ceremonial *dugu* drums of iron. This is the "Drums of Our Fathers Monument," erected in 2003 as a symbol of Garinagu pride—and as a call to war against the ills of society. Turn right to reach the deep dock at Commerce Bight, continue straight ahead for a dip in the ocean, and left to enter Dangriga. Heading north from the drums on St. Vincent Street, the Novelo's Bus Terminal is on your left before the first bridge. Continuing on, you'll find more commercial activity, culminating in the center of town on either side of the North Stann Creek Bridge; crossing the bridge, St. Vincent Street turns into Commerce Street and offers just that, with an informal market often set up along the north bank of the river. Catch a boat out of town from one of several places here. The airstrip is located a mile or so

north of Stann Creek, where you'll also find Pelican Beach, Dangriga's only resort.

SIGHTS

Dangriga is the heart of Garinagu folk culture, and most of the town's attractions involve seeking out some evidence of this. However, until the proposed Garinagu Museum is finally built, you'll have to seek it out on your own. Dangriga does not offer many traditional "sights," per se, but there is plenty going on and the town makes a good base for excursions around the region. Start your tour by browsing several of the crafts and music stores on St. Vincent Street, and ask around for the drum-making workshops—start at the big **Why Not** palapa by the beach. Drums are often heard throughout the town to mark celebrations and funerals; sometimes it's simply a few people practicing the rhythms of their history. Seeking out the town's workshops can be a fun activity, and if you've got the cash, expect to walk away with an instrument of your own. Austin Rodriquez is known for his authentic Garinagu drums. Other local artists of national prominence include

Dangriga laundry dries quickly in the hot ocean breeze.

© DANIELLE VAUGHN

painter Benjamin Nicholas and Mercy Sabal, who makes colorful dolls that are sold all over the country.

Hiking or biking out to watch the sun set from **Gra Gra Lagoon** will kill a few hours, as will renting a canoe to paddle around there for the afternoon; inquire at the Friends of Gra Gra Lagoon office, diagonally across from the bus station. As for other sights, they include a walk along the beach or a hang near the bridge in the center of town where you'll watch Dangriga buzz the day away.

This area is still relatively undeveloped for tourism, which is either a shortcoming or an attraction, depending on what kind of traveler you are. For more ideas and local wisdom, contact **C & G Tours and Charters** (29 Oak St., tel. 501/522-3641 or 522-3379, cgtours@btl.net), a locally owned and highly recommended tour operator.

ENTERTAINMENT

Dangriga is home to the Warribaggabagga Dancers, the Punta Rebels, the Turtle Shell Band, and the Griga Boyz, among other nationally known party bands. The music and dancing, including syncopated African rhythms, is an enchanting mixture of the various cultures of southern Belize. There is often live music on weekends at **Griga 2000,** right near the main bridge, and sometimes at the **Malibu Beach Club** on the north end of town as well. Be advised that karaoke, especially to American country music, is very popular round these parts.

The biggest celebrations of the year are Settlement Day (November 19), Boxing Day (December 26), and New Year's Day, when drumming, dancing, and drinking are common in the streets. At other times of the year, many hotels can arrange a special cultural event for you.

ACCOMMODATIONS
Under US$25
Dangriga's main drag has a handful of low-budget options, like the **Dangriga Central Hotel** (119 Commerce St., tel. 501/522-2008), just

north of the main North Stann Creek bridge, with rooms as low as US$7.50 and balconies overlooking "downtown" 'Griga; you can also see if the **Riverside Hotel** (5 Commerce St., tel. 501/522-2168) suits your fancy (and wallet). For budget on the beach, though, head straight for the three simple cabanas at **Ruthie's** (tel. 501/522-3184, US$25/30 s/d). The **Chaleanor** has a row of economy rooms as well (see later listing under US$25–50).

For just a few more dollars, the **Bluefield Lodge** (6 Bluefield Rd., tel. 501/522-2742, bluefield@btl.net, US$14/17 s/d shared bath; US$19/25 s/d private) is an excellent choice. The owner, Miss Louise, has six attractively furnished rooms with fans and h/c water. Everything about the place bespeaks the pride and care she takes in her lodge and there are great local maps and an information board.

Pal's Guest House (868 Magoon St., tel. 501/522-2095 or 522-2365, palbz@btl.net), on the beach and around the corner from the bus station, has 20 clean, modest cement rooms at the corner of North Havana Road and Magoon Street. Rooms with shared bath in the back building cost US$9/14 s/d; seaside rooms (about US$33 s/d) have linoleum floors, ceiling fans, h/c private showers, TV, and balconies with views of the ocean; louvered windows on both ends of the rooms create good cross-ventilation.

US$25–50
The towering **Chaleanor Hotel** (35 Magoon St., tel. 501/522-2587, chaleanor@btl.net) charges US$27/37 s/d, plus has 8 economy rooms with shared bath for US$10/15 s/d. Friendly and tirelessly accommodating owners Chad and Eleanor offer a homey atmosphere in a residential neighborhood. Ten rooms have private baths, hot water, and some have TV and a/c. Laundry service is available. There's a gift counter in the lobby, and you can also help yourself to the tray with coffee and bananas in the morning. A rooftop restaurant and bar is coming soon. Numerous tour operators book their guests in the Chaleanor, sometimes arranging a drumming or dance session on the roof.

Just a bit up North Stann Creek, but still in the

GARINAGU (GARIFUNA) SETTLEMENT DAY

The hour before dawn, we make our way through the darkness along the edge of the sea heading toward the persistent beat of distant drums. Orange streaks begin to widen across the horizon as we climb over a half-fallen wooden bridge spanning a creek, cutting a muddy path to the Caribbean. We are on our way to Dangriga on Garinagu Settlement Day, one of Belize's lively national holidays, celebrated each year on November 19 to commemorate the arrival of the Garinagu people to Belize.

Rains that had been pouring down for a week subsided only a few hours ago, and by the time we reach the center of town and the river shoreline, crowds of revelers are beginning to gather in the breaking dawn. This is a day of reflection and good times in Belize, a severe contrast to Garinagu beginnings that for decades were filled with misery and tragedy.

Settlement Day is a happy celebration. Everyone dresses in colorful new clothes, and while waiting for the "landing," family, friends, and strangers from all over Belize catch up on local gossip, make new acquaintances, and enjoy the party. Sounds of beating drums emanate from small circles of people on both sides of the river, from the backs of pickup trucks, and from

Garifuna settlement day is celebrated up and down the coast of Belize on November 19.

rooftops. In lieu of drums, young men push through the crowds shouldering giant boomboxes that broadcast the beat. Excitement (and umbrellas) hangs in the air as the assemblage waits for the canoes and the beginning of the pageant.

Now, in the early dawn, the crowd cheers. It spots two dugout canoes paddling from the open sea into the river. Years ago, the first refugees from Roatan crowded into just such boats along with a few meager necessities to start a new life in a new land. Today's reenactment is orchestrated according to verbal history handed down through generations. Leaves and vines are wrapped around the arrivals' heads and waists. Drums, baskets that carry simple cooking utensils, young banana trees, and cassava roots are all among the precious cargo the Garinagu originally brought to start their new lives in Dangriga.

The canoes paddle past cheering crowds; each November is a reminder of the past, and even outsiders are swept along in the excitement and thoughts of what this day represents to the Garinagu citizens of Belize.

The canoes travel up the river and under the bridge and back again so that everyone lining the bank and bridge can see them. When the "actors" come ashore, they're joined by hundreds of onlookers. The colorful procession then winds through the narrow streets with young and old dancing and singing to the drumbeats; they proudly lead the parade to the Catholic church, where a special service takes place. Dignitaries from all over Belize attend and tell of the past and, most important, of the hopes of the future.

The Catholic church plays a unique part in the life of the Garinagu: Some years back, the church reached an unspoken, working agreement with the Garinagu. It's nothing formal, just a look-the-other-way attitude while their Garinagu parishioners mix Catholic dogma with ancient ritual. It wasn't always this way. For generations, the people were forced to keep their religion alive in clandestine meetings or suffer severe punishment and persecution.

Rain, much like time, has not stopped the Garinagu celebrations nor the dancing that is an integral part of the festivities. Street dances (traditionally held along village streets for many nights leading up to Settlement Day) continue and are moved indoors to escape the flooded streets. Small bars and open *palapa* (thatch) structures are crowded with fun-lovers and reverberate with the pounding of exotic triple drums (always three). Drums bring their magic, and parties continue with both modern *punta* rock and traditional dances into the early hours of the morning. The Garinagu are a people filled with music. The songs sung in the Garifuna language tell stories—some happy, some sad—and many melodies go hand-in-hand with daily tasks.

At an open *palapa* hut, three talented drummers begin the beat. The old Garinagu women, heavily influenced by their African beginnings, insist on marshaling the dances the old way. The first tempo is the *paranda,* a dance just for women. A circle is created in the dirt-floored room and the elderly women begin a low-key, heavy-footed, repetitive shuffle with subtle hand movements accompanied by timeworn words that we don't understand but are told tell a tale of survival.

Every few minutes a reveler filled with too much rum pushes through the circle of people and joins the dancing women. He's quickly chased out of the ring by an umbrella-wielding elder who aims her prods at the more vulnerable spots of his body. If that doesn't work, she resorts to pulling the intoxicated dancer off the floor by his ear—a little comic relief that adds to the down-home entertainment.

The *paranda* continues, and little kids energetically join in the dances on the outside of the "circle" or watch wide-eyed from the rafters near the top of the *palapa* roof, entranced by the beat, dim light, and music—the magic of the holiday. The recurring rain adds an extra beat to the exotic cadence of the drums; dance after dance continues.

The *huguhugn* dance is open to everyone, but the sexy *punta* is the popular favorite, with one couple at a time in the ring. Handsome men and beautiful women slowly undulate their bodies with flamboyant grace and sexual suggestion. This is the courtship dance born in African roots. If you miss Settlement Day parties, stop by a bar or nightclub anywhere in Belize and you'll see locals doing a modern version called *"punta* rock."

During Settlement Day, a walk down the narrow streets takes you past small parties and family gatherings under stilted houses where dancing and singing is the rule; others enjoy holiday foods (including cassava bread) and drinks. If invited to share a cup of coffee dipped from an old blue porcelain kettle heavily laced with rum, join in—it could turn out to be the best part of the celebration!

center of town, **Jungle Huts Hotel** (Ecumenical Dr., tel. 501/522-2142, fax 501/522-3166) is run by the local dentist, Arthur Usher, and his wife, Beverly. You'll find hot water, tiled private bathrooms, pleasant furniture, and two double beds in each of the four rooms in the main building. Some have a/c. In addition, there are four basic cabanas of a rustic Belizean design. All feature private h/c baths or showers. The hotel and its cabanas are very secure (behind the Usher home). The whole family is very friendly, and you have more of a feeling of staying with relatives than with strangers. US$25 for basic rooms; US$37 for TV and private bath.

US$75–100

The **Bonefish Hotel** (15 Mahogany St., tel. 501/522-2243, US$50/75 s/d) is near the water with 10 rooms and a second-floor lobby and bar. It caters to active travelers who want to tour the area, fish, or dive. The resort is allied with Blue Marlin Lodge on South Water Caye. Rooms are clean and carpeted. Upstairs rooms have private h/c water baths, minibar, cable TV, and a/c; the Bonefish accepts Visa and MasterCard.

'Griga's high end is found at the north end of town, at the end of Ecumenical Drive, right next to the airstrip: The **Pelican Beach Resort** (tel. 501/522-2044, fax 501/522-2570, sales@pelicanbeachbelize.com, www.southwatercaye.com) rests comfortably on the Caribbean and makes a wonderful base for exploring both offshore and inland sights. Various rate packages are available that include meal plans, excursions, and time spent at the Pelican's sister resort on South Water Caye (see the Islands Near Dangriga section). Rooms run from US$63/85 s/d, with fan and no porch, up to US$80/101 s/d, with a/c, TV, and phone; prices include all taxes.

FOOD

Most of Dangriga's eateries are open only during meal times, so expect some closed doors in the middle of the afternoon and, of course, on Sundays. Your best value is probably **N King Burger,** located on the left as you cross the North Stann Creek bridge from the south (7 A.M.–3 P.M. and

5 P.M.–11 P.M. Mon.–Sat.). There's an excellent breakfast menu, fresh juices, sandwiches, shakes, and dinners.

Another standby is the **Riverside Café** (7 A.M.–9 P.M. six or seven days a week), run by sisters Ronnie and MJ. It's popular with travelers (boats to the cayes leave from right outside), and a gathering spot for local fishermen and folks with tourist businesses on the cayes. If you want to witness a real slice of Dangriga, set up camp at the bar here, order a Guinness with your eggs and beans, and watch the deals go down. If, however, you agree with a number of locals (both Belizeans and expats) that the Riverside is overhyped and over-priced, walk back to the main drag and grab a fistful of street tacos for pennies. Street barbecues are another common sight, offering a plate of grilled chicken served with flour tortillas, beans, and coleslaw for about US$2.50.

There's also **Ruby's Rainforest Café,** just downstream from the Riverside, on a breezy corner where North Stann Creek flows into the Caribbean. Ruby's serves casual breakfast, lunch, and dinner. Opening hours vary; stew lobster with rice is US$5.

Tired of rice and beans? There is a plethora of Chinese restaurants, the highest rated of which is the **N Starlight** (8 A.M.–11 P.M., closed afternoons), on the north side of Commerce Street; plus fried chicken to go at any number of Chinese shops. Dangriga's most upscale restaurant is found a short cab ride away at the **Pelican Beach Resort;** delicious food is prepared by Creole cooks and served in the dining room or in an open beachside eating area.

SERVICES

Belize Bank (8 A.M.–1 P.M. Mon.–Thurs., 8 A.M.–4:30 P.M. Fri.) and **Scotia Bank** (similar hours, but open 9 A.M.–noon Sat.,) are on St. Vincent Street near the bridge and **First Caribbean** is across the bridge; all have ATMs. Mail your postcards at the **post office** on Mahogany Road.

Val's Laundry and Internet (tel. 501/502-3324, www.valsbelize.com, 7:30 A.M.– 7 P.M.

South Stann Creek meets the Caribbean in Dangriga Town.

Mon.–Sat., plus Sun. mornings) is near the post office on Sharp Street. Fast and friendly satellite Internet is available for US$2.50 an hour, as well as FedEx service, local information, and organic, fresh-squeezed juices.

Health and Emergencies

Southern Regional Hospital, "the only fully air-conditioned hospital in the country," is located just out of town and services the entire population of Stann Creek District (tel. 501/522-2078 or 522-2225, dannhis@btl.net).

GETTING THERE AND AWAY

Dangriga is on the coast, only 36 miles south of Belize City as the crow (or local airline) flies. However, the land trip is much longer, roughly 75 miles along the Manatee Road or 100 miles via the Hummingbird Highway.

By Air

Maya Island Air (US tel. 800/225-6732, Bel. tel. 501/223-1140, mayair@btl.net, www.mayaislandair.com) and **Tropic Air** (US tel. 800/422-3435, Bel. tel. 501/226-2012, reservations@tropicair.com, www.tropicair.com) have a number of daily 20-minute flights between Belize City and Dangriga. It's also possible to fly between Dangriga, Placencia, Big Creek, and Punta Gorda.

By Boat

Boat service from Belize City is entirely custom-arranged—they tried running a regularly scheduled shuttle, but it didn't make money. Ask around the docks by the Texaco station, at your hotel, or at the Belize Tourism Board. Expect to pay a decent sum for this trip (probably US$100 each way). Service to and from local cayes or other coastal villages is also dependent on how many people want to go; only two passengers are required to make the trip to Tobacco Caye (US$15 each); ask around the Riverside Café or Texaco Station Tackle Stop.

By Bus

From Belize City, the non-express ride takes close to three hours, including a stop in Belmopan, and costs US$5 each way; better hold

Dangriga & Southern Coast

off for the 6 A.M. express (two hours or so); that's followed by hourly local service till 5 P.M., with additional expresses at 2:30 P.M. and 4:30 P.M.

Double check the schedule with Novelo's (tel. 501/502-2160, posted at the ticket window) in Dangriga. The first return trip to Belize City is 5 A.M., the final one is an express at 6:45 P.M.; there are expresses at 8 A.M. and 8:30 A.M. as well.

There are eight daily buses to Punta Gorda, from 9 A.M. to the day's only express at 6:45 P.M.— a three-hour trip. As of press time, there are only two daily buses to Placencia: 12:15 P.M. and 5:15 P.M., 2.5 hours "to reach." Three buses go to Hopkins and Sittee River: 10 A.M., 12:15 P.M., and 5:15 P.M.

By Car

From Belize City, take the Western Highway to either the Coastal (Manatee) Road or Hummingbird Highway, which you'll follow till it ends.

Manatee Road (a.k.a. Coastal Road)

The alternate route to Dangriga and points south may shave 20 minutes off the Hummingbird route—but the rutted, red dirt surface may also destroy your suspension and jar your fillings loose. In any case, the unpaved road is flat and relatively straight, and is occasionally graded into a passable highway, but you better have a sturdy ride. Be prepared for lots of dust in the dry season and boggy mud after a rain. Numerous tiny bridges with no railings cross creeks flowing out of the west and the landscape of pine savannah and forested limestone bluffs has nary a sign of humans (except for the crappy road, of course). About half way to the junction with the Hummingbird Highway, you'll find a pleasant place to stop and take a dip at Soldier Creek; just look for the biggest bridge of your trip and pull over. Watch out for snakes in the bush and, once you reach your destination, try not to spend those hard-earned 20 minutes all in one place.

Islands near Dangriga

 TOBACCO CAYE

A tiny island perched practically on top of the Belize Barrier Reef, Tobacco Caye is just north of the cut with the same name (a "cut" is a break in the reef through which boats navigate). If your tropical island dream includes sharing that island with a few dozen fellow wanderers, snorkelers, divers, rum drinkers, and hammock-sitters, this is your place. Shoppers can seek out hand-sewn gifts by Phillipa (behind Lana's). Other activities include a number of caye-hopping or underwater excursions to surrounding reef spots or even to Glover's Atoll, less than an hour's boat ride away. Check with the dive shop at Reef's End.

Long considered a backpacker and Belizean tourist destination, Tobacco Caye's six "resorts" have lately diverged a bit in price, but still offer similar packages. All six places are Belizean-run family affairs, each a bit different according to the owner's vision, and are comfortably crowded together on the five-acres of sand. Apart from some

There are six friendly, family-run accommodations on Tobacco Caye

basic differences in room quality, the more you pay, the better food you'll be eating—a pretty important thing when checking into a room that also locks you into a meal plan. The following prices are all per person per night and include three meals.

Gaviota's Coral Reef Resort welcomes you to "the Lifestyle of a Chosen Few" in one of four rooms or nine cabanas (tel. 501/509-5032, US$30, shared bath); the **Paradise Lodge** occupies the northern tip of the island with rooms from US$25 and cabins for US$35; **Lana's** (tel. 501/520-5036 or 522-2571) has four basic rooms for US$40.

Stepping things up a notch, find **Reef's End Lodge** on the southern shore (tel. 501/520-5037 on island, 522-2419 in Dangriga, US$65); owner of the caye's dive shop which can be utilized by anyone on the island. **Tobacco Caye Lodge** (tel. 501/520-5033 or 227-6247, tclodge@btl.net, www.tclodgebelize.com, US$120 a couple plus tax) occupies a middle strip of the island and offers three units. Find Belizean-Brooklynites Raymond and Brenda Lee at **Ocean's Edge** (oceansedge@btl.net, US$50/95 s/d) to rent one of seven rooms and enjoy a flag-draped bar and some of the best food on the island.

Tobacco Caye is the only island in the area that offers semi-regular water taxi service, with boats leaving Dangriga around mid-afternoon from the Riverside Café or the Tackle Stop farther upstream. Captains Buck and Compa are spoken of as the most reliable, just ask around; the trip costs US$15 each way, with a return trip usually made mid-morning. Be advised, if you need a boat after 3 P.M., you'll pay a lot more—seas get rough and a private charter is necessary; plan accordingly.

SOUTH WATER CAYE

South Water Caye is another postcard-perfect, privately owned island 14 miles offshore from Dangriga and 35 miles southeast of Belize City. The reef crests just a stone's throw offshore, providing relaxing surf sounds throughout the day and night and sitting atop a 1,000-foot coral wall awash in wildlife. The island stretches .75

mile from north to south and .25 mile at its widest point.

The **Pelican Beach Resort** (US$130/195 s/d, including all taxes and three delicious meals) occupies the entire southern end of the island, with five second-story rooms in the old convent building, plus three cabins, including a honeymoon cottage. The beach is available to other island guests and offers prime walk-in snorkeling sites. Power is from the sun, and composting toilets help protect the fragile island ecology. The owners also have a strip of island toward the north end that is home to **Pelican's University,** which hosts student research groups throughout the year. Contact the mainland hotel for reservations (tel. 501/522-2044, sales@pelicanbeachbelize.com, www.southwatercaye.com). Plenty of day trips are available with Pelican's guides, or with one of the island dive shops.

Lesley Cottages is the common name for **International Zoological Expeditions** (IZE, US tel. 800/548-5843, Bel. tel. 501/523-7076, izebelize@starband.net, www.ize2belize.com, US$135/person). Named for an old local fisherman, Dan Lesley, the compound here specializes primarily in dealing with student groups and "educational tourism," with their own dive shop, classroom, etc. Beautiful rooms are nestled on the shoreline; included are three meals and transport—a great spot for couples (check to see if you'll be sharing with student groups).

Blue Marlin Lodge (US tel. 800/798-1558, Bel. tel. 501/520-5104, marlin@btl.net), sister resort of the Bonefish Hotel in Dangriga, offers a variety of rooms, air-conditioned igloos (you'll know when you see 'em), and cabanas just steps away from the sea, prices from US$88 s/d to US$150 for a cabin. The bar/dining room over the sea serves meals, snacks (included), and drinks (three meals roughly US$60). The Blue Marlin specializes in fishing trips, plus has a full dive shop, cable TV, and Internet (in case you thought you were on a desert island).

CARRIE BOW CAYE

This dot of sand and palms, close to both the reef and mangrove systems, is home to the

Smithsonian Natural History Museum's Caribbean Coral Reef Ecosystems Program which, since 1972, has produced over 800 published papers. The caye houses up to six international scientists at a time, as well as a real-time weather station, available online at www.nmnh.si.edu/biodiversity/ccre.htm. The public is welcome to check things out, but only if you arrange something first through your host on South Water Caye or elsewhere.

GLOVER'S REEF ATOLL

True, this coral uprising and five-caye phenom could be lumped together with the other islands, but if you've ever cruised 36 miles over an ocean of warm glass and seen the bright seagreen strip of Glover's Reef shine from the horizon, you would agree that this is truly a place apart from the rest of the world. The southernmost of Belize's unique atolls, Glover's

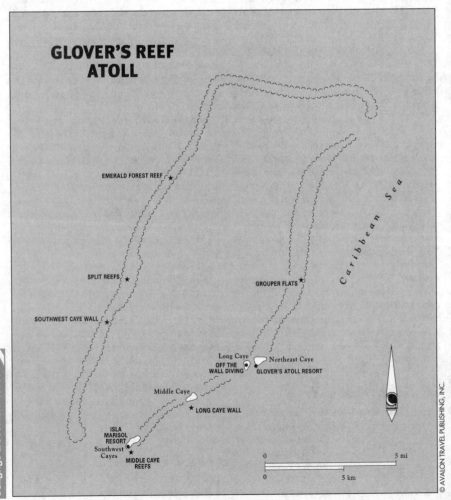

GLOVER'S REEF ATOLL

EMERALD FOREST REEF

SPLIT REEFS

SOUTHWEST CAYE WALL

GROUPER FLATS

Caribbean Sea

Long Caye
OFF THE
WALL DIVING
Northeast Caye
GLOVER'S ATOLL RESORT

Middle Caye
LONG CAYE WALL

ISLA MARISOL RESORT
Southwest Cayes
MIDDLE CAYE REEFS

0   5 mi

0   5 km

© AVALON TRAVEL PUBLISHING, INC.

(named for a pirate, of course) is an 80-square-mile nearly continuous ring of brilliant coral, flanked on its southeastern curve by five tiny islands. The atoll is 18 miles long and 6 miles across at its widest point; to the east, the ocean bottom drops sharply and keeps on dropping, eventually to depths of 15,000 feet at the western end of the Caiman Trench, one of the deepest in the world.

The southern section of the atoll around the cayes serves as a protected marine reserve—however, someone should remind the government Fishery Department Rangers on Middle Caye of this fact, as they reportedly regularly skip patrols and ignore illegal fishing activity (although they're very efficient at collecting tourist fees).

Divers and snorkelers will find a fabulous wall surrounding the atoll, plus more than 700 shallow coral patches within the rainbow-colored lagoon. There are wreck dives and an abundance of marine life, especially turtles, manta rays, and all types of sharks, including reefs, hammerheads, and whale sharks. The names of the dive sites speak for themselves: Shark Point, Grouper Flats, Emerald Forest Reef, Octopus Alley, Manta Reef, Dolphin Dance, and Turtle Tavern.

Anglers will have a chance at bonefish and permit, as well as the big trophies, including sailfish, marlin, wahoo, snapper, and grouper. Also fantastic paddling, sailing, and anything else you can dream up. Glover's is a special place indeed.

Southwest Cayes

The first bit of land you'll reach from the mainland used to be a single island until Hurricane Hattie carved a channel through it in 1961. Now the southern part is the defunct Manta Resort, while the northern bit is owned by the Usher clan and consists of a high-end dive resort called **Isla Marisol Resort** (tel. 501/520-2056, sales@islamarisol.com, www.islamarisol.com). If you're serious about world-class diving and fishing, look into a stay here; there are many all-inclusive packages available.

Island Expeditions (US/Can. tel. 800/667-1630, www.islandexpeditions.com) is an adventure travel outfitter with a tent camp on the north tip of Southwest Caye; it's a well-run, professional operation.

Middle Caye

No accommodations here, unless you're a Fisheries

Glover's Reef: Another sunset to reflect on a day's work of diving and kayaking

© JOSHUA BERMAN

© JOSHUA BERMAN

There are scores of picture perfect islands off Belize's southern coast.

Department Ranger or marine biologist with the Wildlife Conservation Society. If staying on one of the surrounding cayes, ask your host about arranging a trip to see what's going on here.

Long Caye

The 13 acres here form the gorgeous backdrop to **Slickrock Adventures'** thatch-roof base camp (US tel. 800/390-5715, www.slickrock.com) and **Off the Wall Dive Center** (tel. 501/614-6348, offthewall@btl.net, www.offthewallbelize.com), Jim and Kendra Schofield's dive shop and resort. Slickrock has a veritable armada of kayaks, sailboards, and other water toys; conditions and equipment will cover beginners and experts alike (also see Tour Operators in the Practicalities chapter). Guests stay in very private rustic beach cabins or palapa tent platforms overlooking the reef and equipped with kerosene lamps, foam pad mattresses, and great views. Outhouse toilets are of the *plein air* variety, surrounded by palm leaf "walls"—possibly the best views from a WC in the entire country. Book a trip to their island,

or link it with wild inland adventures as well (call for catalog).

Off the Wall's facilities consist of a top-notch dive shop, bar, and gift shop, plus a couple of cabins to accommodate six people on week-long charter trips—US$1,600 includes 7 days' lodging, transport, all meals, and 12 dives. Diving, snorkeling, and fishing are available as well, and yachties are welcome to come ashore and browse the gift shop.

Northeast Caye

At the longstanding **Glover's Atoll Resort,** run by the Lamond family out of their Glover's Guest House in Sittee River (tel. 501/520-5016 or 614-7177, glovers@btl.net, www.glovers.com.bz), you'll get a true Gilligan's Island experience. They've got a new 68-foot catamaran to whisk you out to Glover's most remote caye, where you will camp or shack up for the cheapest rates on the atoll: US$99 camping, $149 dorm, $199 cabin. The price includes transport and a week's worth of primitive lodging, nothing more. Show up at the Bunkhouse in Sittee River at 7 A.M. Saturday, and be prepared for the week—this means asking plenty of questions so you know *exactly* what is available and what will cost you extra once you're out there. You're welcome to bring all your own food (a kitchen is available) and drinking water, or shell out about US$30/day or more to be served. A reputable dive shop and kayak rentals are also available, right on the reef.

OTHER NEARBY CAYES

Man-O-War Caye (Bird Isle) is a bird-choked, raucously chirping clump of protected mangroves that is a crucial nesting site for frigates and boobies. **Coco Plum Caye** (tel. 501/520-2041, www.cocoplumislandresort.com) hosts a cluster of bright cabins that is part of the Jaguar Reef Lodge in Sittee, but the public is welcome to dock up and enjoy the gorgeous sand bar—and the wet bar perched above it. The island was dredged and mangroves cut to form the development, so sand flies may be bad, and the cottages appear to be sinking into the imported sand.

Wee Wee Caye hosts another educational center, featuring a neat system of raised catwalks through the mangroves (beautiful, but lots of bugs). The caye also hosts a population of boa constrictors; contact Paul and Mary Shave (tel. 501/523-7021, possumpt@btl.net).

South of Dangriga

◪ HOPKINS

One foreign volunteer described this lazy seaside village about eight miles south of Dangriga as "the edge between paradise and poverty." Hopkins, which was created in 1942 after a hurricane washed away Newtown just up the coast, is a traditional fishing village steering more and more toward tourism—just not quite as quickly as other places in Belize. Not by long shot. Still, there are a variety of places to stay up and down the two-mile beach strip that is home for some 1,100 Belizeans, mostly Garinagu.

There's not much shopping to do here, nor any sights beyond those that make up everyday village life. On a Saturday night, this usually means drinking some beer and bitters, playing drums and dominoes, and laughing away another hot, breezy day. Of course, things pick up considerably on festival days, especially Settlement Day, Christmas, and Easter Week (expect rooms to be in high demand during these times).

As for orientation, the road that carries you into town also splits Hopkins into Northside (or "Baila") and Southside (or "False Sittee"), with the Northside being a bit more dense with local flavor. Be advised: sand flies can get vicious along this stretch of beach, especially between November and February.

Recreation and Entertainment

If you don't feel like hooking up with a dive shop at one of the nearby resorts to plan a serious offshore outing, you can rent a number of water toys right here in Hopkins, starting with various kayaks and other small craft at several hotels. **Oliver Guthoff** (www.windsurfing-belize.com, oliver@windsurfing-belize.com) has a fine quiver of windsurfing boards of various sizes for rent, and offers lessons for all levels. Or, find **Reilly** (tel. 501/523-7127, www.underthesunbelize.com) nearby—he offers sail charters on his two catamarans.

The central pulse of Hopkins beats at **King Kasava's** (Mark Nuñez, tel. 501/608-6188, 7 A.M. to midnight, with a two-hour afternoon break, daily), occupying the intersection where the road from Dangriga meets the sea. Here you'll find a bar, a restaurant, a taxi stand, a charter service, an information center, a pool hall, a bus stop, and more. Lobster dinners go for US$8, shots of bitters are a buck, and there are finger lickin' barbecues. A great place to meet the parade of local characters.

The **Lebeha Drumming Center** (tel. 501/608-3143), way up on the northside (*lebeha* means "the end" in Garifuna), is a bar, a café, and the site of many a drum jam. You'll find free daily lessons for the neighborhood kids as well as late-night, Guinness-fueled skinfests—grab a drum and join on in.

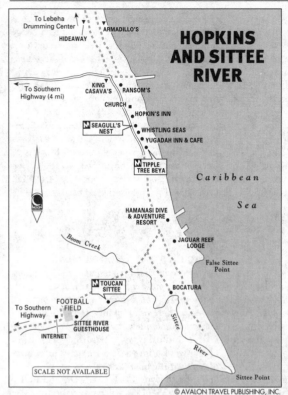

HOPKINS AND SITTEE RIVER

To Lebeha Drumming Center
ARMADILLO'S
HIDEAWAY
To Southern Highway (4 mi)
KING CASAVA'S
RANSOM'S
CHURCH
HOPKIN'S INN
SEAGULL'S NEST
WHISTLING SEAS
YUGADAH INN & CAFE
TIPPLE TREE BEYA
Caribbean
Sea
HAMANASI DIVE & ADVENTURE RESORT
Boom Creek
JAGUAR REEF LODGE
False Sittee Point
TOUCAN SITTEE
BOCATURA
FOOTBALL FIELD
To Southern Highway
SITTEE RIVER GUESTHOUSE
INTERNET
Sittee
River
Sittee Point
SCALE NOT AVAILABLE

© AVALON TRAVEL PUBLISHING, INC.

You have not experienced Hopkins until you have enjoyed at least one cold beverage while leaning over the lapping ocean at **The People's Republic of Swinging Armadillos** (Tues.–Fri.). Actually, be careful with that railing—this stilted, open dock of a bar may fall into the sea at any minute. Until then, enjoy.

Accommodations

Lebeha Drumming Center has campsites (US$2.50) and a cabana for rent by the month, week, or night. There are a few other North-side options near Kasava's; take a few minutes to walk up the road, inquiring at all the random "rooms" signs.

Southside offers considerably more options; all of the following are within about a mile of each other, spread along the beach south of Kasava's, starting with the eccentric, garden-

choked **Ransom's Cabana** (cabanabelize@hotmail.com, US$20/30 s/d). Continuing south on the road (or beach), there are several groups of new, clean, beachside cabins, including **M Seagull's Nest** (tel. 501/523-7015, jc-seagulls@yahoo.com, from US$10/18 s/d, shared bath) and **Whistling Seas Vacation Inn** (tel. 501/608-0016, whistlingseas@btl.net, US$46 d), with its five private cement rooms with fridge and fan. Whistling Seas is classy for the neighborhood, with a new restaurant. **Jungle Jeanie's** (tel. 501/523-7047, US$15–20) was the first hotel on the block and is still pleasant. There's a cluster of beach cabins with kayaks for rent, and camping is available.

Probably the most attractive budget option, **M Tipple Tree Beya** (tel. 501/520-7006 or 603-7613, info@tippletree.com, from US$20 s/d, camping US$5) has a range of excellent rooms on the beach with lovely hammock-adorned porches and palapas.

The top of the line is undoubtedly the **Hopkins Inn Bed & Breakfast** (tel. 501/523-7013, hopkinsinn@btl.net, www.hopkinsinn.com, US$40/50 s/d) with four fully furnished cabanas. They're a bargain for what you get.

Food

Lack of numerous options should make finding food relatively simple. **M Kasava's** is the most obvious, but don't overlook **The Hideaway Restaurant and Cool Spot,** which is tucked off to the left as you walk north and is open most evenings. Down on Southside, you'll find good but slow food at **Innie's** (tel. 501/608-4813, ask about Laruni Cabins for rent); also check out the **Yugadah Café** and **Iris's**—all have similarly relaxed menus and atmospheres.

SITTEE RIVER

Continuing south on the road from Hopkins, you'll pass through False Sittee, followed by the village of Sittee River, occupying a few bends of the slow, flat river of the same name. The road turns upstream, looping westward, about six miles back to the Southern Highway. Sittee River qualifies as a village only in the loosest sense, with a few houses, **Reynold's Store,** a few jungly places to stay, a few dive shops and upscale resorts, and more often than not, a few bugs.

The water just off the beach can be a bit muddy at times because of the close proximity of emptying rivers and streams, and depending on the time of year, flies and mosquitoes can get fierce. However, a couple of miles up the river from the ocean, you'll find a variety of fully screened accommodations from which to soak up the thick, tropical tranquility around you. There are dive shops and boats to whisk you out to the cayes, excellent fishing (snook, tarpon, peacock bass, sheepshead, and barracuda), and only 12 miles to the east, the entrance to the Cockscomb Basin Wildlife Sanctuary.

On the road to Bocatura you'll also find **Second Nature Divers** and the **Diversity Cafe** (contact Martin or Jeanette at tel. 501/523-7038).

Accommodations and Food
Under US$25
Glover's Guest House (tel. 501/520-5016, fax 501/223-6087, glovers@btl.net, www.glovers .com.bz) provides cheap, spartan lodging for both passersby and guests of the owners' Glover's Atoll Resort on the farthest of Glover's cayes (cozy bunkhouse on stilts US$8 a night, US$29 for a private cabin, meals and cooking area available; camping US$3, tents provided). Reasonably priced local tours are available, plus a wide variety of boat trips; please see the Glover's Reef Atoll section earlier in this chapter for information about their budget-priced, week-long primitive island packages.

US$25–50
A short distance farther down the river, **M Toucan Sittee** (tel. 501/522-2888) offers great value rooms and has a well-deserved reputation for providing a hospitable and pleasant stay. Very nice cabins (US$25/30 s/d) and camping (US$5) sit amid the hundreds of fruit and other trees planted by owners Neville ("from South Africa via Sweden") and his wife, Yolita (Guatemalan–Belizean). They can arrange expertly guided river and lagoon fishing, a riverside wine and cheese session, or any number of canoe trips, including a spectacular and spooky night paddle up Boom Creek, a canopied waterway choked with wildlife and jaw-dropping vegetation. They serve delicious and generous locally inspired meals (expect seafood, curries, or maybe *sere,* a savory fish cooked in coconut milk).

Tucked a mile or so up a spur road, on the still river bank, you'll find Alan Stewart tending his **Bocatura Cabins** and 40-foot catamaran (tel. 501/603-8334, bocatura@aol.com). Three apartment-cabins and one tree house (US$45 for the tree house, up to US$95 for a fully furnished apartment with queen beds, TV/VCR, stereo, h/c water, and private bath). Alan offers very reasonable rates to charter a sailing trip anywhere in the western Caribbean (from US$250–300 a night, sleeps up to three couples, diving, fishing available).

Over US$100
On the road back toward Hopkins, the highly rated **Jaguar Reef Resort** (US tel. 800/289-5756, Bel. tel. 501/520-7040, jaguarreef@btl.net) is a full-service resort with seven cottages and 14 a/c rooms with fridge. All are spacious and comfortably furnished. There's a good restaurant, but for a night of romance, enjoy a candlelit dinner on the patio. A pool can cool you off since the beach waters—although pretty—are often muddy and might not be inviting to everybody. Rates for cabanas are US$185; for one-bedroom suites, US$275 (cheaper during the summer season). Mountain bikes, kayaks, and a sand volleyball court are available.

Just up the beach, **Hamanasi Resort** (US tel. 877/522-3483, Bel. tel. 501/520-7073, info @hamanasi.com, www.hamanasi.com, US$160 including breakfast and taxes) is the area's premier diving operation. Sitting on 17 acres, including

400 feet of beachfront, Hamanasi offers eight rooms and four suites, all with a view and tiled bathrooms, a/c, fans, porches, and colorful Guatemalan bedspreads. Meals include good pasta and, of course, fresh seafood.

Services

High-speed, air-conditioned Internet—and coffee, juice, and gifts—can be found at **Sittee River** (9 A.M.–6 P.M. Mon.–Sat., till 1 P.M. Sun., closed Tues., US$6/hr). This is the home of local guide **Horace Andrews** (www.belizebyhorace.com) and is right across from his dock, where he hopes to open a bar and the village's first restaurant. Horace does river tours on the Sittee River, snorkel trips to the cayes, fishing trips to the cayes or lagoons, and inland tours such as Cockscomb, Mayflower, and Red Bank to see the scarlet macaws in season. Up the road toward the highway are a couple of stores, plus **Sew Much Hemp,** whose organic, hemp oil–based bug dope you may wish to try instead of drowning yourself in more DEET.

MAYFLOWER BOCAWINA NATIONAL PARK

The Belize park system's newest jewel is more than 7,100 acres of Maya Mountains. Hike through the jungle searching for waterfalls and green-fringed ancient ruins on newly constructed loop trails, courtesy of a British-based volunteer organization called Trekforce. A walk in Mayflower, located near the **Silk Grass Village,** can be combined with a day trip to Cockscomb (just to the south), or can easily fill a whole day—there's mad wildlife.

The biggest logistical challenge to enjoying Mayflower is simply getting to the trailhead, which lies 4.5 miles west of the Southern Highway with no public transport of any kind making the trip. Who knows, maybe they'll pull something together by the time you're reading this; in the meantime, buy an extra liter of water, lace up them walkin' shoes, and enjoy your reward that much more. Or, contact Horace Andrews in Sittee River or **C & G Tours and Charters** (29 Oak St., tel. 501/522-3641 or 522-3379, cg-tours@btl.net) in Dangriga, who specialize in the area.

Accommodations

Contact the park office in Dangriga (tel. 501/522-3641) and ask about the great camping or about the homestay program with the **Silk Grass Village Women's Group.** Probably the best way to visit Mayflower—and all the other parts of the Cockscomb Basin—is to stay at **Mama Noots Backabush Jungle Resort** (tel. 501/603-4612, mamanoots@lincsat.com, www.mamanoots.com); the price is about US$90 per couple. It's located on the same road to Mayflower, where you'll find amazing hiking, swimming, bird-watching, and more. Well-recommended.

KANANTIK REEF & JUNGLE RESORT

Just a bit farther down the highway, you'll see a turnoff for the Kanantik Resort (tel. 501/520-8048, info@kanantik.com, www.kanantik.com, US$475/315 pp s/d), a high-end, all-inclusive luxury resort on 300 acres that include a beach and forest.

The Cockscomb Basin

The land rises gradually from the coastal plains to the Maya Mountains; the highest point in the Cockscomb Basin range is Victoria Peak (3,675 ft.). Geologists believe that Victoria Peak is four million years old, the oldest geologic formation in Central America. Mountain climbers find this peak a real adventure. The first climbers (a party that included Roger T. Goldsworth, governor of then-British Honduras) reached the peak in 1888; British soldiers recorded another climb in 1986. Heavy rain along the granite peaks of the Maya range (as much as 160 inches a year) runs off into lush rainforest thick with trees, orchids, palms, ferns, abundant birds, and exotic animals, including peccaries, anteaters, armadillos, tapirs, and jaguars. Until recently, the jaguar was a prize for game hunters. Today, the beautiful cat has thousands of acres to roam protected from man in the Cockscomb Basin Wildlife Sanctuary.

The archaeology buff should check out the ruins in the vicinity of Cockscomb Basin: **Pomona** on North Stann Creek, **Kendal** on the Sittee River, and **Pierce** on South Stann Creek.

ⓜ COCKSCOMB BASIN WILDLIFE SANCTUARY

Also commonly called the Cockscomb Jaguar Preserve or simply the Jaguar Preserve, this is one of the best undisturbed natural centers in the country, and easily one of the most beautiful. A large tract of approximately 155 square miles of forest was declared a forest reserve in 1984, and in 1986 the government of Belize set the region aside as a preserve for the largest cat in the Americas, the jaguar. The area is alive with wildlife, including the margay, ocelot, puma, jaguarundi, tapir, deer, paca, iguana, kinkajou, and armadillo (to name just a few), hundreds of bird species, and some unusual reptiles, including the red-eyed tree frog. And though you probably won't see the large cats roaming during the day (they hunt at night), it's exciting to see their prints and other signs—and to know that even if you don't see one, you'll probably *be seen* by one.

Hiking the Trails

From the visitors center, many trails go off in different directions into the park. The trails are well cared for. Check out the front of the visitors center building for a detailed map. If you wish to take a guide for trekking farther afield, ask about availability at the center, or up the road in Maya Center, where excellent guides are found who grew up in these forests. Bring your swimsuit; you'll find cool natural pools for a refreshing plunge, especially along Stann Creek.

If you climb **Ben's Bluff,** you're not just looking out over a park where jaguars live—you're at the entrance of a forest that goes all the way into the Guatemalan Petén, part of the largest contiguous block of protected forest in Central America. It's an easy one-day hike, and the park managers are planning to build a lookout tower.

Visitors Center and Accommodations

Just past the entrance gate into the sanctuary is a small gift shop and office where you'll be asked to sign in. There is also a small museum, picnic area, and outhouse. You'll also find an "office" of the **World Wildlife Fund,** an important sponsor of the park along with the **Belize Audubon Society** and the government.

The overnight accommodations are in a couple of clapboard buildings with about a dozen bunks and metal roofs (US$8 for a bunk, private cabins available for US$18, $48 with more beds and a kitchen, and the "white house," up the road, for US$54). A walled-off washing area has buckets, and a separate cooking area has a gas stove and a few pots and such. Or, bring your own tent to stay at the excellent campground (US$3).

Be prepared if you plan to stay a few days; the only food for sale in the visitors center includes chips, cookies, candy bars, and soft drinks. There are a couple of bigger stores in Maya Center, so feel free to stock up there before catching your cab into the park. You may also be able to arrange for meals to be cooked in Maya Center and brought in.

LOOKING FORWARD: THE JAGUAR'S FUTURE

The first scientist to research the jaguar population in Belize, Dr. Alan Rabinowitz, thought it would take several generations to see any ecological or cultural benefits of the Cockscomb Basin Wildlife Sanctuary's creation—but it happened much more quickly. This was, he admits, partly due to luck: The formation of a protected area based on the jaguar's natural habitat (which was the first of its kind in the world) happened at a fortuitous time in Belize's history, basically at the very beginning of the country's efforts to attract more tourists. Cockscomb helped set the stage for the local preservation movement, giving a crucial boost to the country's fledgling ecotourism efforts.

Jaguar research continues in the Cockscomb Basin, only now the animals are tracked using infrared-triggered camera traps. Current data supports original density estimates that were based on radio-telemetry, which necessitated the invasive, sometimes harmful practice of physically capturing and collaring the cats, and then tracking them from dangerous, low-flying airplanes. "The jaguar's prey are back," reports Rabinowitz, from behind a tiny, cluttered desk in his cramped office at New York's Bronx Zoo, where he is now Director of Science and Exploration for the Wildlife Conservation Society (WCS). "There are peccary all over the place and the jaguars are eating a lot, but their population density has stayed level—it's maxed out—even after 20 years. Also, we've found that the more protected area you give the jaguar, the less complaints there are of jaguars coming out after dogs and cattle—the opposite of what you'd expect."

He notes how the Maya in the Cockscomb area have supplanted natural curiosity of the big cats and other animals for the fear they used to express when he was there. Whereas before, locals never entered the bush without a rifle, today, they carry binoculars, pointing out jaguar tracks and exotic birds to groups of tourists. "Now I go back to Cockscomb and I see these teenagers—sons of people I worked with—working as tour guides. They've known Cockscomb as a protected area since they were children and they realize how important it is, both economically and ecologically. Plus, the women are empowered, with the money from their crafts sales, and you don't see children walking around with parasites and swollen bellies."

Rabinowitz tracked the area's cat population while living in a small clearing of jungle (now the site of the park's visitors center) for nearly two years in the early 1980s, and recounted his story in his fascinating "eco-memoir," *Jaguar: One Man's Struggle to Establish the World's First Jaguar Preserve* (reprinted by Island Press in 2000). He has traveled extensively since then, studying jaguars, clouded leopards, tigers, and other large mammal species in Borneo, Taiwan, Thailand, Laos, and Myanmar (Burma).

And while he has moved on from Cockscomb, the restless biologist does not see the Belizean park as a mere thing of the past. Quite the contrary. His ambitious goal now is to save jaguars throughout their entire range—from Mexico to Argentina—by creating and securing a natural, unbroken corridor of wildland on both public and private lands where jaguars can thrive into the future. "We've already made tremendous strides toward that objective," he says, "with jaguar surveys and rancher outreach programs."

The **Save the Jaguar** project is dependant on private and corporate donations (Jaguar Cars has been extremely supportive). You can learn more about current studies and projects—and about how to help—by logging onto www.savethejaguar.com and also by checking out WCS's **Adopt-a-Jaguar Project** at www.wcs.org/adoptajaguar. Another organization that specializes in big-cat research and protection in Belize is **liFeline** (www.li-feline.com), who has a field station in the Mountain Pine Ridge.

Getting There

Driving into the Cockscomb is best done with a 4WD vehicle, especially after a rain. And if you do get stuck, on a slow day it could take a long time and a few bucks before you are discovered and pulled free. By bus, just hop off any Novelo's or James Bus traveling south from Dangriga (or north from Placencia or Punta Gorda).

MAYA CENTER

You'd do well not to just drive through this small village that stands at the turn-off for the famous Cockscomb Basin Wildlife Sanctuary. Many of the 300 or so Mopan Maya here were relocated when Cockscomb was given protected status. Since then, they have changed their lifestyles; instead of continuing to clear patches of rainforest for short-term agriculture, many men now work as guides and taxi drivers, while the women create and sell their artwork. Still, the people of Maya Center are struggling to support their town with tourism. Ever since they were prohibited from using the now-protected jungle that surrounds them for subsistence farming, tourism's their only hope, aside from working for slave wages at the nearby banana and citrus farms. The village now boasts some wonderfully homey places to stay, eat, and experience village life.

At the very least, make sure that you—or the driver of your tour bus—stop at one of the two Maya crafts stores. At the turnoff from the Southern Highway, you'll find the village women's co-operative **Craft Store and Visitor's Center** (7:30 A.M.–4:30 P.M.); a quarter mile toward the park is the **Nu'uk Che'il Gift Shop.** Both offer fine jewelry, slate carvings, baskets, herbs, and other crafts.

Right across the road from the women's co-op, look for the sign and trail across the creek to William Saqui's **Butterfly Farm** (7 A.M.–5 P.M. daily, US$2.50, possible fee to take photos), boasting several dozen species.

Julio Saqui runs the store next to the women's co-op, and offers satellite Internet access (US$4/hr.) and taxi service.

Accommodations

There are presently three guesthouses that will host and feed you in Maya Center, each owned by a different family who offers transport in

© DANIELLE VAUGHN

Cockscomb was just the beginning...

There are several unique accommodations near Cockscomb, like this guest house in Maya Center.

and out of the preserve plus guides, meals, and other services.

Located right on the highway, about 100 meters north of the entrance to Cockscomb, you'll find **Tutzil Nah Cottages** (tel. 501/520-3044, www.mayacenter.com, US$15/24 s/d), owned and operated by the Chun family (they helped Dr. Alan Rabinowitz in his original jaguar studies and appear in his book, *Jaguar*). There are four wooden rooms with shared bath and shower boasting queen beds, ample space, nice furniture, and a raised deck. Meals are US$6–12, as is camping on the grounds or in a separate campground about a quarter mile into the bush. Inventive trips are available as an alternative to the standard fare, including kayak floats and night hikes.

Located just inside the Cockscomb entrance road is **Mejen Tzil** (tel. 501/520-3032, lsaqui@btl.net), run by Yoli and Liberato Saqui and offering a handful of raised rooms for US$20 with private bath, or US$8 for a bunkbed; camping/hammock US$5, with a grill available for your BBQ needs. The Saquis welcome all kinds of groups (their bunk rooms sleep 12) and can also provide home cooked meals, Mayan language lessons, and cultural presentations. Liberato is a teacher at the town school and offers reduced rates for volunteers looking to help in the school or other projects around town.

Nu'uk Che'il Cottages and Hmen Herbal Center (tel. 501/520-3033 or 615-2091, nuukcheil@btl.net) offers tranquil accommodations removed from the highway, with bunks for US$10 with shared bath and private rooms for US$20 s/d, hot showers available, tax not included; camping US$7. Proprietress Aurora Garcia Saqui's husband, Ernesto, is Director of the Cockscomb Basin Wildlife Sanctuary, and her late uncle, Don Eligio Panti, was a famous healer; she took over his work when he died in 1996. Aurora offers Mayan spiritual blessings, prayer healings, acupuncture, and massage (each for under US$13). Aurora also has a four-acre botanical garden and medicine trail (US$2.50 entrance), herbs for sale, and can arrange homestays in the village (US$20 includes a one-night stay with a local family, one dinner and one breakfast per person).

Getting There

Maya Center is easily accessed by hopping off any bus passing between Placencia or Punta Gorda and points north. Taxis will take you the 6.5 miles from the village to the Cockscomb Basin Wildlife Sanctuary for about US$12.50.

The Placencia Peninsula

This ribbon of barrier beach and mangroves extends from the coastal village of Riverside to Placencia Town proper, 16 miles away on the southern tip of a serpentine barrier beach. The area used to be a forgotten cul-de-sac on the tourist trail, but no more. Traveling to nearby cayes (sailing, snorkeling, diving, paddling) is a snap from anywhere on the peninsula. So is transport to inland attractions like the Cockscomb Basin Wildlife Sanctuary, Maya villages, and ruins—a quick boat trip across the lagoon brings you to waiting tour vehicles at the dock at Mango Creek. You'll have the full range of accommodations from which to choose—whether you prefer to mingle with backpackers in Placencia Town, or rub elbows with fellow well-to-do guests at any number of both established and new beach resorts, each with its own personality.

The road that runs the length of the peninsula is notoriously bad, especially in the wet season, and government promises to pave it (which only come in election years) have—to date—resulted in only a few paved miles from the airstrip into the town at the extreme southern end.

MAYA BEACH

This is the first cluster of homes you'll come to as you drive south from Riverside. This loose stretch of mid-peninsula resorts and homes provides an out-of-the-way option for those who wish to avoid the busier parts of Placencia but still enjoy the beach and have access to the myriad day trips in the area. A few miles before you get to Maya Beach from the north, however, you'll pass through a sketchy strip of soon-to-be-developed (or not) plots of land. There are several resorts in the area that have been known to book pre-paying guests into rooms on hotel grounds surrounded on three sides by destroyed mangrove and swampy landfill. If considering a stay this far up the peninsula, ask careful questions about what you should expect to find.

Most places in Maya Beach are of the beach cabana/apartment variety, many with kitchens for cooking on your own; some provide meals as well, plus kayaks. The first place you'll come to is **The Green Parrot Beach Houses** (tel. 501/523-2488, greenparot@btl.net, www.greenparrot-belize.com, US$140 d plus tax), featuring thatch-roof honeymoon cabanas and two-story A-frame cabanas with large decks and loft bedrooms facing the ocean. The A-frames sleep four people and include multiple beds, couches, a kitchen, and of course hammocks. Green Parrot offers honeymoon packages, courtesy airport shuttles, continental breakfast, and Internet access. There's a restaurant and beach bar.

The **Maya Breeze Inn** (US tel. 888/458-8581, Bel. tel. 501/523-8012, info@mayabreezeinn.com, www.mayabreezeinn.com, US$85–125) offers three cabins on stilts with kitchenettes, two suites with full kitchens, and four deluxe hotel rooms with small fridge, cable TV, and a/c. All are close to the beach, and there's fresh local seafood at adjoining **Monarch Café.** These are great options for families and multiple couples. Internet available.

Catering to couples and honeymooners, **Barnacle Bill's Beach Bungalows** (tel. 501/523-8010, taylors@btl.net, www.gotobelize.com/barnacle, US$95) consists of two comfortable, *fully* equipped apartment cabanas on the beach with a host of creature comforts—you can even order ahead and have a fully stocked fridge awaiting your arrival.

PLACENCIA PENINSULA NORTH OF THE AIRSTRIP

To Riversdale

GREEN PARROT

MAYA BREEZE INN

MANGO'S RESTAURANT

BARNACLE BILLS BEACH BUNGALOWS

SINGING SANDS INN

MARKET/CAFE

MAYA PLAYA

Maya Beach

BAR

BLUE CRAB RESORT

DAVE'S SUPERMARKET

NAUTICAL INN

Seine Bight Village

POLICE

LOLA'S ART

WAMASA BEYABU BAR

WHITE SANDS BAR & ROOMS

VERN'S RESTAURANT

LUCKY'S MARKET

KULCHA SHACK

LUBA HATI BEACH RESORT

DIVE SHOP

INN AT ROBERT'S GROVE

HABANERO'S RESTAURANT

MILLER'S LANDING

SERENITY RESORT

BAMBOO ROOM

RUM POINT INN

AIRSTRIP

KITTY'S PLACE

Rum Point

SCALE NOT AVAILABLE

Placencia Lagoon

PLACENCIA RD.

Caribbean Sea

Inset map

0   4 mi
0   4 km

Maya Beach
False Caye
False Point

Seine Bight Village

Rum Point

Placencia

Placencia Caye

Placencia Lagoon

© AVALON TRAVEL PUBLISHING, INC.

HURRICANE IRIS

Like most Caribbean towns, Placencia's recent history is anchored to a devastating storm, with all events placed either "before" or "after" "The Hurricane." In this case, it was Iris that wiped the town clean off the sand in 2001, leaving only a few cement foundations in its wake. The tourism industry, which was in the middle of a newfound boom, had to start from scratch. It took two years to rebuild and in November 2003, the smell of fresh paint and sound of banging hammers touching up various projects signaled the final preparations before Placencia's first real tourist season since the blow.

Interestingly, things look just as clustered and haphazard as before, and it's amazing to think that nearly every single one of these buildings is brand new. The biggest and most unfortunate change though, agree most townsfolk, is the vegetation, or lack thereof. In addition to homes and hotels, Iris ripped away thousands of trees, but the replanting effort continues, and you'll still find plenty of palm fronds rustling in the sea breeze which, until the next history-altering sou'easter, is gentle and dry.

Orchid lovers will enjoy the garden sanctuary of the **Singing Sands Inn** (tel. 501/520-8022 or 523-8017, singingsands@direcway.com, US$70–135 d), a beautiful, shady, family-friendly resort with six cabanas and an apartment that sleeps four. All units have a fridge, screened windows and doors, ceiling fan, private bath, and h/c water. A continental breakfast is provided and there is a pool. A canoe, snorkel gear rental, and bikes are complimentary to guests, and broadband Internet is available; weddings and groups welcome.

The most economic way to go, **Maya Playa** (tel. 501/523-8020, mayaplaya@btl.net, US$75) offers three rustic two-story cabanas on the beach equipped with loft, private outdoor bath, and hot water. There's no restaurant, but a bare-bones kitchen area is provided overlooking the ocean and owner Chuck offers complimentary fruit and coffee.

If not cooking in your cabana's kitchen, dine out by hopping between the other resorts, or visiting the **Hungry Gecko** (6:30 A.M.–9 P.M.), which serves a cheap and delicious menu of Honduran goodies, fresh seafood, and kick-ass smoothies and juices. Across the street, dine on the beach and even play a match of volleyball at **Mango's,** a restaurant and full bar that offers daily drink and meal specials. The one store in town, the **Maya Point** market, is open mornings and afternoons, closed Sundays.

SEINE BIGHT

Continuing south, a couple more miles of dirt road will put you in the Garinagu village of Seine Bight (rhymes with "rain tight"). In this town of about 600, most of the men are fishermen, and the women tend family gardens. Some are attempting to clean up the town, with hopes it will someday become a prime, low-key tourist destination, and a few foreigners have already put their money on it. There are some locally owned gems here as well, and you are welcome to explore as the town goes about its casual daily business.

Strolling through Seine Bight, you'll realize the people here are different than they are in other parts of Belize; they have a carefree, intact culture that reflects both tribal customs and modern adaptations. Supposedly, men and women lead split lives here; the women claim to have their own language that the men don't understand.

Accommodations

As with Maya Beach, accommodations are growing in Seine Bight; the resorts described here are the most obvious (and expensive) options, but asking around at any of the stores or bars will find you the latest budget option—there are always a few local families with relatively cheap rooms for rent.

Just north of town is the **Nautical Inn** (US tel.

a tea party on the beach at Seine Bight Village

© DANIELLE VAUGHN

800/688-0377, Bel. tel. 501/523-595, nautical@btl.net, $140 d plus tax). A dozen family-friendly rooms surround a pool, beach, and the famous coconut bowling alley (games Wednesday nights during the weekly BBQ); the rooms have multiple beds, mini kitchens, a/c, TV, and porthole-motif mirrors. The Nautical also has its own dive shop and offers all the basic trips, including a sunset booze cruise. On the beach, a catamaran, canoes, and volleyball net await energetic guests. Beyond the beach stretches a 100-foot dock with a *palapa* at the end.

On a clean, shallow beach about a half-mile north of Seine Bight is **Blue Crab Resort** (tel. 501/523-3544, fax 501/523-3543, sales@bluecrabbeach.com, www.bluecrabbeach.com). American-owned, the resort offers a four rooms with a/c (US$95 plus tax) and two cabanas (US$85) with high thatch roof, louvered windows, h/c water, private bath, and three fans. Children under 16 stay free in adult's room. The small restaurant (only three tables, call for reservations) is usually full during the busy season (Dec.–May) with Blue Crab guests. Specials include Lobster

Cordon Bleu, Pork Tenderloin Mandarin, and Caribbean Conch Soup.

Food and Culture

Grab a couple of "dark and lovelies" (Guinness) or a glass of locally brewed bitters at the reggae-colored **Wamasa Beyabu Bar,** which greets you as you enter town from the north. Nightlife, live music, beachside drinks, and basic bar food are available at **White Sands,** where you can also find apartment-style rooms above the bar.

Lola's Art Gallery and Cat's Claw Bar and Café is a must-stop (located behind the soccer field—follow the well-marked signs). Lola sells handmade dolls, as well as a selection of whimsical artwork, including cards and paintings on canvas. Open 8 A.M.–8 P.M.

Habanero's is a lagoon-side Mexican restaurant, near the Inn at Robert's Grove Dive Shop (see next section).

SOUTH TO PLACENCIA: THE RESORTS

The string of high-end accommodations along the beach between Seine Bight and Placencia could be grouped with either of the two towns, but they can just as easily be set aside on their own (as they are here), since each offers its own unique, isolated version of paradise. The following accommodations are listed as they appear on the peninsula from north to south.

M Luba Hati Beach Resort (tel. 501/523-3402, fax 501/523-3403, info@lubahati.com, www.lubahati.com) is a Mediterranean-inspired villa offering simple elegance on a quiet strip of perfect beach (a bit narrow, like everywhere else in the area); walking the grounds, you'll get hints of the Central American vs. Caribbean identity crisis that typifies all of Belize. The eight spacious rooms (US$170) have king or queen beds, full bathrooms with hot water, and semi-private balconies with swinging shutter doors. A third-story viewing platform is perfect for stargazing and contemplating the Mayan meaning of the resort's name: *House of the Moon;* you can also arrange for a private dinner here. The four exclusive beach casitas (US$200) and a massive two-

low-key luxury at Kitty's Place

bedroom executive suite on the second floor of the main lodge (US$500 for four people) are also available. Rates, which go up a bit during the holidays, include a modest continental breakfast; meal plans available. Special packages include a full moon "celestially inspired indulgence for two," featuring a midnight kayak trip and "lunar body scrub."

Perched on eight acres of beachfront, **The Inn at Robert's Grove** (US tel. 800/565-9757, info@robertsgrove.com, www.robertsgrove.com) is a grand affair, owned and operated by easygoing, transplanted New Yorkers. The 20 rooms are spacious with high ceilings and king-sized beds (from US$170 plus tax, more for luxury suites). Enjoy two pools, tennis court, a trio of rooftop hot tubs, and a wonderful open air restaurant. Robert's Grove has its own dive shop on the lagoon side, and offers all kinds of underwater, offshore, and inland trips as well as lots of creative packages; check the website for more information.

Rum Point Inn (tel. 501/523-3239 rupel @btl.net, www.rumpoint.com, US$185) offers

richly decorated condo-style rooms and cabanas with family-style dining. There's a fantastic lounge, a library, a gift shop, and a bar. Placencia Town is a 20-minute walk away. Tours to the cayes and reef are available, as well as bikes to ride into town or to Seine Bight.

After hitting the pavement and rounding the airstrip, look on your left for the vegetation-tunnel of a driveway to **Mariposa Beach Suites** (tel. 501/523-4069, foxbuddy@btl.net, www.mariposabelize.com, US$125), with three spacious, quiet suites.

N Kitty's Place (tel. 501/522-3227, fax 800/886-4265, info@kittysplace.com, www.kittysplace.com) is one of the best and most unpretentious resorts on the block—call it "low-key luxury," and check your shoes at the front desk. A variety of resort accommodations, including shared bath, veranda-equipped rooms (US$30/40 s/d); airy "garden rooms" (US$135 per couple); plush, fully furnished, hardwood beach cabanas (US$175); and nearly a dozen complete apartments in the immediate area are all available for short or long-term stays. Be sure to schedule a day

Dangriga & Southern Coast

Margarita anyone?—the bar at Turtle Inn

© DANIELLE VAUGHN

trip or overnight on Kitty's private isle, **French Louis Caye,** 12 miles offshore with great snorkeling and upscale accommodations (rent your own island for US$300 per night per couple). Swimming pool, beach bar, and restaurant with nightly specials, including a weekly chicken *pibil* (Garinagu dish served with conch fritters) on Sundays. If you're biking through the area, feel free to stop in for a look at the gift shop and a Belikin at the Sand Bar.

A short walk down the beach (or road) will quickly lead you to yet another variation of paradise. Even if you can't afford to stay in one of the 18 cottages at the **Turtle Inn** (tel. 501/523-3244 or 523-3150, www.turtleinn.com)—prices start at US$250 a night, and go up to US$1,500 a night for the master two-bedroom pavilion—you should swing by the beach bar for a drink or treat yourself to a fine meal with beautifully framed views of the ocean. Indeed, the place is so aesthetically pleasing to look at, with artwork and crafts brought in from all over the world, you'd think it was designed by a world-renowned film producer or something—wait a sec, it was—this is one of Francis Ford Coppola's two Belizean projects. Click on the proper scrapbook on Francis's desk at www.turtleinn.com for more information on booking. If staying at a nearby resort, feel free to wander in to the beachside bar and incredible gift shop.

Placencia Town

A longtime fishing village since the time of the Maya and periodically flattened by hurricanes, Placencia continues rebuilding and redefining itself, in large part to accommodate the rather sudden influx of curious foreigners who arrive in increasing numbers every year. Placencia is still worlds away from the condo-dominated landscape of San Pedro, and most locals claim it will never go that way, but time will tell. Chances are, this will be the *tranquilo,* ramshackle beach village it is today for many years to come. Set up camp, book some day tours, pencil in a massage and facial, and relax.

ORIENTATION

The north–south Placencia Road runs the length of the peninsula then dog-legs around the airstrip, runs along the lagoon, and parallels the famous central sidewalk as it enters town; you'll see the soccer field on your right before the road curves slightly to the left, terminating at the Shell station and main docks. If there is a "downtown" Placencia, it would probably be here, in front of the gas station and ocean—this is where buses come and go, taxis hang out, and most boats are caught. It's also the site of the tourism office and several of the dive and tour shops.

◪ THE SIDEWALK STRIP

Aside from the long, beautiful beach, the main attraction in Placencia is the world-renowned main street "sidewalk," cited in the *Guinness Book of World Records* as "the world's most narrow street." It's 24 inches wide in spots and runs north–south through the sand for over a mile. Homes, hotels, open-air shops, and vendors line both sides.

Oh yeah, feel free to drink the tap water as you explore: Placencia's *agua* is piped in from an artesian well across the lagoon in Independence, reportedly the result of an unsuccessful attempt to drill for oil.

RECREATION

Snorkeling and Diving

Although the beach in town is wonderful for swimming and lounging, you won't see much with a mask and snorkel except sand, seagrass, a few fish, and other bathers. A short boat ride, however, will bring you to the reef and the kind of underwater viewing you can write home about. Snorkel gear is available for rent everywhere (US$5 a day), as are trips to the cayes and reefs (around US$40/half-day, depending on distance).

Belize's famous Barrier Reef reaches down past Placencia, ending in a graceful hook known as the Sapodilla Cayes farther south. There are currently six dive shops servicing the area, with more sure to come (and go). Prices are comparable between them all, and unless you want to just let your hotel arrange everything, you should ask around about different reputations. Highly recommended for knowledge and safety, Vance and Lance at **Advanced Diving** (office in a blue shack midway up the sidewalk, tel. 501/523-4037, advancdive@btl.net, 7 A.M.–7 P.M., closed for lunch) run a pretty tight ship, so to speak. The other main in-town operation is **Seahorse,** located on their own dock by the Shell station (tel. 501/523-3166, seahorse@btl.net). To the north, you'll find a handful of serious dive operations linked to their respective resorts: there are dive shops at The Inn at Robert's Grove, Rum Point Inn, Turtle Inn, and Nautical Inn.

Sea Kayaking

A great, underrated way to explore the near-shore cayes, mangroves, creeks, and rivers is in a kayak. Open, plastic kayaks are available to guests at most resorts and many tour operators and dive shops have some for rent as well. Boats are also available for rent at the **Sugar Reef Bar** and are perfect for putting in and paddling up the lagoon in search of birds, manatees, and dolphins. If you're into extended expedition sea kayaking, see Dave at **Toadal Adventure** (tel. 501/523-3207 or 606-1399, debanddave@btl.net). He'll

AIRSTRIP

RUM POINT INN

MARIPOSA BEACH SUITES

Rum Point

Placencia Lagoon

Mango Creek

PLACENCIA RD.

KITTY'S PLACE

TURTLE INN

PLACENCIA TOWN

Caribbean Sea

THE SIDEWALK STRIP

LYDIA'S GUESTHOUSE

JUNGLE JUICE BAR & RESTAURANT

PARKING

SEA SPRAY HOTEL

DAISY'S ICE CREAM

RANGUANA LODGE

DEB AND DAVE'S LAST RESORT

JULIA'S GUESTHOUSE

PLACENCIA MARKET

COZY CORNER

JOHN THE BAKERMAN

POLICE

SCOTIA BANK

BTL

WESTWIND HOTEL

PICKLED PARROT BAR & GRILL

MEDICAL CENTER

OMAR'S GUEST HOUSE

HARALD WALLEN'S MARKET

OMAR'S DINER

THE SIDEWALK STRIP

Placencia

TRADEWINDS HOTEL

FISHERMAN'S CO-OP

PURPLE SPACE MONKEY VILLAGE CAFE

TUTTIFRUTTI ICE CREAM

WENDY'S

ICE HOUSE

SOCCER FIELD

BJ'S RESTAURANT

PLACENCIA BUS STOP

PLACENCIA TOURISM CENTER

THE GALLEY RESTAURANT

PHONE

J-BYRD'S BAR

DIANNI'S GUEST HOUSE

SEA HORSE DIVE SHOP

CAFE MERLENE

SOULSHINE RESORT AND SPA

Placencia Harbour

Big Creek

SCALE NOT AVAILABLE

↓ To Monkey River

0   4 mi
0   4 km

Placencia Lagoon

Maya Beach

False Caye
False Point

Seine Bight Village

Rum Point

Placencia

Placencia Caye

© AVALON TRAVEL PUBLISHING, INC.

© DANIELLE VAUGHN

Another day ends on the Placencia Peninsula.

take you on any of a number of overnight paddling trips, such as a three-night Monkey River tour or a week-long caye exploration. They also rent boats for US$25 a day, with which you can paddle out to any number of cayes and make your own adventure.

Fishing

Placencia has always been a fishing town for sustenance, but with the advent of tourism it has gained a worldwide reputation for sportfishing. Deep water catches include wahoo, sailfish, marlin, kingfish, and dolphin fish; fly-fishing can hook you bonefish, tarpon, permit, and snook (all catch-and-release). Fortunately, serious angling also means serious local guides, several of whom (like the Godfrey brothers Earl and Kurt) have been featured on ESPN and in multiple fishing magazines. Hire Earl at **Trip 'N Travel Southern Guides Fly Fishing and Saltwater Adventures** (located in the Placencia Office Supply building, tel. 501/523-3433, lgodfrey@direcway.com). Most tour operators offer fishing trips, and a few specialize in it, including **Kingfisher's Tarpon Caye Lodge,** boasting 30 years of experience (tel. 501/523-3323, cell 501/600-6071, fax

501/523-3322, kingfisher@btl.net, www.tarpon-cayelodge.com). Charlie Leslie Sr., owner and head guide, has a great reputation and will take you to a wide variety of spots, from inshore places that include nearby flats to Tarpon Caye, and the remote Ycacos area. Also ask about their cabanas for rent. **P&P Sports** (tel. 501/523-3132, permit@btl.net) is another; check www.placencia.com for the latest options.

Sailing

Opportunities abound for day trips and sail charters. Check www.sailingbelize.com (tel. 501/523-3138 or 600-2508) or the high-end **The Moorings** (US tel. 800/535-7289, www.moorings.com), which has a base in Placencia for their multiple catamaran adventures.

Massage, Acupuncture, and Yoga

Spa treatments are the latest trend in Placencia, starting with the facilities at **Soulshine** (tel. 501/523-3347, www.soulshine.com, massage US$65/hr) for body treatments and "soul soothers." **Shangri-La** (near Dianna's Guesthouse, no phone, 9 A.M.–6 P.M. daily) offers massage and other treatments in a stilted house.

Dangriga & Southern Coast

There's also **Ted's Acupuncture and Massage** (no phone), just up from the Purple Space Monkey Internet Café and right before the Secret Garden Day Spa. Ted's mother, Bianca, is currently the only working yoga instructor in Placencia. She's lived a full life (she was a dancer with the New York City Ballet and Metropolitan Opera Companies) and continues to do so, offering class in her cute stilted studio on Monday, Wednesday, and Friday mornings. Look for signs or pay them a visit for more details.

Secret Garden Day Spa (tel. 501/523-3420) sits behind Wallen's Market and offers a full range of services. In addition, there are an increasing number of spas in the resorts, including Turtle Inn and The Inn at Robert's Grove.

Tour Guides

There's no shortage of guide services to whisk you across the water to various adventures. Most Placencia tour operators offer service to *all* the latest nearby day trip destinations: Cockscomb Basin Wildlife Sanctuary, Monkey River, snorkeling and fishing trips with lunch on a beautiful caye, the Maya ruins of Lubaantun and Nim Li Punit, and a variety of paddling tours. For any of these trips, please also refer to the dive shops and fishing guides listed in this chapter.

Many tour operators have their offices/shacks clustered by the main dock, just past the gas station; most are subcontracted by the hotels that offer tours to their guests. If you're going it on your own, ask around and know that prices often rely on a minimum number of passengers. Prices vary little, but it's definitely worth comparing. Monkey River day trips, for example, range US$37–45 pp, depending on whether lunch is included and the size of the boat.

Right by the main dock is **Nite Wind** (tel. 501/523-3487 or 523-3176, renidrag_99@ yahoo.com); just up the sidewalk you'll find **Ocean Motion** (tel. 501/523-3363 or 523-3162, oceanmotion@btl.net, www.ocean-motion.com). Hubert and Karen Young's **Joy Tours** (tel. 501/523-3325, joytours@btl.net, www.belize-withjoy.com) is located next to the Western Horizon Chinese restaurant. There are also some individual guide gurus lurking around town, notably the famed **David Wesby,** who, according to one local, knows more than any living man "bout everyt'ing out dere" (pointing to the ocean). Ask around your hotel or at restaurants.

Dave Vernon of **Toadal Adventure** (tel. 501/523-3207 or 606-1399, debanddave@ btl.net) is considered one of the best guides in Belize. He offers numerous unique trips and each year he seems to come up with something even better and more adventurous than the last. Dave is a walking encyclopedia and a must-speak for the eco-traveler. Call for information or stop by **Deb 'n' Dave's Last Resort.**

Funday Adventure Tours (tel. 501/606-3870 or 523-3536, bensadventures@yahoo.com, www .fundaybelize.com) is another reliable service.

Local **Sam Burgess** drives a taxi in town, but his main occupation is as a guide for his company, **Jaguar Tours,** which you can reach at his **Sea Shell Giftshop** (tel. 501/523-3139). He has a 12-passenger van and escorts guests to Garinagu villages, nearby caves, rivers, and to the Cockscomb Basin Wildlife Sanctuary and Maya ruin sites.

ENTERTAINMENT AND EVENTS

Placencia's bars, restaurants, and resorts do a decent job of coordination so that special events like beach barbecues, horseshoe tournaments, karaoke, and live music are offered throughout the entire week—especially during the high season. Your best bet is to check *The Placencia Breeze* newspaper and look for current schedules.

The most consistently happening bar in town is probably **J-Byrd's** (10 A.M.–midnight daily), right on the water behind the gas station, with live bands most Fridays and Sundays. **Sugar Reef** is a mellow hang (on the road to Soulshine, lagoon-side) with weekly horseshoe tourneys. **Jungle Juice** (short walk north of town, lagoonside, 3 P.M.–10 P.M., live music till midnight Sun., closed Tues.) is popular as well. The town's main disco was washed away by Hurricane Iris, and the loud music at the **Tipsy Tuna Sports Bar** is a poor substitute, although the white monstrosity of a building is right on the beach. Keep an

Sunrise from the Placencia Peninsula; there are dozens of resorts and hotels from which to view it, day after day...

eye out for parties and dances in Seine Bight or at nearby resorts.

The biggest party of the year happens the third week of June, in Placencia's wildly successful **Lobsterfest.** The whole south end of town closes down for all things, well, lobster. Lobster-catching tournaments, dances, food booths, and, if my imagination were allowed to run wild, lobster-eating contests and lobster-shaped balloon-tying races by red, lobster-costumed clowns.

Easter weekend is insanely popular as well, as Placencia is a destination for many Belizeans as well as foreign visitors; they typically book their rooms months in advance, so be prepared for the crowds. Look for a Halloween celebration, complete with parade and trick-or-treating. Another annual gig, the **Mistletoe Ball,** wanders to a different hotel before Christmas every year and doubles as a fundraiser for the local BTIA chapter. The town Humane Society organizes various fundraising events as well; keep an eye out.

SHOPPING

Most gift stores feature Guatemalan crafts and clothes, plus local jewelry and sea-inspired art-work. In addition to the numerous shops, stalls, and tables along the sidewalk, **Myrna's** by the gas station has a huge, colorful selection.

ACCOMMODATIONS

All of Placencia's budget lodgings are found on (or within shouting distance of) the sidewalk and most of the high-end resorts are strung along the beach north of town. Options continue to grow and change, and each guesthouse, hotel, and resort reflects the personality of its respective owner, encompassing the visions of born-and-bred humble Placencians as well as rich foreigners and film moguls. In addition, it seems that, no matter what their primary business, everyone and their mother also rents a couple of extra rooms; please treat the following listings as the tip of the iceberg. Remember, these are high-season prices only; expect significant discounts and negotiable rates between May and November.

Under US$25

Omar's Guest House has five small, bare-bones rooms with shared bath for US$13/18 s/d, private bath for $20/25 s/d. The rooms are on the second floor above the restaurant and porch, and get a decent breeze from the ocean, about 200 feet away. Omar and his family are a wonderful wealth of local knowledge and will gladly sit and laugh with you over a lobster burrito and lime juice. They are also devout 7th Day Adventists and close down their office and restaurant during their Sabbath (sunset Friday to sunset Saturday); if you need a room while they're off, Myra's got a key in her gift shop across the "street."

Lydia's Guesthouse (tel. 501/523-3117, fax 501/533-2335, lydias@btl.net, US$14/23 s/d) has eight clean rooms with shared tile-floor bath. There's a sociable two-story porch, communal kitchen, fans, hammocks, and a 63-second walk to the beach. Miss Lydia will make you breakfast if you make arrangements the day before; she also bakes popular Creole bread. **Julia**

and Lawrence Guest House has seven rooms (from US$27/35, s/d) stringing right back from the beach and including a furnished house (US$60, two couples or a family); laundry service available 7 A.M.–7 P.M.

Deb 'n' Dave's Last Resort (tel. 501/523-3207 or 606-1399, debanddave@btl.net, US$22 s/d shared bath) is on the left side of the road into town, with four small, clean rooms surrounding a gorgeous sand courtyard and garden. Owner Dave is head guide for Toadal Adventures (see Tour Operators in this section) and is renowned for his local knowledge and trip-leading skills.

US$25–50

The ⓜ **Sea Spray Hotel** (tel./fax 501/227-0849, seaspray@btl.net, US$25–55) is a good bet—30 feet from the ocean, 18 rooms, all with private bath, refrigerators, h/c water, and coffeepots. The people are warm and friendly. For land- or sea-based tours, owner Jodie will help with details. De Tatch restaurant on the premises serves breakfast, lunch, and dinner and offers email and Internet services. **Dianni's Guest House** (located back by The Moorings dock, tel. 501/523-3159, dianni@btl.net, US$38/43 s/d) has six rooms with private bath, fan, and coffee maker, plus Internet, tour service, bikes, and a book exchange.

The Cozy Corner (tel. 501/523-3280 or 523-3540, cozycorner@btl.net, US$27 s/d) has 10 cement rooms with private bath and basic amenities, located right behind their bar/restaurant on the beach, with a nice breezy second-story porch. Also check out **Mahogany Beach Cabins,** right next door for US$40 s/d, or US$23 further back from the beach.

The **Serenade Guesthouse** (tel. 501/523-3380, serenade@btl.net, US$23–55) is a two-story cement building right off of the path. There are 10 simple, clean rooms, upstairs and down, all either triples or quads. The upstairs rooms catch great breezes; air-conditioning is more. A tiny but breezy restaurant and bar is on the top floor and serves three meals a day. Owners also operate **Frank Caye,** 28 miles away. The four-and-a-half-acre island has three ca-

banas that sleep four each. A caretaker on the island cooks meals, utilizing the abundant conch and lobster—US$50 per person a night; transportation to get there is extra.

Look for the **Tradewinds Hotel** (tel. 501/523-3122 or 523-3412, trdewndpla@btl.net) on five acres near the sea, offering six cabanas and three rooms. Cabanas have spacious rooms, fans, refrigerators, coffeepots, and private yards just feet away from the ocean. The rooms are smallish, but have private bath with hot water, fans, and a small porch with a hammock. The cabanas cost US$55; the rooms about US$25.

US$50–100

Rent one of four fully furnished, air-conditioned apartments starting at US$80/100 s/d at **Easy Living Apartments** (tel. 501/227-6464 or 523-3524, fax 501/227-0849, info@easyliving.bz). You should book two–four weeks in advance, and there's a three-bedroom house also available.

The **Ranguana Lodge** (tel. 501/523-3112), right off the strip, has five private cabanas, three of them on the beach. All are spacious with beautiful wood floors, walls, and ceilings, US$60. They also have simple accommodations on their caye—cabins are about US$30 a night and camping is US$10/night. As with all of the offshore islands, getting there is the expensive part, but worth it if you want your own island for a night or two.

Westwind Hotel (tel. 501/523-3255, westwind@btl.net, US$45–55) has eight rooms with great views, sunny decks, h/c water, private baths, and fans. This resort provides all the amenities of some of the resorts north of town, right in the heart of the village. **Serenity Resort** (tel. 501/600-1447, serenity@btl.net) is an attractive family resort sitting on 21 acres of land with 12 cabanas and 10 rooms. Cabanas have tiled roofs and floors, high ceilings, h/c water, ceiling fans, private bathrooms, and patios and go for US$85. Generous packages are great for kids.

US$100–150

The Soulshine Resort and Spa (tel. 501/523-3347, bookings@soulshine.com, www.soulshine.com, $155 s/d includes breakfast) is a tucked-away retreat across the canal on the southwest corner of the peninsula. It is comprised of seven spacious, well-supplied thatch-roof cabanas, plus a restaurant, a pool, a bar, and a full-service spa offering a wide array of treatments. Soulshine is a great choice for privacy-seeking couples (or individuals) who don't mind being on the lagoon side (i.e., no beach) and within earshot of the parties at Sugar Reef. It's still a nice spot, just a short walk to town, and all kinds of tours around the area are available.

FOOD

It's all here: seafood cooked in coconut milk and local herbs, Creole stews and "fry chicken," sandwiches, burritos, burgers, chow mein, and Italian (and adequate vegetarian options nearly everywhere you go). Just like the hotels, the simpler to moderate options are right in town and the fancy foreign chefs are all up the road in their respective resorts.

Cafés, Bakeries, and Ice Cream

Check near the Shell station for **Flavours Café and Bakery** (5:45 A.M.–9 P.M. daily), where you can get cheap breakfasts (including a US$2.50 "Backpacker Special") and dinners for US$7.50, not to mention coffee and baked goods. Next door, **Tutti Frutti Gelatería** (10 A.M.–8 P.M. daily) serves up some of the best homemade Italian ice cream you've ever had in your life (a bold statement, but we stand by it). **John the Bakerman** makes great breads; look for his sign on the sidewalk. **Daisy's,** toward the north end of the sidewalk, makes her own ice cream and offers cakes, pies, and other goodies.

Restaurant, Diners, and Bar Food

Ⲛ Omar's Diner (7 A.M.–11 P.M. but closed Fri. night to Sat. sunset, no booze) will take care of you all day, with a US$5 seafood omelet and handmade Maya corn tortillas to start the day off, then a US$3 burrito for lunch and a fish plate from US$7.50 for dinner (or pork chops, conch steak, or lobster). **BJ's** (on the corner of the soccer field, 7 A.M.–10 P.M., closed at 4 P.M. on Sun.) has an outdoor porch and cheap fare: sandwiches from US$2, seafood and stir-fry dinners

from US$9. Walking toward the gas station, **Ⲛ Wendy's** offers a similar menu, reasonable prices, plus a glassed-in, air-conditioned eating area and a full bar. **The Cozy Corner** is one of the nicer beach bars with a lobster burger for US$5, fish dinners from US$9, and good bar food, open 11 A.M.–10 P.M. daily.

The **Galley** is a family restaurant offering a range of reasonable dinner plates from 6 P.M.–10 P.M. (and sometimes other meals as well), plus wonderful jazz music and the occasional impromptu concert by owner and musician Cleveland, handy with a guitar, flute, or keyboard. Try the Galley's famous Seaweed Drink—it claims to have created this common Placencia concoction in its present frothy form. It's similar to eggnog, with a pleasing flavor and a shot of brandy for good measure: "It's good for de back, mon!"

The **Pickled Parrot** (between the sidewalk and main road, just off from the soccer field, pickledparrotbz@yahoo.com, 8 A.M.–11 P.M.) is good for seafood (US$11 fish plate, US$15 lobster), burgers (US$6), and blender drinks (including a US$6, three-rum "Parrot Piss" cocktail). The owner, Wendy, also rents a couple of nice hardwood cabanas out back.

Step into the round thatch rancho next to the soccer field to get out of the sun and enjoy a cold drink or a hot espresso before checking your email; the **Purple Space Monkey Internet Café** serves up three meals a day (but is closed between lunch and dinner) plus high-speed wireless Internet access via satellite for US$5/hr. They've got a jewelry-making and fly-tying workshop next door as part of their expanding "village."

Note: Keep your good sense about you if you run into **Brenda,** a former restaurant owner that reportedly used to make the best spicy conch stew around. She is known to hustle travelers for money for meals that never get cooked. Her rustic kitchen is still on the beach between J-Byrd's and The Moorings and hasn't been licensed to serve food for years.

Haute Cuisine

Most of the resorts north of town have restaurants—and foreign chefs—to brag about. At **The**

Turtle Inn, Chef Antonio, from Sicily, prepares meals with greens from his own organic garden; nouveau Belize cuisine (designed by a Beverly Hills chef) at **Luba Hati** is quickly building a great reputation (entrees from US$15); **The Inn at Robert's Grove** serves mouthwatering seafood and imported U.S. steaks. Grab a fistful of dollars and a taxi and *bon appetit.*

INFORMATION

Before leaving for your trip, check for updates on the town's official and regularly updated website, www.placencia.com. Upon arriving, go straight to the **Tourism Office** (tel. 501/523-4045, placencia@btl.net, 9 A.M.–5 P.M. Mon.–Fri., closed 1.5 hours at lunchtime) next to the Shell station and, after reading the various party postings on the wall, pick up a copy of the latest *The Placencia Breeze,* a monthly village rag with many helpful schedules and listings for you, the traveler. The office also sells books, maps, music CDs, and postcards and has a mail drop.

SERVICES
Money
Atlantic Bank, near the gas pump, is open 9 A.M.–2 P.M. The new **Scotia Bank** branch brings a long-awaited ATM, just north of the BTL office.

Communications
The **BTL office,** located at the bottom of the big red-and-white antennae, is open 8 A.M.–5 P.M. Monday–Friday but closes for lunch.

Placencia Office Supply, just around the corner from the gas station (tel. 501/523-3433, fax 501/523-3205, 8:30 A.M.–7 P.M. Mon.–Sat., closed lunchtime) has a copy machine, Internet service, fax, and more—they'll let you plug into their Ethernet line or use their WiFi as well. More wireless broadband (and cappuccino) is available at the **Purple Space Monkey Internet Café.**

Groceries
At **Olga's Market** and **Wallen's Market,** both on the main road, you can find almost all of your needs, including groceries, dry goods, and sundries. **Everyday Supermarket,** in the center of town, is open 7 A.M.–9 P.M.

GETTING AROUND

The town itself is small enough to walk and if you're commuting on the sidewalk, walking is your only option—riding a bike can earn you a US$50 fine. Speaking of two-wheel options, there are plenty of bicycle rentals in town; check with any tour provider or hotel or visit **G & G,** right behind BTL, who rents bikes for US$13 a day. Bikes for rent are of the beach cruiser, Pee-Wee Herman variety and are a good way to go if you find yourself wandering up the peninsula to Seine Bight. Mopeds are another option. Seine Bight, by the way, is 5 miles from Placencia, and Maya Beach another 2.5, so plan to sweat if you're pedaling in the hot part of the day. The cheapest way (besides walking) to get up and down the peninsula is to hop on a bus as it travels to or from Dangriga (see Getting There and Away).

There used to be a free shuttle service, but no more; perhaps it'll be reinstated. In the meantime, there are at least a dozen green-plated taxis hanging around the Shell station or the airport. Rides between town and the airstrip cost a minimum of US$5 for one or two people, US$10 to the Seine Bight area, one way. Ask around the gas station and tourist office and look for posted rate lists to know what you should be paying. The more trusted and long-standing taxi services include **Sam Burgess** (tel. 501/523-3310 or 603-2819), **Cornell** (tel. 501/609-1077), **Percy Neal** (tel. 501/523-3202 or 614-7831), **Radiance Ritchie** (tel. 501/600-6050 or 523-3321), and **Traveling Gecko** (tel. 501/603-0553 or 523-4078).

GETTING THERE AND AWAY

There are a number of ways to travel the 100-plus miles between Placencia Town and Belize City. The tip of the long peninsula is not as isolated as it used to be, and various options exist for continuing on to points south and west, including Guatemala and Honduras.

By Air

At last check, there were over 20 daily flights in and out of the little airstrip north of town, to and from various destinations throughout Belize. For current schedules and fares check directly with the two airlines: **Maya Island Air** (US tel. 800/225-6732, Bel. tel. 501/223-1140, mayair@btl.net, www.mayaislandair.com) or **Tropic Air** (US tel. 800/422-3435, Bel. tel. 501/226-2012, reservations@tropicair.com, www.tropicair.com).

By Bus

Placencia is serviced by Novelo's (still painted "Southern Transport") Dangriga line, with three daily departures and arrivals (in high season, spotty service the rest of the year). Buses come and go from the Shell station, and current schedules are posted there at the Tourism Office. You'll need to change in Dangriga to reach Belize or Belmopan. Cost is about US$5 each way. At press time, buses were leaving Placencia at 5:30 A.M., 6 A.M., and 1:30 P.M.; Dangriga to Placencia departures are at 12:15 P.M., 3:30 P.M., and 5:15 P.M., with some schedule changes on Sundays.

By Car

If driving on the Hummingbird from the north, turn right onto the Southern Highway, then look out for a left turn to the coast at Riverside where you'll begin the peninsula road. If it's been raining, four-wheel-drive is a good idea.

By Boat to/from Mango Creek (Independence Village)

For those traveling to points south like Punta Gorda or Guatemala, and for those who wish to avoid the Placencia Road, a boat/bus combo will get you back to the mainland and on your way. **Hokey Pokey Water Taxi** (tel. 501/523-2376) is the only regular service between the town dock (by Shell station) and the dilapidated landing at Mango Creek, charging US$5 one way for the 15-minute trip through bird-filled mangrove lagoons. Boats leave Placencia at 6:45 A.M., 10 A.M., 4 P.M., and 5 P.M., and Mango Creek at 6:30 A.M., 7:30 A.M., 8 A.M., 2:30 P.M., and 4:30 P.M.

Bus connections to all points are coordinated with the 10 A.M. and 4 P.M. boats from Placencia, so that the traveler need only worry about stepping onto the correct bus as soon as her boat lands in Mango Creek (after the quick taxi shuttle to the bus depot by Sherl's Restaurant, US$.50). Hokey Pokey is a reliable family-run operation, proudly steered by Captains Pole, Lito, and Caral.

By Boat to Honduras

The **Gulf Cruza** ship leaves like clockwork for Puerto Cortes every Friday at 9:30 A.M., returning Monday afternoon at 2 P.M. (tel. 501/202-4506 or 603-7787, in Honduras tel. 504/665-1200). The trip costs US$50 and takes roughly four hours, stopping in Big Creek, Belize for immigration purposes, and carrying a maximum of 50 passengers.

Near Placencia

 MONKEY RIVER

An easy 35-minute boat ride from Placencia brings you to the mouth of the Monkey River and the village by the same name. Founded in 1891, Monkey River Village was once a thriving town of several thousand loggers, *chicleros,* banana farmers, and fishermen; that was then. Now, the super-sleepy village of 30 families (about 150 people) makes its way with fishing and, you guessed it, tourism. Some 50 villagers are trained and licensed tour guides who work with hotels in Placencia to provide a truly unique wildlife-viewing experience. The handful of daily trips are also a welcome source of income for Monkey River's three eateries.

Ninety percent of the structures you see have been rebuilt since Hurricane Iris flattened the town in 2001. The village is accessible only by boat—most often through the mangroves from Placencia, but there is also an eight-mile road from the Southern Highway that ends across the river from the village. Park your car and honk, and a boat will come pick you up.

The Monkey River Day Trip

After negotiating the mangrove maze, your guide will take you into the river's mouth and dock up in town for a bathroom break and a chance to place your lunch order for later in the day. Then you'll be off upstream, all eyes peeled for animals. You'll beach up at the trailhead to explore a piece of **Payne's Creek National Park,** a 31,000-acre reserve that is surrounded by even more protected area. You'll hike through the dense brush, now a regenerating broadleaf forest which will take decades before reaching its pre-Iris glory. Then it's back down the river for lunch and a stroll through the village. Most head back to their rooms in Placencia, but you may wish to consider staying a night or two, either to experience the village life, or to get some serious fishing time in.

Accommodations

The options in Monkey River are casual inns, best appreciated by those who enjoy isolation and primitive surroundings. Most offer a set menu (a different entrée served each day). Reservations are required for meals, though all of these small cafés will serve drop-ins something such as a burger or a beer.

Near the breezy part of town by the mini-basketball court, **Alice's Restaurant** (tel. 501/720-2033) offers meals for about US$5, served in a large dining room with a view of the sea; renting one of her airy wood rooms in a neighboring building costs US$23 with fan and shared bath with h/c water. A room with private bath is planned. **Sunset Inn** (tel. 501/720-2028, US$30 s/d) is a two-story structure with eight musty rooms with private bath, fan, and h/c water. Decent meals can be had for about US$8. The **Black Coral Gift Shop, Bar, and Restaurant** offers simple fare, local crafts, and, by the time you read this, Internet service.

© DANIELLE VAUGHN

You'll see more than "baboons" on Monkey River.

All hotels and resorts offer sea and land tours and trips. Local guides and fishermen are experts. Sorry, no dive shop yet, but bring your snorkeling gear. Overnight caye trips are available, as are river camping trips (you're dropped off at the Bladen bridge and canoe down the river, stopping at night to camp).

LAUGHING BIRD CAYE

Managed primarily by the NGO **Friends of Nature** (near Placencia Village dock, tel. 501/523-3377, folbc@btl.net), Laughing Bird Caye National Park is an important protected area encompassing over 10,000 acres of sea, and it's a popular day-trip destination from Placencia. It's easy to see why. Swaying palms, small but beautiful beaches, an absence of biting bugs, shallow sandy swimming areas on the leeward side of the island, and interesting diving on the ocean side add up to a lot of pleasure in a relatively small package.

This particular kind of caye is referred to as a *faro* island, and the arms on each end make a kind of enclosure around a lagoon area on the leeward side. In this way the island acts much like a mini-atoll. That's good news for those wishing to dive the eastern side of the island. You'll find a lot of elkhorn coral and fish life. Grunts, damselfish, parrot fish, houndfish, bonefish, and even rays and nurse sharks are to be found here.

This site was designated in December 1991. The reserve is visited regularly, mostly by researchers and tourists carried out by tour operators from Placencia for picnics, snorkeling, and diving. Previously, the reserve was used for overnight camping, but no longer due to the lack of toilet or other waste disposal facilities. Some mooring buoys have been installed to prevent anchor damage to the surrounding reef. Private yachts and sea kayaks also use the site regularly. There is one trail through the center of the caye.

OTHER NEARBY ISLANDS

Many small islands off the Placencia coast are privately owned and accessed only through a specific resort or tour company. Others can be visited by anyone—here are a couple. **Ranguana Caye** (tel. 501/503-8452, or book through The Inn at Robert's Grove) does not allow camping on this tiny isle, but there are three wood cabins

© DANIELLE VAUGHN

island for one: a private caye off Placencia's southern tip

with two beds each that rent for US$107 a night. There's decent walk-in snorkeling, barbecue capability, kayaks, and a fulltime caretaker.

It takes 1.5 hours in a motorboat to reach Ranguana, and it costs roughly US$100 each way. The nearest island to Ranguana is **Pompion Caye,** a dot on the horizon some six miles north. Camping is allowed there; contact Kingfisher's Tarpon Caye Lodge (tel. 501/523-3323, kingfisher@btl.net, www.tarponcayelodge.com) in Placencia.

Ask at Kitty's (tel. 501/522-3227, fax 800/886-4265, info@kittysplace.com, www.kittysplace.com) on the way to Placencia about a trip to **French Louis Caye,** where you'll find a simple cabin to get away from it all. The caye is about 12 miles off the coast. It's never crowded—only a few beds. The snorkelers from Kitty's stop here for lunch, but other than that it's all yours (you do have to share with the caretaker—a great cook). US$300 per night per couple.

The **Sapodilla Cayes** refer to the multitude of cayes that make up the southern tip of Belize's Barrier Reef as it fishhooks back up on the coast side. Ask local tour operators about possibilities for getting out here, especially **Seal Caye,** one of the nicer ones (see also the information on Sapodilla Cayes Marine Reserve in the East and South of Punta Gorda section of the Punta Gorda chapter).

MANGO CREEK (INDEPENDENCE VILLAGE)

This coastal population and transport hub began as Mango Creek and later expanded into Independence Village; it is referred to alternately by both names. This is a dispersed community with a sweltering climate and no attractions aimed at tourism, except as a transportation stop. The only reason a traveler will find himself here for any length of time is if he is waiting for a boat or bus, or volunteering in one of the medical facilities. Independence has the nearest 24-hour clinic to Placencia and if an air-evac to Belize City is not possible, this is where a patient will be taken in an emergency. The private clinic (tel. 501/601-2769) is located on Water Side Street; there is also a public hospital providing health care to the poor. Independence is also the site of the area's secondary school, and a boat-load of students from Placencia makes the daily trip to conduct their studies, as there is no high school on the peninsula.

Practicalities

There are a few hotels in Independence, including **Ursella's Guest House** (up the street behind the basketball court, tel. 501/503-2062, US$13/19 s/d shared bath); **Hotel Hello** (near the bus "station," tel. 501/523-2428, US$25/40 s/d), which has a restaurant; and on the main road to the highway, **Hotel Cardie's** (tel. 501/523-2421, US$32), where rooms have a/c, private bath, and TV.

There are a number of places to eat, the most obvious of which is **Sherl's** (6:30 A.M.–9 P.M.), behind the gas station where you'll board or get off your bus. There are cheap plates of food and a bathroom and cheap plates of food. Also try the Chinese restaurant by the park. There is an **Alliance Bank** branch by the park (tel. 501/523-2588, 8 A.M.–2 P.M. Tues.–Fri.).

Bus service through Independence is provided by both James and Novelo's (Southern Transport) in a perplexing timetable. You probably won't have to worry about bus times though, since your boat will hook you right onto your bus; the best we could make out, the last bus to Punta Gorda leaves at 8 P.M. and the last ride to Dangriga and Belize City is at 5:30 P.M.

TO HONDURAS

A quick hop and a skip away, Honduras, the original banana republic, offers a wealth of less-trammeled destinations for those travelers with enough time on their hands to make the trip. Most-visited are the Copan archaeological site, near the country's western border, and the Bay Islands, off the coast from the city of La Ceiba. Either one can be reached in a day from Belize. Less-known are the treasures surrounding Lago de Yojoa, less than two hours south of the city of San Pedro Sula.

If you choose not to fly to San Pedro Sula from Belize City, you can go by direct boat across the Bay of Honduras to Puerto Cortes, Honduras from either Dangriga or Placencia. From Dangriga, the sleek *Nesymein Neydy* (tel. 501/223-1235, 203-1128, or 203-4955, Honduras tel. 504/984-9544) makes the three-hour trip for US$50, leaving Saturdays at 9 A.M. and returning Tuesdays. **Gulf Cruza** (tel. 501/202-4506 or 603-7787, Honduras tel. 504/665-1200) departs from the main dock at Placencia every Friday 9:30 A.M., returning Monday afternoon at 2 P.M. The trip costs US$50 and takes about 4–5 hours, stopping in Big Creek, Belize for immigration purposes. Most travelers hook the trip into their own schedules, but at least one tour company in Belize City will book your seat on the Gulf Cruza boat *and* arrange for a shuttle to Placencia (US$15); Mundo Maya can even have the van pick you up at your hotel (call or visit them for details, they can book you on the Dangriga boat as well, but there's no shuttle).

See *Moon Handbooks Honduras* for more information.

Punta Gorda and the Toledo Villages

There's a lot going on down south—wild, remote attractions that you'll have to work to discover. Even with improvements to the Southern Highway and daily air service to and from the town of Punta Gorda, the majority of Toledo District's real gems lie hidden away in remote villages, caves, waterfalls, and offshore cayes. Official tourism representatives want to change the region's motto from the "Forgotten" corner of Belize to the "Unforgettable" corner, but this is still about as off the beaten track as you can get in Belize.

Toledo is also the poorest district in the country and the most expensive in which to live. Money earmarked for development and tourism rarely finds its way south, although the first signs of development and real estate–swapping around Punta Gorda are showing themselves and there are finally a few upscale lodges in the area in addition to the cheap flophouses and backpacker digs that have been around a lot longer. Up till now, tourism has been coming to the district in small, interesting doses: Student groups, researchers, and independent travelers have shown

a great interest in the network of Maya villages and the world-famous ecotourism programs hosted there. Of course there are also Garinagu, Mennonites, and your typical assortment of foreigners, including the biggest concentration of Peace Corps Volunteers in the country.

Big changes may be afoot for sleepy Toledo. The controversial Plan Puebla Panama, a massive big-business–oriented infrastructure project that is part of hemisphere-wide free trade agreements, may use the area as part of a new isthmus-long super highway, opening up the Southern Highway for international trade across the new Guatemalan border crossing at Jalacte. For travelers, this would mean additional options to loop back up into Guatemala. For the local Maya, however, who have always been the most marginalized people in Belize, it could be disastrous. Many Maya families who came to Belize as unofficial homesteaders have never needed to accept traditional Western ideas of landownership; efforts to secure them titles are now underway before their plots get snatched away from under their feet.

PLANNING YOUR TIME

Start by factoring in all the moving around necessitated by a southern foray. If you are coming to the area by bus, plan on nearly a full day of travel on either end of your trip south (at least five to six hours from Belize City); consider taking the quick flight between Belize City (or Placencia or Dangriga) and Punta Gorda. If you plan on heading into the upcountry Toledo villages, you'll have to come to Punta Gorda first and set the trip up, usually necessitating at least one night in town, maybe more, depending on the limited village bus schedules. Basically, if you really want to explore Toledo District, one or two days ain't gonna cut it. You'll need to set aside at least four or five days, or more if you'd like to get out to the cayes or down to Livingston, Guatemala. Some Placencia-based tour operators offer day trips to the archaeological sites of Toledo District, with several hours of travel on either end of the trip. You'll have a pleasant tour of the ruins on these trips, but you won't see much of the region, and you won't get to see Punta Gorda.

HISTORY
Maya Mysteries

The first Maya built several ceremonial centers in the Toledo area. Little is known about this group of people. However, as archaeologists continue to make discoveries, they learn more and more— some fact, and some fiction. One favorite mystery is that surrounding the crystal skull found by the daughter of explorer Benson Hedges on her 17th birthday. Experts have vacillated about the authenticity of the perfectly formed crystal skull for years. Was it made by the Maya? Does it have inexplicable powers? Is it a phony? Where did it really come from? Did Hedges plant it for the pleasure of his daughter? The questions persist over the decades. The skull resides outside Belize, somewhere in Canada. A book by Richard Garvin (*The Crystal Skull*, Doubleday, 1973) even suggests the involvement of Atlantis and Extraterrestrials.

Southerners Meet Southerners

During the American Civil War, arms dealers became familiar with the Belizean coast. In the 1860s, British settlers encouraged Americans to come and begin new lives in Belize. Hundreds of Confederates did arrive after the Civil War and began clearing land to develop. However, it was not to last. Most of the American settlers returned to the United States, though one group of Methodists from Mississippi stayed in Toledo District long enough to develop 12 sugar plantations. By 1910, most of the Mississippians were gone. During the U.S. Prohibition, boats decked out as fishing crafts ran rum from Belize to Florida.

Today's Toledo

Today, the district is a blend of many unrelated cultures—Q'eqchi' and Mopan Maya, mestizo, Garinagu, Creole, Caucasian, Chinese, Palestinian, and East Indian. More than 10,000 Q'eqchi' and Mopan Maya are subsistence farmers in the Toledo countryside.

ust-Sees

Look for **M** to find the sights and activities you can't miss and **N** for the best dining and lodging.

M The Waterfront: Start your walking tour of lazy **Punta Gorda** along the Caribbean, then wander over to the central park for ice cream (page 209).

M Lubaantun: The ancestors of today's Maya used this sacred place as a ceremonial center. Lubaantun and the nearby sites of **Nim Li Punit** and **Uxbenka** boast stunning views, thick surrounding forests, and several long-standing legends, including the mystery of the Crystal Skull (page 215).

M Village Guesthouses and Homestays: Head "upcountry" to experience these world-renowned cultural immersion programs in one of a dozen simple country villages. In addition to the cultural adventure, expect guided hiking, swimming, caving, and river trips (page 218).

M Blue Creek and Blue Creek Cave: Near the village of Blue Creek, the cave of the same name is the source of the Río Blanco—you can swim 600

© JOSHUA BERMAN

The ruins at Lubaantun are distinguished by intricate brick work and rounded corners.

yards inside it. Also check out nearby Río Blanco National Park, Ho Keb Ha Caves, and the Fallen Stones Butterfly Ranch (page 220).

M Barranco: This small, riverside village of Belize's southernmost Garinagu population is accessed by boat or bus and available as a homestay site with many cultural and music program possibilities (page 221).

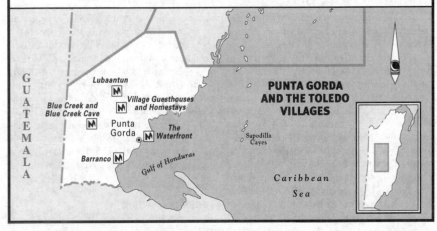

Lubaantun
M

Blue Creek and
Blue Creek Cave
M

Village Guesthouses
and Homestays
M

Punta
Gorda ⊙

The
M Waterfront

Barranco **M**

Gulf of Honduras

GUATEMALA

Sapodilla
Cayes

**PUNTA GORDA
AND THE TOLEDO
VILLAGES**

*Caribbean
Sea*

Punta Gorda & Toledo

PUNTA GORDA AND THE TOLEDO VILLAGES

Punta Gorda

Toledo District's county seat and biggest town, "PG" is simultaneously the lazy end of the road and an exciting jumping off point for forays to upland villages, offshore cayes, Guatemala, and Honduras. PG's 5,000 or so inhabitants live their daily lives, getting by from hurricane to hurricane, while a humble, seasonal trickle of unrushed tourists wander through the streets, sampling local food and taking lots of pictures. Besides the lively market, one of the biggest draws in town is the Toledo Ecotourism Association's central office, where people sign up for their village excursions.

Punta Gorda is a simple port, not super-clean, with no real beach to speak of, and its crooked streets are framed by mostly old, di-lapidated wooden buildings. Most folks in

town speak English, including the Maya in outlying villages. The majority of inhabitants in town are of Garinagu and East Indian descent. Fishing was the main support of the local people for centuries; today many fisher-men work for a high-tech shrimp farm. Farm-ers grow rice, mangoes, bananas, sugarcane, and beans—mainly for themselves and the local market.

ORIENTATION

This is a casual village—many people know only a few street names. Coming into Punta Gorda across **Joe Taylor Creek** from the north, the looming Sea Front Inn greets you as you skirt the Caribbean on the left. Fifty or so

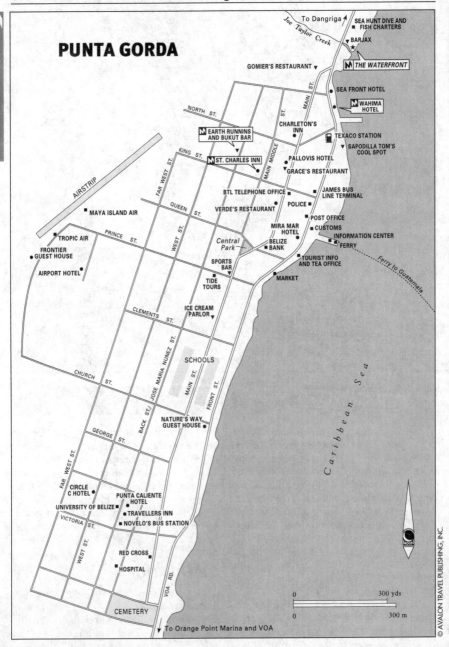

Punta Gorda & Toledo

PUNTA GORDA

To Dangriga

Joe Taylor Creek

SEA HUNT DIVE AND FISH CHARTERS

★ BARJAX

GOMIER'S RESTAURANT ▼

MAIN ST.

M THE WATERFRONT

SEA FRONT HOTEL

M WAHIMA HOTEL

NORTH ST.

ST.

CHARLETON'S INN

TEXACO STATION

▼ SAPODILLA TOM'S COOL SPOT

M EARTH RUNNINS AND BUKUT BAR

MAIN MIDDLE ST.

KING ST.

M ST. CHARLES INN

PALLOVIS HOTEL

GRACE'S RESTAURANT

FAR WEST ST.

BTL TELEPHONE OFFICE

JAMES BUS LINE TERMINAL

QUEEN ST.

VERDE'S RESTAURANT

POLICE

AIRSTRIP

MAYA ISLAND AIR

PRINCE ST.

WEST ST.

Central Park

POST OFFICE

CUSTOMS

INFORMATION CENTER

FERRY

Ferry to Guatemala

TROPIC AIR

MIRA MAR HOTEL

BELIZE BANK

FRONTIER GUEST HOUSE

AIRPORT HOTEL

SPORTS BAR

TOURIST INFO AND TEA OFFICE

TIDE TOURS

MARKET

CLEMENTS ST.

ICE CREAM PARLOR ▼

Caribbean Sea

JOSE MARIA NUNEZ ST.

SCHOOLS

MAIN ST.

FRONT ST.

CHURCH ST.

BACK ST.

NATURE'S WAY GUEST HOUSE

GEORGE ST.

FAR WEST ST.

CIRCLE C HOTEL

PUNTA CALIENTE HOTEL

VICTORIA ST.

UNIVERSITY OF BELIZE

TRAVELLERS INN

WEST ST.

NOVELO'S BUS STATION

RED CROSS

HOSPITAL

VOA RD.

CEMETERY

To Orange Point Marina and VOA

0   300 yds
0   300 m

MOON

© AVALON TRAVEL PUBLISHING, INC.

yards down the way, the road splits at a Texaco station, forming **North Park Street** (a diagonal street a block long) on the right and **Front Street** on the left. Following Front will take you through town past the ferry pier, the Mira Mar Hotel, and several eating establishments; continue south to Nature's Way Guest House at the bottom of **Church Street.** The municipal dock and town plaza, just a couple blocks in, form the town center.

SIGHTS
☒ The Waterfront
Even though there is no real lounging beach, people still go swimming off (and sunbathing on) the dock just north of Joe Taylor Creek. The waterfront is quiet and tranquil, with small waves lapping the shoreline, and a walk along its length, especially at sunrise, should be considered a top priority of your visit.

Central Park
The town park, on a small triangle of soil roughly in the center of town, has an appropriately sleepy air to it. At the north end is a raised stage dedicated to the "Pioneers of Belizean Independence." In the center of the park is a dry fountain, and here and there are some green cement benches. A clock tower on the south end has hands everlastingly stuck as if holding time at bay. On Monday, Wednesday, Friday, and Saturday, this is an especially pleasant spot to take a break, enjoy the blue sky, and watch the activities of the villagers who have come in to sell their produce.

Market Days
Although there are four weekly market days, Wednesdays and Saturdays are the biggest. Friday and Monday are smaller, but still interesting. Many Maya vendors sell wild coriander, yellow or white corn, chiles of various hues, cassava, tamales wrapped in banana leaves, star fruit, mangoes, and much more. Many of the women and children bring handmade crafts as well. Laughing children help their parents. If you're inclined to snap a photo, ask permis-

sion first—it wouldn't hurt to buy something, as well. If refused, smile and put your lens cap in place.

RECREATION
Tour Operators
Green Iguana Eco Adventures (tel. 501/608-0431, ecoiguana@yahoo.com) comes well-recommended; contact Wilfred and Alex for trips to the cayes, sportfishing, river trips, fly-fishing, kayaking, bird-watching, camping, and cultural tours. **Tide Tours** (www.tidetours.org) offers a great many local trips, including kayaking, biking, island-hopping, fishing, to villages, and more. This is the customer service branch of the Toledo Institute for Development and Education (TIDE), Belize's only "ridges to reef" NGO; they do much of the guide training in the area, helping to teach people sustainable, often tourism-related skills. Half-day kayak/bird-watching trips run less than US$30, or for a full day trip to the cayes, US$50 a person. TIDE also supports local cultural events, buying uniforms for the Garinagu dance troops, for example. At **Wild Encounters** (tel. 501/722-2716 or 722-2300), Roberto and April Echeverría are currently the only diving operators in PG.

ENTERTAINMENT
There are many small bars scattered around town, some with pool tables, all with lots of booze.

"Entertainment Lives" at the **PG Sports Bar,** on the southern end of Central Park, and whether you are inside or out you can hear the loud cheers of the crowd watching whatever game is on—or the crooning of the karaoke singers.

Waluco's (it means "son of the soil" in Garifuna) is right across from the ocean, a short walk north of town, and is usually the happening spot to be, especially during festival times and after soccer games. The **Infinity Night Club** is 2.5 miles north of town, and opened up with a big Christmas Eve bash in 2003. For spectator sports, be sure to check out the weekly Sunday soccer games at **Union Field.**

© CRISSIE FERRARA

The market is in Punta Gorda four days a week, located near the seawall and town dock.

SHOPPING

Tienda La Indita Maya (24 Main Middle St.) lies just north of Central Park (the end opposite the clock tower). This store has arts and crafts by Maya Indians from Belize, Guatemala, and El Salvador. It also carries footwear and clothing. Also check the **Fajina Craft Center of Belize,** on Front Street near the ferry pier. It's a small co-op for quality Maya crafts run by the Q'eqchi' and Mopan women. Baskets, slate carvings, textiles, and embroidered clothes are available; it's only open occasionally, ask around to get it opened up. The **Sea Front Inn** has a nice selection of handmade wood frames and other crafts.

ACCOMMODATIONS

Accommodations are very simple but relatively plentiful in Punta Gorda. *Most* rooms are clean,

some only have cold water, offer shared bathrooms (a few are not much more than outhouses), and don't take credit cards. The majority of accommodations in PG are family-run, and that alone can be a great experience. However, do check out your room, sit on the bed, and take a peek into the bathroom before you sign the register.

Under US$25

PG's seedier options occupy the block of Front Street near the main dock; a good rule of thumb is not to book a room that is accessed via a smoky bar and pool hall (e.g. the Mira Mar Hotel). Quieter options are not far, though. Walk a couple of blocks north along Front Street (past the Texaco) to find the **Wahima Hotel** (tel. 501/722-2542), right on the ocean, with five unpretentious rooms, including bunks for US$10 and rooms with private baths for US$15 (up to three people, an excellent deal); they should have hot water and meals by the time you read this.

You're apt to run into all sorts of interesting travelers from around the world who have somehow heard of **Nature's Way Guest House** (tel. 501/702-2119, US$10). Rooms and furnishings are simple and comfortable, clean with pleasant surroundings, and fan-cooled; good breakfast is served on a regular basis, and you'll have access to all activities in the area. The place is run by Chet Schmidt and his Belizean wife. Chet is an American expat and Vietnam veteran who has been here for over three decades, including 13 years teaching in the surrounding villages. He often sits in the common area in the mornings and is very willing to answer questions on what to do, and to give his opinion on life in the area, in particular the challenges faced by the Maya villagers. Ask about kayak trips, jungle treks, camping, exploring uninhabited cayes, visits to archaeology sites, and Maya and Garinagu guesthouse stays.

Another great option is the centrally located **St. Charles Inn** (tel. 501/702-2149, US$15/20 s/d), with a plethora of comfortable rooms and a shady veranda that allows you to observe village life below. Rooms include private bath, fan, and a small TV.

A block west of the Novelo's bus station, the **Circle C Hotel** (tel. 501/722-2726, US$11 shared bath, US$18 private) is run by a local family in a very quiet but convenient part of town, but the rooms are a bit gloomy. **Pallavi's Hotel** (tel. 501/702-2414, US$16–21) has nine basic, clean rooms with a small common balcony overlooking a courtyard. Walk through a messy yard or Grace's Restaurant next door to get to the stairs to reach the rooms with private bath, fan, and TV.

For those traveling by bus, **Punta Caliente Hotel** (tel. 501/702-2561, US$22 with fan, US$33 with a/c and TV) delivers great location, value, and food. Next door to the Novelo's bus station, it offers eight rooms, on-site laundry service (air dried, about US$5 per bag of laundry), a second-story common balcony, and a rooftop sundeck overlooking the ocean. The bright, airy rooms have cold water, private baths, cross-ventilation, and ceiling fans. As you step off the tarmac at the airport, you'll see the **Frontier Guest House** (tel. 501/722-2450), a two-story white cement building with good value, tile-floored rooms with TV, private bath, and hot water. Four rooms have a/c for US$25/30 s/d; two fan-cooled rooms are US$15/20 s/d.

US$25–50

Charleton's Inn (tel. 501/722-2197), at the north end of town, is close to everything, and James buses stop across the street. The 22 rooms are a bit worn but have h/c water, private baths, TV, and either a/c or fans. US$30 with a/c; US$25 or US$18 for rooms with fans, depending on their size.

Tate's Guest House (34 Jose Maria Nunez St., tel. 501/722-0147, teach@btl.net, US$25) is a comfortable lodging with five double rooms in a neighborhood setting. Rooms without a/c are considerably less. Ask for rooms 4 or 5; they are spacious with ceiling fans, remote-controlled color TV, sunrooms, louvered windows, and tile floors, and each has an additional entrance through the backyard.

The **Sea Front Inn** (tel. 501/722-2300, info@seafrontinn.com, www.seafrontinn.com) consists of the two towering stone buildings that

greet you as you drive into the north end of town. The 13 rooms start at US$60, and apartments are also available for monthly rentals. The restaurant serves a locally popular breakfast. Guests find comfortable, spacious rooms, no two alike, with cable TV, fans, a/c, private bath, handmade furniture built with hardwoods. The third floor is the kitchen/dining room/common area that overlooks the ocean.

Next to the Novelo's bus station, the cavernous **Traveler's Inn** (tel. 501/702-2568, US$40/54 s/d) offers eight luxury rooms (by PG standards, anyway) with h/c water, private bathrooms, a/c, cable TV with remote, and ceiling fans. One room is family-size. The carpet is a bit faded and worn but clean, and the staff is efficient. Rates include tax and breakfast.

TC's by the Sea Bed and Breakfast (tel. 501/722-2963, tcbythesea@btl.net) is about a mile and a half north of town and has seven rooms, four with water beds; all have cable TV and rates include breakfast. The cement building appears worn on the outside, but once inside you'll find spacious and comfortable rooms, starting at US$30 for shared bath, going up to US$90 for a/c, private bath, and the works. Meat lovers, enjoy! The restaurant offers some of the biggest steaks in Belize. A 22-ounce porterhouse costs about US$17. Other menu choices are chicken-fried steak, hush puppies, and smoked ham. TC's can also arrange all tours, and swimming off the town dock is a stone's throw away.

FOOD

Punta Gorda offers a great variety of cheap, local eats, with the added benefit of fresh seafood and a few excellent vegetarian options. The town has several good bakeries, and fruit and veggies are cheap and abundant on market days. Ask at any corner store for a sampling of the local Mennonite yogurt—it's excellent, and good for your tummy. (Note: Many of these places are closed on Sunday.) The tortilla factory, located just south of the bank, makes fresh tortillas every day. The best johnnycakes (and other treats) are baked across the street from the fire station.

One of the best restaurants, bars, and all-around

hangout spots in PG is undoubtedly **Earth Runnins and Bukut Bar,** a feel-good shady spot with Internet, good coffee, a unique menu (hummus!), and relaxing lounge area. **Nature's Way Guest House** and the **Sea Front Inn** both serve filling breakfasts, although the Sea Front may make you wait a while for it. Another option is **El Café,** around the corner from Charlton's Inn, with cheap, diner-style Belizean food all day long. **Merenco's,** next to the **Ice Cream Parlor** (1.5 blocks south of the park), has super-cheap burritos, famous fishbowl-size natural fruit juices, and a selection of dinners as well as sandwiches and snacks. **Grace's Restaurant** is a longtime favorite with typical Belizean fare like stew chicken (US$4), tasty conch soup (US$5) and great fry jacks with breakfast.

Located on a spit of land between Joe Taylor Creek and the Caribbean Ocean, you'll find **Barjax,** an unassuming hut belonging to a Belizean–English couple named Barbara and Jack. Although not an official restaurant, you can usually find delicious baked treats here and, if you've got the time, they can cook up a full meal as well. Both are very involved in the community and are great to talk with as you wait for your food.

Try **Sapodilla Tom's** on Front Street, or **Emery's** around the corner, both with excellent local reputations for a variety of good cooking. A few Chinese restaurants offer reliable Chop Suey, especially **Tai Song** and **Fei Wang,** although the latter is sometimes frequented by sloppy drunks. **Punta Caliente Restaurant** offers generous and delicious plates of seafood, stewed pork (US$4), and fried chicken (US$7), with sautéed vegetables and coleslaw; the conch soup (US$5) is particularly good. The restaurant is open seven days a week. You can arrange early breakfasts (6–7 A.M.) for groups.

Gomier's Restaurant, located at the north entrance to town right across from the PG welcome sign, offers a delicious veggie menu oozing with whole grains, homemade tofu, and good karma. The restaurant is tiny and has tasty and creative daily specials, such as barbecued tofu

Refreshment is never far away—there are many cheap eateries and juice bars in Punta Gorda.

served with baked beans, grain bread, and coleslaw, plus a veggie grain casserole, served with a salad (about US$5); bulging soysage burger only US$3, and tofu pizza. There are also fresh fruit juices, soy milk, and soy ice cream. Gomier opens around 8 A.M. and closes around 7 P.M., closed on Sundays.

For cahume cabbage and iguana, there's only one place: **Marian's,** behind the market on Saturday, overlooking the ocean under the Titanic Bar (there are drinks and other foods, too). Keep an eye out for **Mr. Buns,** who pedals around on his bike with homemade cinnamon rolls and cheese buns.

INFORMATION

Look for the **Toledo Visitors' Information Center** at the Town Dock. Here you'll find the owners of **Dem Dats Doin',** who come into town every Monday, Wednesday, Friday, and Saturday and are willing to answer questions about Punta Gorda and the entire Toledo District, especially the "host family network," or Maya homestays. This is not to be confused with the **Toledo Ecotourism Association** (TEA, tel. 501/722-2096, ttea@btl.net, http://ecoclub .com/toledo), whose office is around the corner. TEA is where you sign up to stay in one of the nine village guesthouses (and where you can learn a great deal more about activities in the area). Also, contact the Toledo branch of the **Belize Tourism Industry Association** (tel. 501/722-2119) and look for a copy of *Total Toledo* magazine.

You can also call the **Belize Tourism Board** at tel. 501/722-2531.

SERVICES

Near the municipal dock, you'll find the **Immigration** office (tel. 501/722-2247). Opposite that are a couple of government buildings, including the **post office. PG Laundry,** across from the Belize Bank, is open 8 A.M.–5 P.M., closed Sundays, and charges by the pound. Fill your gas tank at the **Texaco** station at the north end of Front Street, right across from

the ocean; they accept travelers checks and credit cards.

Health and Emergencies

Contact the police at tel. 501/722-2247, fire department at tel. 501/722-2032, and the hospital at tel. 501/722-2026.

Money

The **Belize Bank** (tel. 501/722-2326, 8 A.M.– 1 P.M. Mon.–Thurs., 8 A.M.–1 P.M. and 3–6 P.M. Fri.) is right across from the town square; it is still the only bank in town and has a new ATM. Grace is also a licensed *Casa de Cambio* and can change dollars, *quetzales,* or travelers checks—stop by her restaurant. You may also find a freelance moneychanger hanging around the dock at boat time.

Internet Access

As of press time, PG was still in the dial-up stone age, with only a few options available, like the **The Cyber Café** (coffee, homemade cookies, fresh bread, and used books for sale, US$6 an hour) next door to the Sea Front Inn. Chances are, however, that broadband is coming soon—keep an eye out near Johnson's Store.

GETTING AROUND

Any of PG's couple dozen cabs will take you within city limits for about US$2.50. It's US$10 to drive the six miles to El Pescador or US$12.50 to Jacintoville and the Tranquility Lodge. Look for the green plates. One reliable provider is **Pablo Bouchub's Taxi and Tour Service;** he is also a natural healer and can get you all manner of medicinal herbs and roots (tel. 501/722-2834 or 608-2879). Also call **Galvez's Taxi Tours** (tel. 501/722-2402).

GETTING THERE AND AWAY
By Air
Daily southbound flights from Belize City to Dangriga continue to Placencia and then to Punta Gorda. This is the quickest and most comfortable way to get to Punta Gorda. For

© CRISSIE FERRARA

Life is unrushed on the streets of PG.

the return trip, **Tropic Air** (US tel. 800/422-3435, Bel. tel. 501/226-2012, reservations @tropicair.com, www.tropicair.com) and **Maya Island Air** (US tel. 800/225-6732, Bel. tel. 501/223-1140, mayair@btl.net, www.mayaislandair.com) each offer five daily flights to Placencia, Dangriga, and Belize City, from 6:45 A.M. to 4 P.M.

By Land

Punta Gorda is just under 200 miles from Belize City, a long haul by bus, even with the newly surfaced Southern Highway speeding things up. Count on three to four hours by car, five to six hours by express bus, or seven hours in a non-express. **James Bus Lines** (tel. 501/702-2049 or 702-2625) has a centrally located terminal across from the police station and runs four daily buses between PG and Belize City; first departure from Belize City is a 5:30 A.M. express, then continuing service until 3:30 P.M.; US$11 one-way. Nov-

elo's (Southern, tel.) has its terminal on the south end of town near the hospital and offers 6 A.M. and 4 P.M. express runs from Belize City, with a number of normal buses in between.

From PG to Belize City, James offers a 6 A.M. express and Novelo's goes at 5 A.M. and 4 P.M., with both offering various other options throughout the day.

To the Maya Villages

Every day has a different schedule, but buses go to the Maya villages on Monday, Wednesday, Friday, and Saturday, generally around noon, and depart from the Central Park. From here it's possible to get to the villages of **Golden Stream, Silver Creek, San Pedro, San Miguel, Aguacate, Blue Creek, San Antonio** and the others. Some buses drop you off at the entrance road, leaving a walk of a mile or two. Check at the TEA office or the Toledo Visitors' Information Center for updated village bus schedules.

Vicinity of Punta Gorda

The wild, unique, and stunning southwestern chunk of Belize is referred to as "up-country" or simply "the villages." There are dozens more waterfalls, caves, trails, and hills to climb than appear in these pages—some of them are already locally famous around each village, but the majority are yet to be discovered by intrepid explorers like yourself.

Punta Gorda is also the gateway to the southern hook of the Belize Barrier Reef, a swoosh of tiny cayes and coral that are the least-visited of any of Belize's Caribbean jewels.

THE CAYES

There are some 138 islands off the coast, although only a handful are actually made of sand and palm trees. This is where you'll find the **Port of Honduras Marine Reserve** (PHMR), the largest protected area in the country, spanning 500 square miles of ocean. The southernmost reach of Belize's Barrier Reef lies just offshore, as do the **Snake Cayes** and a few other accessible island paradises. There is a week-long raging party on **Hunting Caye** at Easter time, and camping and simple accommodations on **Lime Caye.**

You've also got the **Sapodilla Cayes Marine Reserve,** declared a World Heritage Site in 1996 as part of the Belize Barrier Reef Reserve System. The reserve covers about 80 square miles and is co-managed by the Fisheries Department and the **Toledo Association for Sustainable Tourism and Empowerment** (TASTE, 53 Main St., Punta Gorda Town, tel. 501/722-0191, taste_smcr@btl.net), an NGO that focuses on using the reserve to educate local youths about their environment. Contact their office to find out about volunteering or possible tourism-related projects centered around these stunning islands.

ARCHAEOLOGICAL SITES
Nim Li Punit

At about Mile 75 on the Southern Highway near the village of Indian Creek, 25 miles north of Punta Gorda town, you'll find Nim Li Punit (a 15-minute walk from the highway along a trail marked by a small sign). The site saw preliminary excavations in 1970 that documented a 30-foot-tall carved stela, the tallest ever found in Belize—and among the tallest in all the Maya world. A total of about 25 stelae have been found on the site, most dated A.D. 700–800. Although looters damaged the site, excavations by archaeologist Richard Leventhal in 1986 and later by the Belize Institute of Archaeology (IOA) in the late '90s and early 2000s uncovered several new stelae and some notable tombs. The stelae and artifacts are displayed in the very nice visitors center built by the IOA. If you don't have a car, it's best to make arrangements to see these ruins and the villages with a guide.

Lubaantun

On a ridge between two creeks, Lubaantun ("Place of the Fallen Stones") consists of five layers of construction, unique from other sites because of the absence of engraved stelae. The site was first reported in 1875 by Civil War refugees from the southern United States and first studied in 1915. It is believed that as many as 20,000 people lived in this trading center.

Game to the death, anyone?—the ball court at Nim Li Punit

JOSHUA BERMAN ©

Lubaantun was built and occupied during the Late Classic period (A.D. 730–890). Eleven major structures are grouped around five main plazas—in total the site has 18 plazas and three ball courts. The tallest structure rises 50 feet above the plaza, from which you can see the Caribbean Sea 20 miles distant. Lubaantun's disparate architecture is completely different from Maya construction in other parts of Latin America.

Most of the structures are terraced, and you'll notice that some corners are rounded—an uncommon feature throughout the Mundo Maya. Lubaantun has been studied and surveyed several times by Thomas Gann and, more recently in 1970, by Norman Hammond. Distinctive clay whistle figurines (similar to those found in Mexico's Isla Jaina) illustrate lifestyles and occupations of the era. Other artifacts include the mysterious crystal skull, obsidian blades, grinding stones (much like those still used today to grind corn), beads,

shells, turquoise, and shards of pottery. From all of this archaeologists have determined that the city flourished until the 8th century A.D. It was a farming community that traded with the highland areas of today's Guatemala, and the people worked the sea and maybe the nearby cayes just offshore.

To get to Lubaantun from Punta Gorda, go 1.5 miles west past the gas station to the Southern Highway, then take a right. Two miles farther, you'll come to the village of San Pedro. From here, go left around the church to the concrete bridge; cross and go almost a mile—the road is passable during the dry season.

Uxbenka

Found relatively recently (1984), Uxbenka has revealed more than 20 stelae, seven of which are carved. One dates from the Early Classic period, an otherwise nonexistent period in southern Belize and a rare date for stelae in the entire Maya area. The site is perched on a ridge overlooking the traditional Maya village of Santa Cruz and provides a grand view of the foothills and valleys of the Maya Mountains. Here you'll see hillsides lined with cut stones resembling massive structures. This method is unique to the Toledo District. Uxbenka ("Old Place") was named by the people of nearby Santa Cruz. It's located just outside Santa Cruz, about three miles west of San Antonio Village. The most convenient way to see the site is with a rental car. However, if you're staying in San Antonio or Punta Gorda, ask around town—a local may be willing to take you and act as a guide.

RÍO BLANCO NATIONAL PARK

Located between Santa Cruz and Santa Elena Villages in Toledo, this park is 105 acres and encompasses a spectacular waterfall that is 20 feet high and ranges from a raging 100 feet wide during the rainy season to about 10 feet during the dry season. The pool that the waterfall empties into has been deemed bottomless by the locals (one claims to have dived 60 feet and never touched bottom). If you

© JOSHUA BERMAN

The ruins at Lubaantun are distinguished by intricate brick work and rounded corners.

are adventurous, you can jump off of the surrounding rocks and fall 20 feet into the crystal clear water. There is also a nature trail you can traverse.

Surrounding the falls is a beautiful forest with thriving flora and fauna populations and a possibility of jaguar sightings. The park is co-managed by the **Río Blanco Mayan Association,** comprised of seven executives from Santa Elena and Santa Cruz who volunteer their time as the park wardens. The Park is as community-based as it gets, and 10 percent of all entrance fees collected at the park goes back to each village.

The surrounding villages are made of indigenous Maya and a trip to the park allows visitors to drive through Santa Cruz, a very traditional village where women wear traditional dresses and there are thatch huts and no electricity.

SOUTHERN JUNGLE LODGES

For those who choose not to participate in the guesthouse or homestay programs, there are a handful of upscale and unique resorts from which you can also base your southern wanderings. Discover the villages by day and then kick back and soak in the surroundings by night, in a hammock or over a candle-lit dinner to the sound of birds and crickets.

Near Punta Gorda

There will surely be more resorts popping up in the area, but for now, **El Pescador** (tel. 501/722-0050, info@elpescadorpg.com, www.elpescadorpg.com, US$180, packages available) is a gorgeous lodge five miles north of Punta Gordaa and the only high-end game this close to town. Perched above the Río Grande, "The Fisherman" is primarily a fishing lodge and encompasses 470 acres of rainforest and citrus farm, including 1.5 miles of riverfront. The ocean is a quick 20-minute ride down the river. Nature trails in the surrounding forests and access to local guides will keep guests busy—unless they'd rather lounge by the pool, the restaurant, or the veranda of their plush cabin.

Near Jacintoville

Tucked away on the San Felipe Road, about eight miles outside PG, **Tranquility Lodge** (no phone, mspennyl@yahoo.com, www.tranquility-lodge.com) offers four surprisingly luxurious rooms that have hosted many avid bird-watchers and orchid lovers; both types have plenty to explore right here on Tranquility's 20 lush acres (only five of which are developed at the lodge area). There were 75 species of orchids at last count—both planted and volunteers—and over 200 identified species of birds. Rates, which include breakfast, are US$50 a night, with one larger family room for US$65, all with clean tile floors, private bath, a/c, and fan; when there are no other guests, it's like having your own private lodge. Upstairs from the rooms is a beautiful, screened-in (but very open) dining room where you'll enjoy gourmet dinners for US$13 (one of the owners is a chef, his wife is a retired nurse). All rates are negotiable off-season. There's direct access to an excellent swimming hole on the Jacinto River, as well as a number of walking trails.

Cuxlin Ha (tel. 501/614-2518, cuxlinha@hotmail.com) is an upscale "timeshare resort retirement village" with a swimming pool, a volleyball court, and a number of fully furnished apartments. There's also a dorm intended for both church groups and members of a worldwide timeshare-swapping organization (RCI). There is an interesting community of Maya homes next to the resort.

Near Big Falls

Hugging a lush bend of the Río Grande as it sweeps past the roadside village, **The Lodge at Big Falls** (tel. 501/722-2878, info@thelodgeatbigfalls.com, www.thelodgeatbigfalls.com, about US$150 s/d) is an upscale retreat. In a peaceful, well-manicured, and vividly green clearing, the six cabanas (more are planned) are ideal for the nature-loving couple or family looking for a comfortable base from which to explore the surrounding country. Special rates for multiple nights and families.

Near San Pedro Columbia

Fallen Stones Jungle Lodge (tel./fax 501/722-

2167, about US$105) is the other most notable option for accommodations in the San Pedro Columbia area. This handsome lodge features thatch-roof cabanas scattered about 42 acres of jungle hillside; there's a covered wooden outdoor deck/dining area. The cabanas are built along the lines of traditional Q'eqchi' Maya homes, using rustic wood with high-pitched ceilings and deep, shady verandas. Screened, louvered windows provide bug protection. The food is delicious and meal plans are available (US$23 for a four-course dinner.)

Butterflies flutter about the grounds, but the real work with the winged creatures takes place in buildings down the hill, where they are fed and bred. The Fallen Stones and its famous **Butterfly Ranch** is only one and a half miles from San Pedro, yet it could be a hundred; as far as the eye can see are rolling jungle hills and valleys stretching off into the Maya Mountains. The various trails about the property lead through heliconia groves, forest trees, and many native plants that appeal to the appetites of butterflies.

ⓜ VILLAGE GUESTHOUSES AND HOMESTAYS

For the culturally curious traveler who doesn't mind using an outhouse, the unique experiential accommodation programs in the Toledo District offer a three-fold attraction: 1) first-hand observation of daily rural life in Central America, 2) a chance to closely interact with one of several proud, distinct cultures while participating in a world-renowned model of ecotourism, and 3) a unique way to go deep into the lush, natural world of the forests, rivers, caves, and waterfalls of southwestern Belize.

Simple guesthouse and family home networks in participating villages offer a range of conditions and privacy, but most are simple, primitive, and appreciated most by those with an open mind. Activities include tours of the villages and surrounding natural attractions. For nighttime entertainment, traditional dancing, singing, and music can usually be arranged; otherwise it's just stargazing and conversation.

These are poor villages and the local brand of ecotourism provides an alternative to total dependency on subsistence farming that entails slashing and burning the rainforest. Additionally, the community-controlled infrastructure helps ensure a more equitable distribution of tourism dollars than most tour operations (members rotate duties of guiding, preparing meals, and organizing activities). Some of the villages where homestays might be available are described in the next section, Maya Villages.

How Do I Sign Up?

Toledo Ecotourism Association (TEA) is the umbrella organization for the guesthouse program, cooperatively-managed and employing 13 village representatives in their respective towns. All participants must arrange their visit from the central office in Punta Gorda (tel. 501/722-2096, ttea@btl.net, http://ecoclub.com/toledo), where you will pay, be assigned to a village and briefed, and be told about transport. Another organization, **Dem Dats Doin'**, is based out of a tourist information booth at the town dock and has a network of families offering more primitive (and cheaper) packages than TEA, in which you stay in a partitioned off room of someone's home, or maybe even in a hammock.

Prices and Practicalities

For the TEA program, a registration fee, one night's lodging, and three meals runs about US$22 pp; all guide services, storytelling, crafts lessons, paddling trips, and music/dance sessions are extra, but extremely reasonable—especially with a group.

Bring comfortable walking shoes, bug repellent, a poncho, a swimsuit, a flashlight with extra batteries, and lightweight slacks and a long-sleeved shirt. Photos of your own family and home—or postcards of your hometown—are appreciated and good icebreakers. Be sure to fill out the evaluation form at the end to help them improve the program.

Meals

Breakfast in Maya villages is generally eggs, homemade tortillas, and coffee or cacao drink. All meals are ethnic and lunch is the largest meal of the day; it is often chicken *caldo* (like a stew cooked with Maya herbs), although it isn't unusual to get local dishes like iguana or gibnut (paca, a large rodent). Fresh tortillas round out the meal. Supper is the lightest meal of the day and generally includes "ground" food (a root food such as potatoes) that the guide and visitors might "harvest" along the jungle trail. The *comal* (tortilla grill) is always hot, and if you're invited to try your hand at making tortillas, go ahead— this is a wonderful way to break the ice with the usually shy Maya women. In a Garinagu village, be prepared for simple but traditional cooking. It can be tasty, but guaranteed to be different. We especially like the *sere,* or fish in coconut milk.

MAYA VILLAGES

Inhabitants of the thatch-hut villages of San Pedro Columbia and San Antonio, the Q'eqchi' and Mopan Maya, are people who fled to Belize to escape from oppression and forced labor in their native Guatemala at the turn of the century. The older folks continue to maintain longtime traditional farming methods, culture, and dress. No modern machinery here—they use a simple hoe to till the soil, and water is hand-carried to the fields during dry spells.

San Pedro Columbia

To get there, take the main road in Punta Gorda that goes inland about 10 miles toward San Antonio. Just before you get to San Antonio, a dirt track to the right breaks off to the village of San Pedro. If you're without a vehicle, take the bus, which makes this trip about three times a week. Or you can hire a cab by day—a bit pricey, but the most convenient way to come and go according to your personal schedule. The owner of the Shell station you pass once in the general area has also been known to take people into the villages for a fee.

San Pedro is one of the biggest of the villages. On the outskirts of town, the dwellings are rather primitive; they often have open doorways covered by a hanging cloth, and hammocks and dirt floors. Chickens and sometimes dogs wander through the houses in search of scraps. People use the most primitive of latrines or just take a walk into the jungle. They bathe in the nearest creek or river, a routine that becomes a source of fun as well as a cleaning procedure. Electricity is found in some of the villages.

As you walk into town past the thatched homes on each side of the road, it becomes apparent that the effects of modern conveniences are only beginning to arrive. When a family can finally afford electricity, the first things that appear are a couple of lights and a refrigerator—the latter allows the family to earn a few dollars by selling chilled soft drinks and such. After that, it's a television set; you can see folks sitting in open doorways, their faces lit by the light inside.

A small Catholic church in town has an equally small cemetery. It sits on a hilltop surrounded by a few thatched dwellings. Not far away is a prefab-looking school that was erected, we were told, with the assistance of National Guardsmen from the United States who were getting jungle training.

Local guides take visitors out of their village past a towering ceiba tree and into what appears to be secondary forest. If there's been rain, the going is muddy. We slogged up and down hilly trails, over little streamlets, and through glens. It's worth it. Everywhere is a stunning parade of life. Hummingbirds, toucans, parrots, and other birds flit about the canopy. Our guide pointed out a jaguar's track, plainly imprinted in the mud of the trail. We were able to follow it for a spell before it led off into the bush. We were impressed by the coolness of the jungle interior and more impressed with the guide's knowledge. He could point out and name every variety of flora and fauna along the path. He plucked wild coriander for us to savor and led us to a farmer's *milpa,* where corn was drying under a *palapa.* What a difference between the oppressive heat in the open cornfields and the cooling relief in the dark shadows of the jungle.

San Antonio

After leaving San Pedro and returning to the main road, make a right turn and you'll soon be in San Antonio just down the road. The village of San Antonio is famous for its exquisite traditional

SPEAKING Q'EQCHI':
IS THERE HAPPINESS IN YOUR HEART?

Nearly all of southern Belize's people of indigenous descent are recognized as Q'eqchi' Maya. You may see the word Q'eqchi' spelled different ways. "Kekchi" is how protestant missionaries described the Maya of southern Belize, and British colonial officials wrote "Ketchi." Today, in neighboring Guatemala, the indigenous leaders of the Guatemalan Academy of Maya Languages (ALMG) have developed a standard Maya alphabet that the Q'eqchi' leaders in Belize have begun to use as well.

Making even a small attempt to speak and learn the language of your Maya hosts will deepen your experience with them. Never mind the laughs your funny accent will attract—your noble attempts are an amusing novelty and no one means any harm. Persist, and you will be rewarded in ways you would never have expected—indeed, learning another language in such an immersing setting is one of the most humbling and empowering experiences a traveler can have.

Basic Phrases

One of the first things you will probably be asked is, "B'ar xat chalk chaq?" (bar shaht chalk chok) to which you can respond, "Xin chalk chaq sa' New York" (sheen chalk chok sah New York).

In Q'eqchi', there are no words for "Good morning," "good afternoon," or "good evening." You simply use the standard greeting, *Ma sa sa' laa ch'ool* (mah sah sah laa ch'ohl), literally, "Is there happiness in your heart?" (In Q'eqchi' however, you wouldn't use a question mark because the "Ma" indicates a question.) A proper response would be "Sa in ch'ool" (sah een ch'ohl), "Yes, my heart is happy."

Although it is falling out of custom with the younger generation, if you are speaking with an older woman or man, they would be delighted if you greeted them with the terms of respect for the elderly: "Nachin" (nah cheen) for an elder woman, and "Wachin" (kwah cheen) for an elder man.

If you decide to go swimming in one of Toledo's beautiful rivers, you might want to ask first, "Ma wan li ahin sa' li nima'" (mah kwan lee aheen sa li neemah), which means "Are there crocodiles in the river?"

Ani laa kab'a? (anee lah kabah) means "What's your name?", to which you can respond: "Ix (eesh)

Q'eqchi' embroidery. However, the younger generation is being whisked right along into 21st-century Belizean society, so who knows how much longer it will survive.

There should be a local tourism representative in San Antonio who can give helpful advice about the area, and direct you to local guides in town willing to take you to **Ho Keb Ha Caves** and **Blue Creek** (bring your swimsuit). This is great bird-watching country.

From here the road is passable as far as Aguacate ("Avocado"), another Q'eqchi' village. But if you intend to visit the ruins at **Pusilha,** near the Guatemala border, you must travel either on foot or horseback. Another ruin, **Uxbenka** (described earlier in this chapter), is west of San Antonio near the village of Santa Cruz, and easy to get to via the trucks that haul supplies a couple of times a week. Not known by anyone but locals until 1984, Uxbenka is where seven carved stelae were found, including one dating from the Early Classic period.

Check out a tiny guesthouse that's been around for a long time, **Bol's Hilltop Hotel.** No electricity, very simple. One mile before reaching San Antonio, you'll find the entrance to **Charlie Foreman's Farm,** an out-of-the-way clearing that boasts precious views of the surrounding hills; Charlie may soon have a campground here, if not, he'll be happy to show you his tree house and chat about the spot, named "Karino Hill" by the British soldiers.

Blue Creek and Blue Creek Cave

This village of some 275 Q'eqchi' and Mopan Maya was first settled in 1925 and is also called

WOMAN's NAME in kab'a (een kabah)" or "Laj MAN's NAME in kab'a (een kabah)."

More Phrases and Vocabulary

Chan xaawil? (chan shaa kwil)—What's up?

Jo xaqa'in (hoe shakaeen)—Not much, Just fine.

B'an usilal (ban ooseelal)—Please.

B'antiox (ban teeosh) or *T'ho-kre*—Thank you.

Us (oos)—Good

Yib' i ru (yeeb ee rue)—Bad, ugly.

Hehe (eheh)—Yes.

Ink'a (eenk'ah)—No.

K'aru (kaieeroo?)—What?

B'ar (bar)—Where?

Joq'e (hoekay)—When?

Jarub' (hahrueb)—How many?

Jonimal tzaq (hoeneemahl ssahq)—How much does it cost?

Chaawil aawib (chah kwil aakweeb)—Take care of yourself (a good way to say goodbye).

Jowan chik (hoekwan cheek)—See you later.

Wi chik (kwee cheek)—Again

Wa (kwah)—tortilla

kenq (kenk)—beans

molb' (mohlb')—eggs

kaxlan wa (kashlan kwah)—bread

tib' (cheeb)—meat

tzilan (sseeelan)—chicken

kuy (kue-ee)—pork/pig

kar (car)—fish

chin (cheen)—orange

kakaw (cacao)—chocolate

ha' (hah)—water

woqxinb'il ha' (kwohk sheen bill hah)—boiled water

cape (kahpay)—coffee

sulul (suelul)—mud

ab' (ahb)—hammock

chaat (chaht)—bed

nima' (neemah)—river

kokal (kohkahl)—children

chaab'il (chahbill)—good

kaw (kauw)—hard

najt (nahjt)—far

nach (nahch)—close

(Thanks to Liza Grandia, Department of Anthropology, University of California, Berkeley.)

"Ho Keb Ha"—"the place where the water comes out," describing this spot where the Río Blanco emerges from the side of a mountain, becoming Blue Creek and home to an extensive cave system. You'll need a guide who's familiar with these caves; ask at Punta Gorda or at one of the nearby Maya villages. Many of these folks know the nearby caves well. Go prepared with flashlights. You can swim up to 600 yards into the cave; it's pretty stunning.

M Barranco

Barranco is an isolated Garinagu village where activities include fishing along the river as well as traveling by dugout canoe up the river into the Sarstoon-Temash Forest Reserve to see howler monkeys, hicatees, and iguana. Return for a refreshing glass of *hiu* (a spicy drink made

of cassava and sweet potato) and an evening of drumming. Get there by bus from the park in PG, or by boat from the PG dock. Ask for times, as transportation is scarce; charter boats can be arranged.

Numerous individuals of Barranco's 600 inhabitants have traveled far from their village to become some of Belize's most renowned musicians, painters, and researchers.

GETTING UPCOUNTRY

To get to Maya country from Punta Gorda, you have several choices. If you plan on an overnight with the homestay or guesthouse programs, TEA will assist you. They may simply direct you to the appropriate village bus from Punta Gorda.

FEAST OF SAN LUIS

There is no question that the Feast of San Luis celebration is symbolic, but of what? It's doubtful that anyone really knows. So much of the ancient traditional culture has been mixed with the Christian religion that even the Maya aren't sure. We do know that an all-night vigil begins the festival, during which traditional masks and costumes are blessed with smoke from burning incense and food offerings. According to Maya belief, a great power resides in the masks and it can be directed toward good or evil.

Drums announce the procession to the home of the *prioste* (holy man) on each of the next nine days. Leading the marchers is a man dressed as the "holy deer," followed by the other characters of the dance, including *el tigre* (the jaguar), women portrayed by men, dogs, and finally, the hunters dressed in black. Four men carry an instrument called the marimba, which is played all the way into the *prioste*'s house and intermittently during respites in the ceremonial dances. Some of the men shake rattles and an ongoing chant adds an exotic tone to the music of the dance.

The Tiger Dance

The ancient legend of the tiger is performed in a square. The four corners and the center of the space represent the Maya's five cardinal directions—north, south, east, west, and the center. Slowly and with grace, the story of *el tigre* unfolds. With active movements, the tiger chases and is chased by the men in red from each of the four corners and around the center. Were they the *bacabs,* the Maya guardians of directions? As a clown, the tiger impishly teases the hunters throughout the dance, stealing their hats or their rattles. At the finale the tiger is captured and killed; the hunters pantomime the killing and skinning of the tiger while the dancer steps out of his costume and runs away. Though performed with exaggerated elements of sincerity, it's a comedic performance, a warm-up of more serious things to come.

The Holy Deer Dance

The story of the holy deer, on the other hand, is performed with reverence instead of comedy, and continues for several days. The festivities include a lively procession to the San Antonio village church. The deer dances proudly, head high, acknowledges each of the other dancers, and then disappears into the forest. Enter the dogs sent by the hunters to seek out the deer. After a while the frightened deer/dancer is chased back by the dogs and with great drama the hunters kill the noble animal.

The Greased Pole

Preparations for the finale start two days ahead of time with an all-night vigil for the men who will cut down a tall tree to be used in the pole-climbing festivities. The pillar is about 60 feet long and made from a special tree, called *sayuc* in Maya. The tree is trimmed and the dancing continues, drawing larger and larger audiences. A great procession follows as the huge pole and a statue of San Antonio (which has been in the *prioste*'s home) are carried to San Antonio's church on the top of the hill. Occasionally, the long line of people stops and lays the pole on the ground. In silence and great solemnity, the pole is "blessed" by the statue of San Antonio while women manipulate censers of burning incense, sending wisps of aromatic smoke wafting around the pole. Once at the church, saints are traded. The statue of San Antonio is returned to its place, more prayers are said, and the statue of San Luis, under a protective colorful canopy and flanked by a dozen flags, is carried out on a wooden platform to "bless" the pole. The procession of people, including the statue, then makes its way to the *prioste*'s house for another night of social dancing.

The Finale

It's September 25, the climax day—and the end of the celebration. Preparations for raising the pole begin early in the morning to the steady, low beat of a drum. Under the watchful eyes of many anxious children, bars of soap are flattened with rocks, broken into small pieces, and dissolved in buckets of water. Next, melted lard is added and thoroughly mixed. The oily compound is then generously spread on the pole. How anyone could accomplish an upward movement on this mess is a mystery, although the first has the most slips. Prizes that have been stored at the *prioste*'s house—a generous hand of bananas, a bottle of rum, and a small sum of money—are placed at the top of the pole for the climber who makes it all the way. He will earn it!

After a slow procession, eating, dancing, and more blessings, the grand finale (under the watchful eye of the saint) begins.

The pole-raising brings a still moment: The only sound is the low beat of the drums. The aroma of incense permeates the air. Fifty men hold ropes while others hold forked sticks and the pole slowly begins to rise, but not without a few slippery sways that bring gasps from the anticipating crowd. Finally the long pole slips neatly into the hole.

Now the fun begins—at least for the onlookers. The tiger and the hunter characters are the first to attempt to climb the pole, followed by a dozen other men; to make it more difficult each has his feet tied together. Everyone has a good laugh watching the slipping and sliding. Finally, a successful challenger with great determination inches his way to the top and reaches for his prize; the crowd cheers and the church bells ring out.

The **Chun Bus** (tel. 501/722-2666) makes the run to San Antonio Monday, Wednesday, and Friday, returning to Punta Gorda Tuesday, Thursday, and Saturday (about US$4 round trip). This bus doesn't stop in San Pedro; instead you will have to leave the bus at the road and trek in several miles. You can also catch a bus as far as Pueblo Viejo, "the edge of the known world." Catch the Chun Bus at Central Park to ensure getting a seat. Remember: no buses run on Sunday.

If traveling by car, you have the option of exploring every little road you see (4WD recommended). From the turnoff for Punta Gorda at Mile 86 on the Southern Highway, take the road north. At about Mile 1.5 there will be a turnoff on the right that heads for San Pedro and other villages.

Across the Border

LIVINGSTON, GUATEMALA

A day trip or overnight to the coastal town of Livingston can be an exciting breath of activity after sleepy PG. One of the many Central American backpacker routes involves entering Belize after a visit to Tikal, then reentering Guatemala via boat from southern Belize; from there, one can travel up the Río Dulce, take a bus to Guatemala City, or a series of hired cars to the Honduran border.

Livingston is a popular destination for vacationing Guatemalans and foreign tourists alike. Prices of everything from beer to hotel rooms are easily half what they are in Belize, and many budget accommodations (and a few fancy ones) are available. Livingston also boasts numerous restaurants, open-air street cafés, and a rich Garinagu presence (most readily experienced at the rasta-colored **Abafu Bar**, where you'll find live drumming, potent bitters, and lots of reggae). Livingston is situated on the Caribbean shore and the wide mouth of the Río Dulce, making it an ideal base for upriver jungle explorations.

Puerto Barrios, on the other hand, is a trash-strewn, rough-and-tumble port town. Primarily a deep-water banana-loading dock, Puerto Barrios provides the curious traveler and merchant marine alike with plenty of hard drugs, prostitution, and bar fights. Stay and play or else make your boat connection and get the hell out. Express buses to Guatemala City leave the **Terminal de Autobuses Litegua** (eight blocks from the dock in Puerto Barrios, a 10-minute walk or US$1.50 cab ride); the 5.5-hour ride costs about US$5.

Getting There and Away

A triangular boat run between the municipal docks of Punta Gorda, Puerto Barrios, and Livingston shuttles travelers across this section of Central American coastline. The trip is done in rather small boats with minimal shelter, so prepare for cold, wet, and rough seas during the rainy season. The direct leg between Livingston and Punta Gorda is only done Tuesdays and Fridays, leaving 7 A.M. from Livingston, then shoving off from Punta Gorda at 10 A.M. If you miss that boat, you'll have to travel first to Puerto Barrios (the hour-long trip costs US$15), then catch a regular *colectivo* water taxi to Livingston (leaves about every hour, the 40-minute trip costs under US$4). There are two trips every day between PG and Puerto Barrios, one based in Belize (**Requena's Charter Service,** tel. 501/722-2070, watertaxi@btl.net), the other based in Guatemala (**El Chato,** tel. 502/948-5525, pichilingo2000@yahoo.com). Boats leave PG at 9 A.M. and 4 P.M. daily and depart from Puerto Barrios at 10 A.M. and 2 P.M.

Customs and Fees

Before leaving Punta Gorda, you'll get your passport stamped at the customs office there at the municipal dock; you'll also be charged a US$4 PACT fee to help support Belize's protected areas—or maybe you won't. If traveling directly to Livingston, be sure to walk up the hill from the dock to check in at the **Migracion Office,** where you'll get stamped and pay a tiny fee (less than US$2); if you fail to do this, you'll have problems leaving Guatemala. In Puerto Barrios, Migracion is located 1.5 blocks east of the dock and is open 24 hours. If leaving for Belize, you'll need to pay a US$10 exit fee here when you get your passport *ponchada* (stamped). Be sure to do this *before* buying your boat ticket to PG. There is no fee to enter Belize.

HONDURAS FROM PUNTA GORDA

To get to Honduras, you'll first take a daily boat shuttle from PG to Puerto Barrios. Buses and taxis in Puerto Barrios can whisk you to the Honduran border. Look for one of the many minivans trolling for passengers around the docks and market; it's about an hour to the border at Corinto, then another 1.5 hours to the coastal backpacker hideout of Omoa, Honduras. From there, it is under an hour to Puerto Cortes and San Pedro Sula, where you'll find connecting buses and flights to Copan, the Bay Islands, or points farther south.

We found no direct boat service to Honduras from the PG docks.

Northern Belize

Comprised of the Orange Walk and Corozal Districts, this area is as overlooked by most tourists as is far southern Belize, yet it is just as filled with hidden surprises—and is a great deal more accessible. The wilds of Belize's northwest corner host some of the highest densities of jaguar and rare bird populations in the country, and the extensive coastal lagoons of the northeast are largely undeveloped, home to manatee, dolphin, and thick flocks of both native and migratory birds.

The second-largest district of Belize, Orange Walk encompasses vast tracts of wilderness, peaceful waterways, Maya ruins, and Orange Walk Town, one of the largest commercial and farming centers in the country. Belize's northern region is blessed with a wide array of habitats and wildlife: riverine lagoons, marshes, and deep tropical forests. In Orange Walk, you'll find the New River Lagoon, the Río Bravo Conservation Area, and the high country around Chan Chich Lodge. The vast New River Lagoon, over which you must travel to reach the Lamanai Ruins, is Belize's largest body of fresh water (28 miles long). Its dark waters are smooth and reflective, changing with every cloud that passes over the sun.

Must-Sees

New River Lagoon

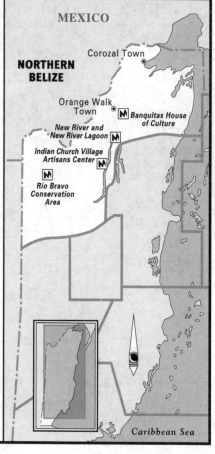

M Banquitas House of Culture: Located in **Orange Walk Town** and featuring exhibits on history, industry, and culture, this is one of the country's premier museums (page 231).

M New River and New River Lagoon: A fabulous wildlife-viewing float trip can also take you to Lamanai and Indian Church Village Artisans Center (page 231).

M Indian Church Village Artisans Center: Much of the craftwork you'll find at this community-based initiative is inspired by the ancient designs of the nearby archaeological site of **Lamanai** (page 236).

M Río Bravo Conservation Area: Go deep into the northwest to explore this area as well as the ruins and lodge at Chan Chich; getting there necessitates a sturdy truck or a chartered flight (page 238).

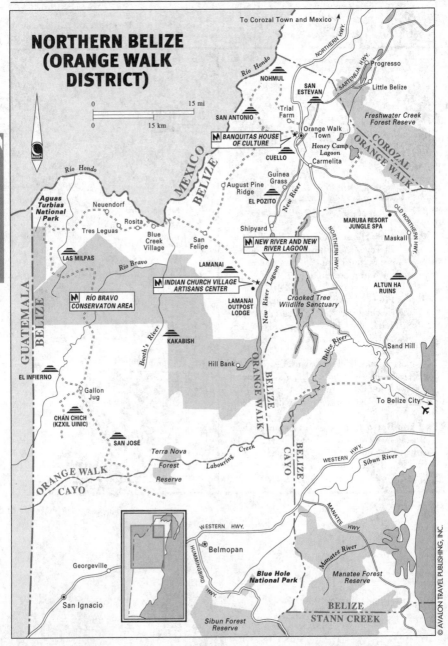

NORTHERN BELIZE (ORANGE WALK DISTRICT)

To Corozal Town and Mexico

NORTHERN HWY.

Río Hondo

Progresso

SARTENEJA HWY.

NOHMUL

SAN ESTEVAN

Little Belize

Freshwater Creek Forest Reserve

SAN ANTONIO

Trial Farm

Orange Walk Town

M BANQUITAS HOUSE OF CULTURE

Honey Camp Lagoon

Carmelita

COROZAL

ORANGE WALK

CUELLO

Guinea Grass

August Pine Ridge

EL POZITO

New River

MARUBA RESORT JUNGLE SPA

Maskall

OLD NORTHERN HWY.

Río Hondo

Aguas Turbias National Park

Neuendorf

Rosita

Tres Leguas

Blue Creek Village

San Felipe

Shipyard

M NEW RIVER AND NEW RIVER LAGOON

NORTHERN HWY.

MEXICO BELIZE

LAS MILPAS

Río Bravo

LAMANAI

M INDIAN CHURCH VILLAGE ARTISANS CENTER

ALTUN HA RUINS

GUATEMALA BELIZE

RÍO BRAVO CONSERVATON AREA

LAMANAI OUTPOST LODGE

Crooked Tree Wildlife Sanctuary

New River Lagoon

Booth's River

KAKABISH

Belize River

Sand Hill

Hill Bank

ORANGE WALK

BELIZE

EL INFIERNO

Gallon Jug

To Belize City

CHAN CHICH (KZXIL UINIC)

SAN JOSÉ

Terra Nova Forest Reserve

Labouring Creek

BELIZE

CAYO

WESTERN HWY.

Sibun River

ORANGE WALK

CAYO

WESTERN HWY.

HUMMINGBIRD HWY.

Belmopan

Georgeville

San Ignacio

Blue Hole National Park

Sibun Forest Reserve

MANATEE HWY.

Manatee River

Manatee Forest Reserve

BELIZE

STANN CREEK

0   15 mi
0   15 km

MoGN

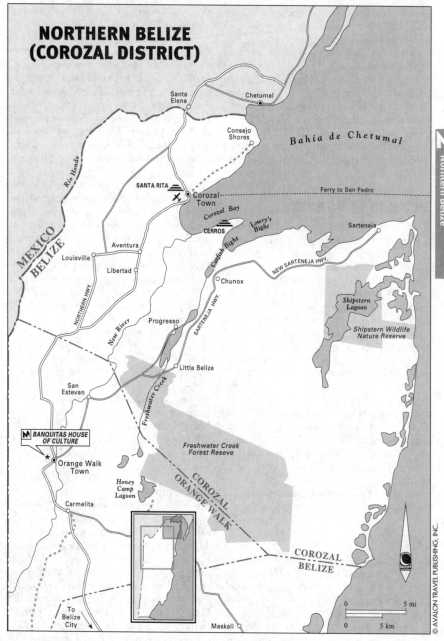

NORTHERN BELIZE (COROZAL DISTRICT)

Santa Elena

Chetumal

Consejo Shores

Bahía de Chetumal

Río Hondo

SANTA RITA

Corozal Town

Ferry to San Pedro

Corozal Bay

CERROS

Lowry's Bight

Sarteneja

MEXICO
BELIZE

Louisville

Aventura

Libertad

Catfish Bight

NEW SARTENEJA HWY.

Chunox

Shipstern Lagoon

Shipstern Wildlife Nature Reserve

New River

Progresso

SARTENEJA HWY.

Little Belize

San Estevan

BANQUITAS HOUSE OF CULTURE

Orange Walk Town

Honey Camp Lagoon

Freshwater Creek Forest Reserve

Freshwater Creek

COROZAL
ORANGE WALK

Carmelita

COROZAL
BELIZE

To Belize City

Maskall

0   5 mi

0   5 km

Northern Belize

© AVALON TRAVEL PUBLISHING, INC.

Morelet's crocodiles and hicatee turtles inhabit these waters, along with numerous species of fish and waterfowl.

In the oceanside town of Corozal, just nine miles from the Río Hondo (which forms the border between Belize and Mexico) and 96 miles north of Belize City, you'll enjoy a peaceful stroll along the seawall as you plot your possible paths from here: North to Chetumal, Mexico? East to the remote Shipstern Wildlife Nature Reserve? West to Chan Chich and Gallon Jug Estates? Or southeast to San Pedro? Take your time and enjoy the view.

PLANNING YOUR TIME

This is one of the areas that most travelers blow right through, or else only spend a night or two in either Orange Walk or Corozal Town. But, the two towns offer entirely different vibes and are small enough to be explored in a day each. There are a few day trips here, including Chetumal, Mexico and the Shipstern Reserve. To really dig into the north, plan on at least a night or two at the Lamanai Outpost Lodge or in the village nearby; by being situated so close and not having to travel hours to reach them, this is the best, fullest way to experience the Lamanai ruins and the jungle around them. If this doesn't fit your plan, Lamanai is also offered as a day trip from Belize City, the North Cayes, Orange Walk, and Corozal. Add an extra couple of days if you attempt to venture into the extreme northwest, to the Río Bravo Conservation Area or Gallon Jug Estates. Some travelers choose to link Corozal into loops that include Ambergris Caye—making this trip by boat gives you a chance to stop off at Sarteneja, a small, remote fishing village.

HISTORY

Belize's northern region was settled in the 19th century by refugees from southern Mexico during the Caste War, and you'll still hear more Spanish than English. What's left of two forts, Mundy and Cairns, in Orange Walk Town reminds one that this was the scene of violent battles between Belizean settlers and war-minded Maya trying to rid the area of outsiders. The last battle took place in 1872.

For centuries, before settlement by farming-inclined mestizo refugees from Yucatán (Mexico) in 1849, this was timber country. Logs from the north and middle districts of Belize were floated down the New River to Corozal Bay, and then to Belize City; from there they were shipped all over the world. If you travel about two miles south past Orange Walk Town, you'll find a toll bridge over the New River. Tree harvesting is still going on, and you'll encounter large logging trucks crossing the toll bridge.

At one time, sugarcane was the most important Belizean crop. Now farmers grow more and more citrus, and beef producers supply not only the local market but are tapping into the export market. Caribbean rum (a product of sugarcane) is still big business in this area. During the cane harvest, the one-lane highway is a parade of trucks stacked high with sugarcane and waiting in long lines at the side of the road to get into the Tower Hill sugar mill. Night drivers beware: The trucks aren't new and often have no lights.

Another interesting tidbit of northern agricultural history: before the thriving Belizean marijuana industry was shut down by the United States government in 1983, massive amounts of high-grade "Belize Breeze" were grown and shipped from this area. The product was loaded by the ton onto airplanes that landed right on the Northern Highway. Anti-drug officials tried to hamper this method by raising poles along the sides of the highway which would clip the pot planes' wings.

Mennonite Country

The picturesque Mennonite farming areas of Orange Walk seem strangely out of place as you ride through the countryside, but there is no doubt that they are some of the most productive communities in the country. At times you could believe you were in North Dakota or eastern Pennsylvania as you near Blue Creek and the mountains that straddle the Mexican border behind it. Today's Mennonite farmers have created lovely green pastures and rich gardens; they specialize in cattle, dairy, and egg industries.

Orange Walk Town

Located 66 miles north of Belize City and 30 miles south of Corozal Town, Orange Walk Town is one of the larger communities in Belize. Its 15,000 inhabitants work predominantly in local industry and agriculture, providing yet another facet of Belize with its own history and style. If passing through, stop and look around. The town has two banks, a few hotels, and a choice of many small, casual cafés. Roads from Orange Walk Town enable you to explore, in four directions, as many as 20 villages and numerous Maya ruins. Elsewhere in Orange Walk District, you'll find several interesting historic sites including **Indian Church Village;** a 16th-century Spanish mission; and the ruins of Belize's original sugar mill, a 19th-century structure built by British colonialists.

Heading west and then southwest, you'll find **Blue Creek,** a Mennonite development where Belize's first hydroelectric plant is located. While Orange Walk Town has changed little in recent years, change is coming. A new bypass is being built that should be completed by spring 2005 and will make the town center much more quiet and pedestrian-friendly. New development at **Banquitas Plaza,** including a cultural museum, extends a welcome to tourists interested in the regional way.

SIGHTS AND RECREATION

Banquitas House of Culture

Banquitas Plaza (tel. 501/322-0517, 10 A.M.–6 P.M. Tues.–Fri., 8 A.M.–1 P.M. Sat.) is an exhibition hall that presents a broad exhibit about Orange Walk–area history, culture, industry, and the work of local artisans. They also host special traveling exhibits on Maya and African archaeology, and the modern culture of Central America. This is the place for a slow evening watching the light die on the New River and the landscaped grounds of the Banquitas Plaza. The plaza comes alive on Friday and Saturday nights when young Orange Walk couples stroll the river walk enjoying the cool evening together. The nearby amphitheater hosts monthly cultural activities.

New River and New River Lagoon

Trips up and down the New River and around the New River Lagoon are fun adventures for the entire family, with a chance to see Morelet's crocodiles and iguanas sunning on a bank. Night safaris can be equally exciting. It's a chance to see the habits of animals that come out to play only after the sun sets; you'll need the help of a good guide and a spotlight.

By day you'll see the sights of verdant jungle and wildlife along the river. Many people combine a river trip with a visit to the ruins of Lamanai. It is the most impressive way to approach the site, and a time-saver as well compared to going by land. Contact any of the guide companies listed in the Lamanai section.

Honey Camp Lagoon

About twenty minutes south of Orange Walk Town on the old Northern Highway, you can join the locals to indulge in white sandy beaches and shady coconut trees as nice as any on the Cayes.

Nohmul

This major Maya ceremonial center means "Great Mound," and the top of the pyramid is the highest point in the Orange Walk and Corozal Districts. Twin ceremonial groups are connected by a *sacbe* (raised causeway). The center shows it once catered to a thriving population in the Late Pre-Classic and Late Classic periods (350 B.C.–A.D. 250 and A.D. 600–900, respectively) and controlled an area of about 12 square miles. Nohmul ("Big Hill") was named by the people living in the vicinity of the site.

Not much has been consolidated for tourists here. The entrance to the site is about 10 miles north of Orange Walk Town, in the sugarcane fields west of the village of San Pablo; it is one mile from the center of the village. Public transportation from Belize City, Orange Walk Town, and Corozal passes through the village of San Pablo several times daily.

ACCOMMODATIONS

Don't expect upscale accommodations like you'll find in more touristed regions of the country, but there are some decent basic options.

Under US$25

M Akihito Hotel (22 Belize/Corozal Rd., tel. 501/302-0185 or 302-3018, akihitolee@msn .com) charges US$12/20 s/d, more for a/c; all rooms have shared bath. Soon, they'll offer dorm beds for US$9. Run by the Lee couple, this is a good sleep for the dollar. It's clean, with cool tiled interiors and a downstairs shop serving beverages and a few necessities, and offers just about every amenity the basic traveler needs: laundry service, credit card phone calls, high speed Internet, cable television, and a whirlpool tub. The Lees are an excellent source of information about the Orange Walk area, what restaurants are good, and what bars to avoid. By press time they may have completed the rooftop dormitories and terrace. Did we mention the whirlpool tub?

Lucia's Guesthouse (68 San Antonio Rd., tel. 501/322-2244) is a basic traveler's rest house with rooms from US$10. Most with private baths, a/c available. Coming from Belize City, hang a left at the fire station downtown, and then it's about a half mile down on the left.

US$25–50

Run by four sisters that take good care of things, **Hotel St. Christopher's** (10 Main St., tel. 501/322-2420) is an ideal stop for those driving; it has colorful, traditional Spanish-feeling rooms with tiled floors and private bath for US$27 with fan, US$46 with a/c. A few of the rooms have shared balconies with a view of the river flats.

D Star Victoria (40 Belize Rd., tel. 501/322-0518, dvictoriahotel@btl.net) charges from US$23 single with fan up to US$54 for a triple with a/c. All rooms have a private bath. There's a pool, second story terrace, and thatch-roof awnings for hammock hanging. The Victoria has been an Orange Walk regular for many years, but is starting to show its age. As you come into town, it is hard to miss with its coral and white exterior.

FOOD

One good reason to linger in Orange Walk Town is **M The Diner** (on the far side of town behind the hospital, tel. 322-3753). The owner, Ms. Terry, runs a family-style restaurant with excellent cuisine. Here you'll find a surprising menu: peppermint steak (US$5), smoked pork chops (US$8), filet mignon (US$12.50), lobster thermidor, and grouper in bechamel sauce (US$15). Her deserts are unique Maya fruits and pastries with special Ochote and Blackberry desert wines that she makes herself. Many of her staff are hired out of difficult home situations—she helps them financially while providing practical restaurant training. Although she says she never turns away tourists, Ms. Terry often hosts parties of the Belizean elite. If you're headed over to The Diner, give her a call first letting her know when you'll be showing up.

Another choice for a night out in Orange Walk is **Ft. Mundi Bar & Grill,** located at Banquitas Plaza (tel. 501/302-0011, 8 A.M.–midnight). Meals are US$3–7, including grilled seafood, steaks, barbequed chicken, and other Belizean and American dishes.

Central Park Restaurant (New Market near the bus terminal, 6 A.M.–9 P.M. Mon.–Thurs., till 11 P.M. Fri. and Sat., US$1–3) is actually a collection of six restaurants styled after the old-school open market located next door. They serve everything a hungry traveler could want: burgers, tacos, empanadas, pizza, hot dogs, eggs & bacon breakfasts, sweet cakes, waffles, and the usual assortment of beverages.

It's easy to find Chinese food in Orange Walk Town: **Lee's Chinese Restaurant,** near the fire station, serves passable versions of chicken chow mein (US$3.25), sweet and sour fish (US$7.50), black soybean lobster or shrimp (US$12), and cocktails from a colorful bar on Yo Street. Another traveler's standard for a basic Belizean meal is **Juanita's** (8 Santa Anna St., tel. 501/322-2677, 6 A.M.–2 P.M. then open again at 6 P.M. for dinner Mon.–Sat., US$2–5). There are many other cafés in town offering cuisines of many nationalities. Check any of them out, but you might first make sure the restaurant meets your hygiene standards.

Central Park Plaza restaurants, the place for a quick burrito or beer in downtown Orange Walk

© JAMES SAVAGE

Northern Belize

Entering town on the Belize/Corozal Road you will see a **service station/convenience store** on the left. This store has light snacks, cold drinks, and a few staples. If you are headed by car to Río Bravo or Chan Chich, this is a good place to top off the gas tank.

GETTING THERE AND AWAY

By Bus

Novelo's and **Venus** travel between Chetumal and Belize City with stops in Orange Walk and Corozal—they pass about every hour until 6 P.M. Some of the buses are express, but it's often hard to tell which one. Sunday service is about every two hours. At press time, there was a daily bus to Indian Church about 5 P.M. daily, and it leaves Indian Church at 5 A.M. There are hourly buses to San Felipe to the west, and Sarteneja to the east.

By Boat

Going by boat is a pleasant way to get anywhere, especially to Lamanai. Enjoy nature's best along the shore of the river. You never know what you will see next—long-legged birds, orchids growing in tall trees, flitting hummingbirds—it's like a treasure hunt. Bring your binocs. Ask at your hotel for directions to the boat dock.

Tours and Transport

If you're in Orange Walk Town and need help arranging some transportation logistics, contact Freddy Gomez, the owner of **Transport Services** (21 St. Peters St., tel. 501/322-2037 or 609-9641). Not only does he own a 15-passenger van and a Crown Vic, he's also a highly knowledgeable local that can arrange insightful tours anywhere in Orange Walk District.

Lamanai Archaeological Zone

THE RUINS

Set on the edge of a forested broad lagoon are the temples of Lamanai. One of the largest ceremonial centers in Belize, it is believed to have served as an imperial port city encompassing ball courts, pyramids, and several more exotic Maya features. Hundreds of buildings have been identified in the two-square-mile area. Today, visitors can see four large temples, a residential complex, and a reproduction stela of a Maya elite, Lord Smoking Shell. Excavations reveal continuous occupation and a high standard of living into the Post-Classic period, unlike other colonies in the region. Lamanai is believed to have been occupied from 1500 B.C. to the 19th century—Spanish occupation is also apparent with the remains of two Christian churches, and the sugar mill that was built by British colonialists.

A few sites to look for:

The Mask Temple N9-56: Here two significant tombs were found, as well as two Early Classic stone masks.

The High Temple N10-43: At 33 meters (10 feet) tall, this is the tallest securely dated Pre-Classic structure in the Maya area. Among many findings was a dish containing the skeleton of a bird and Pre-Classic vessels dating to 100 B.C.

Temple N10-9: Dated to the 6th century A.D., this temple had structural modifications in the 8th and 13th centuries. Jade jewelry and a jade mask were discovered here, as was an animal-motif dish.

The Ball Court: The game played in this area held great ritual significance for the Maya. In 1980, archaeologists raised the huge stone disc marking the center of the court and found lidded vessels containing miniature vessels with

Pre-Classic carving of a Mayan God on the Mask Temple at Lamanai

© JUDY & JAN WILSON

© SHERRY GIBBS

Belize's original sugar mill, built by British colonialists in the 18th century, is an interesting example of the different cultural occupations at the Lamanai archeological site.

small jade and shell objects on top of a mercury puddle.

Archaeologist David Pendergast headed a team from the Royal Ontario Museum that, after finding a number of children's bones buried under a stela, presumed that human sacrifice was a part of the residents' religion. Large masks that depict a ruler wearing a crocodile headdress were found in several locations, hence the name Lamanai ("Submerged Crocodile").

The landscape at the site is overgrown, and trees and thick vines grow from the tops of buildings—the only sounds are birdcalls echoing off the stone temple. To see above the thick jungle canopy, you can climb to the top of the temple on ancient steps that are still pretty much in place, and don't be surprised if you find Indiana Jones's hat at the top—it's that kind of a place.

Wildlife

The trip to the site is great; it's located in Orange Walk District on the high banks of New River Lagoon about 50 miles northwest of Belize City. Most people travel by boat through tropical flora and fauna, and on the way you might see such exotics as black orchids, old tree trunks covered with sprays of tiny golden orchids, and a multitude of bird life, possibly even the jabiru stork (the largest flying bird in the New World).

This area is a reserve, so look for some wildlife you may not see in other, more-inhabited areas. On the paths you'll see numbered trees that correspond to a pamphlet of information available from the caretakers at the entrance of Lamanai Reserve.

Bird-watchers, look around the Mask and High temples for the **black oropendola.** The **black vulture** is often spotted slowly gliding over the entire area. A woodpecker with a distinct double-tap rhythm and a red cap is the male **Guatemalan ivorybill.** Near the High Temple, the **collared *aracari,*** a variety of toucan, sits on the highest trees and chirps like an insect. The **citreoline trogon** is covered with color: a yellow chest, black-and-white tail, and a back of blue and green. Though it looks as if the **northern jacana** is walking on water, it's the delicate floating vegetation that holds the long-toed bird above the water as it searches along the water's edge for edible delicacies.

Other fauna spotted by those who live there are jaguarundi, agouti, armadillo, hicatee turtle, and the roaring howler monkey.

Visiting Lamanai

The ruins of Lamanai huddle to one side of New River Lagoon near the village of Indian Church. It's reachable by boat from Orange Walk or by road during the dry season from San Felipe. The Institute of Archaeology has done a great deal of reconstruction at this site, so the temples are impressive even to the uneducated eye. The High Temple can be climbed to yield a 360-degree view of the surrounding jungle.

By press time, a new visitors center, a special dock for tours from cruise ships, and a museum should have been completed. This is a popular site for day-trippers from the cruise ships and can be quite crowded in the middle of the day, especially during the week. If you want a more solitary experience, go early in the morning or late in the afternoon. The reserve is open to the public 8 A.M.–5 P.M. Don't forget to save time to visit the nearby ruins of **Cuello** and **Nohmul.**

M Indian Church Village Artisans Center

Consider contributing directly to the local economy by shopping at this community-based organization, founded in 2000 with the assistance of professional archaeologists, artisans, and architects that were working at the nearby Lamanai site. The center has provided workspace, tools, material, craft training, and English classes to interested villagers. The center has a small shop at the Lamanai site, or you can check out their wares at their workshop in the village.

Artisans working at the center have produced silver and bronze jewelry, hand-sewn purses, bags, embroidered pillowcases, and fired clay statues. Most of the artwork emulates artifacts found at the Lamanai site, including silver pendants of Lord Smoking Shell stela. Stop by the village workshop or ask your guide to take you by their shop at the Lamanai site.

Tour Operators

All regional tour operators in Orange Walk, Corozal, and Belize City offer tours to Lamanai. They usually include the entrance fee, drinks, and a catered lunch as part of the deal. Prices range US$35–40 per person. The cruise down the river is far more pleasant and faster than driving or riding on the dirt road. All these operators can offer night safaris, bird-watching tours, and other trips up and down the New River. Most will pick you up at your hotel around 9 A.M. and return you around 4 P.M.

Jungle River Tours (20 Lovers Ln., tel. 501/302-2293 or 615-1712) is the oldest operating guide service, with the reputation of giving the best tours of Lamanai. Their boats leave from docks near Banquitas Plaza in Orange Walk. **Reyes & Sons Tour Guides** (tel. 501/322-3327) has a dock at the Tower Hill Toll Bridge. **Lamanai EcoAdventures** (tel. 501/322-3653 or 610-1753) also has a dock just south of the

Tower Hill Toll Bridge, as does **New River Cruises.**

Lamanai Outpost Lodge's (see listing in next section) ongoing archaeological program allows guests of the lodge to get involved at Lamanai as well.

ACCOMMODATIONS

Right next door to Lamanai Reserve along the shore of the New River Lagoon, **Lamanai Outpost Lodge** (US tel. 888/733-7864, Bel. tel. 501/223-3578, fax 501/220-9061, outpost @lamanai.com, www.lamanai.com) offers a peaceful jungle retreat for a relaxing adventure, with rooms US$120–190, three meals US$49. From the moment the manager, Blanca, greets you at the boat dock, you know you're in capable, welcoming hands. The lodge boasts 16 elegantly rustic thatch-roof cabanas made of natural wood and detailed with converted oil lamps, brass desk lamps, and other amenities that contribute to an old-fashioned feel. Outside, the grounds are lushly landscaped with orchids, ceiba trees, and palmettos providing cooling shade and visual delight. Below the resort's lodge and dining room lies the shore of the lagoon, where you'll find a dock, swimming area, canoes, boats of various types, hammocks, and an assortment of beach chairs. The dock is particularly peaceful at sunset.

This is a low-key, escape-to-nature kind of setting, perfect for the bird-watcher, Mayaphile, naturalist, or traveler who wants to get away from the tourist trail for a while. The area is rich in animal life, including more than 300 species of birds as well as crocodiles, margays, jaguarundis, anteaters, arboreal porcupines, and the fishing bulldog bat.

The owners are involved in several scientific research projects that also allow nature-study opportunities for guests. The study topics include local bats, archaeology, howler monkeys, Morelet's crocodiles, and ornithology. Guests with programs such as Elderhostel and Oceanic Expeditions can participate in the work. Ask about daily herbal and bird-watching walks as well as night safaris. There are all-inclusive packages that include meals and transit to and from Belize City and allow guests to take advantage of all the guided tours.

Donna Blanca Cabins (tel. 501/606-7244 or 309-1015) is, at US$25 per person, currently the only budget lodging in the area, with a handful of dark, basic cabins. There may be other accommodations opening in the Lamanai area soon, but these things can take time in rural Belize. Check out www.lamanaisouth.com, or if you have good enough Spanish you may be able to rent a room or a spot to hang your hammock in the local village of Indian Church.

FOOD

The **Blue Bird Ceviche Bar** on the San Carlos Road is open 10 A.M.–midnight; Roy, the British expat owner, offers handmade ceviche, burritos, empanadas, and tacos. With a sand floor, thatch roof, and a collection of Michael Bolton CDs, the Blue Bird keeps it real.

West of Orange Walk Town

CUELLO RUINS

Four miles west of Orange Walk Town on Yo Creek, on the property of a Caribbean Rum warehouse, are the minor ruins of **Cuello.** Check in at the gate office (tel. 501/322-2141, 8:30 A.M.–4:30 P.M.), then investigate these relatively undisturbed ruins consisting of a large plaza with seven structures in a long horizontal mound. There are three temples; see if you can find the uncovered ones. These structures (as in Cahal Pech) have a different look than most Maya sites. They are covered with a layer of white stucco, as they were in the days of the Maya.

The ruins of Cuello were studied in the 1970s by a Cambridge University archaeology team led by Dr. Norman Hammond. A small ceremonial center, a proto-Classic temple, has been excavated. Lying directly in front is a large excavation trench, partially backfilled, where the archaeologists gathered the historical information that revolutionized previous concepts of the antiquity of the ancient Maya. Artifacts indicate that the Maya traded with people hundreds of miles away. Among the archaeologists' out-of-the-ordinary findings were bits of wood that proved, after carbon testing, that Cuello had been occupied as early as 2600 B.C., much earlier than ever believed; however, archaeologists now find that these tests may have been incorrect, and the age is in dispute.

Also found was an unusual style of pottery—apparently in some burials, clay urns were placed over the heads of the deceased. It's also speculated that it was here over a long period that the primitive strain of corn seen in early years was refined and developed into the higher-producing plant of the Classic period. Continuous occupation for approximately 4,000 years was surmised, with repeated layers of structures all the way into the Classic period.

Continuing West

As the road meanders west from there, numerous small villages dot the border region. Occasionally you see a soft drink sign attached to a building, but there's not much in the way of facilities between Orange Walk and Blue Creek. Heading west from San Felipe, you soon find flat, open farmland, with Mennonite accoutrements, dominating the landscape. Low, open rice paddies provide great bird-watching opportunities as well as placid scenery.

Soon, however you hit the foothills of the Maya highlands near **Blue Creek** village. Climbing up into the foothills you can see the flatlands of the Río Hondo and New River drainages to the east. The small village to the right is **La Union,** on the other side of the Mexico border. This part of Orange Walk district is much hillier, and has an increasingly wild feel to it. In the village of Blue Creek you'll find **The Hillside Bed & Breakfast** (tel. 501/323-0155, US$30/40 s/d) on the left coming up the hill. At the top of the hill is the **Linda Vista Credit Union** and a gas station/general store. Fill the tank if you're driving on to Río Bravo or Chan Chich, as this is the last gas station until you come back this way.

As you continue further west, the area becomes progressively more forested until you reach the dramatic boundary of the Programme for Belize Río Bravo Conservation Area. Here, the cleared pastureland runs smack dab into a wall of jungle and there is a gate at the border. If you aren't expected, the guard won't let you pass. Once inside the gate, you've entered the Río Bravo Conservation Area.

☒ RÍO BRAVO CONSERVATION AREA

Río Bravo provides the chance for visitors to experience the outdoors while supporting a worthy environmental effort. You have opportunities to experience the wilderness and see archaeological work underway at La Milpa, the ancient Maya ruins on the property. Activities include nature walks (both day and night); in-depth study of local birds, mammals, and reptiles; and swims in the Río Bravo. Visitors may or may not see crocodiles, deer, peccaries, fer-de-lances, coatis, boa constrictors, margays, and jaguars in the surrounding jungle. Bird life is plentiful, with waterfowl and jungle birds represented. Scientists, research volunteers, donors, and interested travelers are encouraged to contact the Belizean conservation group **Programme for Belize** (US tel. 617/259-9500, Bel. tel. 501/207-5616 or 207-5635, pfbel@btl.net, www.pfbelize.org), which runs two field stations in Río Bravo (Hill Bank and La Milpa).

Within the conservation area, the research station is housed in a cluster of small thatch-roof buildings. Programme for Belize is dedicated to scientific research, agricultural experimentation, and the protection of indigenous wildlife and the area's Maya archaeological locations—all this while creating self-sufficiency through development of ecotourism and sustainable rainforest agriculture such as *chicle* production. A scientific study continues to determine the best management plan for the reserve and its forests.

Another focus is on environmental education.

Every year the organization, which receives support from the Massachusetts Audubon Society, the Nature Conservancy, and the World Wildlife Fund, expends a goodly effort in educating Belizeans and eco-specialists from abroad. In one program, young Belizean students are recruited to become field biology trainees. This one-year program allows young people the opportunity to work alongside international researchers in gathering knowledge of the jungle and its inhabitants. Another program, sponsored through Save the Rain Forest, Inc., brings in groups of high school teachers and students to experience and learn about the forest and its ecosystems.

CHAN CHICH
Chan Chich Ruins

In the northwestern corner of Belize in Orange Walk District, near the Guatemala border, an old overgrown logging road, originally blazed by the Belize Estate and Produce Company (logging operators), was reopened. Here, the Maya site of Chan Chich (Kaxil Uinich) was rediscovered. As recently as 1986, the only way in (for rare adventurers, pot farmers, or grave robbers, for the most part) was with machete in hand and a canoe to cross the swiftly flowing river. After sweating and cutting into dense jungle to the end of the barely visible track, the adventurer's sudden reward was a 100-foot-tall, rock-strewn hill—an introduction to another Maya ceremonial site! This complex has two levels of plazas, each with its own temples, all surrounded by unexcavated mounds.

When found, three of the temples showed obvious signs of looting with vertical slit trenches—open just as the looters had left them. No one will ever know what valuable artifacts were removed and sold to private collectors all over the world. The large main temple on the upper plaza had been violated to the heart of what appears to be one or more burial chambers. A painted frieze runs around the low ceiling. Today, the only temple inhabitants greeting outsiders are small bats.

The ruins provide opportunity for discovery and exploration and the population and diversity of wildlife here is probably greater than

FIRE ON THE (MAYA) MOUNTAIN

Driving through the village of San Felipe during the dry season, you may see distant plumes of smoke rising into an otherwise cloudless blue sky. The smoke may be from agricultural fires, set by descendants of the Maya—or it may be the result of controlled blazes, set and monitored by professional firefighters (a.k.a. "fire managers") working in the Río Bravo Conservation Area.

San Felipe and many villages in the upland regions of Belize reside in an ecosystem known as upland pine savanna, consisting of gangly Caribbean pines and open grassland. Fire plays an instrumental role in this ecosystem, causing both destruction and renewal for vegetation and wildlife. Grasses, palmettos, and pine trees adapt quite successfully to both nature- and human-caused fires, but some species, like the endangered yellow-headed parrot, are not faring as well (although their demise is as much due to habitat destruction as predation by locals for the exotic pet trade).

Fire is used not only to clean fields of brush before planting; it has also been used by rural folk for thousands of years to encourage grazing for such game species as peccary, deer, and gibnut (or paca, a large rodent). Locals also burn the upland savanna in order to provide access to the riverine lowland forests, which yield highly profitable timber harvests. Also, sugar cane farmers have come to rely on fire to dry their fields and prepare them for harvest.

For many years, the professionals of the Río Bravo Conservation Area suppressed all fires when they were capable, because the general cultural belief was that all wildfire was bad for wildlife as well as a risk to human settlements. However, recent studies have revealed the interdependency between the yellow-headed parrot nest trees, and low-intensity, high-frequency fires. In response, the Río Bravo Conservation Area managers have begun a program of controlled burns that will restore the savanna to a state that is beneficial for the nesting trees. This burning is implemented in a controlled manner on allotted acres in order to rejuvenate the grasslands, prevent invasion of broadleaf trees, and prevent damage to the nest trees.

The foresters of the Hill Bank Field Station have conducted successful burns for several years with the help of the Nature Conservancy and the United States Forest Service. The Caribbean pine savanna is extensive throughout Belize and many Central American countries, and the Río Bravo fire program serves as a model for potential future savanna management throughout the region.

So not only is the preservation of the yellow-headed parrot served by the smoke you see in the sky, but entire ecosystems and additional rare species are served by this scientific management as well. The prescribed fire program is an integral tool in habitat management, serving to reduce fire-suppression costs, recycle nutrients, and prevent invasion by non-native vegetative species. As you eye the tops of the rough-barked pine trees, looking for yellow-headed parrots, give a moment of thanks to the hard, dirty work of the Río Bravo firefighters—*maybe* you'll be blessed with a sighting.

(Contributed by James Savage, a firefighter for the U.S. National Park Service with extensive experience in prescribed fire management.)

Northern Belize

© JAMES SAVAGE

coffee beans after roasting at the Gallon Jug estate

anywhere else in Belize. The nine miles of hiking trails wind through the verdant jungle, and give ample chance to sight wildlife, especially jaguars. There is evidence of Gallon Jug Estate's previous incarnation as the hub of the British Belize Estate & Produce Company's mahogany logging operation.

Chan Chich Lodge

The ruins' new steward is Belizean-born Barry Bowen, owner of the property, who has built a group of simple thatch cabanas in one of the plazas of the Maya site. Though deplored by some archaeology buffs, these cabanas are very popular with bird-watchers and Mayaphiles who agree with Bowen that they serve as a deterrent to temple looters who think nothing of defiling the ancient stone cities, as well as marijuana growers who find these isolated spots perfect hiding places for their illegal crops.

This lodge, which began in 1987 as a tool shed, has blossomed into an elegant and luxurious retreat set amongst the plazas of the Chan Chich Maya ruins and the expansive surrounding jungle. The family of staff running the lodge offers top-notch service in everything that they do. The landscaped grounds, quietly lit pool, and sunset view from the unexcavated Maya ruins would lead one to think this is an easy place to relax. Even more so with the cabanas with modern amenities including water cooler, refrigerator, huge tiled bathrooms, and natural insulation and ventilation that keep it cool all day long. However, there is so much to do that managers Nick and Brigitte can schedule your days to bursting. In addition to exploring the ruins and hiking trails, activities include canoeing at the nearby Laguna Verde; horseback riding from the Gallon Jug stables; and unique bird-watching opportunities to see trogons, oscellated turkeys, toucans, and other birds. Tours of the current-day coffee plantation and experimental farm at Gallon Jug provide the opportunity to learn all the steps in the coffee making process as well as other sustainable agricultural initiatives taking place here. The smell of roasting coffee is especially enticing. Finally, the day ends at the

the manicured grounds of the Chan Chich
Jungle Lodge

© JAMES SAVAGE

perhaps a night safari or a swim in the intimate pool before you finish off at the Looter's Trench Bar, where you might get to hear jungle tales from Nick, or stories from the bartenders Erma or Norman.

The history of this area is deep, from the time of the Maya to the present inhabitants. Relax, breathe it in, and keep in mind that your presence here is serving to protect all this.

The offices of the lodge are located near the water in Belize City at 1 King Street (US tel. 800/343-8009, Bel. tel./fax 501/223-4419, info@chanchich.com, www.chanchich.com). The remarkable experience here does not come cheap: room rates range from US$175 single to US$230 for a deluxe suite, meals for $55/day, plus more for tours and guides. Ask about inclusive packages to bring the cost and complications down.

Chan Chich is 130 miles from Belize City (plan an all-day drive to get there) on all-weather roads from the international airport, or (much easier) a 30-minute charter flight to nearby Gallon Jug. Call or write for more information; they can make all your travel arrangements.

peaceful dining veranda where you enjoy excellent cuisine to the sounds of the jungle. Then

Norhtern Belize

Corozal Town

Corozal's 9,000 or so inhabitants casually get by while the bay washes against the sea wall running the length of town. While English is the official language, Spanish is just as common since many are descendants of early-day Maya and mestizo refugees from neighboring Quintana Roo in Mexico. Historically, Corozal was the scene of many attacks by the Maya Indians during the Caste War. What remains of the old fort can be found in the center of town (west of Central Park).

The town was almost entirely wiped out during Hurricane Janet in 1955 and has since been rebuilt. As you stroll through the quiet streets, you'll find a library, a museum, town hall, government administrative offices, a Catholic church, two secondary schools, five elementary schools, three gas stations, a gov-

ernment hospital, a clinic, a few small hotels, a couple of funky bars and discos, and several restaurants. Not a whole lot of activity goes on here, unless you happen to be in town during special holidays. The biggest excitement is during the Mexican-style "Spanish" fiestas of Christmas, Carnaval, and Columbus Day; there are also a few local fiestas around mid-September.

Many houses are clapboard, raised on wooden stilts to avoid possible floods and to catch the wind, creating a cool spot for the family to gather. More of the newer houses are built out of cement blocks.

The Corozal District economy has for years depended on the sugar industry and its local processing factory. One of the oldest (no longer in operation), the **Aventura Sugar Mill**, began

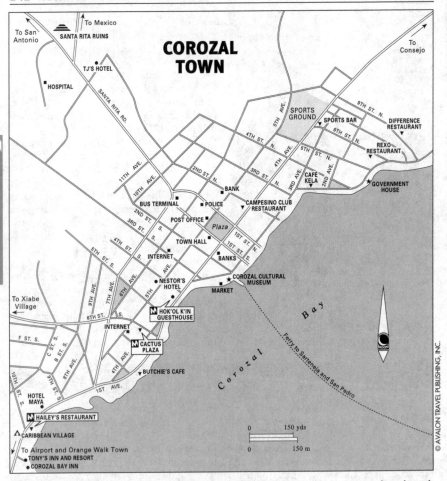

CABBEAN VILLAGE
To Airport and Orange Walk Town
TONY'S INN AND RESORT
COROZAL BAY INN

© AVALON TRAVEL PUBLISHING, INC.

operating in the 1800s. Little is left today, but you can still see the antiquated chimney when driving past the village of Aventura on the New Northern Highway, seven miles from Corozal Town.

ORIENTATION

Most visitors enter Corozal either from the north (traveling from Mexico), from the south on the Northern Highway, or from Ambergris Caye to the east by boat or airplane. Getting oriented to Corozal is easy since it's laid out on a grid

system with avenues running north and south (parallel to the sea wall) and streets running east and west. Corozal's two primary avenues, 4th and 5th, run the length of town. The majority of restaurants and stores of interest to travelers lie on, or adjacent to, these streets.

SIGHTS AND RECREATION

Corozal Town is a great base camp for fishing, nature watching, and water sports. Lots of folks just hang out for a couple of days, wander over to the town square, have a drink or two somewhere,

Northern Belize

Corozal's wonderful waterfront looks out over Corozal Bay.

and strike up a conversation with the locals and a few of the expats who've come to love the laid-back lifestyle.

Be sure to go into the town hall and take a look at the dramatic historical **mural** painted by Manuel Villamour. The flamboyantly colored mural depicts the history of Corozal, including the drama of the downtrodden Maya, their explosive revolt called the Caste War, and the inequities of colonial rule.

Some trips include day trips to the Shipstern Wildlife Nature Reserve, Sarteneja Village, and the Maya sites of Cerros and Santa Rita (see sidebar "Maya Archaeological Sites" later in this chapter).

River Trips

A favorite excursion from Corozal is a boat ride up the New River to Lamanai in Orange Walk District. It's about an hour drive to the put-in on the river, then another 30 miles past mestizo, Maya, and Mennonite settlements on a sun-dappled, jungle-lined river until you come to a broad lagoon and then to the temples of Lamanai (see earlier in this chapter for more on Lamanai). The trip is through tropical flora and fauna, and you might see such exotics as black orchids and jabiru storks, the largest flying birds in the New World with a wing span of 10–12 feet. This is an all-day trip. The price runs about US$65 pp (check with Manuel Hoare, tel. 402-2744). During the dry season (Jan.–Apr.), you can reach Lamanai by road from San Felipe, preferably in a 4WD.

Local Guides and Tour Companies

Henry Menzies Travel & Tours (tel. 501/422-2725, menziestours@btl.net) will arrange custom tours depending on your or your group's needs, specializing in Lamanai and Shipstern trips, Chetumal transfers (and other Mexican attractions), and local ruins. Also check at the **Hok'ol K'in Hotel** or with **Herman Pollard** (tel. 501/422-3329). For travel agencies, stop by the **Hotel Maya** or **Jal's Travel Agency** (tel. 501/422-2163, ligializama@hotmail.com).

bird-watching in downtown Corozal

ACCOMMODATIONS

Under US$25

Try your luck at **Marvinton Guest House** (tel. 501/608-0476). Rooms start at US$18 plus tax; there's also a queen bed with private bath for US$25. Once the standby budget hotel in town, **Nestor's Hotel** (123 5th Ave., tel. 501/422-2354, nestorshotel@belizemail.net) has suffered from a series of management changes over the last few years and is overpriced at US$56 s/d, or dorm beds for US$20; all this may change soon, so check it out. Rooms are small, simple, and have fans, a/c, and private baths. Laundry service is available. Downstairs, a sometimes-lively restaurant and bar with karaoke, audio, and video systems attracts locals and travelers.

　　Caribbean Village RV Park and Campground (tel. 501/422-2725, menziestours@btl .net) offers full RV hookups for US$20 a night, camping US$5, and an apartment with kitchen for US$25, a bargain if you have a family or a group of friends.

US$25–50

Just two blocks south of town center, and right across from the water, the  **Hok'ol K'in Guest-house** (tel. 501/422-3329, maya@btl.net) was begun by an ex–Peace Corps Volunteer with the intention of supporting local Maya community endeavors. In Yucateca Mayan, "Hok'ol K'in" means the "Coming of the Rising Sun," a sight you'll see from your window if you're up early enough—follow your sun salutations with an excellent breakfast (and real coffee!) on the patio downstairs. Hok'ol K'in's 10 immaculate rooms have private baths, veranda, and fan and cost US$30–55; the more expensive ones have a view and cable TV. One budget room has beds for US$12.50. Ask about available trips and homestays (or visits) with local families; the staff are very helpful in arranging things to do. This is one of the few lodgings in Belize that's equipped to handle a wheelchair—one room only, so be sure to specify if it's needed. The restaurant serves a variety of good meals.

　　On the road leading into town from the south, the **Hotel Maya** (tel. 501/422-2082 or 422-2874, www.stayathotelmaya.com) offers 16 rooms with a/c, TV, and private bath for US$50 for two double beds; restaurant serves breakfast only. The hotel is fairly well-maintained and the help is friendly; you can swim at the shore across the street. There is also a gift shop and travel agency that can arrange trips to local destinations as well as transport across the borders to Tikal, Chetumal, or even Cancún. Near the road out of town to Mexico, **TJ's Hotel** (tel. 501/422-0150, tjshotel@red83.com.mx) has six small but clean well-furnished rooms with tiled floor, a/c, private bath, h/c water, cable TV, mini-fridge and coffee makers for US$40/50 s/d; there's also a Tex-Mex restaurant and bar set next to a lovely raised pool.

US$50–100

Two seaside options reside on the south end of town. At **Tony's Inn and Beach Resort** (tel. 501/422-2055 or 422-3555, tonys@btl.net, US$45–75), "beach" may be stretching it a bit, and the 24 rooms are set up more like a Motel 6 than a resort. Still, the large rooms have a/c, private baths, and h/c water. The Y-Not Bar and Grill is in a nice setting on the water, and the hotel has its own marina and runs a variety of local trips.

Right next door, you'll find a couples-oriented cluster of 10 cute, thatch-roof cabanas set around 396 truckloads of sand from Belize's Pine Mountain Ridge; the **Corozal Bay Inn** (tel. 501/422-2691, www.corozalbayinn.com, US$70) has a swimming pool, a lively bar, and rooms with a/c, big screen TV, private bath, and fridge.

A bit more to the south in a very quiet, out-of-the-way spot, the **Copa Banana** (tel. 501/422-0284, relax@copabanana.bz) charges about US$50 for lovely, tropical-décor rooms open to the sea breeze but also air-conditioned. There's a shared living room and kitchen area.

FOOD

For solid, super-cheap Mexican snacks and meals, be sure to hit **M Cactus Plaza,** with a very popular streetside café; drinks, beers, and juices are served all night (till the club inside closes anyway). Another mellow waterfront affair, **Butchie's** has steaks, seafood, Mexican, and appetizers; dinners about US$6.

Le Café Kela offers one of Belize's only truly French dining experiences, albeit with a relaxed Caribbean twists and at very reasonable prices; the only complaints come from the long waits (ser-

COROZAL ONLINE

N early all of the businesses mentioned in this chapter have websites found on Corozal's main portals: **www.corozal.bz** is more tourist and business-related, while **www.corozal.com** is an ongoing community school project.

vice is occasionally spread thin). The food is excellent, though, especially the fish fillet almandine (US$7) and shrimp crepes.

M Hailey's Restaurant, located right on the water across from Caribbean Village on the south end of town, serves up some of the best local food around, including "the best rice-and-beans and potato salad in the whole damn country." It's a bold statement by the owner, for sure, but well deserved; steaks for US$7.50, burgers, and breakfast too (10 A.M. till around midnight).

SERVICES

Corozal has lots of little shops, grocery stores, bookstores, and a few gift shops. You'll find locally made jewelry, pottery, wood carvings, clothing, textiles, and a host of other mementos here and there, but it's not overrun with gift shops yet. **U Sav Supermarket** is near the Hok'ol K'in Guesthouse. Gifts, books, and other supplies can be obtained at **BASIX** (#69 7th Ave.).

Money

If you need to change money, go to the **Casa de Cambio** (tel. 501/422-2516, 8 A.M.–5 P.M. Mon.–Fri., 8 A.M.–noon Sat.), a block south of the park, where you're guaranteed a better exchange rate than the banks, even for travelers checks. For other needs, Corozal has several ATMs and branches of **Belize Bank, Nova Scotia Bank,** and **Atlantic Bank** (all open 8 A.M.–2 P.M. Mon.–Thurs., 8:30 A.M.–4:30 P.M. Fri.).

Health and Emergencies

Emergency numbers are fire tel. 501/422-2105, police tel. 501/422-2022, and hospital tel. 501/422-2076. There are several clinical laboratories in town, including **Selby's Medlab** (tel. 501/422-3252), a few blocks from the park at 103 5th Avenue.

Internet Access
The two main places to get online are **Charlotte's Web,** with a bulletin board, book exchange, and coffee; and **M.E. Computer Systems** (3rd St. S, 9 A.M.–9 P.M., closed Sun.).

GETTING AROUND
There are a few taxi stands in town: one at the bus station (tel. 501/422-3626) and another closer to the water (tel. 501/422-2345). You can get around town for US$2.50, to the border for US$10, or to Chetumal and Cerros for US$30, all convenient ways to go if you have a few people to split the costs.

GETTING THERE AND AWAY
By Air
There are five daily inexpensive flights on each airline between Corozal and San Pedro only. Call Tropic Air (US tel. 800/422-3435, Bel. tel. 501/226-2012, reservations@tropicair.com, www.tropicair.com) or Maya Island Air (US tel. 800/225-6732, Bel. tel. 501/223-1140, mayair@btl.net, www.mayaislandair.com) for schedules.

By Bus
Buses from Novelo's in Belize City alternate between Corozal and Chetumal; expresses take about 2.5 hours to Corozal and leave at 6:15 A.M., 9 A.M., 11 A.M., 5 P.M., and 6 P.M., US$6. Expresses from Corozal (check schedule with the Novelo's station, tel. 501/402-3030) leave at 6 A.M., 7 A.M., noon, 3 P.M., 4 P.M., 6 P.M., and 7:30 P.M., all of them originating an hour or so previously in Chetumal. There is one bus that goes all the way to the Guatemalan border at Benque, leaving Friday–Monday at 4 P.M. Typically, Novelo's Sunday service is less frequent.

By Boat
Thunderbolt (tel. 501/422-0026 or 610-4475, crivero@btl.net) has daily 7 A.M. runs to San Pedro for US$23 pp, arriving at 8:45 A.M. It leaves San Pedro at 3 P.M. for the return trip. Stops in Sarteneja are possible going either way.

Near Corozal

CONSEJO VILLAGE
Nine miles north of Corozal, the tiny fishing village of Consejo is home to a beach hideaway, an upscale hotel, and a retirement community called **Consejo Shores.** The dock at Consejo is also the place to catch a boat to Chetumal—the ride is only five minutes long and you'll avoid the overland border fees.

Hole up in one of three bayside units at **Smuggler's Den** (two miles northwest of Consejo, tel. 501/614-8146, smugglersdenbelize @belizeweb.com), nicely furnished and with h/c water—quite a bargain if you're looking for isolation. Two have private bath and kitchenette (US$40 plus tax), the unit without a kitchen goes for US$20. Smuggler's is locally famous for their Sunday night roast beef dinners.

Right in Consejo, **Casablanca by the Sea** (US tel. 781/235-1024, Bel. tel. 501/423-1018, www.casablanca-bythesea.com) is an intimate hotel with lovely grounds and views of the Bay of Consejo. Eight stately rooms with queen-size beds, private bathrooms, a/c, h/c water, and TV start at US$65. The bar and dining room offers excellent seafood dishes and other meals, eaten while watching the lights of Chetumal, just across the bay. There's rooftop stargazing, volleyball, and top-notch conference/group facilities.

SHIPSTERN WILDLIFE NATURE RESERVE
In Corozal District, Shipstern is in the northeastern corner of the Belize coast. Thirty-two

MAYA ARCHAEOLOGICAL SITES

The nearby ruins of **Santa Rita** and **Cerros** are not as immediately awe-inspiring as, say, Lamanai or Caracol, but they are still interesting and easy to visit.

Santa Rita

This site was still a populated community of Maya when the Spanish arrived. One mile northeast of Corozal, the largest Santa Rita structure was explored at the turn of the century by Thomas Gann. Sculptured friezes and stucco murals were found along with a burial site that indicates flourishing occupation in the Early Classic period (about A.D. 300), as well as during the Late Post-Classic period (A.D. 1350–1530). Two significant burials were found from distant periods in the history of Santa Rita: one from A.D. 300 was a female and the other was a king from a period 200 hundred years later.

In 1985, archaeologists Diane and Arlen Chase discovered a tomb with a skeleton covered in jade and mica ornaments. It has been excavated and somewhat reconstructed under the Chases' jurisdiction; only one structure is accessible to the public. Post-Classic murals, mostly destroyed over the years, combined Maya and Mexican styles that depict the ecumenical flavor of the period. Some believe that Santa Rita was part of a series of coastal lookouts. Santa Rita is probably more appealing to serious archaeology buffs than to the average tourist.

Cerros

Cerros is especially intriguing as it looms over the jungle on a peninsula across from Corozal Town. Cerros was an important coastal trading center during the Late Pre-Classic period (350 B.C.–A.D. 250). Magnificent frescoes and stone heads were uncovered by archaeologist David Friedel; these signify that elite rule was firmly fixed by the end of the Pre-Classic period. The tallest of its temples rises to 70 feet, and because of the rise in the sea level the one-time stone residences of the elite Maya are partially flooded.

It would appear that Cerros not only provisioned oceangoing canoes, but was in an ideal location to control ancient trade routes that traced the Río Hondo and New River from the Yucatán to Petén and the Usumacinta basin. A plaster-lined canal for the sturdy, oversized ocean canoes was constructed around Cerros. Archaeologists have determined that extensive fishing and farming on raised fields took place, probably to outfit the traders. But always the question remains: Why did progress suddenly stop?

You can reach Cerros by boat—hire one at **Tony's Inn** in Corozal or check with a travel agent. If you travel during the dry season (Jan.–Apr.), you can get to Cerros by car.

square miles of moist forest, savanna, and wetlands have been set aside to preserve as-yet-unspoiled habitats of well-known insect, bird, and mammal species associated with the tropics. The reserve encompasses the shallow **Shipstern Lagoon,** which, although hardly navigable, creates a wonderful habitat for a huge selection of wading and fish-eating birds. The reserve is home to about 200 species of birds, 60 species of reptiles and amphibians, and nearly 200 species of butterflies (they began the production of live butterfly pupae through intensive breeding).

The Audubon Society and International Tropical Conservation Foundation have been extremely generous in their support. As at most reserves, the objective is to manage and protect habitats and wildlife, as well as to develop an education program that entails educating the local community and introducing children to the concept of wildlife conservation in their area. Shipstern, however, goes a step further by conducting an investigation of how tropical countries such as Belize can develop self-supporting conservation areas through the controlled, intensive production of natural commodities found within such wildlife settlements. Developing facilities for the scientific study of the reserve area and its wildlife is part of this important program. For information about a few cabins at the reserve for US$10, email the Belize Audubon Society at base@btl.net.

It's essential that visitors go first to the visitors center. A guided tour costs US$5 per person. The forest is alive with nature's critters and fascinating flora, and the guides' discerning eyes spot things that most city folk often miss even though they are right in front of them. Hours for touring are 9 A.M.–noon and 1–3 P.M. daily except for Christmas, New Year's Day, and Easter.

Botanical Trail

This lovely trail starts at the parking lot by the visitors center and meanders through the forest. You will have the opportunity to see three types of hardwood forests and 100 species of hardwood. Many of the trees are labeled with their Latin and Yucatec Maya names. Before starting your 20- to 30-minute walk, pick up a book with detailed descriptions of the trail and the trees at the center's headquarters.

Getting There

Easiest is to take a boat from Corozal, or to hire a local tour guide to arrange travel. From Corozal and Orange Walk, figure a little more than an hour to drive there. The road takes you through **San Estevan** and then to **Progreso.** Turn right just before entering Progreso, to **Little Belize** (a Mennonite community). Continue on to **Chunox. Sarteneja** is three miles beyond Shipstern. Don't forget a long-sleeved shirt, pants, mosquito repellent, binoculars, and a camera for your exploration of the reserve.

SARTENEJA

This small fishing village in northern Belize was established by Yucatán settlers from Mexico in the 19th century. The fishermen follow the fishing and boat-building skills handed down over the years. Obviously, the immigrants were not the only people who felt that Sarteneja's location on the Corozal District coast was ideal for the seafaring life; it is apparent that the ancient Maya spent many years here also.

To date, only one Maya structure has been partially restored, and archaeologists note that the remains of more than 350 structures have been discovered—but not excavated. For generations, the people of nearby villages have robbed the Maya sites of building materials such as stone blocks and limestone to make plaster and cement. As the scavengers picked and dug around the structures over the years, artifacts made of gold, copper, and shells continued to turn up. Scientists believe Sarteneja was occupied by the Maya from the Early Classic period into the 1700s.

Today, Sarteneja is home to a few hundred fishermen and farmers. Pineapples grow well and for years were transported to Belize City by boat twice a week to be sold at the Belize City wharf. But since the all-weather road from Sarteneja opened, the fruit can be delivered more frequently by truck. Farmers are planting other crops, and with the freedom of coming and going to Belize City more easily, this may develop into a major agricultural community—if tourism doesn't beat it out first! Already there are sport fishermen who prefer Sarteneja's mild climate (with rich catches of fish) to the southern, more humid part of the country.

Accommodations

Inexpensive, simple accommodations can be found at **Fernando's Seaside Guesthouse** (tel. 501/423-2085), US$30 for a room with private bath. There may be other options by the time you read this.

Getting There

Thunderbolt boats can stop here on their Corozal–San Pedro run, charging US$15 pp, about 40 minutes from the dock in Corozal. There are also two daily buses between Sarteneja and Belize City. They leave from a riverside lot on North Front Street in Belize City, across from the Holy Redeemer School, at noon and 4 P.M. Three early morning buses depart Sarteneja each day; the ride takes a little over three hours.

Chetumal, Mexico

An exciting dose of culture shock is an easy 15 miles from Corozal. Chetumal, capital of the Mexican state of Quintana Roo, is a relatively modern, mid-sized city of about 200,000—nearly as many people as in the entire country of Belize! If you don't come for the culture (wonderful museums, a few parks, a zoo, and a delicious seafront), then you must be here to shop in the new American-style mall, or see a first-run film in Chet's brand new air-conditioned Cineplex, located in the **Plaza de las Americas** mall.

Chetumal can be done as a day trip from Corozal, or used as a base from which to visit the many Yucatecan archaeological sights, like Tulum, just up the coast. It's also a gateway to Mexico's well-known Caribbean resorts: Cancún, Cozumel, Playa del Carmen, and Akumal. Chetumal is without the bikini-clad, touristy crowds of the north and presents the businesslike atmosphere of a growing metropolis. A 10-minute walk takes you to the waterfront from the marketplace and most of the hotels. Modern, sculpted monuments stand along a breezy promenade that skirts the broad crescent of the bay. Also explore the back streets, where worn, wooden buildings still have a Central American/Caribbean look. The largest building in town—white, three stories, close to the waterfront—houses most of the government offices. Wide, tree-lined avenues and sidewalks front dozens of small variety shops.

SIGHTS

Do not miss the **Museo de la Cultura Maya** (9 A.M.–7 P.M. Sun., Tues.–Thurs., 9 A.M.–8 P.M. Fri. and Sat., US$5), located at the new market and an impressive and creative experience by any standards. The **Museo Municipal** is excellent as well, with a great deal of contemporary Mexican art.

Norhtern Belize

© JOSHUA BERMAN

Chetumal

On Avenida Heroes, five miles north of the city, is **Calderitas Bay,** a breezy area for picnicking, dining, camping, and RVing. Tiny **Isla Tamalcas,** 1.5 miles off the shore of Calderitas, is the home of the primitive capybara, the largest of all rodents.

Twenty-one miles north of Chetumal (on Highway 307) is **Cenote Azul,** a circular *cenote* 61.5 meters deep and 185 meters across and filled with brilliant blue water. This is a spectacular place to stop for a swim, lunch at the outdoor restaurant, or just to have a cold drink.

ACCOMMODATIONS AND FOOD

Chetumal has quite a few hotels in all price categories (including a Holiday Inn near the new market), as well as many fine cafés specializing in fresh seafood. Check out *Moon Handbooks Yucatán Peninsula* for details.

GETTING AROUND

Taxis are available from the old market into town for under US$1; if going to the mall, ask to be let off at the Plaza de las Americas before arriving at the station. Bus travel is a versatile and inexpensive way to travel the Quintana Roo coast—there are frequent trips to Playa del Carmen and Cancún, and a new fleet of luxury express buses are a treat after Belize's school-bus system. Chetumal is part of the loop between Campeche, Cancún, and Mérida. Fares and schedules change regularly; currently the fare to Cancún is about US$30.

GETTING THERE AND AWAY

Buses between Belize City, Corozal, and Chetumal travel throughout the day, taking you all the way through the border (you'll need to get off twice to pass through Immigration and pay a US$19 exit fee) to the Mercado Viejo in Chetumal. A local Chetumal bus from Corozal costs US$1.50, a taxi to the border US$10. The express trip to Chetumal from Belize City takes about four hours and costs US$10. Also check with the various kiosks in the Water Taxi Terminal by the Swing Bridge in Belize City for direct bus service to Chetumal with **S & L Travel and Tours** (tel. 501/227-7593 or 227-5145, sltravel@btl.net, www.sltravelbelize.com); **Mundo Maya Deli, Gifts, Travel & Tours** (tel. 501/223-1235, mundomayatravel@btl.net); **Kaisa International;** and **San Juan Tours.** Most of these companies offer one or two daily buses, leaving between 9 A.M. and noon. Mundo Maya will go one step further and book you to points beyond on the main Mexican bus line (Autobuses del Oriente), all the way to Brownsville, Texas, if you so desire. The trip to Mexico City, by the way, is roughly 20–22 hours from Chetumal.

Also, Corozal-based **Henry Menzies Travel & Tours** (tel. 501/422-2725, menziestours @btl.net) will arrange Chetumal transfers (and other Mexican attractions), and local ruins. Also check other Corozal travel folks: at the **Hok'ol K'in Hotel** or with **Herman Pollard** (tel. 501/422-3329). For travel agencies, stop by the **Hotel Maya** or **Jal's Travel Agency** (tel. 501/422-2163, ligializama@hotmail.com).

Know
Belize

The Land

ⓜ GEOGRAPHY

Belize lies on the east coast of Central America, right at the corner where the Honduran coast takes off to the east. Belize's 8,866 square miles of territory are bordered on the north by Mexico, on the west and south by Guatemala, and on the east by the Caribbean Sea. From the northern Río Hondo border with Mexico to the southern border with Guatemala, Belize's mainland measures 180 miles long, and is 68 miles across at its widest point. Offshore, Belize has more than 200 cayes, or islands. Both the coastal region and the northern half of the mainland are flat, but the land rises in the south and west (in the Maya Mountains) to over 3,000 feet above sea level. Mangrove swamps cover much of the humid coastal plain. The Maya Mountains and the Cockscombs form the country's backbone, rising 3,675 feet to **Victoria Peak,** Belize's highest point.

In the west, the Cayo District contains the **Mountain Pine Ridge Reserve.** At one time a magnificent pine forest, it was destroyed in the lower plains by fires and lumber removal over the decades, and only a few straggler pine trees remain in the arid foothills. However, the upper regions of Mountain Pine Ridge provide spectacular scenery, and thick forest encompasses the **Macal River** as it tumbles over huge granite boulders. **Hidden Valley Falls** plunges 1,000 feet to the valley below. The **Río Frio** cave system offers massive stalactites and stalagmites to the avid spelunker. The diverse landscape includes limestone-fringed granite boulders.

Over thousands of years, what was once a sea in the northern half of Belize has become a combination of scrub vegetation and rich tropical hardwood forest. Near the Mexican border, much of the land has been cleared, and it's here that the majority of sugar crops are raised, along with family plots of corn and beans. Most of the northern coast is swampy, with a variety of grasses and mangroves that attract hundreds of species of waterfowl. Rainfall in the north averages 60

inches annually, though it's generally dry November–May.

Significant rainfall in the mountains washes silt and nutrients into the lower valleys to the south and west, forming rich agricultural areas. In southern Belize, it rains most of the year, averaging 150 inches or more. The coastal belt attracts large farms that raise an ever-expanding variety of crops. A dense rainforest thrives in this wet, humid condition with thick ferns, lianas, tropical cedars, and palms.

CLIMATE

The climate in Belize is subtropical, with a mean annual temperature of 79°F, so you can expect a variance between 50 and 95°F. The dry season generally lasts from December-ish through May and the wet season June–November, although it has been known to rain sporadically all the way into February, when cold fronts from the north arrive from time to time.

The amount of rainfall varies widely from north to south. Corozal in the north receives 40–60 inches while Punta Gorda in the south averages 160–190 inches with an average humidity of 85 percent. Occasionally during the winter, "northers" sweep down from North America across the Gulf of Mexico, bringing rainfall, strong winds, and cooling temperatures. Usually lasting only a couple of days, they often interrupt fishing and influence the activity of lobster and other fish. Fishermen invariably report increases in their catches several days before a norther.

The *"mauger"* season, when the air is still and the sea is calm, generally comes in August; it can last for a week or more. All activity halts while locals stay indoors as much as possible to avoid the onslaught of ferocious mosquitoes and other insects.

Hurricanes

Belize lies in a hurricane belt. Since 1787, 22

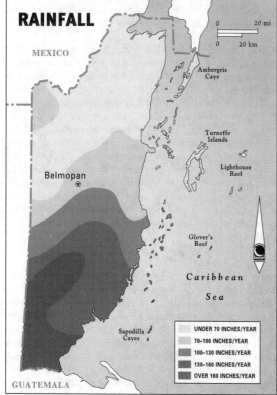

RAINFALL

MEXICO

Ambergris Caye

Turneffe Islands

Lighthouse Reef

Belmopan ⊛

Glover's Reef

Caribbean Sea

Sapodilla Cayes

GUATEMALA

0 20 mi
0 20 km

	UNDER 70 INCHES/YEAR
	70–100 INCHES/YEAR
	100–130 INCHES/YEAR
	130–160 INCHES/YEAR
	OVER 160 INCHES/YEAR

© AVALON TRAVEL PUBLISHING, INC.

City (just 18 inches above sea level) to Belmopan. Then, in 1978, Hurricane Greta took a heavy toll in dollar damage, though no lives were lost. The three most recent hurricanes were Mitch in 1998, Keith in 2000, and Iris in 2001. The Belizeans are survivors—they pick up the pieces of their lives and homes, and build again. What else can they do?

HABITATS OF INLAND BELIZE

Belize has several productive habitats that support a startling variety of life. Each habitat is dependent on the soil and available water.

Marshy Havens

Belize is dotted with rivers, lagoons, and swamps. Low forests grow up around these wetlands and provide an environment for insects, birds, mammals, and reptiles. Bamboo, logwood, red mangrove, and white mangrove are among the species that find footholds in the soggy soil and grow into thickets. Numerous insects, agouti, basilisk lizards, iguanas, paca, and waterfowl are among the many creatures that inhabit these fringe forests. The wetlands themselves play host to many creatures: crocodiles, fish, turtles, and hundreds of bird species. A boat ride into one of the wetlands will give you an opportunity to see a great variety of waterfowl. The lakes of Belize (such as those at Crooked Tree) are wintering spots for many flocks of North American duck species. Among others, you might see the blue-winged teal, northern shoveler, and lesser scaup, along with a variety of wading birds feeding in the shallow waters, including numerous types of heron, snowy egret, and (in the summer) white ibis.

hurricanes have hit the small country in varying degrees of intensity. In an unnamed storm in 1931, 2,000 people were killed and almost all of Belize City was destroyed. The water rose nine feet in some areas, even onto Belize City's Swing Bridge. Though forewarned by Pan American Airlines that the hurricane was heading their way, most of the townsfolk were unconcerned, believing that their protective reef would keep massive waves away from their shores. They were wrong.

The next devastation came with Hurricane Hattie in 1961. Winds reached a velocity of 150 mph, with gusts of 200 mph; 262 people drowned. It was after Hurricane Hattie that the capital of the country was moved from Belize

We once watched a peregrine falcon hunt at Crooked Tree. First, the wary bird slowly circled high above the lake watching its prey, and then it plummeted to attack a flock of American coots. Seconds before the falcon reached the ducks, the flock spotted it and began squawking loudly—warning the whole family—and diving into the water (where the falcon will not follow). After watching the falcon dive for the ducks over and over again, we moved on in our canoe, feeling more secure about the destiny of these American coots.

Broadleaf Jungle and Cohune Forests

By certain scientific definitions, there is no true "rainforest" in Belize; the quantity of rainfall is insufficient and is not evenly spread throughout the year. Instead, the magnificent broadleaf jungle of Belize is considered "moist tropical forest." Depending on its maturity, this forest may have a single, double, or even triple canopy, triple being the oldest and rarest. Definitions aside, the broadleaf jungles of the Maya Mountains and parts of northern and western Belize create beneath their crowns relatively cool, damp environments that yield an explosion of life. Towering mahogany, ceiba, figs, and guanacaste live here. Bromeliads, orchids, and other epiphytes cover the limbs of these jungle giants. Lianas and vines drip from the branches to the ground. Mushrooms of many varieties and other fungi digest the remains of fallen trees. Leaf cutter ants, termites, butterflies, and spiders abound. Hummingbirds, parrots, toucans, and woodpeckers flit between trees. Anteaters, howler and spider monkeys, squirrels, and margays move among the branches. Jaguars and pumas are plentiful. Boa constrictors, fer-de-lance, and other snakes are common, as are many species of lizards.

Broadleaf forests thrive in clay soils enriched by alluvial runoff from streams and rivers. In places, cohune palms, which are typically scattered throughout the forest, grow in thick concentrations. This cohune forest forms a dense cover or canopy. Even so, many of the jungle giants will penetrate it as they reach upward into the sun-light. Many of the same epiphytes, vines, and animals frequent these areas.

Pine Forests and Savanna

Pine forests grow up around areas of low moisture and sandy soil. These conditions exist in certain lowland areas and the low mountains of western Belize. With its typically open canopy, the pine forest allows much more light to reach the ground. Plant and animal life is less diverse here. Palmetto palms, scrub oak, and various grasses grow in close association with pine forests. In fact, standing pines are frequently surrounded by savanna or grassland. Foxes and jaguarundis, deer, mice, squirrels and other rodents, armadillos, hawks and owls, rat snakes, and fer-de-lance frequent these areas.

CAVES

Approximately 200 million years ago, the beginning stages of limestone formation occurred, creating what in part gives Belize its extensive cave system. It was during this Cretaceous period that life under the ocean started to create what is now limestone. Millions of sea creatures left a legacy with their deaths: skeletons formed a thick layer (6,000 feet in some areas) of what is now limestone, the backbone of the cave systems. Sea levels fell and the mountains impelled themselves upward. After 120 million years, and with the help of wind, rain, and faulting, the Maya Mountains were created, and flowing underground rivers carved out channels, rooms, and caverns.

Cenotes are created when the constant ebb and flow of underground rivers and lakes erodes the underside of limestone containers. In certain places, the surface crust eventually wears so thin that it caves in, exposing the water below, and at the same time creating steep-walled caverns—natural wells. Around these water sources, Maya villages grew. Some of the wells are shallow—seven meters below the jungle floor; some are treacherously deep at 90 meters underground. In times of drought, the Maya fetched water by carving stairs into

CAVES AND THE MAYA

Mythology

Large populations of Maya were concentrated in the limestone foothills, where water supplies and clay deposits were plentiful. Caves were a source of fresh water, especially during dry periods. Clay pots of grain were safely stored for long periods of time in the cool air and, thousands of years later, can be seen today. Looting of caves has been a problem for decades, and as a result all caves are considered archaeological sites.

The Maya used caves for utilitarian as well as religious and ceremonial purposes. The ancient Maya believed that upon entering a cave, one entered the underworld, or Xibalba, the place of beginnings and of fright. The Maya believed there were nine layers of the underworld, and as much as death and disease and rot was represented by the underworld, so was the beginning of life. Caves were a source of water—a source of life—for the Maya. Water that dripped from stalactites was used as holy water for ceremonial purposes. The underworld was also an area where souls had hopes of defeating death and becoming ancestors. As a result, rituals, ceremonies, and even sacrifices were performed in caves, evidenced today by many pots, shards, implements, and burial sites.

Caves were important burial chambers for the ancient Maya, and over 200 skeletons have been found in more than 20 caves. One chamber in Caves Branch was the final earthly resting spot for 25 individuals. Many of these burial chambers are found deep in the caves, leading to speculation that death came by sacrificing the living, as opposed to carrying in the dead. Some burial sites show possible evidence of commoners being sacrificed to accompany the journey with an elite who had died—but who really knows?

Spelio-Archaeology

The first written accounts related to cave archaeology began in the late 1800s. A British medical officer by the name of Thomas Gann wrote of his extensive exploration of caves throughout the country. In the late 1920s, he was also part of the first formal study of some ruins and caves in the Toledo District, and his papers provide insight no one else can give to modern-day archaeologists.

Little else was done until 1955, when the Institute of Archaeology was created by the government of Belize. Starting in 1957, excavations were organized throughout the years under various archaeologists. Excavations in the 1970s led to many important archaeological discoveries, including pots, vessels, and altars. In the 1980s, a series of expeditions was undertaken to survey the Chiquibul cave system. Other finds during this time period include a burial chamber and one cave with over 60 complete vessels and other ceremonial implements.

Today, projects are underway in many caves around the country. The Institute of Archaeology does not have a museum—yet—they've been talking about one for years. In the meantime, you may have to get a little wet and dirty to go visit some of these artifacts yourself.

slick limestone walls or by hanging long ladders into abysmal hollows that led to the underground lakes.

The cave systems of Belize are some of the most extensive in the world and have only begun to be explored. Modern-day mapping and research only began in the 1960s. Since then, more than 300 caves have been explored and probably 150 miles of passages have been mapped, including the Cebada and Petroglyph Caves, two of the largest underground chambers in the world. Caves are found all over the country, but most are centered in the southern and western areas of Belize.

Belize's neighbor, Mexico, is renowned for its cave and cenote diving, but so far this is not an option for the visitor to Belize. Researchers have done very little study of cenote diving, in part due to the remote and difficult locations of the cave entrances (but that is slowly changing).

Notable Caves

The most spectacular cave system in Belize is the **Chiquibul,** west of the Maya Mountains and close to the Guatemalan border. Miles and miles of passageways riddle this system, including **Cebada,** the largest in Belize.

The Toledo District has two major cave systems, one near Blue Creek Village and the other north of Blue Creek, **Little Quartz Ridge.** Located in pristine surroundings, the **Blue Creek Cave System** includes a large walk-through cave with some passages that force you to crawl through on hands and knees.

In the Cayo District, north of the Maya Mountains, **Caves Branch** offers tourists easy access to incredible sights. Many hotels and tour operators run trips that include floating on inner tubes in and out of black passageways. Caves Branch is close to the highway, allowing easy access and logistical planning. **St. Herman's Cave, Petroglyph Cave,** and the (inland) **Blue Hole** are part of this system, all part of a nature reserve. Many lodges are situated literally on top of these caves and offer outings and various modes of transport through the caves.

Vaca Plateau is partly in the Mountain Pine Ridge area and includes the **Río Frio Cave,** undoubtedly the most popular cave (due to its easy access) in the Cayo District. Ask at any hotel or at Eva's Cafe in San Ignacio to visit this small cave.

Underwater Caves

Many submerged sinkholes, most notably the Blue Hole, occur in the ocean. **Giant Cave,** off of Caye Caulker, is believed to be one of the longest underwater caves in the world. Other underwater caves are also found off of Caye Chapel, Ambergris Caye, and Columbus Caye. Diving these caves is highly unlikely for the average diver—local dive shops just are not equipped or trained for this type of undertaking, regardless of how much you are willing to spend to go under.

ENVIRONMENTAL ISSUES

Because of Belize's impressive network of protected areas and relatively low population density, the widespread deforestation that occurs in other parts of Central America is not nearly as big a problem. However, Belize faces its own unique set of challenges it will need to overcome if it is to remain as pristine as it is. Perhaps the biggest problem is improper disposal of solid and liquid wastes, both municipal and industrial, particularly agro-wastes from the shrimp and citrus industries.

Mining of aggregates from rivers and streams has negative impacts on local watersheds and the coastal zones into which they empty, where sedimentation can be destructive to reef and other marine systems. Unchecked, unplanned development, especially in sensitive areas like barrier beaches, mangroves, islands, and riverbanks, where changes to the landscape often have wide and unanticipated effects, is another problem. For more information on Belize's environmental challenges, visit the websites of some of the organizations listed in the Internet Resources later in this section.

The Sea

Belize's modest patch of Caribbean Ocean is rich in marine life and a variety of habitats, and much of it has protected status.

THE CAYES AND ATOLLS

More than 200 cayes (pronounced KEEZ and derived from the Spanish *cayo* for "key" or "islet") dot the blue waters off Belize's eastern coast. They range in size from barren patches that are submerged at high tide to the largest, Ambergris Caye—25 miles long and nearly 4.5 miles across at its widest point. Some cayes are inhabited by people, others only by wildlife. The majority are lush patches of mangrove that challenge the geographer's definition of what makes an island (that's why you'll never see a precise figure of how many there are).

Most of the cayes lie within the protection of the Belize Barrier Reef (almost 200 miles long), which parallels the mainland. Without the protection of the reef—in essence a breakwater—the islands would be washed away. Within the reef, the sea is relatively calm and shallow.

Beyond the reef lie three of the Caribbean's four atolls: **Glover's Reef, Turneffe Islands,** and **Lighthouse Reef.** An atoll is a ring-shaped coral island surrounding a lagoon, always beautiful, and almost exclusively found in the South Pacific. The three types of cayes are **wet cayes,** which are submerged part of the time and can support only mangrove swamps; **bare coral outcroppings** that are equally uninhabitable; and **sandy islands** with palm trees, jungle shrubbery, and their own set of animals. The more inhabited cayes lie in the northern part of the reef and include Caye Caulker, Ambergris Caye, St. George's Caye, and Caye Chapel.

THE REEFS

Reefs are divided into three types: atoll, fringing, and barrier. An **atoll** can be formed around the crater of a submerged volcano. The polyps begin building their colonies on the round edge of the crater, forming a circular coral island with a lagoon in the center. Thousands of atolls occupy the world's tropical waters. Only four are in the Caribbean Ocean; three of those are in Belize's waters.

A **fringing reef** is coral living on a shallow shelf that extends outward from shore into the sea. A **barrier reef** runs parallel to the coast, with water separating it from the land. Sometimes it's actually a series of reefs with channels of water in between. This is the case with some of the larger barrier reefs in the Pacific and Indian oceans.

The Belize Barrier Reef extends from the tip of Mexico's Isla Mujeres to Sapodilla Caye in the Bay of Honduras. This 180-mile-long reef is known by various names (Belize Reef is the most common) and is the longest reef in the Western and Northern Hemispheres.

Have a great snorkel, and observe proper reef etiquette.

Coral

Coral is a unique limestone formation that grows in innumerable shapes, such as delicate lace, trees with reaching branches, pleated mushrooms, stovepipes, petaled flowers, fans, domes, heads of cabbage, and stalks of broccoli. Corals are formed by millions of tiny carnivorous polyps that feed on minute organisms and live in large colonies of individual species. These small creatures can be less than half an inch long or as large as six inches in diameter. Related to the jellyfish and sea anemone, polyps need sunlight and clear saltwater not colder than 70°F to survive. Coral polyps have cylinder-shaped bodies. One end is attached to a hard surface (the bottom of the ocean, the rim of a submerged volcano, or the reef itself), and the mouth end is encircled with tiny tentacles that capture its minute prey with a deadly sting.

How a Reef Grows

As these small creatures continue to reproduce and die, their sturdy skeletons accumulate. Over eons, broken bits of coral, animal waste, and granules of soil contribute to the strong foundation for a reef that will slowly rise toward the surface. To grow, a reef must have a base no more than 82 feet below the water's

BELIZE GOVERNMENT FISHERIES REGULATIONS

Bone Fish *(Albulba vulpes)*
Also known locally as Macabi. No person shall buy or sell any Bone Fish.

Conch *(Strombus gigas)*
Shell length should exceed 7 inches, market clean weight should exceed 3 ounces, closed season is from 1st July to 30th September, no diced or fillet.

Coral
It is illegal for any person to take, buy, sell or have in his possession any type of coral. An exception is made in the case of Black Coral (order Antipatharia), which may only be bought, sold, or exported with a license from the Fisheries Administrator.

Hicatee *(Dermatemy mawii)*
No person shall have in his possession more than three or transport on any vehicle more than five such turtles or fish for female Hicatee that are greater than 43 centimeters (17.2 in.), smaller than 38 centimeters (15.2 in.). Closed season: May 1 to May 31, inclusive of any year.

Lobster *(Panulirus argus)*
Minimum cape length is 3 inches, minimum tail weight is 4 ounces, closed season is from February 15th to June 14th, no diced or fillet.

Marine Turtles
No person should interfere with any turtle nest. No person may take any turtle unless with a license from the Fisheries Administrator (traditional use only). No person shall buy, sell, or have in his possession any articles made of turtle shell.

Nassau Grouper *(Epinephelus striatus)*
No person shall take in the waters of Belize, or buy, sell, or have in his possession, any Nassau Grouper between 1st December and 31st March except from Maugre Caye at Turneffe Islands and Northern Two Caye at Lighthouse Reef. At these two places a special license is granted to traditional fishers.

Shrimp
(Trawling) Closed season: 15th April to 14th August, inclusive of any year.

No one should fish using scuba gear except under license from the Fisheries Administrator.

Contact the Fisheries Department for further information: P.O. Box 148, Belize City, Belize, tel. 501/223-2623, 224-4552, or 223-2187, fax 501/223-2983, species@btl.net.

REEF ETIQUETTE

There are a few important guidelines to follow when snorkeling or diving near coral and other marine life. The reef, though massive and impressive, is also extremely fragile and every year is subject to impact from an increasing number of visitors.

Start by getting comfortable with your dive or snorkel gear in a sandy area before venturing out to the reef. Ask your guide to explain the area to you, and give yourself plenty of time to learn how to kick properly, to float on the surface of the water, to practice expelling water from your snorkel, and to clear your mask a couple times.

If you're in doubt about your swimming ability, wear a life jacket around your waist. You don't want to find yourself far from the boat, tired and gulping water. This is dangerous for you and could force you to grab onto the coral and stand on a patch of reef—both of which can seriously damage or even kill the coral.

Here are some more standard guidelines to follow:

• Don't touch the coral! Not only can it sting you, but it is a living thing and can be seriously damaged. The coral lives in a mutually beneficial relationship with a type of algae, and by disrupting that protective layer, the algae can die and the coral won't get all the nutrients it needs. Gloves are not allowed in the Hol Chan Marine Reserve for this reason.

• Watch your fins. It's easy to forget that you have two extensions on your feet when you're in the water, so be sure to keep your distance from the coral heads so that you don't brush against them or break them off.

• Don't stand on the coral. This happens a lot, and it's one of the surest ways to kill coral. Be smart, safe, and don't put yourself in that situation. If you're feeling a little anxious or think you might need to rest, stay near the boat or ask your guide

for help. Hold onto a life ring if you're not sure about your swimming abilities.

• Know the area. Some snorkel sites are located near channels with strong currents, and you don't want to find yourself too far out or struggling to swim back. Stay near your group and listen to your guide.

• If you're in a sandy area, try not to stir up the sand, especially if you're near a coral head. Corals cannot live in murky water, and when sediments land on top of them, the algae they live with are unable to photosynthesize and could easily die.

• Don't touch or feed the marine life. Poking them, prodding them, lifting them out of the water—these activities can cause the animal stress. Feeding them can change their habits and make them more susceptible to predators.

• Don't collect coral. It's tempting to take some of these beautiful creatures home, but all marine life should be left where it is. The only coral that is legal to sell in Belize is Black Coral, and that's only with a special license.

• Always go snorkeling or diving with a guide. Not only is this for your safety, but they know the area better than anyone and will certainly enhance your experience.

• Don't leave any garbage behind. And if you see any, pick it up and take it back to shore with you (but be sure to check it carefully to make sure no animals are using it as a home.)

• When diving, be sure to maintain neutral buoyancy and watch for dragging equipment. This will ensure that you and your gauges won't run into the coral.

surface. In a healthy environment it can grow one to two inches a year. One small piece of coral represents millions of polyps and many years of construction.

ESTUARIES

The marshy areas and bays at the mouths of rivers where saltwater and fresh water mix are called estuaries. Here, nutrients from inland are carried out to sea by currents and tides to nourish reefs, sea-grass beds, and the open ocean. Many plants and animals feed, live, or mate in these waters. Conch, crabs, shrimp, and other shellfish thrive here, and several types of jellyfish and other invertebrates call this home. Seabirds, shorebirds, and waterfowl of all types frequent estuaries to feed, nest, and mate. Crocodiles, dolphins, and manatees are regular visitors. Rays, sharks, and tarpon hunt and mate here. During the wet season, the estuaries of Belize pump a tremendous amount of nutrients into the sea.

MANGROVES

Mangroves live on the edge between land and sea, forming dense thickets that act as a protective border against the forces of wind and waves. Four species grow along many low-lying coastal areas on the mainland and along island lagoons and fringes. Of these, the red mangrove and the black mangrove are most prolific. Red mangrove in excess of 30 feet is found in tidal areas, inland lagoons, and river mouths, but always close to the sea. Its signature is its arching prop roots. Black mangrove grows almost double that height. Its roots are slender, upright projectiles that grow to about 12 inches, protruding all around the mother tree. Both types of roots provide air to the tree.

Mangrove Succession

Red mangroves (Rhizophora mangle) specialize in creating land—its seedpods fall into the water and take root on the sandy bottom of a shallow shoal. The roots, which can survive in seawater, then collect particles from the water and the tree's own dropping leaves to create soil. Once the red mangrove forest has created land, it makes way for the next mangrove in the succession process. The black mangrove (Avicennia germinans) can actually out-compete the red mangrove at this stage due to its ability to live in anoxic soil (without oxygen). In this way, the red mangrove appears to do itself in by creating an anoxic environment. But, while the black mangrove is taking over the upland of the community, the red mangrove continues to dominate the perimeter as it continuously creates more land from the sea. One way to identity a black mangrove forest is by the thousands of dense pneumataphores (tiny air roots) covering the ground under the trees.

Soon, burrowing organisms such as insects and crabs begin to inhabit the floor of the black mangrove forest and the first ground covers, Salicornia and salt wart (Batis maritima) take hold—thereby aerating the soil and enabling the third and fourth mangrove species in succession to move in: the white mangrove (Laguncularia racemosa) and the gray mangrove (Conocarpus erectus), also known locally as buttonwood.

Desalinizers

Each of the three primary mangrove species lives in a very salty environment and each has its own special way of eliminating salt. The red mangrove concentrates the salt taken up with seawater into individual leaves, which turn bright yellow and fall into the prop roots, thereby adding organic matter to the system. The black mangrove eliminates salt from the underside of each leaf. If you pick a black mangrove leaf and lick the back, it will taste very salty. The white mangrove eliminates salt through two tiny salt pores located on the petiole (the stem that connects the leaf to the branch). If you sleep in a hammock under a white mangrove tree, you will feel drops of salty water as the tree "cries" upon you! The buttonwood also has tiny salt pores on each petiole.

Know Belize

SEA-GRASS BEDS

Standing on Ambergris Caye and looking seaward, many tourists are surprised to see something dark in the shallow water just offshore. They expect a sandy bottom typical of many Caribbean islands. However, it is this "dark stuff" that eventually will make their day's snorkeling, fishing, or dining experience more enjoyable. What they are noticing is sea grass, another of the ocean's great nurseries.

Sea grasses are plants with elongated, ribbonlike leaves. Just like the land plants they evolved from, sea grasses flower and have extensive root systems. They live in sandy areas around estuaries, mangroves, reefs, and open coastal waters. Turtle grass has broader, tapelike leaves and is common down to about 60 feet. Manatee grass, found to depths of around 40 feet, has thinner, more cylindrical, leaves. Both cover large areas of seafloor and intermix in some areas, harboring an amazing variety of marine plants and animals. Barnacles, conch, crabs, and many other shellfish proliferate in the fields of sea grass. Anemones, seahorses, sponges, and starfish live here. Grunts, filefish, flounder, jacks, rays, and wrasses feed here. Sea turtles and manatees often graze in these lush marine pastures.

Flora and Fauna

Belize's position at the biological crossroads between North and South America has blessed it with an astonishingly broad assortment of wildlife. Belize's wide ranging geography and habitat have also been a primary factor in the diversity and complexity of its ecosystems and their denizens.

FLORA

Belize is a Garden of Eden. Four thousand species of native flowering plants include 250 species of orchids and approximately 700 species of trees. Most of the country's forests have been logged off and on for more than 300 years (2,000 years, if you count the widespread deforestation during the time of the ancient Maya). The areas closest to the rivers and coast were the hardest hit because boats could be docked and logs easily loaded to be taken farther out to sea to the large ships used to haul the precious timber.

Forests

Flying over the countryside gives you a view of the patchwork landscape of cleared areas and secondary growth. Belize consists of four distinct forest communities: pine-oak, mixed broadleaf, cohune palm, and riverine forests. Pine-oak forests are found in sandy, dry soils. In the same areas, large numbers of mango, cashew, and coconut palm are grown near homes and villages. The mixed broadleaf forest is a transition area between the sandy pine soils and the clay soils found along the river. Often the mixed broadleaf forest is broken up here and there and doesn't reach great height; it's species-rich but not as diverse as the cohune forest. The cohune forest area is characterized by the cohune palm, which is found in fertile clay soil where a moderate amount of rain falls throughout the year. The cohune nut was an important part of the Maya diet. Archaeologists say that where they see a cohune forest, they know they'll find evidence of the Maya.

The cohune forest gives way to the riverine forest along river shorelines, where vast amounts of water are found year-round from excessive rain and from the flooding rivers. About 50–60 tree varieties and hundreds of species of vines, epiphytes, and shrubs grow here. Logwood, mahogany, cedar, and pine are difficult to find along the easily accessible rivers because of extensive logging. The forest is in different stages of growth and age. To find virgin forest, it's necessary to go high into the mountains that divide Belize. Because of the rugged terrain and distance from the rivers, these areas were left almost untouched. Even today, few roads exist. If left undisturbed for

hibiscus

many, many years, the forest will eventually regenerate itself.

Among the plant life of Belize, look for mangroves, bamboo, and swamp cypresses, as well as ferns, vines, and flowers creeping from tree to tree, creating a dense growth. On topmost limbs, orchids and air ferns reach for the sun. As you go farther south you'll find the classic tropical rainforest, including tall mahoganies, *campeche, sapote,* and ceiba, thick with vines.

Orchids

In remote areas of Belize, one of the more exotic blooms, the orchid, is often found on the highest limbs of tall trees. Of all the species reported in Belize, 20 percent are terrestrial (growing in the ground) and 80 percent are epiphytic (attached to a host plant—in this case trees—and deriving moisture and nutrients from the air and rain). Both types grow in many sizes and shapes: tiny buttons, spanning the length of a long branch; large-petaled blossoms with ruffled edges; or intense, tiger-striped miniatures. The lovely flowers come in a wide variety of colors, some subtle, some brilliant. The black orchid is

Belize's national flower. All orchids are protected by strict laws, so look but don't pick.

FAUNA

A walk through the jungle brings you close to myriad animal and bird species, many of which are almost extinct in other Central American countries—and the world. Bring your binoculars, some fast film, and be vewy, vewy quiet.

Following is a short introduction to a few of the creatures you are likely to see in the wild if you spend any amount of time outside your room. This is an incomplete, quite random selection; for more detailed information, find yourself one of the abundant field guides to the various flora and fauna of Belize.

Birds

If you're a serious bird-watcher, you know all about Belize. Scores of species can be seen while sitting on the deck of your jungle lodge: big and small, rare and common, and with local guides aplenty to help find them in all the vegetation. The **keel-billed toucan** is the national bird of

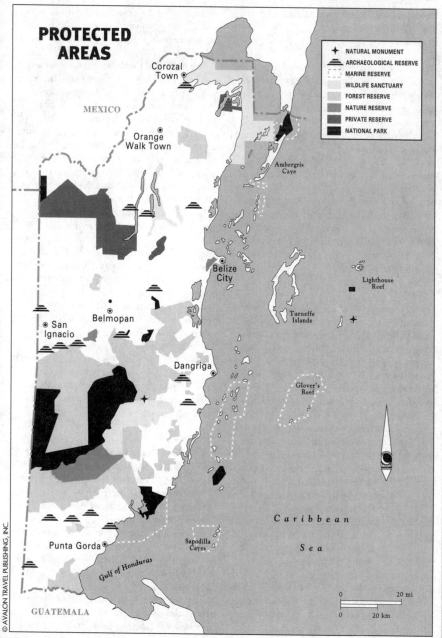

PROTECTED AREAS

+ NATURAL MONUMENT
▲ ARCHAEOLOGICAL RESERVE
MARINE RESERVE
WILDLIFE SANCTUARY
FOREST RESERVE
NATURE RESERVE
PRIVATE RESERVE
NATIONAL PARK

Corozal Town

MEXICO

Orange Walk Town

Ambergris Caye

Belize City

Lighthouse Reef

Turneffe Islands

San Ignacio

Belmopan

Glover's Reef

Dangriga

Caribbean

Sea

Punta Gorda

Sapodilla Cayes

Gulf of Honduras

GUATEMALA

0   20 mi

0   20 km

© AVALON TRAVEL PUBLISHING, INC.

Know Belize

Belize and is often seen perched high on a bare limb in the early morning.

Bats

Bats cling to the ceilings of caves, often attracted to warm pockets of air. Their urine and other bodily secretions slowly eat away at the limestone, creating these holes. The bats' sense of smell attracts them back to these same holes. Bats are harmless to humans (although confused vampire bats, with a risk of rabies, may bite, but only if you are sleeping outside); most that live in the caves are insect-eating bats. Their eyesight is excellent, as is their use of echolocation; fly-bys occur only if they go after the bugs attracted to your headlamp. Some scientists give warning about a pulmonary disease that can be carried in the dry dust of bat droppings. If you are concerned, ask your doctor and perhaps wear a breathing mask of some sort.

Cats

Seven species of cats are found in North America, five of them in Belize. For years, rich adventurers came to Belize on safari to hunt the jaguar for its beautiful skin. Likewise, hunting margay, puma, ocelots, and jaguarundis was a popular sport in the rainforest. All of that has changed. Hunting any endangered species in Belize is not allowed and there is much protected area in which they freely wander.

The **jaguar** is heavy-chested with sturdy, muscled forelegs, a relatively short tail, and small, rounded ears. Its tawny coat is uniformly spotted; the spots form rosettes: large circles with smaller spots in the center. The jaguar's belly is white with black spots. The male can weigh 145–255 pounds, females 125–165 pounds. Largest of the cats in Central America and third-largest cat in the world, the jaguar is about the same size as a leopard. It is nocturnal, spending most daylight hours snoozing in the sun. The male marks an area of about 65 square miles and spends its nights stalking deer, peccaries, agoutis, tapirs, monkeys, and birds. If hunting is poor and times are tough, the jaguar will go into rivers and scoop fish with its large paws. The river is also a fa-vorite spot for the jaguar to hunt the large tapir when it comes to drink. Females begin breeding at about three years and generally produce twin cubs.

The smallest of the Belizean cats is the **margay,** weighing in at about 11 pounds and marked by a velvety coat with exotic designs in colors of yellow and black designs, and a tail that's half the length of its body. The bright eye shine indicates it has exceptional night vision. A shy animal, it is seldom seen in open country, preferring the protection of the dense forest. The "tiger cat," as it is called by locals, hunts mainly in the trees, satisfied with birds, monkeys, and insects as well as lizards and figs.

Larger and not nearly as catlike as the margay, the black or brown **jaguarundi** has a small flattened head, rounded ears, short legs, and a long tail. It hunts by day for birds and small mammals in the rainforests of Central America. The **ocelot** has a striped and spotted coat. Average weight is about 35 pounds. A good climber, the cat hunts in trees as well as on the ground. Its prey include birds, monkeys, snakes, rabbits, young deer, and fish. Ocelots usually have litters of two but can have as many as four. The **puma** is also known as the cougar or mountain lion. The adult male measures about six feet in length and weighs up to 198 pounds. It thrives in any environment that supports deer, porcupine, or rabbit. The puma hunts day or night.

Monkeys

In Creole, the **black howler monkey** is referred to as "baboon" (in Spanish, *saraguate*) though it has no close connection to its African relatives. Because the howler prefers low-lying tropical rainforests under 1,000 feet of elevation, Belize is a perfect habitat. They are more commonly found near the riverine forests, especially on the Belize River and its major branches. The howler monkey, along with its small cousin the spider monkey, also enjoys the foothills of the Maya Mountains.

To protect the howler monkey, the **Community Baboon Sanctuary** was organized in Bermudian Landing to help conserve the lands

SSSH! I'M LOOKING FOR WILDLIFE!

I t takes many years of practice to fine tune your wildlife-viewing skills; hours upon hours of patient sitting and walking sessions to learn some of Mother Nature's more subtle communication skills. Growing up and living off the forest helps—that's why hiring a native guide will guarantee you more sightings than going it on your own. Spending years in the Belizean bush studying jaguars and other cats is a good method as well, the one employed by biologist Alan Rabinowitz in his landmark studies of the Cockscomb Basin. He shares some of his hard-won knowledge in the following passage:

The forest is teeming with wildlife, but you see and hear very little just by walking through it. It often seems simply a quiet, green darkness, but that appearance is deceiving. When you learn to read the signs of an animal's passing, it's like watching the wildlife. A nibbled twig tells you a red brocket deer has been feeding; a muddy wallow says a tapir has been by; chewed nuts from the cohune palm tree indicate that a paca has fed the night before; and a musky smell warns you that a group of peccaries may be closer than you'd like.

Alan Rabinowitz, Jaguar

where it lives. Thanks to an all-out effort involving local property owners, the Belize Ministry of Natural Resources, the U.S. World Wildlife Fund, the Belize Audubon Society, and the Peace Corps, the land that provides for the howler will be saved. The sanctuary is an ideal place for researchers to study its habits and perhaps discover the key to its survival among encroaching humans (and for tourists to get close to these creatures in their natural habitat). In fact, natural breeding was so successful there that troops of howlers have been relocated to Cockscomb and other regions where the monkey was decimated by yellow fever decades ago.

The adult howler monkey is entirely black and weighs 15–25 pounds. Its most distinctive trait is a roar that can be heard up to a mile distant. A bone in the throat acts as an amplifier; the cry sounds much like that of a jaguar. The howler's unforgettable bark is said by some to be used to warn other monkey troops away from its territory. Locals, on the other hand, say the howlers roar when it's about to rain, to greet the sun, to say good night, or when they're feeding.

Howlers live in troops that number four to eight and no more than 10, consisting of one adult male and the rest females and young. Infants nurse for about 18 months, making the space between pregnancies about 24 months. Initially, "mom" carries her young clutched to her chest; once they're a little older, they ride piggyback. The troop sleeps, eats, and travels together. The howlers primarily eat leaves, but include flowers and fruit in their diet (when available). Highly selective, they require particular segments of certain trees and blossoms: sapodilla, hog-plum, bay cedar, fig, and buket trees. The locals even put up with the monkey's occasional invasion of cashew trees. Although the baboon has a couple of natural predators—the jaguar and the harpy eagle—its worst foe is deforestation by humans. An unexpected boon to the area has been the reappearance of other small animals and bird species that are also taking advantage of the protected area.

Spider monkeys are smaller than black howlers and live in troops of a dozen or more, feeding on leaves, fruits, and flowers high in the jungle canopy. Slender limbs and elongated prehensile tails assist them as they climb and swing from tree to tree. With a border of white around their faces, adults look like little old people. Baby spider monkeys are winsome in appearance too, and often are captured for pets. So curious and

Know Belize

Know Belize

BUTTERFLY-WATCHING

A number of butterfly "farms" or "ranches" have been built around Belize, and a visit to one is always a pleasant, educational, and colorful experience. Many began as export businesses, to raise butterflies for foreign zoos and classrooms, but now feature screened-in rooms where you'll see the creatures fluttering about your head as you walk through.

Notable places to see butterflies include the Fallen Stones, in the Toledo District, and Green Hills, at Mile 8 on the Mountain Pine Ridge Road in Cayo District. The latter is a butterfly breeding, educational, and interpretive center. All the butterfly farms pay as much attention to the plants that provide the larval food as to the pupae. And these fussy little creatures often have different tastes. You'll find another small but diverse butterfly reserve at the entrance road to the Cockscomb Basin Wildlife Sanctuary. It's right across the creek from the Women's Craft Co-op in Maya Center. Another readily accessible butterfly farm, with one of the highest numbers of species, is Tropical Wings, located at the Trek Stop, right on the Western Highway, just seven miles or so west of San Ignacio—they have an excellent interpretive center, guided tour, and a Frisbee golf course and café for when you've finished.

Depending on where you are in the country, you'll see the intense blue morpho as well as the white morpho, which is white but shot with iridescent blue. Three species of the owl butterfly (genus *Caligo*) love to come and lunch on the overripe fruit. You'll also see tiny heliconians and large yellow and white pierids, among many, many more.

Chaa Creek Lodge has developed the Blue Morpho Butterfly Breeding Center. A small flight room houses the blue beauties; naturalists on the grounds gladly explain the various stages of life the butterfly goes through.

A butterfly goes from tiny teardroplike egg, to

© JOSHUA BERMAN

Stay calm! The beautiful blue morpho senses fear.

colorful caterpillar, to pupae, and then graceful adult. Butterfly farms gather breeding populations of typical Belizean species in the pupal stage, and then the pupae are carefully "hung" in what is called an emerging cage with a simulated "jungle" atmosphere—hot and humid (not hard to do in Belize). A short time later they shed their pupal skin, and a tiny bit of Belize flutters away to the amazement and joy of all who behold.

Depending on the species, butterflies live anywhere from seven days to six weeks. If you plan to visit a farm, or to go into the rainforest on a butterfly safari to observe the beautiful creatures, go on a sunny day: you'll see lots more butterfly activity than on an overcast day. If it's raining, forget it!

In many areas of Belize, butterfly populations have been almost totally depleted for many reasons, including habitat destruction (from logging, for instance) and changing farming practices, particularly the use of pesticides. Belize's steamy marshes, swamps, and rainforest have been a natural breeding ground for beautiful butterflies for thousands of years and hopefully will continue to be so.

mischievous are they, however, that frustrated owners frequently cage or even release them back into the wild. Without the skills to survive or the support of a troop, such freed orphans are doomed to perish. Unlike howler monkeys, which may allow human proximity during their midday siesta, spider monkeys rarely approve. They usually dissolve into the forest canopy. On occasion, they have been known to aim small sticks, urine, and worse at intruders. Though not as numerous in Belize as howler monkeys because of disease and habitat loss, they remain an important part of the country's natural legacy.

Rodents

A relative of the rabbit, the **agouti** or "Indian rabbit" has coarse gray-brown fur and a hopping gait. It is most often encountered scampering along a forest trail or clearing. Not the brightest of creatures, it makes up for this lack of wit with typical rodent libido and fecundity. Inhabiting the same areas as the paca, these two seldom meet, as the agouti minds its business during the day and the paca prefers nighttime pursuits. The agouti is less delectable than the paca. Nonetheless, it is taken by animal and human hunters and is a staple food of jaguars.

The **paca**, or **gibnut**, is a quick, brownish rodent about the size of a large rabbit with white spots along its back. Nocturnal by habit and highly prized as a food item by many Belizeans, the gibnut is more apt to be seen by the visitor on an occasional restaurant menu than in the wild.

Coati

A member of the raccoon family, the coati—or quash—has a long, ringed tail, masked face, and lengthy snout. Sharp claws aid the coati in climbing trees and digging up insects and other small prey. Omnivorous, the quash also relishes jungle fruits. A sensitive, agile nose helps it sniff out trees bearing these favored goodies. Usually seen in small troops of females and young, coatis have an amusing, jaunty appearance as they cross a jungle path, tails at attention. The occasional solitary male is referred to as a coatimundi or solitary coati.

Peccary

Next to deer, peccaries are the most widely hunted game in Central America. Other names for this piglike creature are musk hog and javelina. Some compare these nocturnal mammals to the wild pigs found in Europe, though in fact they are native to America.

Two species found in Belize are the collared and the white-lipped peccaries. The feisty collared peccary stands one foot at the shoulder and can be three feet long, weighing as much as 65 pounds. It is black and white with a narrow semicircular collar of white hair on the shoulders. In Spanish, *jabalina* means "spear," descriptive of the two spearlike tusks that protrude from its mouth. This more familiar peccary lives in deserts, woodlands, and rainforests, and travels in groups of 5–15.

Also with tusks, the white-lipped peccary or warrie is reddish-brown to black and has an area of white around the mouth. This larger animal, which can grow to four feet long, dwells deep in tropical rainforests and at one time lived in herds of 100 or more. They are more dangerous than their smaller cousins and should be given a wide berth.

Tapir

The national animal of Belize, the South American tapir is found from the southern part of Mexico to southern Brazil. It is stout-bodied (200–300 kgs or 91–136 lbs.), with short legs, a short tail, small eyes, and rounded ears. Its nose and upper lip extend into a short but very mobile proboscis. Totally herbivorous, tapirs usually live near streams or rivers in the forest. They bathe daily and also use the water as an escape when hunted either by humans or by their prime predator, the jaguar. Shy, unaggressive animals, they are nocturnal with a definite home range, wearing a path between the jungle and their feeding area.

Iguanas

Found all over Central America, lizards of the family *Iguanidae* include various large plant-eaters, in many sizes and typically dark in color with slight variations. The young iguana is bright emerald green. The common lizard grows to three feet long and has a blunt head and long flat tail. Bands of black and gray circle its body, and a serrated column reaches down the middle of its back, almost to its tail. During mating season, it's common to see brilliant orange males on a sunny branch hoping to attract girlfriends.

Very large and shy, the lizard uses its forelimbs to hold the front half of its body up off the ground while the two back limbs remain relaxed and splayed alongside its hindquarters. However, when the iguana is frightened, its hind legs do everything they're supposed to, and the iguana crashes quickly (though clumsily) into the brush searching for its burrow and safety. This reptile is not aggressive, but if cornered it will bite and use its tail in self-defense. The iguana mostly enjoys basking in the bright sunshine along the Caribbean. Though they are mainly herbivores, the young also eat insects and larvae. Certain varieties in some areas of southern Mexico and Central America are almost hunted out—for example, the spiny-tailed iguana in the central valley of Chiapas, Mexico. A moderate number are still found in the rocky foothill slopes and thorn-scrub woodlands.

Several other species of iguana live in Belize, from the small to a gargantuan six feet long. Their habits are much the same, however. They all enjoy basking in the sun, sleeping in old hollow trees at night, and eating certain tender plants. The female can lay up to a hundred eggs, and when the pale green or tan hatchlings emerge from the rubbery egg skins, they scoot about quickly. One of the iguana's serious predators is the hawk. If an iguana sunbathing high in the trees senses a winged shadow, it flings itself from the tree either into a river below or the brush, skittering quickly into hiding. However, the human still remains its most dangerous predator.

It is not unusual to see locals along dirt paths carrying sturdy specimens by the tail to put in the cook pot. From centuries past, recorded references attest to the medicinal value of this lizard, partly explaining the active trade of live iguanas in marketplaces in some parts of Belize. Iguana stew is believed to cure or relieve various human ailments, such as impotence. The unlaid eggs of iguanas caught before the nesting season are considered a delicacy. Another reason for their popularity at the market is their delicate white flesh, which tastes much like chicken. If people say they're having "bamboo chicken" for dinner, they are dining on iguana.

Crocodiles

Though often referred to as alligators, Belize has only crocodiles, the American (up to 20 feet) and Morelet's (to eight feet). Crocodiles have a

---

PASS THE PLASTIC, PLEASE

Until 2000, beer and soda came in recycled glass bottles in Belize. But in early 2000, that changed with the introduction of soda in plastic bottles by the country's only major beverage distributor. Bowen & Bowen Ltd promised a recycling center to do something about the tonnage of bottles that is bound to end up in landfills and along the side of the roads, but have done little to make it happen. Some businesses, especially in the Cayo District, refuse to sell plastic bottles until they can be properly disposed of or reused, as glass bottles are. If you'd rather not contribute to Belize's volume of unnecessary solid waste (which is the country's top environmental problem), bring your own water bottle or re-use the first liter you buy as many times as you can (disinfect with a drop of bleach every couple of uses); many hotels have five gallon jugs of purified water from which you can fill your bottle. We know one longtime expat who, to do her part, saves up several duffle bags and briefcases of imported plastic trash, and carries it back with her to the United States once or twice a year.

well-earned bad reputation in Africa, Australia, and New Guinea as man-eaters, especially the larger saltwater varieties. Their American cousins are fussier about their cuisine, preferring fish, dogs, and other small mammals to people. The territories of both species overlap in estuaries and brackish coastal waters. Able to filter excess salt from its system, only the American crocodile ventures to the more distant cayes. Endangered throughout their ranges, both crocs are protected by international law and should be left undisturbed. Often seen floating near the edge of lagoons or canals during midday, they are best observed at night with the help of a powerful flashlight. When caught in the beam, their eyes glow an eerie red. Crocodiles are most abundant in the rivers, swamps, and lagoons of the Belize City, Orange Walk, and Toledo Districts, as well as areas around the Turneffe Islands. Don't miss the Crocodile Reserve at Monkey Bay.

MANGROVES AND HUMANS

The doctor on Christopher Columbus's ship, *Hispaniola,* reported in 1494 that mangroves in the Caribbean were "so thick that a rabbit could scarcely walk through." The mangroves are just as dense today, a wall of bright green along the shore, but their location is probably not the same. Over a period of several hundred years, depending on hurricanes and other localized natural events, the red mangroves may have extended the edge of a coastline a mile or more in their determined march into the sea.

Mangrove islands and coastal forests play an important role in protecting Belize's coastline from destruction during major natural events such as hurricanes. Along with the seagrass beds, they also protect the Belize Barrier Reef by filtering much of the sediment out of river runoff before it reaches and smothers the delicate coral polyps. However, dense mangrove forests are also home to mosquitoes and biting flies. The mud and peat beneath mangrove thickets is often malodorous with decaying plant matter and hydrogen sulfide–producing bacteria. Many developers would like nothing better than to eliminate the mangroves and replace them with seawalls. But such modification to the coastline results in accelerated erosion and destruction of seaside properties during severe storms.

Importance to Wildlife

Birds of many species use the mangrove branches for roosting and nesting sites, including swallows, redstarts, warblers, grackles, herons, egrets, osprey, kingfishers, pelicans, and roseate spoonbills. Along the seaside edge of red mangrove forests, prop roots extend into the water creating thickets that are un-paralleled as nurseries of the sea. Juveniles of commercial fisheries, such as snapper, hogfish, and lobster, find a safe haven here. The flats around mangrove islands are famous for recreational fisheries such as bonefish and tarpon. The roots that extend below the low tide mark provide important substrate (a platform to which organisms settle or attach) for sessile (immobile) marine invertebrates such as sponges, hydroids, corals, tube worms, mollusks, anemones, and tunicates. In many areas, snorkeling along a mangrove is often more colorful and exciting than along a reef.

The three-dimensional labyrinth often created by expanding red mangroves, seagrass beds, and bogues (small channels of seawater flowing through the mangroves) provides the home and often the nursery for nurse sharks, American crocodiles, and manatees.

Protection

Fortunately, the Belize government enforces laws that make it difficult to disturb these natural wonders. Destruction of mangroves is illegal in most areas; cutting and/or removal of mangroves requires a special permit and mitigation. Despite some illegal cutting, you can still see miles and miles of red mangrove forests edging the coast and islands of Belize, in some places as extensive as they were hundreds of years ago when the *Hispaniola* sailed through these waters.

(Contributed by Caryn Self-Sullivan, a marine scientist who, since 1998, has been studying manatee ecology and behavior in the mangrove island habitat of the Drowned Cayes area near Belize City.)

History

Early recorded comments following Columbus's fourth voyage to the New World led the Spaniards to hastily conclude that the swampy shoreline of what is now Belize was unfit for human habitation. Someone should have told that to the Maya, who had been enjoying the area for quite some time already.

ANCIENT CIVILIZATION

Earliest Humans

During the Pleistocene epoch (about 50,000 B.C.), when the level of the sea fell, people and animals from Asia crossed the Bering land bridge into the American continent. For nearly 50,000 years, humans continued the epic trek southward.

As early as 10,000 B.C., Ice Age man hunted woolly mammoth and other large animals roaming the cool, moist landscape of Central America. Between 7000 and 2000 B.C., society evolved from hunters and gatherers to farmers. Such crops as corn, squash, and beans were independently domesticated in widely separated areas of Mesoamerica after about 6000 B.C. The remains of clay figurines from the Pre-Classic period, pre-

sumed to be fertility symbols, marked the rise of religion in Mesoamerica, beginning about 2000 B.C.

Around 1000 B.C., the Olmec culture, believed to be the earliest in the area and the predecessors to the Maya, began to spread throughout Mesoamerica. Large-scale ceremonial centers grew along Gulf Coast lands, and much of Mesoamerica was influenced by the Olmecs' religion of worshiping jaguarlike gods. They also developed the New World's first calendar and an early system of writing.

Classic Period

The Classic period, beginning about A.D. 300, is now hailed as the peak of cultural development among the Maya. Until A.D. 900, they made phenomenal progress in the development of artistic, architectural, and astronomical skills. They constructed impressive buildings during this period, and wrote codices (folded bark books) filled with hieroglyphic symbols that detailed complicated mathematical calculations of days, months, and years. Only the priests and the privileged held this knowledge and continued to learn and develop it until, for some unexplained reason, the growth suddenly halted. A new militaristic society was born, built around a blend of ceremonialism, civic and social organization, and conquest.

A Society Collapses

Priests and noblemen, the guardians of religion, science, and the arts, conducted their ritual ceremonies and studies in the large stone pyramids and platforms found today in ruins throughout the jungle. Consequently, more specific questions arise: What happened to the priests and noblemen? Why were the centers abandoned? What happened to the knowledge of the intelligentsia? They studied the skies, wrote the books, and designed the pyramids. Theories abound. Some speculate about a revolution—the people were tired of subservience and were no longer

BELIZE HISTORY IN A NUTSHELL

The peaceful country of Belize is a sovereign democratic state of Central America located on the Caribbean. The government is patterned on the system of parliamentary democracy and experiences no more political turmoil than any other similar government, such as Great Britain or the United States.

Important Dates

1862: Became a British colony
1954: Attained universal adult suffrage
1964: Began self-government
1981: Attained full independence

WHAT'S IN A NAME?

No one knows for sure where the name Belize originated or what it means. The country was called Belize long before the British took the country over and renamed it British Honduras. In 1973, the locals changed it back to the original Belize as a first step on the road to independence. There are several well-known theories for its meaning. Some say it's a corruption of the name Wallis (wahl-EEZ), from the pirate (Peter Wallace) who roamed the high seas centuries ago and visited Belize. Others suggest that it's a distortion of the Maya word *belix*, which means muddy river. Still others say it could be a further distortion of the Maya word *belikin* (which is also the name of the local beer). And of course it could be another of those mysterious Maya secrets we may never learn.

willing to farm the land to provide food, clothing, and support for the priests and nobles. Another theory is that there just wasn't enough land to farm and provide food and necessities for the large population.

All signs point to an abrupt work stoppage. After about A.D. 900, no buildings were constructed and no stelae, which carefully detailed names and dates to inform future generations of their roots, were erected.

Whatever happened, it's clear that the special knowledge concerning astronomy, hieroglyphics, and architecture was not passed on to Maya descendants. Sociologists who have lived with the indigenous people in isolated villages are convinced that this privileged information is not known by today's Maya. Why did the masses disperse, leaving once-sacred stone cities unused and ignored? It's possible that lengthy periods of drought, famine, and epidemic caused the people to leave their once-glorious sacred centers. No longer important in day-to-day life, these structures were ignored for a thousand years and faced the whimsy of nature and its corroding elements.

Anthropologists and historians do know that perhaps as many as 500,000 Maya were killed

by diseases such as smallpox after the arrival of the Spaniards into the New World. But no one really knows for sure what halted the progress of the Maya culture.

Secrets of the Ruins

With today's technology, astronauts have seen many wonders from outer space, spotting overgrown structures within the thick uninhabited jungle of La Ruta Maya. These large treasures of knowledge are just waiting to be reopened. But until the funds and plans are in hand, these mounds are left unsung and untouched in hopes that looters will not find them before archaeologists are able to open them up. Looters generally are not interested in the knowledge gained from an artifact, just money. Not only has much been lost in these criminal actions, but their heavy-handed methods have also destroyed countless artifacts. As new finds are made, the history of the Maya develops new depth and breadth. Archaeologists, ethnologists, art historians, and linguists continue to unravel the ongoing mystery with constant new discoveries of temples and artifacts, each with a story to tell.

COLONIALIASM

The pre-Columbian history of Belize is closely associated with that of its nearby neighbors: Mexico, Guatemala, and Honduras. The Maya were the first people to inhabit the land referred to as La Ruta Maya. They planted *milpas* (cornfields), built ceremonial centers, and established villages with large numbers of people throughout the region. Hernán Cortés passed through the southern part of the country on his trek northward searching for treasure. In 1530, the conquistador Montejo attacked the Nachankan and Belize Maya, but his attempt to conquer them failed. This introduction of Spanish influence did not have the impact on Belize that it did in the northern part of the Caribbean coast until the Caste War.

Hernán Cortés and Other Explorers

After Columbus's arrival in the New World, other

adventurers traveling the same seas soon found the Yucatán Peninsula. In 1519, 34-year-old Cortés sailed from Cuba against the will of the Spanish governor. With 11 ships, 120 sailors, and 550 soldiers, he set out to search for slaves, a lucrative business with or without the blessings of the government. His search began on the Yucatán coast and eventually encompassed most of Mexico. However, he hadn't counted on the ferocious resistance and cunning of the Maya. The fighting was destined to continue for many years—a time of bloodshed and death for many of his men. This "war" didn't *really* end on the peninsula until the Chan Santa Cruz people finally made peace with the Mexican federal government in 1935, more than 400 years later.

Although the Maya in Mérida, in Yucatán, Mexico, were a long distance from Belize and not directly bothered by the intrusion of the Spanish, the actions of the Spanish Franciscan priests toward the Mérida Maya would have a great influence on Belize in the years that followed. The Catholic priests were wiping out ceremonies and all other traces of the Maya, further setting the stage for the bloodshed to come. The ripple effect that followed eventually exploded into the Caste War, which, in turn, brought both Maya and mestizos across the borders of Belize.

Diego de Landa was the Franciscan priest who, while trying to gather the Maya into the fold of Christianity, leaned on them and their beliefs with a heavy hand, destroying thousands of Maya idols, many of their temples, and all but four of their books. Because his methods were often cruel, in 1563 he was called back to Spain after colonial civil and religious leaders accused him of

A VOICE FROM THE PAST

This passage from John Lloyd Stephens' famous high adventure travelogue was written in the mid-19th century but still speaks volumes about the unique early history of Belize with subtle, important messages regarding the modern course of the country:

The next day we had to make preparations for our journey into the interior, besides which we had an opportunity of seeing a little of Balize. The Honduras Almanac, which assumes to be the chronicler of this settlement, throws a romance around its early history by ascribing its origin to a Scotch bucanier named Wallace. The fame of the wealth of the New World, and the return of the Spanish galleons laden with the riches of Mexico and Peru, brought upon the coast of America hordes of adventurers—to call them by no harsher name—from England and France, of whom Wallace, one of the most noted and daring, found refuge and security behind the keys and reefs which protect the harbour of Balize. The place where he built his log huts and fortalice is still pointed out; but their site is now occupied by warehouses. Strengthened by a close alliance with the Indians of the Moscheto shore, and by the adhesion of numerous British adventurers, who descended upon the coast of Honduras for the purpose of cutting mahogany, he set the Spaniards at defiance. Ever since, the territory of Balize has been the subject of negotiation and contest, and to this day the people of Central America claim it as their own. It has grown by the exportation of mahogany; but, as the trees in the neighbourhood have been almost all cut down, and Central America is so impoverished by wars that it offers but a poor market for British goods, the place is languishing, and will probably continue to dwindle away until the enterprise of her merchants discovers other channels of trade.

John L. Stephens, *Incidents of Travel in Central America, Chiapas and Yucatan,* 1841 "despotic mismanagement." He spent a year in prison, and while his fate was being decided, he wrote a book, *Relaciones de las Cosas de Yucatán,* defending himself against the charges.

Ironically, this book gave extensive information about the Maya, their beliefs, the growth and preparation of their food, the structure of their society, the priesthood, and the sciences—essentially a broad insight into the culture that otherwise would have been lost forever. Fortunately, he included in his book a one-line formula that, when used as a mathematical and chronological key, opened up the science of Maya calculations and their great knowledge of astronomy. De Landa returned to the Yucatán Peninsula and lived out his remaining years, continuing his previous methods of proselytizing until his death in 1579.

Catholicism

Over the years, the majority of Maya were baptized into the Catholic faith. Most priests did their best to educate the people, teach them to read and write, and protect them from the growing number of Spanish settlers who used them as slaves. The Maya practiced Catholicism in their own manner, combining their ancient beliefs, handed down throughout the centuries, with Christian doctrine. These mystic yet Christian ceremonies are still performed in baptism, courtship, marriage, illness, farming, house building, and fiestas.

Pirates and the Baymen

While all of Mesoamerica dealt with the problems of economic colonialism, the Yucatán Peninsula had an additional problem: harassment by vicious pirates who made life in the coastal areas unstable. In other parts of the Yucatán Peninsula, the passive people were ground down, their lands taken away, and their numbers greatly reduced by the European settlers' epidemics and mistreatment.

British buccaneers sailed the coast, attacking the Spanish fleet at every opportunity. These ships were known to carry unimaginable riches of gold and silver from the New World back to the king of Spain. The Belizean coast became a convenient place for pirates to hole up during bad weather or for a good drinking bout. And, though no one planned it as a permanent layover, by 1650 the coast had the beginnings of a British pirate lair/settlement. As pirating slacked off on the high seas, British buccaneers discovered they could use their ships to carry logwood back to a ready market in England. These early settlers were nicknamed the Baymen.

In the meantime, the Spanish desperately tried to maintain control of this vast New World they had grasped from across the ocean. But it was a difficult task, and brutal conflicts continually flared between the Spanish and either the British inhabitants or the Maya. The British Baymen were continually run out but always returned. Treaties were signed and then rescinded. However, the British relentlessly made inroads into the country, importing slaves from Africa beginning in the 1720s to laboriously thrash through the jungles and cut the timber—work that the fiercely independent Maya resisted with their lives.

In 1763, Spain "officially" agreed to let the British cut logwood. The decree allowed roads (along the then-designated frontiers) to be built in the future, though definite boundaries were to be agreed upon later. For nearly 150 years the only "roads" built were narrow tracks to the rivers; the rivers became Belize's major highways. Boats were common transport along the coast and somehow road building was postponed, leaving boundaries vaguely defined and countrymen on both sides of the border unsure. This was the important bit of history that later encouraged the Spanish-influenced Guatemalans to believe that Belize had failed to carry out the 1763 agreement by building roads, so it was their turf. Even after Spain vacated Guatemala, Guatemalans tried for generations to assume ownership across the existing Belize borders. Since 1988, however, the boundary disagreement *appears* to have blown over with the Guatemalan threat of a takeover stopping on their side of the frontier. But because no official agreements have been made, most believe this conflict is still unresolved.

Treaty of Paris

Politically, Belize (or, more to the point, its timber) was up for grabs, and a series of treaties did little to calm the ping-pong effect between the British and the Spanish over the years. One such agreement, the Treaty of Paris, did little to control the Baymen—or the Spanish. With license, British plantation owners continued to divest the forests of logs, leaving Belize with nothing more than a legacy of brutality and tyrannical control over the slaves (who worked under cruel conditions while making rich men of their masters). The Spanish continued to claim sovereignty over the land but never settled in Belize. They continued their efforts to take over by sporadically harassing and attacking the Baymen—only to fail each time when the British returned and held on to their settlement.

The Baymen held on with only limited rights to the area until the final skirmish in 1798 on St. George, a small caye just off Belize City. The Baymen, with the help of an armed sloop and three companies of a West Indian regiment, won the battle of St. George's Caye on September 10, ending the Spanish claim to Belize once and for all. After that battle, Belize was ruled by the British Crown until gaining its independence in 1981.

During the first 400 years after Europeans arrived, nothing much was done to develop the country, not even (as mentioned) roads or railroads, and you can count on one hand how many historic buildings are standing (because few were ever built).

Land Rights

In 1807, slavery was *officially* abolished in Belize by England. This was not agreeable to the powerful British landowners, and in many quarters it continued to flourish. Changes were then made to accommodate the will of the powerful. The local government no longer "gave" land to settlers as it had for years (the British law now permitted former slaves and other "coloureds" to hold title). The easiest way to keep them from possessing the land was to charge for it—essentially barring the majority in the country from landownership. So, in essence, slavery continued.

Caste War

It was inevitable that the Maya would eventually erupt in a furious attack. This bloody uprising in the Yucatán Peninsula in the 1840s was called the Caste War. Though the Maya were farmers and for the most part not soldiers, in this savage war they took revenge on every white man, woman, and child by rape and murder. When the winds of war reversed themselves and the Maya were on the losing side, vengeance on them was merciless. Some settlers would immediately kill any Maya, regardless of his beliefs. Some Maya were taken prisoner and sold to Cuba as slaves; others left their villages and hid in the jungles, in some cases for decades. Between 1846 and 1850, the population of the Yucatán Peninsula was reduced from 500,000 to 300,000. Guerrilla warfare ensued, with the escaped Maya making repeated sneak attacks upon the white settlers. Quintana Roo, adjacent to Belize along the Caribbean coast, was considered a dangerous no-man's-land for more than a hundred years until, in 1974, with the promise of tourism, the territory was admitted to the Federation of States of Mexico.

Growing Maya Power

Many of the Maya who escaped slaughter during the Caste War fled to the isolated jungles of Quintana Roo and Belize. The Maya revived the religion of the "talking cross," a pre-Columbian oracle representing gods of the four cardinal directions. This was a religious/political marriage. Three determined survivors of the Caste War—a priest, a master spy, and a ventriloquist—all wise leaders, knew their people's desperate need for divine leadership. As a result of their leadership and advice from the talking cross, the shattered people came together in large numbers and began to organize. The community guarded the location of the cross, and its advice made the Maya strong once again.

They called themselves Chan Santa Cruz ("People of the Little Holy Cross"). As their confidence developed, so did the growth and power of their communities. Living very close to the Belize (then British Honduras) border, they found they had something their neighbors wanted. The Chan Santa Cruz Maya began selling timber to the British and in return received arms, giving the Maya even more power. Between 1847 and 1850, in the years of strife during the Caste War in neighboring Yucatán, thousands of Maya, mestizo, and Mexican refugees who were fleeing the Spaniards entered Belize. The Yucatecans introduced the Latin culture, the Catholic religion, and agriculture. This was the beginning of the Mexican tradition in northern Belize, locally referred to as "Spanish tradition." The food is typically Mexican with tortillas, black beans, tamales, squash, and plantain (a type of banana that can be cooked). For many years, these mestizos kept to themselves and were independent of Belize City. The colonial administration kept its distance, and a community-appointed headman made and kept the laws. Both Hispanic and non-Hispanic Belizeans who live in the northern area speak Spanish. Today all the towns and cities of Belize come under the jurisdiction of the central Belizean government.

The Sugar Industry

Though most of the refugees ultimately returned to their homes in Mexico, the ones who stayed and began farming the land were making the first real attempt at much-needed agriculture. Large tracts that had been cleared of trees were empty, and rich landowners were willing to rent acreage (cheaply) to the refugees for farming. Until then, almost all foodstuffs had been imported from other countries (and to this day it's not unusual to see many tinned foods from Australia, England, and the United States on market shelves).

The mestizos settled mostly in the northern sections of the country, which is apparent by the Spanish names of the cities: Corozal, San Estevan, San Pedro, and Punta Consejo. By 1857, the immigrants were growing enough sugar to supply Belize, with enough left over to export the surplus (along with rum) to Britain. After their success proved to the tree barons that sugarcane could be lucrative, the big landowners became involved. Even in today's world of low-priced sugar, the industry is still important to Belize's economy.

Timber

For 300 years, Belize was plundered and neglected—and not just by swashbuckling pirates and hard-living buccaneers. Its forests were denuded of valuable logwood (the heart of which provided rich dyes for Europe's growing textile industry until manmade dyes were developed). When the demand for logwood ceased, plantation owners found a viable substitute for their logging interests—removing mahogany trees from thick virgin forests. For three centuries the local economy depended on exported logs and imported food.

In a 1984 Audubon Society report, it was noted that despite the widespread use of slash-and-burn farming by the Maya a millennium ago, and the more recent selective logging of logwood and mahogany since the 16th century, Belize still has extensive forests. The large-scale abandonment of farms with the decline of the Maya civilization about A.D. 900 permitted forest regeneration that has attained what plant ecologists consider to be "climax" status. The removal of logwood had little effect on the forest structure. It's in today's economy that logging can cause serious damage to the forest with the indiscriminate removal of large tracts of trees, no matter the variety, because of modern methods and high-tech equipment.

INDEPENDENCE

In 1862, Belize officially became the colony of British Honduras, though it had been ruled by the British crown since 1798. The average Belizean had few rights and a very low living standard. Political unrest grew in a stifled atmosphere. Even when a contingent of Belizean soldiers traveled to Europe to fight for the British in World War I, the black men were scorned. But when these men returned from abroad, the pot of change began to boil. Over

THE GUATEMALA–BELIZE SOVEREIGNTY DISPUTE

One of the legacies of colonial rule in the Americas, and elsewhere around the world, was a seemingly endless succession of territorial conflicts and border disputes, many of which remain unresolved. One of the most durable is the seemingly interminable struggle between Guatemala and its eastern neighbor Belize, formerly known as British Honduras.

The problem's origins date back more than five centuries. In 1494, only two years after Columbus's "discovery" of the Americas, the papal Treaty of Tordesillas divided the New World into Spanish and Portuguese realms of influence (Portugal got the short end of the stick, as most of the new lands lay west of the line of Tordesillas, beyond the 46th meridian). Nevertheless, northern European interlopers such as England and France showed little respect for Spanish and Portuguese claims, and were soon occupying their own lands in North America and the Caribbean.

Spain claimed the entire Caribbean coast of Central America, but never effectively dominated it entirely because the small, scattered Indian populations made it difficult to exact taxes and tribute. Because Spain enforced a rigid mercantile monopoly on its American colonies, obliging all trade to go directly—and often inconveniently—to Spain, British smugglers found an opening for contraband that led to a foothold on the Cockscomb Coast of present-day Belize. English privateers and traders exploited logwood, which produced red and brown dyes, and the valuable timber from mahogany.

Belize thus traces its origins to the 17th- and 18th-century English activity on the Rimland, as a western extension of its activity in the Caribbean proper. A 1763 treaty between Britain and Spain legalized logwood exploitation but prohibited permanent settlement, so the first permanent farming did not begin until after Spanish colonial rule ended in 1821.

Guatemala argued its successor rights to Spain under the Treaty of Tordesillas, but in the chaos of the early post-colonial years was unable to contest the British presence. A treaty between the two countries in 1859 regularized that presence (though Guatemala argues that Britain never made a £50,000 payment due under the treaty, rendering it null and void). Britain formally established the colony of British Honduras in 1862.

In fact, Guatemala's original claim is ambiguous, as the northern part of Belize may have been part of the Intendencia of Yucatán, part of the Viceroyalty of New Spain whose successor state was Mexico. Mexico in fact renounced this claim in 1893, but reserved the right to reactivate it should Guatemala, which calls its border with Belize an "imaginary line," aggressively pursue its own claim.

In the meantime, Belize has developed in a dramatically different way from Guatemala. With its diverse population of Creoles (the descendants of English-speaking liberated slaves), Garinagu (Black Caribs), Spanish-speaking whites, Maya-speaking indigenes and German-speaking Mennonite immigrants, Belize remains an outlier of the Euro-African Rimland. After nearly two decades of internal self-government it became independent in 1981; English is the official language. It has a British-style parliamentary government, and is a member of the Caribbean Common Market, Caricom.

Despite economic problems—many Belizeans live overseas for economic reasons—Belize has been politically stable even during the Central American upheavals of the 1980s, when it welcomed many Q'eqchi' Maya as refugees from Guatemala.

Despite these broad cultural differences, and Belize's recognition by the United Nations, border incidents have been commonplace and sometimes surreal. In 1958, Guatemalan President Miguel Ydígoras Fuentes made an impromptu and uninvited excursion across the Río Mopán to the (then) British Honduran town of Benque Viejo del Carmen, where he capriciously passed out copies of the Guatemalan constitution. In 1963, Francisco Sagastume Ortiz led an incursion of 19 armed Petén farmers from Poptán into Pueblo Viejo without telling his men they were entering to take down the British flag. After a confrontation with the British army at Punta Gorda, Sagastume was sentenced to 10 years in prison but released later that same year.

More serious incidents took place in 1975, when Britain sent warships to the area after Guatemalan President Gen. Kjell Laugerud García rattled some sabers. In 1977, the British sent 6,000 troops in anticipation of an invasion by Guatemalan Gen. Benedicto Lucas García, brother of President Romeo Lucas García, also a general. In 1982, when Argentina invaded the British-held Falkland Islands, Guatemala enthusiastically supported the Argentine claim, to the limit of its diplomatic influence and in expectation of mutual assistance.

At the same time, of course, Belize supported the British and focused its diplomatic efforts on the Anglophone Caribbean Rimland. Guatemala finally acknowledged Belize's independence in 1991, but still claims 12,272 square kilometers of its neighbor's territory—more than 53 percent—despite an almost total lack of international support.

Militarily, Belize is at an overwhelming disadvantage if it ever came to a fight. Its population of 250,000 is a small fraction of Guatemala's 12.5 million or so, and the difference between the enormous, well-equipped Guatemalan army and the modest Belize Defence Force is even greater, especially since British troops no longer help defend Belize's borders.

Ironically, about 35,000 Guatemalans live in Belize—nearly 15 percent of the country's population—though less than 10 percent of them are legal residents—and their status is often the subject of hysterical articles in the otherwise insipid Guatemalan press. Guatemala's government may no longer be so publicly vociferous about its continuing differences with Belize, but the press has a way of overblowing border incidents to the point where Belize sometimes sounds like a garrison state threatening to overpower its larger neighbor.

The latest disputes surround illegal Guatemalan harvesters of an ornamental palm called *xate* (SHAH-tay), a decorative leaf prized for its longevity and used around the world to supplement floral bouquets. *Xate*'s market (mostly Holland and the United States) demands prices high enough to tempt hundreds of Guatemalans to illegally cut from within Belize's vast western forest reserves; these *xateros*, as they are called, often present "official" papers from their government, giving them rights to cut in Belize. They have a habit of also getting into non-*xate*–related troubles during their visit, making the matter even more touchy.

—by Wayne Bernhardson, from *Moon Handbooks Guatemala*

THE BELIZE NATIONAL ANTHEM

LAND OF THE FREE

O, Land of the Free by the Carib Sea,
Our manhood we pledge to thy liberty!
No tyrants here linger, despots must flee
This tranquil haven of democracy.
The blood of our sires which hallows the sod,
Brought freedom from slavery oppression's rod,
By the might of truth and the grace of God.
No longer shall we be hewers of wood.

Arise! ye sons of the Baymen's clan,
Put on your armours, clear the land!
Drive back the tyrants, let despots flee—
Land of the Free by the Carib Sea!

Nature has blessed thee with wealth untold,
O'er mountains and valleys where prairies roll;
Our fathers, the Baymen, valiant and bold
Drove back the invader; this heritage bold
From proud Río Hondo to old Sarstoon,
Through coral isle, over blue lagoon;
Keep watch with the angels, the stars and moon;
For freedom comes to-morrow's noon.

The colonial system had been falling apart around the world, and when India gained its freedom in 1947 the pattern was set. Many small undeveloped countries soon began to gain independence and started to rely on their own ingenuity to build an economy that would benefit the people.

Even though Belize was self-governing by 1964, it was still dominated by outside influences until September 1981, when it gained its independence from the British Crown. But change comes slowly. This third-world country is learning through hard knocks how to be self-sustaining, self-motivated, self-governing—noncolonial. In the process of finding methods to become financially independent and raise the standard of living, Belizean leaders are discovering that the country's natural assets may indeed hold the key to bringing in dollars in the form of tourism, an industry they never before dreamed of. The government is proceeding slowly to design the proper tourist growth to fit into its scheme to preserve the ethnic cultures, the animals, the reef, and the forests. Belize is becoming a role model for other developing countries that need tourism dollars but are not willing to sacrifice their cultures and natural resources. In September 1981, the Belizean flag was raised—the birth of a new era! Belize joined the United Nations, the Commonwealth, and the Non-Aligned Movement. Its work is cut out for it.

the next 50 years, the country struggled through power plays, another world war, and economic crises. But always the seed was there—a growing desire to be independent.

Government and Economy

GOVERNMENT

The infant country's first parliamentary elections were held in 1984. The government is directed by a prime minister; a bicameral legislature, the National Assembly, comprises an appointed Senate and an elected House of Representatives. Belize has two active political parties, PUP (People's United Party) and UDP (United Democratic Party). George Price and Manuel Esquivel have been elected prime minister back and forth. As in most democracies, the rhetoric can get very animated, but Belize is a peaceful country and its citizens are proud to rule themselves.

ECONOMY

The economy of Belize was traditionally based on export of logwood, mahogany, and *chicle* (the base for chewing gum, from the *chicle* tree). Today, tourism, agriculture, fisheries, aquaculture (shrimp farming), and small manufactured goods give the country an important economic boost, but it is still dependent on imported goods to get by. The main exports are sugar, citrus, bananas, lobster, and timber.

Foreign Investment

Thanks to tax concessions given to foreign investors, Belize has experienced a diversification of manufacturing industries, such as plywood, veneer manufacturing, matches, beer, rum, soft drinks, furniture, boat-building, and battery assembly.

The *Belize Investment Code* states, "Foreign investment is welcome as long as it creates jobs and expands Belizean talent and skills; infuses foreign financial resources and good managerial

© JOSHUA BERMAN

Wigs and robes are the day's fashion for a parade of lawyers up North Front Street in Belize City.

© JOSHUA BERMAN

These conch fisherman, unloading their harvest in Mango Creek, spend weeks at sea diving for shellfish.

skills into Belize; produces for export markets; utilizes indigenous raw materials; and engages in environmentally sound projects which make technological advances and increase the capital stock of the nation." Developing and improving the country's infrastructure promises big changes. For example, the government has brought electricity to 98 percent of outlying villages.

However, some critics in the country say Belize should take a hard look at what's happening. These locals are questioning how much of the country they are willing to give away to enter mainstream economics.

Tourism

Say what you will about the inefficiencies and nepotism of developing-world government agencies—the **Belize Tourism Board** (BTB) is doing *something* right. They started promoting tourism, basically from scratch, and in only a decade or so, have gotten the word "Belize" buzzing on the lips of hundreds of thousands of potential visitors

who, only a few years ago, had never even heard of the tiny country. Hiring a slick New York PR firm probably didn't hurt, not to mention all the natural and cultural qualities that make Belize such a viable destination in the first place.

In fact, Belize is the *only* country within the Caribbean to experience consistent increases with respect to overall tourist arrivals since 1998. Tourism is quickly heading to the top of the list of moneymakers in the country, responsible for one out of every four jobs in 2004.

Tourism, of course, is a dangerous beast, a double-edged machete in these parts, especially when its success is measured solely by visitor number increases, a practice most apparent in the sudden, high-impact arrival of the cruise ship industry to Belize's shores. Here are a couple of numbers for you: In 2003, the month of December recorded an unprecedented 93,173 cruise passengers visiting Belize, an increase of 66.2 percent over the previous year's figure for that month. The year-end figures for 2003 showed a whopping 80 percent increase in the total number of cruise ship day-trippers from the previous year, surging to 575,196. Belize has, in fact, recorded the highest growth in cruise ship arrivals for 2003 in the entire region, according to the latest statistics from the Caribbean Tourism Organization (CTO), and continued increases are planned.

If you'd like to bring this matter up at a Belizean cocktail party, prepare to open an enormous can of worms. There is no doubt that Belize desperately needs the money that cruise passengers are expected to bring, but the question is: Who is benefiting? So far, it's only a handful of rich stakeholders, with a large percentage of spending money going back into the giant cruise ship companies, which own the majority share of the cruise terminals of Belize City's Tourism Village. More importantly, Belize is barely equipped to handle the enormous numbers of visitors. How do you balance those cruise-ship dollars against the impacts to Belize's tiny infrastructure, such as damage to roads by bus traffic, stress on bathroom facilities and septic systems, bus exhaust, trail/garbage impact, and more?

For updated information on developments and events in Belize's tourism industry, or to offer comments/advice, contact the Marketing Department of the Belize Tourism Board (tel. 501/223-1913 in Belize City, info@travelbelize.org, www.travelbelize.org).

© JOSHUA BERMAN

As many as 10,000 cruise ship passengers disembark in Belize City's "Tourism Village" some days, a highly controversial issue within the tourism industry.

Tourism Development Project (TDP)

The TDP, a Government of Belize initiative in collaboration with the Institute of Archaeology and the Ministry of Tourism and Culture to enhance and develop Belize's archaeological sites as primary tourism destinations, is funded to the tune of US$14 million over four years. This loan from the Interamerican Development Bank and other institutions has made possible astounding excavations at the primary site, Caracol, as well as at Xunantunich, Lamanai, Altun Ha, and Cahal Pech.

The People

The extraordinary diversity of Belize's relatively tiny population is similar to the rainbow of skin colors one finds in a New York City subway car—except in Belize, they're all making direct eye contact and talking and laughing with each other. Belizeans are doubly proud of their heritage: once for their family's background (Maya, Creole, Garinagu, etc.) and again for their country, Belize. An official webpage (CIA) with 2003 data breaks it down: mestizo 48.7 percent, Creole 24.9 percent, Maya 10.6 percent, Garinagu 6.1 percent, and other 9.7 percent.

Here's a bit of background about Belize's diverse demography, but keep in mind that every one of these groups continues to mingle with the others, at least to some extent, ensuring continuing "creolization."

THE CREOLES

Comprising about 60 percent of the population of Belize, Creoles share two distinctive traits: some degree of African–European ancestry and the use of the local English-Creole dialect. Skin color runs from very dark to very light, but some old trace of English logger or buccaneer is back there. Many Creoles are also descended from other groups of immigrants.

The center of Creole territory is Belize City. Half of Belize's ethnic Creoles live here, and they make up more than three-fourths of the city's population. Rural Creoles live along the highway between Belmopan and San Ignacio, in isolated clusters in northern Belize District, and in a few coastal spots to the south—Gales Point, Mullins River, Mango Creek, Placencia, and Monkey River Town.

Cheap labor was needed to do the grueling timber work in thick, tall jungles. The British failed to force it on the maverick Maya, so they brought slaves from Africa, indentured laborers from India, and Caribs from distant Caribbean islands, as was common in the early

16th and 17th centuries. "Creolization" started when the first waves of British and Scottish began to carnally know their imported slaves and servants.

MESTIZOS

Also referred to as "Ladinos" or "Spanish," this is the quickest-growing demographic group in Belize and encompasses all Spanish-speaking Belizeans, descended from some mix of Maya and Europeans. These immigrants to Belize hail from the nearby countries of Guatemala, El Salvador, Honduras, and Mexico. Once the predominant population (after immigration from the Yucatecan Caste War), mestizos are now the second-most populous ethnic group of Belize. They occupy the old "Mexican-Mestizo corridor" that runs along New River between Corozal and Orange Walk. In west-central Belize—Benque Viejo and San Ignacio—indigenous people from Guatemala have recently joined the earlier Spanish-speaking immigrants from Yucatán.

THE MAYA

Small villages of Maya—Mopan, Yucatec, and Keq'chi—still practicing some form of their ancient culture dot the landscape and comprise roughly 12 percent of Belize's population. Records show that after the Europeans arrived and settled in Belize, many of the Maya moved away from the coast to escape hostile Spanish and British intruders who arrived by ship to search for slaves. The independent Maya refused to be subjugated, so traders brought boatloads of African slaves into the Caribbean. Both the Maya and the Africans had religious beliefs that were inconsistent with the lifestyles of European settlers, who considered them subhuman. As a result, the Maya and the Garinagu for years kept to themselves.

Many Maya communities continue to live

BELIZEANS IN THE UNITED STATES

By some estimates, there are as many Belizeans living in the United States as there are in Belize. They are concentrated mostly in New York City, Chicago, Los Angeles, and New Orleans. Of these, many young Belizeans serve in the United States Armed Forces. The money these emigrants send home is an important source of income for their Belizean families. Some Belizean expats stay in the States, but many return to settle in Belize with new skills and contribute to the development of the nation. On the flip side are those who have been deported back to Belize because of illegal activities in the United States, bringing the negative impacts of U.S. gang culture with them.

The most well-organized community of Belizean expats is the Belize Association of Louisiana (BAL, tel. 504/465-0769, www.belizeassociationlouisiana.com), a great group of people living in Louisiana who were born in Belize or whose parents are from Belize. It is a social club—everyone gets together at parties, dances, fashion shows, and other special events. But the best part is that the profits all go to Belize and accepts donations. The group doesn't want cash. Instead, members donate toys for Christmas, books for Belizean libraries, summer clothes for adults and children, and sports equipment of all kinds; TACA airlines graciously hauls the goods to Belize. Medical supplies are always needed, even if it's just aspirin. And BAL tries to help one very special charity in Belize, HelpAge, a home for older folks in need. For this the group is always happy to get used bedding, sheets, blankets, pillows, etc.—hotels that turn over their bedding periodically are contacted in the hopes that they will donate the linens to BAL.

much as their ancestors did and are still the most politically marginalized people in Belize, although certain villages are becoming increasingly empowered and developed, thanks in part to tourism (although some would argue at a cultural cost).

Most modern Maya practice some form of Christian religion integrated with ancient beliefs—in southern Belize, the Keq'chi have their own Mennonite church. But ancient Maya ceremonies are still quietly practiced in secluded pockets of the country, especially in southern Belize.

The Mundo Maya

For several years, five Latin American nations (Mexico, Belize, Guatemala, Honduras, and El Salvador) have discussed the need to preserve the remaining culture of the Maya, one of the greatest civilizations of all time. The Maya were dynamic engineers who created architecturally flamboyant buildings, massive reservoirs, more cities than were in ancient Egypt, and innovative farmlands. They developed a written language, tracked and recorded movements of the universe, and at its zenith the society numbered more than

five million people. Present-day descendants of the Maya, along with thousands of structures hidden in thick tropical jungles, continue to tell the story of the past.

An ambitious project, tagged Mundo Maya ("World of the Maya"), has been designed to both exhibit and preserve, so that the rapid growth of population—and tourism—will not destroy what has been quietly enduring nature and her elements for hundreds of years (and in some cases as long as three thousand years). Many factors are involved in project decisions that will affect millions of people; not only the Maya who have lived in isolated pockets and out-of-the-way villages for centuries, but also the people of each country involved, plus thousands of visitors who are discovering this culture for the first time. **La Ruta Maya** ("The Maya Route") will be an area marketed for tourism that encompasses the entire area that was once inhabited by the Maya.

The project requires the cooperation of five countries, concentrating on the preservation of natural resources and rainforests, including the birds and animals that live within their

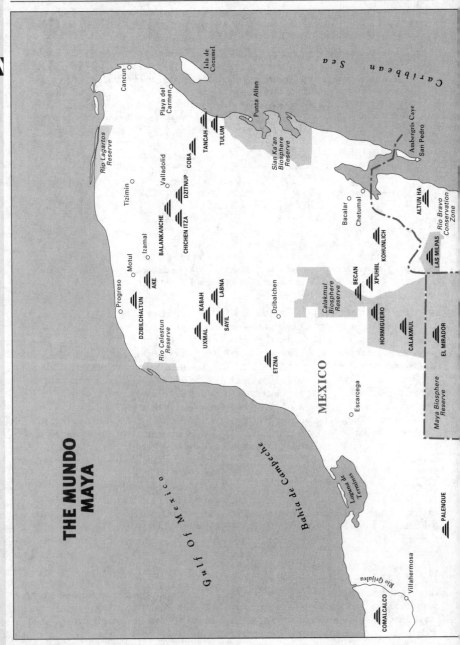

THE MUNDO MAYA

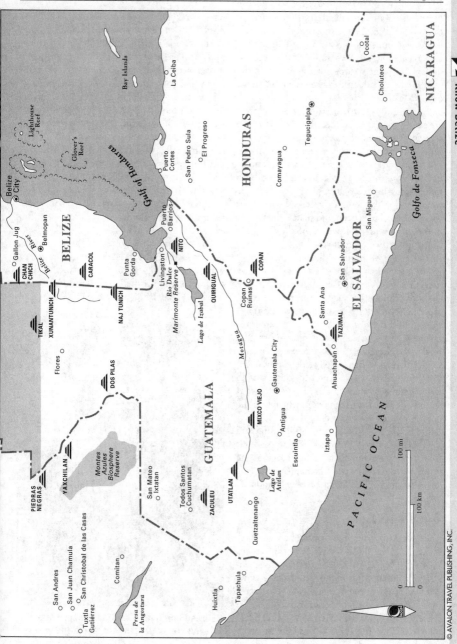

© AVALON TRAVEL PUBLISHING, INC.

boundaries (already extinct in other parts of the world). Perhaps the most important challenge the countries face is to come up with a way to encourage the development that tourism dollars can bring without infringing upon the cultural, historical, and environmental heritage of the Maya people.

Community-based, sustainable alternatives are being sought to induce the population to stop cutting the rainforest to create pastureland for raising crops and grazing cattle. Options include harvesting and selling such rainforest products as coffee, cacao, medicines, and fruits, and raising water buffalo (which survive nicely in the wet rainforest) rather than cattle—the meat is a viable substitute for beef. And maybe the biggest moneymaker for the people of the future is tourism—rather, ecotourism.

The five governments first met in October 1988 in Guatemala City, at an event hosted by then-President Vinicio Cerezo Arevalo. One of the most innovative suggestions was to build monorail-type transportation that would travel the 1,500-mile route throughout the environmentally precarious landscape to avoid bringing roads into these areas. Road development invariably brings uncontrolled settlement and destruction. There was talk of a regional Mundo Maya tourist visa and a Eurail-type pass that would allow visitors to move freely across the borders of the five countries.

No doubt it will take years of planning and agreements before these ideas come to pass, but Mexico and Guatemala have made one of the first moves by creating two adjoining biosphere reserves totaling 4.7 million acres of wildlands.

GARINAGU

The Garinagu, as a race, are relative newcomers to the world. They are also commonly referred to as "Garifuna," which, technically, refers to their language, a fascinating blend of African tribal, Arawak, Spanish, and other tongues. They came to exist on the Lesser Antillean island of San Vicente (Saint Vincent), which in the 1700s had become a refuge for escaped slaves from the sugar

plantations of the Caribbean and Jamaica. These displaced Africans were accepted by the native Carib islanders, with whom they freely intermingled. The new island community vehemently denied their African origins and proclaimed themselves Native Americans. As the French and English began to settle the island, the Garinagus (as they had become known) established a worldwide reputation as expert canoe navigators and fierce warriors, resisting European control. The English finally got the upper hand in the conflict after tricking and killing the Garinagu leader, and in 1797, they forcefully evacuated the population from San Vicente to the Honduran Bay Island of Róatan. From there, a large part of the Garinagu migrated to mainland Central America, all along the Mosquito Coast.

On November 19, 1823, so the story goes, the first Garinagu boats landed on the beaches of what is now Dangriga, one of the chief cultural capitals of the people. They landed in Belize under the leadership of Alejo Beni and a small

Belizean Garifuna culture is kept alive in part by a number of dances throughout the year.

Garinagu settlement grew in Stann Creek, where they fished and farmed. They began bringing fresh produce to Belize City, but were not welcome to stay for more than 48 hours without getting a special permit—the Baymen wanted the produce but feared that these free blacks would help slaves escape, causing a loss of the Baymen's tight control.

Traditions

Garifuna language is a mixture of Amerindian, African, Arawak, and Carib, dating from the 1700s. The Garinagu continued to practice what was still familiar from their ancient African traditions—cooking, dancing, and especially music, which consisted of complex rhythms with a call-and-response pattern that was an important part of their social and religious celebrations. An eminent person in the village is still the drum maker, who continues the old traditions, along with making other instruments used in these singing and dancing ceremonies that often last all night.

One of the most enduring customs, the practice of black magic known as *obeah,* was regarded with great suspicion and concern by the colonialists in Belize City, even after laws were enacted that made it illegal "for any man or woman to take money or other effects in return for fetishes or amulets, ritual formulas, or other magical mischief that could immunize slaves from the wrath of their masters." The practice continues—mostly in private. The *obeah* works through dances, drumbeats, trances, and trancelike contact with the dead.

There are a number of old dances and drum rhythms still used for a variety of occasions, especially around Christmas and New Year's. If you are visiting Dangriga, Hopkins, Seine Bight, Punta Gorda, or Barranco during these times (or during Settlement Day, November 19), expect to see (and possibly partake in) some drumming. Feel free to taste the typical foods and drinks. If you consume too much "local dynamite" (rum and coconut milk) or bitters, have a cup of strong chicory coffee, said by the Garinagu "to make we not have goma" (a hangover).

RASTAFARIANS

Belizean Rastafarians are part of a religion that believes in the eventual redemption of blacks and their return to Africa. They wear dreadlocks as a sacrament. Their beliefs, according to the biblical laws of the Nazarites, forbid the cutting of their hair. Rastafarians use ganja (marijuana) in their rituals and venerate Haile Selassie I, late emperor of Ethiopia, as their god. Selassie's precoronation name was Ras Tafari Makonnen, hence the name (Ras is simply an honorific title). He allegedly descended from King Solomon and the Queen of Sheba.

Belizean Rastas are a difficult group to quantify, as the religion and customs are found throughout the country's sundry cultures, including Bob Marley–worshipping Latinos, Creoles, and Maya alike. A great Rasta greeting or goodbye which is practiced by many people in Belize (Rasta or not) involves bumping fists, then bringing your clenched fist to your heart and saying, "One Love."

Many Rastas are strict vegetarians and cook wonderful "ital" dishes, as they refer to their diet. Particularly tasty ital joints are the Wildside Café and Teahouse in Cayo and Gomier's in Punta Gorda.

EAST INDIANS

From 1844 to 1917, under British colonialism, 41,600 East Indians were brought to British colonies in the Caribbean as indentured workers. They agreed to work for a given length of time for one "master." Then they could either return to India or stay on and work freely. Unfortunately, the time spent in Belize was not as lucrative as they were led to believe it would be. In some cases, they owed so much money to the company store (where they received half their wages in trade and not nearly enough to live on) that they were forced to "reenlist" for a longer period. Most of them worked on sugar plantations in the Toledo and Corozal Districts, and many of the East Indian men were assigned to work as local police

Know Belize

GRINGOS IN BELIZE

Population numbers of white foreigners fluctuate widely throughout Belize—and throughout the year as well, depending on a variety of factors like seasons, sand flies, and the global economy; but their presence as a full-time part of the cultural landscape in many areas of Belize is undeniable.

gringos sunning themselves at the split, Caye Caulker

© JOSHUA BERMAN

"Gringo" generally refers to any pale non-Belizean, although some locals reserve the term exclusively for the North American sub-species, preferring to distinguish this variety from the less common "Euro." The word is purely descriptive and does not have negative connotations, unless preceded by an adjective such as "bloody," "*pinche,*" or "damn."

While many gringos travel independently, many more tend to cluster, especially during their peak migratory season (mid-December through May). Over the years, such groups have established distinct colonies throughout Belize. For instance, the quickly breeding community in San Pedro Town are generally distinguished as politically conservative rummies, while those farther south along the Placencia Peninsula are more likely to vote liberal and are less excited about country music. The two are much more difficult to distinguish from each other than they are from the more mature, pink-skinned retiree gringos occupying Corozal Town and Consejo Shores, both in the extreme northeast of the country and only a 20-minute drive from the new Walmart in Chetumal, Mexico.

Gringos are just as numerous in the western district of Cayo, especially in the streets of San Ignacio, where they typically graze on vegetarian fare with beatific smiles on their faces. This western specimen is more idealistic, more tolerant of the cold, and more prone to blonde dreadlocks than his cousins on the coast. Generally more transient as well, Cayo gringos are sometimes found foraging as far as the reefs near Caye Caulker and the southern villages of Punta Gorda—but they always return to the highlands.

Then there is the red-breasted cruise ship passenger, an entirely distinct and little studied strain of gringo. When not sunning themselves aboard floating cities, cruise ship passengers travel either on foot in Belize City's Tourism Village or in large, air-conditioned buses to nearby attractions, identified by video cameras resting atop exposed, peeling beer bellies.

Of course, most gringos in Belize have a few things in common, particularly their lust for real estate and physiological inability to dance *punta*. Gringo habits and behavior varies widely, but sightings are guaranteed in beach bars, restaurants with espresso machines, and Internet cafés.

in Belize City. In a town aptly named Calcutta, south of Corozal Town, many of the population today are descendants of the original indentured East Indians. Forest Home near Punta Gorda also has a large settlement. About 47 percent of the ethnic group live in these two locations. The East Indians usually have large families and live on small farms with orchards adjacent to their homes. A few trade in pigs and dry goods in ma-and-pa businesses. East Indians normally speak Creole and Spanish—apparently descendants from the original immigrants do not speak Hindi today. A small number of Hindi-speaking East Indian merchants live in Belize City and Orange Walk Town, but they are fairly new to the country and have no cultural ties with the descendants of earlier immigrants.

MENNONITES

German-speaking Mennonites are the most recent group to enter Belize on a large scale. This group of Protestant settlers from the Swiss Alps wandered over the years to northern Germany, southern Russia, Pennsylvania, and Canada in the early 1800s, and to northern Mexico after World War I. For some reason, the quiet, staid Mennonites disturbed local governments in these other countries, and restrictions on their isolated agrarian lifestyle led to a more nomadic existence.

Most of Belize's Mennonites first migrated from Mexico between 1958 and 1962. A few came from Peace River in Canada. In contrast to other areas where they lived, the Mennonites bought large blocks of land (about 148,000 acres) and began to farm. Shipyard (in Orange Walk District) was settled by a conservative wing; Spanish Lookout (in Cayo District) and Blue Creek (in Orange Walk District) were settled by more progressive members. In hopes of averting future problems with the government, Mennonites made agreements with Belize officials that guarantee them freedom to practice their religion, use their language in locally controlled schools, organize their own financial institutions, and to be exempt from military service. Over the 30-plus years that Mennonites have been in Belize, they have slowly merged into Belizean activities. Although they practice complete separation of church and state (and do not vote), their innovations in agricultural production and marketing have advanced the entire country. Mennonite farmers are probably the most productive in Belize; they commonly pool their resources to make large purchases such as equipment, machinery (in those communities that use machinery), and supplies. Their fine dairy industry is the best in the country, and they supply the domestic market with eggs, poultry, fresh milk, cheese, and vegetables.

The Culture

CONDUCT AND CUSTOMS

Concept of Time

Like many other Central American and Caribbean cultures, the Belizean clock is not quite as rigidly precise as it is in other parts of the world. "Nine o'clock A.M." is not necessarily a moment in time that occurs once a morning, as it is in the United States or Europe; rather, it is a general guideline that could extend an hour or two in either direction (usually later). The Creoles say "Time longa den da roop" ("time is longer than the rope"), which means the same as the Spanish, *"Hay mas tiempo que vida"* ("there is more time than there is life")—both of which boil down to the unofficial motto of Caye Caulker: "Go slow!"

A great deal of patience is required of the traveler who wishes to adapt to this looser concept of time. Buses generally leave when they are scheduled, but may stop for frustratingly long breaks during the journey. Don't use Belize Time as an excuse to be late for your tour bus pickup, but don't get angry when your taxi driver stops to briefly chat and laugh with a friend.

THE ARTS

In 2003, the Government of Belize created the **National Institute for Culture and History** (NICH, www.nichbelize.org), to bring together diverse government departments which had historically worked to preserve and promote different aspects of Belizean culture, from painting and music to archaeology. It falls under Belize's Ministry of Culture and Tourism and encompasses **The Institute for the Creative Arts** (ICA), which is responsible for the promotion of the performing, plastic, and visual arts. The ICA is headquartered at the newly renovated Bliss Center for the Creative Arts and is headed by musical artist Andy Palacio.

© JOSHUA BERMAN

There are always plentiful modern Mayan crafts for sale at the entrance to most of Belize's ancient Mayan ruins.

CRAFTS

You'll always have a wide selection of Belizean and Guatemalan crafts to choose from when visiting any archaeological site, as vendors typically set up rows of stalls with similar gifts, crafts, textiles, and basket work. See the travel chapters for more local information about where to shop for Belizean crafts. A few things you'll find are described as follows.

Slate Carvings

Maya and Belizean motifs set out in slate have become very popular and, in some cases, costly. Among the leading artists are **The Garcia Sisters, Lesley Glaspie,** and the **Magana family.** Their work can be found in several Cayo shops as well as elsewhere in the country (especially Aurora's shop near the entrance to Cockscomb). The Garcia sisters helped revive the slate craze, and their quality has always been high. Slate carvings require a lot of time to create. Now more artists produce them and wise shopping will net a treasured piece without draining your personal treasury.

Wood Furniture

Mennonite furniture is becoming increasingly popular as a take-home item. Cleverly executed chairs and small tables in mahogany and other tropical woods are the mainstays. In San Ignacio you can have them conveniently boxed and ready for baggage check at the airport.

MUSIC

The music of Belize has been heavily influenced by the rhythmic, exotic syncopations of Africa. If you manage to get to Belize during one of the festivals such as the Battle of St. George's Caye, National Independence Day, or Settlement Day, you'll have an introduction to the raucous, happy music of a **jump up** (a street dance); *punta* **rock** (a spin-off from the original *punta*, a traditional rhythm of the Garinagu settlers in the Stann Creek District); **reggae** (Bob Marley is King in Belize); *soka* (a livelier interpretation of reggae); and *brukdown*. *Brukdown* began in the timber camps of the 1800s, when the workers, isolated from civilization for months at a time, would let off steam with a full bottle of rum and begin the beat on the bottle—or the jawbone of an ass, a coconut shell, a wooden block—anything that made a sound. Add to that a harmonica, guitar, and banjo, and you've got *brukdown*.

In the southern part of Belize, in Toledo District, you'll likely hear the strains of ancient Maya melodies played on homemade wooden instruments designed before memory: Q'eqchi' harps, violins, and guitars. In Cayo District in the west, listen for the resonant sounds of marimbas and wooden xylophones—from the Spanish influence across the Guatemala border. In Corozal and Orange Walk Districts in the north, the infatuations of old Mexico are popularized with romantic lyrics and the strum of a guitar.

Stonetree Records (www.stonetreerecords .com) has the most complete catalogue of truly Belizean music, including Aziatic, Griga Boyz, Titiman Flores, Mohobub, and of course, Andy Palacio and Paul Nabor. They also offer several collections such as *Garifuna Women Voices* and *The Creole Experience*.

LANGUAGE

English is the official language, although Belize Creole English (or Kriol) serves as the main spoken tongue among and between groups. The **Belize Kriol Project** (tel. 501/225-3320, www.kriol.org.bz) would like to see Kriol established as a literary language as well, and they have produced dictionaries and phrasebooks, and promoted Kriol literature to that effect. There is an increasing number of Spanish speakers in Belize as Central American immigrants continue to arrive. Spanish is the primary language of many native Belizean families as well—descendants of Yucatecan immigrants who inhabit the Northern Cayes, as well as Orange Walk and Corozal Districts. The Garinagu people speak Garifuna, and the various Mennonite communities speak different dialects of Old German. Then there are Mopan, Yucateca, and Qe-q'chi Mayan tongues.

ENTERTAINMENT AND EVENTS

When a public holiday falls on Sunday, it is celebrated on the following Monday. If you plan to visit during holiday time, make advance hotel reservations—especially if you plan to spend time in Dangriga during Settlement Day on November 19 (the area has limited accommodations).

Note: On Sundays and a few holidays (Easter and Christmas), most businesses close for the day, and some close the day after Christmas, which is Boxing Day; on Good Friday most of the buses do not run. Check ahead of time.

St. George's Caye Day

On September 10, 1798, at St. George's Caye off the coast of Belize, the British buccaneers fought and defeated the Spaniards over the territory of Belize. The tradition of celebrating this victory is still carried on each year, followed by a weeklong calendar of events from religious services to carnivals. During this week, Belize City (especially) feels like a carnival with parties everywhere. On the morning of September 10, the whole city parades through the streets and enjoys local cooking, spirits, and music with an upbeat atmosphere that continues well into the beginning of Independence Day on September 21.

National Independence Day

On September 21, 1981, Belize gained independence from Great Britain. Each year, Belizeans celebrate with carnivals on the main streets of downtown Belize City and district towns. Like giant county fairs, they include displays of local arts, crafts, and cultural activities, while happy Belizeans dance to a variety of exotic rhythms from *punta* rock to *soka* to reggae. Again, don't miss the chance to sample local dishes from every ethnic group in the country. With this holiday back to back with the celebration of the Battle of St. George's Caye, Belize enjoys two weeks of riotous, cacophonous partying.

Baron Bliss Day

On March 9, this holiday is celebrated with various activities, mostly water sports. English sportsman Baron Henry Edward Ernest Victor Bliss, who remembered Belize with a generous legacy when he died, designated a day of sailing and fishing in his will. A formal ceremony is held at his tomb below the lighthouse in the Belize Harbor, where he died on his boat. Fishing and sailing regattas begin after the ceremony.

Ambergris Caye Celebration

If you're wandering around Belize near June 26–29, hop a boat or plane to San Pedro and join the locals in a festival they have celebrated for decades, **El Dia de San Pedro,** in honor of the town's namesake, St. Peter. This is good fun; reservations are suggested. **Carnaval,** one week before Lent, is another popular holiday on the island. The locals walk in a procession through the streets to the church, celebrating the last hurrah (for devout Catholics) before Easter. There are lots of good dance competitions.

Garinagu (Garifuna) Settlement Day

On November 19, Belize recognizes the 1823 arrival and settlement of the first Garinagu (also

NATIONAL HOLIDAYS IN BELIZE

January 1	New Year's Day
March 9	Baron Bliss Day
March or April	Good Friday
March or April	Easter Sunday
May 1	Labour Day
May 25	Commonwealth Day
September 10	National Day
September 21	Independence Day
October 12	Columbus Day
November 19	Garinagu (Garifuna) Settlement Day
December 25	Christmas Day
December 26	Boxing Day

called Garifuna) to the southern districts of Belize. Belizeans from all over the country gather in Dangriga, Hopkins, Punta Gorda, and Belize City to celebrate with the Garinagu. The day begins with the **reenactment** of the arrival of the settlers and continues with all-night dancing to the local Garinagu drums and live *punta* rock bands. Traditional food—and copious amounts of rum, beer, and bitters—is available at street stands and local cafés.

Maya Dances

If traveling in the latter part of September in San Antonio Village in the Toledo District, you have a good chance of seeing the **deer dance** performed by the Q'eqchi' Maya villagers. Dancing and celebrating begins around the middle of August, but the biggest celebration begins with a *novena,* nine days before the feast day of San Luis.

Actually, this festival was only recently revived. The costumes were burned in an accidental fire some years back at a time when (coincidentally) the locals had begun to lose interest in the ancient traditions. Thanks to the formation of the **Toledo Maya Cultural Council,** the Maya once again are realizing the importance of recapturing their past.

Getting There

BY AIR

To Belizeans, flying in and out of Belize was a far-fetched idea when American hero Charles Lindbergh paid a dramatic visit to the small Caribbean nation as part of his ongoing effort to promote and develop commercial aviation. At the time (1927), Lindbergh had just completed his famous nonstop flight across the Atlantic. On his visit to Belize, the Barracks Green in Belize City served as his runway, and the sound of his well-known craft, *The Spirit of St. Louis,* attracted hundreds of curious spectators.

Today, there dozens of daily flights in and out of the country, served by American, Continental, and TACA Airlines. Airfares range from okay to exorbitant; try to use a Latin America travel specialist like **Exito Travel** (US tel. 800/655-4054, www.exitotravel.com) or **Me-Again Travel** (US tel. 718/852-9410 or 800/321-3711, meagaintravel@aol.com), both skilled at finding special fares and "open jaw" flights (flying into one city in Central America and out of another).

When departing Belize, don't forget to carry enough cash for your US$20 departure fee and for generic Viagra and Valium from the drugstore kiosk out front.

Philip Goldson International Airport

Most travelers to Belize arrive at Philip Goldson International Airport, nine miles from Belize City, outside the community of Ladyville. The medium-sized airport (by Central American standards) offers basic services like gift shops, currency exchange, and two restaurants; Internet is available in the **Sun Garden Restaurant** upstairs from the American terminal. Check the "waving deck" upstairs by the other bar/restaurant.

Arriving in Belize

After clearing customs, you'll be besieged by taxi drivers offering rides into town, for a fixed US$20 (and rising); split the cost with fellow travelers if

© JOSHUA BERMAN

Belize's two local airlines are small but safe and reliable.

Know Belize

you can. If you are not being picked up by a resort or tour company and you choose to rent a car, look for the 11 rental car offices, all together on the same little strip, across the parking lot.

BY BOAT

Daily boats from Punta Gorda travel back and forth to Puerto Barrios, Guatemala, and there are two boat services from Puerto Cortes, Honduras (one leaves from Placencia, the other from Dangriga). Please see the appropriate travel chapters for more information.

Boat owners should note that vessels traveling to the area must have permission from the Belize Embassy in Washington, D.C.

VIA MEXICO

Because airfares to Belize City are sometimes high, traveling there via Mexico's state of Quintana Roo on the Yucatán Peninsula can be cheaper. Combining vacations in both countries is a way to see a little more than usual.

If traveling by car all the way from the States, the route from Brownsville, Texas to the border of Belize is just under 1,400 miles. If you don't stop to smell the flowers along the way, you can make the drive in a few days. The all-weather roads are paved, and the shortest route is through Mexico by way of Tampico, Veracruz, Villahermosa, Escarcega, and Chetumal (check with Mexican authorities beforehand to find out the latest hoops you'll have to jump through).

The drive is easy between Belize and Mexico on the Northern Highway. A good paved road connects Chetumal, Mexico with Mérida, Campeche, Villahermosa, and Francisco Escarcega; Highway 307 links all of the Quintana Roo coastal cities. Expect little traffic, and you'll find that gas stations are well-spaced if you top off at each one. **Car rentals** are scarce in Chetumal; go to the Hotel Los Cocos for Avis. Chetumal is

an economical place to rent your car (if one is available), since the tax is only 6 percent. If you're driving, watch out for No Left Turn signs in Chetumal.

Driving from Cancún: Yes, it is possible to rent a car in Cancún and continue south on a Belizean adventure, but it'll cost you both money and patience. Still, with the money you save with the cheaper airfare into Cancún, the mobility may be worth it. Cancún is 369 kilometers from the border at Santa Elena, roughly 4.5 hours in car on Route 307. Here's what you need to know:

Big, international rental companies will not let you take their vehicles across the border, so you'll have to find a more accommodating Mexican company, like **J.L. Vegas,** with one office near the airport and another in the Crystal Hotel. Next, you'll need to "make the papers," as the car guy will surely remind you. The most crucial part of this is a letter of permission from the car's owner; customs will scrutinize this document. Next, to avoid being turned back at the border, be sure to get the vehicle sprayed with insecticide from one of the roadside sprayers near the border—it's tough to pick them out; look for a little white shack near the bridge and be sure to get a certificate. When presenting paperwork to customs, you'll have to remove all luggage from the car for inspection. If you don't buy insurance on the Mexican side, be advised that the offices in Belize close at 6 P.M., although with a little convincing you can drive through and promise to buy it in Corozal. It costs US$20 for two weeks' insurance; you get a sticker on your window that police will check.

Crossing the border without your own vehicle is a cinch. Many buses travel from the main terminal in Chetumal all the way to Belize City. You'll have to get out to wait in various lines, but just follow the crowd and you'll be fine. There are also several Mexican lines that run between Chetumal, Belize City, Cayo, and Guatemala.

Getting Around

BY AIR

Both of the Belizean commuter airlines have an outstanding record of safety. Pick up a complete timetable at any local office around the country (located at each town's humble airstrip), or make reservations directly with either **Tropic Air** (US tel. 800/422-3435, Bel. tel. 501/226-2012, reservations@tropicair.com, www.tropicair.com) or **Maya Island Air** (US tel. 800/225-6732, Bel. tel. 501/223-1140, mayair@btl.net, www.mayaislandair.com).

Regularly scheduled flights leave Belize City's municipal and international airports for Caye Caulker, San Pedro, Dangriga, Placencia, Punta Gorda, and San Ignacio; the flights usually combine several of these destinations, so if you're traveling to PG, you may have to land and take off in Dangriga and Placencia first. Ditto for

Caulker and San Pedro, the two of which are linked together. There are also regular flights to Flores, Guatemala, and you can fly between Corozal and San Pedro; ask about new service to San Ignacio. If your scheduled flight is full, another will taxi up shortly and off you go. Chartered flights can be arranged at any time and to less frequented stops like Lighthouse Reef Resort on Northern Caye, Blancaneaux Lodge in the Mountain Pine Ridge, and Gallon Jug airstrip near Chan Chich.

Some Belizean airstrips are paved and somewhat official-looking (Belize City and San Pedro, for example); the rest are more like short abandoned roadways or strips of mown grass, but they work just fine. Because such small planes are used, you not only watch the pilot handle the craft, you may also get to sit next to him. Coming in for a landing, you have an

It only costs a little bit more to cross San Pedro's cut in a golf cart.

excellent vantage point from which to observe the runway looming large on approach. Best of all, flying low and slow in these aircraft allows you to get a panoramic view of the Belize Barrier Reef, cayes, coast, and jungle (keep your camera handy).

BY BUS

The motley fleet of buses that serves the entire country ranges from your typical run-down, recycled yellow school bus to a handful of plush, air-conditioned luxury affairs. Belize buses are relatively reliable, on time, and less chaotic than the chicken-bus experience in other parts of Central America and Mexico. Still, most buses make a maddening amount of stops, stretching seemingly short distances into long journeys that make Belize feel a lot bigger than it really is. For anyone who wants to meet the Belizean people, this is the way to go. Most of these buses make frequent stops and will pick up anyone on the side of the road anywhere—as long as space permits and even when it doesn't. The drivers will also drop you off wherever you wish if you holler when you want off.

Note that all buses between Belize City and points west and south—even expresses—stop in Belmopan for anywhere from five to thirty minutes. They'll do the same at any other city terminal that gets in their way, like Dangriga or Orange Walk; it's a good time for a bathroom break. Travel time from Belize City to Corozal or San Ignacio is about two hours, to Dangriga two–three hours, and to Punta Gorda five–six hours. Fares average about US$2–4 to most destinations, about US$7–12 for the longer routes.

Nearly all of Belize's scattered regional bus lines have been eaten up by Novelo's, with a couple of small companies still holding out. The consolidation makes things simpler than they once were for the average foreign traveler. Nearly all buses in Belize begin and end their runs at the main **Novelo's Terminal** (tel. 501/207-4924, 207-3929, or 227-7146, novelo@btl.net), located on West Collett Canal Street in one of Belize City's many run-down areas and reached by

ROAD DISTANCES FROM BELIZE CITY	
Belmopan:	55 miles
Benque Viejo:	81 miles
Corozal Town:	96 miles
Dangriga:	105 miles
Orange Walk Town:	58 miles
Punta Gorda:	210 miles
San Ignacio:	72 miles

walking west on King Street until it crosses Collett Canal and ends at the terminal—definitely use a taxi at night. **James Bus** still runs their daily Punta Gorda service, using the street in front of the Shell station on Vernon Street (two blocks north of the Novelo's) as their terminal.

Express direct bus service to Guatemala and Mexico leaves from the hectic intersection in front of the Water Taxi Terminal and Swing Bridge; this is the place to catch one of several private direct buses to Belize's borders and beyond. Boat-bus connections are convenient here, but it's all happening in the middle of one of Belize's busiest intersections, and at press time city officials were reportedly about to prohibit buses from operating here. If they succeed, these buses will be moved somewhere close by, but their various ticket counters will remain inside the water taxi terminal.

Other small lines, which don't have phone numbers, are **Jex Buses,** which departs from 34 Regent Street and from the Pound Yard Bridge to Crooked Tree, and **Pooks** and **Russell's,** which go to the Bermudian Landing.

BY RENTAL CAR

Driving Belize's four highways (Northern, Western, Southern, and Hummingbird) certainly gives you the most independence when traveling throughout the country, but it is also by far the most expensive, with rental fees running US$75–125 per day. You'll also have the added responsibility of taking care of the vehicle, finding places to park, and being sure not to hit any of the obstacles you'll encounter on the roads, like farm animals, cyclists, iguanas, and cruise ship passengers on mopeds.

In some areas, like the Mountain Pine Ridge and other back roads in the hinterlands, there is no public transportation and a 4WD rental car is a good way to go if you're into traveling on your own schedule. Alternatively, all jungle lodges arrange airport and town transfers for their guests (sometimes for free, sometimes for exorbitant amounts), and taxis can be chartered as well.

Your Options

One of the first things you'll see upon walking out of the arrival lounge at the International Airport is a strip of 11 car rental offices offering small, midsize, and large 4WD vehicles. Vans and passenger cars are also available, some with air-conditioning—they cost more. Insurance is mandatory but (like taxes) not always included in the quoted rates. If you know exactly when you want the car and where, it's helpful to make reservations—and often cheaper. Note the hour you pick up the car and try to return it before that time: a few minutes over could cost you another full-day's rental fee.

Budget Rent a Car (tel. 501/223-2435 or 223-3986, fax 501/223-0237, reservations@budget-belize.com, www.budget-belize.com) is reliable and offers new cars that are well maintained. You'll find a few other foreign heavy-hitters, like **Hertz** and **Avis,** as well as a number of locally owned agencies. **Crystal Auto Rental** (tel. 501/223-1600, www.crystal-belize.com) is the only company that will allow you to drive across the border, but you won't be insured.

Driving in Belize

Drive defensively! Expect everyone else out

BETA NO LITTA

Whether in Creole or plain English, the message comes through—Keep our country clean. The Belize Eco-Tourism Association (BETA), along with businesses, resorts, and individuals, is sponsoring an anti-littering campaign to clean up the roadsides and to protect the environment. Where you see the green signs, someone has adopted that portion of the road and makes certain it is kept clean.

---

there to make stupid passes and unexpected moves—they probably will and it's your job to stay out of their way (especially when they are bigger than you, like the buses and trucks that speed crazily around blind curves and over one-lane bridges). Driving rules are U.S.-style, and it wouldn't hurt to obtain an international driver's license before you leave home (about US$10 at most auto clubs), although this is not necessary by law. Gasoline is also costly, topping US$3 a gallon.

Expect police checkpoints anywhere around the country: They'll check your seatbelt (US$25 fine), car papers, driver's license, and, courtesy of the United States Drug Enforcement Agency, dogs will sniff for that dime-bag of weed in your shaving kit (easier to find than stopping the tons of cocaine flowing through the country, apparently).

Using your odometer from Belize City will help you track your location and mileage. The mileage signs are easy to see alongside the road. If you're driving the **Western Highway,** start your trip odometer at the cemetery; if you're driving the **Northern Highway,** start the odometer at the northern edge of town just north of the intersection of the highway with Central American Boulevard/Princess Margaret Drive.

Visas and Officialdom

You *must* have a current passport that will be good for six months beyond your planned departure date from Belize. You may be asked at the border to show a return ticket or ample money to leave the country. You do not need a visa if you are a British Commonwealth subject or a citizen of Belgium, Denmark, Finland, Greece, Iceland, Italy, Liechtenstein, Luxembourg, Mexico, Spain, Switzerland, Tunisia, Turkey, the United States, or Uruguay, provided you have valid documents (although onward or return air tickets and proof of sufficient funds are required).

If you are planning on staying more than 30 days, you can ask for a new stamp at any immigration office in the country, or you can cross the border and return. The first few times are free, then there may be various fees to extend (the most we've been charged was US$12.50 for an extra 30 days). Visitors for other purposes must obtain a visa. U.S. citizens are encouraged to register at the Consular section of the U.S. Embassy in Belize City, where updated information on travel conditions and security in Belize is available (you can do this online as well).

FOREIGN EMBASSIES IN BELIZE

Only a handful of countries have official embassies in Belize. The **United States Embassy** (29 Gabourel Lane, P.O. Box 286, Belize City, tel. 501/227-7161 or 223-1862, fax 501/223-0802, embbelize@state.gov, www.usembassy.state.gov/belize) is open 8 A.M.–noon and 1 P.M.–5 P.M. Monday–Friday, and the **British High Commission** (Embassy Square, P.O. Box 91, Belmopan, tel. 501/822-2146 or 822-2147, fax 501/822-2761, brithicom@btl.net) is open 8 A.M.–noon and 1 P.M.–4 P.M. Monday–Thursday, and 8 A.M.–2 P.M. Friday. China (tel. 501/227-8744, embroc@btl.net), Cuba (tel. 501/223-5345), Mexico (www.embamexbelize.gob.mx), and El Salvador (tel. 501/223-5162) are also represented.

LIVING IN BELIZE

It's a typical story—the gringo who vacationed in Belize and never left. There are a number of ways to do it, from starting a business, investing in land, retiring, or working online; there are a number of helpful resources as well. For more detailed information on becoming an expat, pick up a copy of *Adapter Kit: Belize* by Lan Sluder (Avalon Travel Publishing), or search for the Belize page at **www.escapeartist.com.** To learn how to qualify for retirement incentives, check www.belizeretirement.org (US tel. 800/624-0686).

EMBASSIES AND CONSULATES OF BELIZE IN SELECTED NATIONS

Canada

Consulate of Belize in Ontario
c/o McMillan Binch, Suite 3800
South Tower, Royal Bank Plaza Toronto
Toronto, Ontario M5J 2JP, Canada
416/865-7000, fax 416/864-7048

Consulate of Belize in Quebec
1800 McGill College, Suite 2480
Montreal, Quebec H3A 3J6, Canada
514/288-1687, fax 514/288-4998
dbellemare@cmmtl.com

Consulate of Belize in Vancouver
2321 Trafalgar Street
Vancouver, British Columbia V6K 3T1 Canada
604/730-1224
dwsmiling@hotmail.com

Costa Rica

Consulate of Belize in San José
Apartado Postal 11 121-1000
San José, Costa Rica
tel. 506/253 5598, fax 506/233 6394
gprisma@sol.racsa.co.cr

Europe

High Commission of Belize in London
22 Harcourt House 19, Cavendish Square
London, W1G 0PL United Kingdom
tel. (44 20) 7499-9728, fax (44 20) 7491-4139
bzhc-lon@btconnect.com

Embassy of Belize and Mission of Belize
to The European Communities
Boulevard Brand Whitlock 136
1200 Brussels, Belgium
tel. (32-2) 732-6204, fax (32-2) 732-6246
embelize@skynet.be

Permanent Mission of Belize
to the UNESCO in France
1 Rue Miollis, Room M339
75015 Paris, France
tel. (33-1) 45-68-32-11, fax (33-1) 47-20-18-74

dl.belize@unesco.org

Permanent Mission of Belize to the
United Nations in Geneva, Switzerland
7 Rue du Mont-blanc
CH 1201 Geneva, Switzerland
tel. (022) 906-8420
mission.belize@ties.itu.int

Japan

Embassy of Belize in Tokyo, Japan
No. 38 Kowa Bldg., 4-12-24-907
Nishi-Azabu Minato-ku
Tokyo 106-00 31, Japan
tel. (81-3) 3400-9106, fax (81-3) 3400-9262
belize@mxd.mesh.ne.jp

Mexico

Embassy of Belize in Mexico
215 Calle Bernardo de Galvez,
Col. Lomas de Chapultepec
Mexico D.F. 11000
tel. 52-5/520-1274
embelize@prodigy.net.mx

Consulate of Belize in Cancún
Ave. Nader 34
Cancún, Quintana Roo, Mexico
tel. 52-9/887-8417
nel.bel@prodigy.net.mx

United States

Consulate of Belize in Chicago
c/o Ezetech Manufacturing, Inc.
1200 Howard Drive West
Chicago, IL 60185
708/293-0010
eztecmfg@aol.com

Consulate of Belize in Florida
4173 S. Le Jeune Road
Coconut Grove, FL 33146
tel./fax 305/666-1121
bzconsulmi@mindspring.com

(continued on next page)

Know Belize

EMBASSIES AND CONSULATES OF BELIZE IN SELECTED NATIONS (cont'd)

Consulate of Belize in Illinois
201 N. Church Street, Room 200
Belleville, IL 62223
618/234-4410

General Consulate of Belize in Los Angeles
5825 Sunset Boulevard, Suite 206
Hollywood, CA 90028
323/469-7343, fax 323/469-7346
belizeconsul@earthlink.net

Consulate of Belize in Louisiana
c/o Westbank Optical, Inc.
419 Lapalco Boulevard
Gretna, LA 70056

504/392-3655, fax 504/392-3809
jsbenard@hotmail.com

Consulate of Belize in Michigan
24984 Glen Orchard Drive
Farmington Hills, MI, 48336-1732
810/477-8768
lennox-p@prodigy.net

Permanent Mission of Belize to the United
Nations in New York
885 Second Avenue
1 Dag Hammarskjöld Plaza, 20th Floor
New York, NY 10017
212/593-0999, fax 212/593-0932

Tips for Travelers

ALTERNATIVE TRAVEL

A number of visitors come to Belize with time and energy to do more than drink alcohol and waste away on the beach (not that there's anything wrong with that). There are many nonprofit organizations that cater to those travelers looking to study, volunteer, research, or work during their time in Belize. Following are just a few that we've identified—be sure to research a bit deeper on your own before committing. Some organizations offer full funding and support, others expect you to pay tuition to participate. Find out how much (if any) money you are expected to pay and of that, how the is money divided between the community where you'll be working and the organization's overhead costs. Look for specific opportunities that may suit your skills and experience; check websites like www.studyabroaddirectory.com, www.volunteerabroad.com, and www.teachabroad.com, as well as resources like *Transitions Abroad* magazine and books specializing in volunteering and studying abroad.

Field Research and Educational Travel

There are numerous opportunities to learn, teach, and volunteer at **The Belize Zoo and Tropical Education Center** (tel. 501/220-8004, fax 501/220-8010, info@belizezoo.org, www.belizezoo.org); take a good look at the education part of their website. The **Maya Mountain Lodge** in the Cayo District (tel. 501/824-2164, www.mayamountain.com) offers talks covering a range of subjects, including Maya ceramics. The **Blackbird-Oceanic Society Field Station** (US tel. 800/326-7491, fax 415/474-3395, office @oceanic-society.org, www.oceanic-society.org) allows guests to participate in a dolphin research project. **Lamanai Field Research Center** (www.lamanai.com) offers the opportunity to study howler monkeys. Outside the village of Sarteneja, **Wild Tracks** (tel. 501/423-2032 or 423-2162, wildtracks@btl.net) is a research center that accepts both undergraduate and graduate students.

The **Belize Foundation for Research and Environmental Education** (BFREE, bfree@btl.net, www.bfreebelize.org) offers student programs

ECO-*WHAT?*

Belize is generally acknowledged as one of the world's freshest and most successful models of ecotourism. If you're not entirely sure what that means, you're not alone.

The word "eco-tourism" was created in the 1980s with the best of intentions—ostensibly, to describe anything having to do with environmentally sound and culturally sustainable tourism, the "business" of both preventing tourism from spoiling the environment and using tourism as an economic alternative to spoiling the environment for some other reason.

The success of the concept—and its marketing value—led directly to a worldwide boom in the usage of that prefix that we know so well, even if its actual practice has sometimes fallen short of original intentions. "Eco" has been used, abused, prostituted, and bastardized all over the world, and Belize is no exception. Surely, anything "eco" has something to do with the outdoors, but that's about all we can promise. We've limited our eco-writing, not because we don't believe in its precepts, but because we're wary of what it means in this day, age, and place. Some word-savvy tourism marketers have tried to freshen things up by using "alternative" or "adventure" tourism, but, when trying to describe an operation that practices the original definition of ecotourism mentioned above, we prefer "sustainable," "responsible," "ethical," or even "fair trade" tourism.

Semantics aside, as a visitor, you should never forget how the choices you make can have a variety of immediate (and long-term) effects on how well Belizean natural areas remain preserved in their original state. The concept of protected areas is still relatively new in Belize and is still at times viewed with skepticism—especially by rural folk who live near (or sometimes actually within) these areas. Left to their own devices, the desperately poor use the wilderness to supplement their paltry income, by chopping wood for fuel, cutting out farmland acres, or hunting wild game (as they always did before the advent of tourism).

That's where you come in. By spending money among the people who live near these protected areas, nature-loving visitors give Belizeans a viable incentive not to cut into the forest. This means hiring a local guide, buying a meal from a family, or paying a few dollars to pitch a tent or hang a hammock outside a farmer's hut—and feel free to tip people like the ferry guy at Xunantunich.

Those going on a trip with a tour company are not exempt from any of this—you must be sure that the company you go with leaves some money behind, rather than using their own guides, transportation, and food. Just imagine how a self-sufficient trip must look to the locals—rich foreigners are out enjoying their forest again, forests they are no longer supposed to touch.

The Belize Eco-Tourism Association (BETA) and Belize Audubon Society (BAS) are two of the many organizations concerned with keeping the "eco" in tourism—and in keeping pressure on the Government of Belize to do the same. BETA was created on Earth Day in 1993 by a small group of members of the Belize Tourism Industry Association (BTIA). Find out more at www.bzecotourism.org.

from one week to a whole semester, with lots of activities and cultural immersion programs available. Also, the **Belize Rainforest Institute** (jungle@mayamountain.com, www.mayamountain .com) provides week-long courses and workshops covering a variety of activities and workshops. You've also got the **Tropical Education Center** (www.belizezoo.org) and a wide variety of environmental education programs at **Monkey Bay Wildlife Sanctuary** (mbay@btl.net, www .monkeybaybelize.org).

The **Programme for Belize** (1 Eyre St., US tel. 617/259-9500, Bel. tel. 501/227-5616, pfbel @btl.net) is the group that manages the Río Bravo Conservation Area and has a full menu of ecology and rainforest workshops.

For Mayaphiles and archaeology students, the **Belize Valley Archaeology Reconnaissance Project** (BVAR, www.bvar.org) conducts research and offers field schools at several sites in western Belize.

Volunteer Opportunities

The **Belize Audubon Society** (www.belize audubon.org) accepts qualified volunteers and interns for a variety of land and marine projects. **Habitat for Humanity Belize** (tel. 501/227-

6818, habelize@btl.net), a worldwide leader in providing low-income housing, operates from Belize City.

Pro-Belize (tel. 501/601-9121, info@pro-belize.org, www.probelize.org) offers volunteer positions for anywhere from two weeks to six months or longer. Your weekly tuition includes room, board, work placement, and weekend excursions—work areas of focus are health, environment, micro-business, youth sports, fine arts, journalism, and women's issues.

An organization that specializes in big-cat research and protection is **www.li-feline.com.**

In San Pedro, **Green Reef** (www.greenreefbelize.com) is a private, non-profit organization dedicated to the promotion of sustainable use and conservation of Belize's marine and coastal resources; they're always interested in hearing from potential volunteers, especially those that have skills in web design, photography, fundraising, community outreach, and environmental education. They won an award from the Belize Tourism Board for Environmental Organization of the Year in 2003.

Itzamna Society (tel. 501/820-4023, life @epnp.org) is based in San Antonio, Cayo District, and was set up "for the protection and con-

THE PEACE CORPS IN BELIZE

The Peace Corps (www.peacecorps.gov) is a United States government program created by John F. Kennedy in 1961. Its original goal was to improve America's image in the Third World by sending young, idealistic volunteers deep into the countryside of developing countries. Forty-something years later, there are some 7,000 Volunteers serving in more than 90 countries around the world, with a standing order from Washington to double the number of Volunteers. Participants who are accepted serve a two-year tour (preceded by three months of intensive language and cultural training) and receive a bare-bones living allowance during their stay in-country.

The first group of Peace Corps Volunteers arrived in Belize in 1962. Since that time, more than 1,600 Volunteers have worked in Belize in a variety of projects. Currently, there are approximately 70 Volunteers providing assistance in education, youth development, rural community development, and environmental education. Pre-service training is conducted in rural Creole and mestizo villages. Training lasts nine weeks and includes technical training as well as an introduction to Creole. Volunteers are placed throughout the country's six districts to work with both government agencies and non-governmental organizations.

servation of the environment and cultural patrimony" of the local Maya community and national park.

The **Cornerstone Foundation** (tel. 501/824-2373, peace@btl.net) is a humanitarian NGO based in the Cayo District whose volunteer opportunities include HIV/AIDS education and awareness, special education, adult literacy, working with youth or women, and teaching business skills.

Trekforce Belize (8 Saint Mark St., tel. 501/223-1442, info@trekforce.org.uk, www.trekforce.org.uk) offers challenging conservation, community, and scientific expeditions to volunteers, often combined with other activities like Spanish school in Guatemala followed by an eight-week teaching placement in a rural Belizean school.

SPECIAL CONCERNS

Travelers with Children

Though lodges and hotels may offer discounts on accommodations for small children, Belize is best-suited for families with kids old enough to enjoy outdoor activities and learning about nature. However, many small children may do well at resorts that offer safe beaches, games, and of course a visit to the zoo (and free lodging for under a certain age). Any of the tranquil beaches are a great place to give them their first look through a dive mask at the unique underwater world.

Women Travelers

For the independent woman, Belize is a great place for group or solo travel. Its size makes it easy to get around, English is spoken everywhere, and if you so desire, you won't be lacking for a temporary travel partner in any part of the country. You'll meet many fellow travelers at the small inexpensive inns and guesthouses. Belizeans are used to seeing all combinations of travelers; solo women are no exception.

That said, sexual harassment of females traveling alone or in small groups can be a problem, although most incidents are limited to no more

than a few catcalls—just keep on walking; usually, some minor acknowledgment that you have heard them will shut them up more quickly than totally ignoring them. Although violent sexual assault is not a common occurrence, it does occur (like anywhere in the world). Several American travelers were the victims of sexual assaults in recent years. At least one of these rapes occurred after the victim accepted a ride from a new acquaintance, while another occurred during an armed robbery at an isolated resort. Never give the name of your hotel or your room number to someone you don't know.

When away from the beach towns and cayes, know that revealing clothes *will* attract lots of gawking attention, possibly more than you want. Most of the small towns and villages are safe even at night, with the exception of Belize City—don't walk anywhere there at night, even with friends. The best protection to bring is common sense.

Feminine supplies are found everywhere, with the exception of the smallest outlying villages and some of the remote lodges.

Some international tour companies specialize in trips for independent, active women; **Mariah Wilderness Expeditions** is one, with a special Belize adventure package (US tel. 800/462-7424, rafting@mariahwe.com). For "uncommon advice for the independent woman traveler," pick up a copy of Thalia Zepatos' *A Journey of One's Own* (Eighth Mountain Press, Portland, OR), a highly acclaimed women's travel resource.

Senior Travelers

Active seniors enjoy Belize. Some like the tranquility of the palm-studded cayes. Many come to learn about the jungle and its creatures or about the ancient Maya ruins. **Elderhostel** (US tel. 877/426-8056, www.elderhostel.org) has a number of tours to Belize.

Gay and Lesbian Travelers

Although there are plenty of out-and-about gay Belizean men (in Creole, "Batty-Men" or "Benque Boys"), there is no established community or any

TRAVEL AGENTS AND TOUR COMPANIES

International tour companies and travel specialists offer a huge variety of trips, from afternoon city tours, to weeklong cruises and treks in the farthest reaches of the country, the logistics of which would be next to impossible for the solo traveler. These adventures cost money, and of course, as part of a group, you lose some independence. But then again, you are provided with security, freedom from logistics, and, with some companies, downright luxury.

Tour operators in Belize are numerous enough to cover a wide range in their levels of responsibility—both to the environment and to the Belizean communities with which they interact. This is surely in large part a result of demands made by their clients. Before choosing a tour company, research it well and ask lots of questions: Will you interact with the communities through which you'll be traveling? If so, are the people of those communities benefiting in some way other than the opportunity to watch you pass through their villages in air-conditioned vehicles with the windows rolled up? Will your tour operator create an environment that allows you to practice the tenets of ethical tourism as listed in this section?

Tour Operators

For those interested in letting someone else do the driving (and planning, booking, etc.), various tour operators are reliable. In Belize City, Sarita and Lascelle Tillet of S & L Travel and Tours (91 N. Front St., tel. 501/227-7593 or 227-5145, sltravel@btl.net, www.sltravel-belize.com) operate as a husband/wife team. They drive late-model air-conditioned sedans or vans and travel throughout the country with airport pickup available. The Tillets have designed several great special-interest vacations and will custom design to your interests, whether they be the Maya archaeological zones (including Tikal), the cayes, or the caves and the countryside.

Toucan Travel (US tel. 800/747-1381, fax 504/464-0325) is run by Dulce, a transplanted Belizean living in Louisiana. She relays her intimate knowledge of the country to tourists and specializes in Placencia.

InnerQuest Adventures (www.innerquest.com) has over 14 years of experience leading wildlife-viewing trips with local guides around the country. They've been featured in dozens of magazines. Magnum Belize Tours (US tel. 800/447-2931, information@magnumbelize.com, www.magnumbelize.com) is one of the bigger companies, with an extensive network of resorts across the country.

Sea & Explore (US tel. 800/345-9786, seaexplore-belize@worldnet.att.net) is run by owners Sue and Tony Castillo, native Belizeans who take pleasure and pride in sharing their country with visitors. They know every out-of-the-way destination, and make every effort to match clients with the right areas of the country to suit their interests. Susan worked with the Belize Ministry of Tourism before coming to the United States.

Mary Dell Lucas of Far Horizons Cultural Discovery Trips (US tel. 800/552-4575, journey@farhorizon.com, www.farhorizon.com) is known throughout the Maya world for her excellent archaeological knowledge and insight. Her company provides trips into the most fascinating Maya sites, regardless of location. Although Mary is an archaeologist herself, she often brings specialists along with her groups. You can be assured that the trips with Far Horizons all have an archaeological or cultural emphasis.

Also check Jaguar Adventures Tours and Travel (4 Fort St., tel. 501/233-6025, jaguaradv@btl.net), located at the Fort Street Hotel and offering night walks at the Belize Zoo, cave tubing trips, visits to Maya ruins, snorkeling the reef, and diving the atolls, to name a few.

Adventure Travel

Dangriga- and Vancouver-based Island Expeditions (US/Canada tel. 800/667-1630, mail@islandexpeditions.com, www.islandexpeditions.com) has been leading exciting sea kayaking, rafting, ruins, nature, and snorkeling adventures in Belize since 1987. It's a very experienced and professional outfit, and they have a stunning island camp in Glover's Reef Atoll with canvas-wall tents on platforms.

Slickrock Adventures (US tel. 800/390-5715, slickrock@slickrock.com, www.slickrock.com), based on their primitively plush camp on a private island in Glover's Reef Atoll, offers paddling trips of various lengths and specializes in sea kayaking, windsurfing, and inland activities like mountain biking.

With 17 years of experience as a premier land operator in Belize, International Expeditions (US tel. 800/633-4734, belize@ietravel.com, www.ietravel.com) has a full-time office in Belize City. They offer group and independent nature travel in sturdy, comfortable vehicles, and are staffed by travel and airline specialists, naturalists, and an archaeologist. Trips run 7–14 days with two- and three-day add-ons available.

Travel Specialists

Various independant travel agents, specializing in all kinds of niche, group, and solo travel within Belize, await your call.

Belize Trips (tel. 501/610-1923, www.belize-trips.com) founder Katie Valk's greatest asset as a Belize travel specialist is her ability to pinpoint exactly what kind of experience her clients want, and then, through an impressive latticework of friends and acquaintances, make that experience happen. Katie is an ex-New Yorker who has lived full time in Belize for over 16 years and you'll often find her swinging a machete in the bush or paddling her kayak down some wildlife-choked river, as she seeks out and test-drives every adventure she promotes.

Barb's Belize (US tel. 888/321-2272, fax 915/760-6497, escape@barbsbelize.com, www.barbsbelize.com) is a small operation that offers custom itineraries for any budget, from backpacker to decadently deluxe. They are specialists in unique interests such as traditional herbal medicine, jungle survival, and extreme adventure expeditions.

gay clubs, per se. The gay travelers we've seen were totally accepted by both their fellow lodge guests and Belizean hosts. Still, the act of "sodomy" is illegal in Belize (only between men) and a bit of discretion is advised.

Travelers with Disabilities

There are probably about as many wheelchair ramps in all of Belize as there are traffic lights (three); disabled travelers will generally be treated with respect, but expect logistics to be a bit challenging in places. At least one tour operator, **Belize Special Tours** (tel. 501/600-4284 or 824-4748, suga_brown34@yahoo.com), based in Cayo, caters specifically to travelers with disabilities, offering tours of the city and to Belize Zoo, Maya ruins, and various wildlife sanctuaries. Hokol Kin Hotel in Corozal and Red Jaguar Lodge in San José de Succotz both have very nice wheelchair-accessible suites and facilities.

CAMERAS AND PHOTOGRAPHY

Film Processing

Most larger cities in Belize have one-hour photo labs, but technicians often know nothing more than how to feed your film into their big machines, so print quality may be wanting. Kodak film mailers are another option, but most photographers won't let their film out of sight until they reach their favorite lab at home.

If you've already gone digital, your big concern will be finding places to download those memory chips. Many Internet cafés provide the service, but few have figured out how to provide easily accessible, up-to-date software for your particular camera, and they may or may not allow you to download it yourself onto their computer. The software allows you to transfer your camera's images onto a computer so that you can then burn them on a CD or store them on a memory card to take home. Your best bets are to find the most modern Internet café you can, which will probably be able to accommodate you; travel with a laptop and regularly upload your photos to clear your memory card;

GETTING MARRIED IN PARADISE

Belize is gaining quite the reputation as the perfect place to tie the knot and/or honeymoon. A huge number of resorts cater to both activities, some quite creatively (such as ceremonies underwater or atop Maya pyramids). If getting married, you must be in Belize three days before submitting your paperwork to the registry office on the fourth business day. The Government of Belize charges US$100 for the license (Registrar General's Office tel. 501/227-7377), and you'll need a birth certificate or passport. Several wedding specialists can facilitate paperwork and help with ministers, flowers, accommodations, receptions, and more, including Iraida Gonzales on San Pedro (www.belizeweddings.com), Lee Nyhus in Placencia (www.secretgardenplacencia.com), and Katie Valk, who handles anywhere in the country (www.belize-trips.com).

or travel with plenty of memory (this option can be quite expensive).

Photo Etiquette

Cameras can be a help or a hindrance when trying to get to know the local people. When traveling in the backcountry, you'll run into folks who don't want their pictures taken. Keep your camera put away until the right moment. The main thing to remember is to ask permission first and then if someone doesn't want his/her picture taken, accept the refusal with a gracious smile and move on. Especially sensitive to this are Mennonites and Maya. Remember, you are a guest in their land and capturing somebody's image (or artwork) on film for your own purposes is a gained privilege, not your "right" as a tourist.

Underwater Photography

One of the delights for the amateur photographer is shooting the creatures of the Belizean reef in living color. Most travelers use disposable under-

KNOW YOUR RATES

Exact hotel rates are an elusive thing in Belize; seasonal fluctuations are compounded by various hotel taxes and service charges, sometimes as much as 25 percent additional; occasionally, using a credit card will score you another 3–5 percent charge. Universal standards for presenting prices are absent in Belize's hotel industry. Always make sure the rate you read about or are quoted is actually the same amount you will be asked to pay.

The high season is loosely considered to last from mid-December through the end of April, and is marked by a rise in both the number of visitors and the price of most accommodations. A minority of hotels keep their rates the same year-round, but it's rarely that simple. In this book, high (or winter) season rates only (for doubles) are provided, so calculate cheaper figures (30–40 percent lower) if traveling during the low/rainy season (roughly May through early December). On the same note, be advised that some places kick their rates up even higher during Christmas, New Year's, and Easter, calling these "holiday" or "peak" rates.

Independent travelers who make their plans on the fly will have no problem, except during the holidays listed above in San Pedro, Caye Caulker, and Placencia. It's a good idea to make reservations as soon as you decide to travel to the cayes. If you show up to one of these towns with no booked room, chances are you'll find *something*, but you'd better be open minded.

water cameras, but if you're looking to publish, you'll need a bit more under the hood.

Some hotels, resorts, and shops in Belize rent underwater cameras or housings for your camera. Don't expect a large selection. Remember when buying film that the best for underwater is natural-, red-, or yellow-tint film; film such as Ektachrome with a bluish cast does not give the best results. A strobe or flash is a big help if shooting in deep water or into caves. Natural-light pictures are great if you're shooting in fairly shallow water. It's best to shoot on an eye-to-eye level when photographing fish. Be careful of stirring up silt from the bottom with your fins. Try to hold very still when depressing the shutter, and if you must stabilize yourself, *don't* grab onto any bright-colored coral—you will kill it and you may hurt yourself as well. If it's colored, it's alive, so grab only the drab gray coral.

Accommodations

There are currently about 500 hotels of all types licensed by the Belize Tourism Board to lodge visitors, the vast majority of which are small (less than 12 rooms), often family-run operations.

BUDGET

Budget accommodations are ample in Belize, but you may have to readjust your idea of what's "cheap." In this book, anything under US$25 is considered reasonable, a shock to backpackers arriving from Mexico and Guatemala who are accustomed to paying US$3 (or less) a night. In Belize, rates under US$10 per person per night usually mean a significant sacrifice in safety and/or cleanliness. At press time, US$10 is the accepted bottom line for low-cost lodging, and it'll get you anything from a cramped, stuffy concrete box in most towns to a generous wooden cabin at the Trek Stop and other backpacker hotspots. Guesthouses and budget hotels often offer a dormitory or bunkroom, which you'll share with fellow travelers; this option is always cheaper, but obviously you give up privacy and security. Expect community bathrooms and cold water in such places. Sometimes, nicer hotels offer a few "economy rooms," which are considerably cheaper than normal rates. And, of course, great deals are abundant in the low season, when room rates plummet across the board.

Many villages around the country are trying to emulate the wildly successful guesthouse and homestay networks available in the Toledo villages. Sometimes calling themselves "bed-and-breakfasts," such options are usually primitive in every sense of the word, often lacking electricity, running water, and flush toilets.

UPSCALE

The sky's the limit when it comes to mid-range and luxury accommodations in Belize. A great many Belizean families and foreign investors have attempted to bring their personal visions of paradise to life. Belize's amazing selection of truly creative beach resorts and jungle lodges have been featured in international travel magazines around the world, and with good reason.

Food and Drink

Throughout this book (and throughout Belize), you will find references to "Belizean" food, often preceded by words like "simple" and "cheap." It should be noted that the very idea of a national cuisine is as new as every other part of Belizean identity. Since the times of the Baymen, Belize has been an import economy, surviving mostly on canned meats like "bully beef" and imported grains and packaged goods. With independence, however, came renewed national pride, and with the arrival of tourists seeking "local" food, the word "Belizean" was increasingly applied to the varied diet of so many cultures. Anthropologist Richard Wilk writes, "The crucible of Belizean national cooking has been the *transnational* arena; the flow of migrants, sojourners, tourists and media which increasingly links the Caribbean with the United States."

Nobody will argue about the common denominator of Belizean food: **rice and beans.** The starchy staple is pronounced altogether with a heavy accent on the first syllable: *"RICE-n-beans!"* Belizeans speak of the dish with pride, as if they invented the concoction, and you can expect a massive mound of it with most midday meals. Actually, Belizean rice and beans *is* a bit unique: they use red beans, black pepper, and grated coconut, instead of the black beans and cilantro common in neighboring Latin countries. The rest of your plate will be occupied by something like **stew beef** or **fry chicken** (or some other meat), plus a small mound of either

Belizean breakfast of champions: salbutes and Marie Sharp's Hot Sauce

potato or cabbage salad. Be sure to take advantage of so much fresh fruit: oranges, watermelon, starfruit, mangoes, and papaya, to name a few.

The omnipresent **Chinese restaurants** are, in addition to being providers of authentic Chinese cuisine of varying quality, also famous for their cheap "fry chicken" and are just as Belizean

KULCHA SHACK MENU—
A FEW GARINAGU DISHES

True to their unique heritage, the Garinagu have a variety of dishes that are distinctly theirs, although you'll have to search hard to find an actual Garinagu-themed restaurant. More commonly, you'll find their dishes at local cafés in Dangriga, Hopkins, Seine Bight, and Punta Gorda. Fish in coconut milk, cooked with local spices, is called *sere*. In many dishes, plantains or green bananas are grated into various recipes, and seaweed is used now and then.

Traditionally, and continuing today, the Garinagu raise cassava to make *eriba*, a flat bread made from the meal of the cassava root. The large bulbous roots of the shrubby spurge plant are peeled and grated (today mostly by electric graters, but formerly by hand—a long, tedious job on a stone-studded board). The grated cassava is packed into a six-foot-long leaf-woven tube that is hung from a hefty tree limb, then weighted and pulled at the bottom, squeezing and forcing out the poisonous juices and starch from the pulp. The coarse meal that remains is dried and used to make the flat bread that has been an important part of the Garinagu culture for centuries.

Here are a few dishes to try:

- *hudut:* fish simmered in thick coconut milk with herbs and cooked over an open fire—served with *fu-fu* (beaten plantain)
- *tapow:* green banana cut in wedges and simmered in coconut milk with fish, herbs, and seasonings—served with white rice or *ereba* (cassava bread)
- *seafood gumbo:* a combination of conch, lobster, shrimp, fish, and vegetables, cooked in coconut milk, herbs, and grated green banana or plantain—served with rice or *ereba* and also called "boil-up."

To wash it down, how 'bout a seaweed shake, or a shot of bitters?

as anyone else on the block. These are often your only meal options on Sundays and holidays and we've done our best to ask locals and expats in each town which one is the best.

For breakfast, try some **fry jacks** (fluffy fried-dough crescents) or **johnnycakes** (flattened biscuits) with your eggs, beans, and bacon. Unfortunately, most coffee served in the country is still instant or, if brewed, just plain horrible. This is changing, however, mostly because of demanding tourists like yourself who insist on a real mug o' Joe—or a soymilk, double-decaf latte, for that matter, which you'll find in the finer restaurants and cafés.

One of the cheapest and quickest meal options, found nearly everywhere in Belize, is Mexican "fast-food" snacks, especially **taco stands,** which are everywhere you look, serving as many as five or six soft-shell chicken tacos for US$1. Also widely available are *salbutes,* a kind of hot, soggy taco dripping in oil; *panades,* little meat pies; and *garnaches,* which are crispy tortillas under a small mound of tomato, cabbage, cheese, and hot sauce.

Speaking of hot sauce, you'll definitely want to try and to take home **Marie Sharp's** famous habanero sauces, jams, and other creative products. Marie Sharp is a classic independent Belizean success story and many travelers visit her factory and store in Dangriga (her products are available on every single restaurant table and gift shop in the country). Her sauce is good on pretty much everything.

Then, of course, there's the international cuisine, in the form of many excellent (and many not-so-excellent) foreign-themed restaurants. San Pedro and Placencia, in particular, have burgeoning fine dining scenes, and Cayo has excellent Indian and vegetarian fare.

Many restaurants in Belize have flexible hours of operation, and often close for a few hours between lunch and dinner.

Know Belize

Seafood

One of the favorite Belize specialties is fresh fish, especially along the coast and on the islands, but even inland Belize is never more than 60 miles from the ocean. There's lobster, shrimp, red snapper, sea bass, halibut, barracuda, conch, and lots more prepared in a variety of ways.

Conch (pronounced KAHNK) has been a staple in the diet of the Maya and Central American communities along the Caribbean coast for centuries. There are conch fritters, conch steak, and conch stew; it's also often used in *ceviche*—uncooked seafood marinated in lime juice with onions, peppers, tomatoes, and a host of spices. In another favorite, conch is pounded, dipped in egg and cracker crumbs, and sautéed quickly (like abalone steak in California) with a squirt of fresh lime. Caution: If it's cooked too long, it becomes tough and rubbery. Conch fritters are minced pieces of conch mixed into a flour batter and fried—delicious.

On many boat trips, the crew will catch a fish and prepare it for lunch, either as *ceviche;* cooked over an open beach fire; or in a "boil up," seasoned with onions, peppers, and *achiote,* a fragrant red spice grown locally since the time of the early Maya.

Know Your Seasons

Don't order seafood out of season: Closed season for lobster is February 15–June 15, and conch season is closed July 1–September 30. The ocean is being over-fished, due in large part to increasing demand from tourists. The once-prolific lobster is becoming scarce in Belizean waters. And conch is not nearly as easy to find as it once was. Most reputable restaurateurs follow the law and don't buy undersized or out of season seafood; however, a few have no scruples.

NON-ALCOHOLIC BEVERAGES

Although U.S. corporate soft drink companies will undoubtedly continue trying to push

catch of the day on Ambergris Caye

© JOSHUA BERMAN

their brown sugar-water down your throat as they do back home (and as they have successfully done with most locals), there are wonderful natural fruit drinks to be had throughout Belize. Take advantage of fresh lime, papaya, watermelon, orange, and other healthy juices during your travels—just be sure the drinks are made with purified water.

ALCOHOLIC BEVERAGES

Beer

Perhaps the most important—or at least best-tasting—legacy left by nearly three centuries of British imperialism is a national affinity for dark beer. Nowhere else in Central America will you find swill as hearty and *morena* as you will in any bar, restaurant, or corner store in Belize, where beer is often advertised separately from stout, a good sign indeed for those who prefer more bite and body to their brew.

At the top of the heap are the slender, undersized (280 ml) bottles of **Guinness Foreign**

Extra Stout, known affectionately by Belizeans as "short, dark, and lovelies." Yes, that's right, Guinness—brewed in Belize under license from behind the famous St. James's Gate in Dublin, Ireland, and packing a pleasant 7.5 percent punch. No, this is not the same sweet nectar you'll find flowing from your favorite Irish pub's draught handle at home, but c'mon, you're in Central America, enjoy.

Next up is **Belikin Stout,** weighing in with a slightly larger bottle (342 ml) and distinguishable from regular beer only by its blue bottle cap. Stouts run 6.5 percent alcohol and are a bit less bitter than Guinness, but still a delicious, meaty meal that goes down much quicker than its caloric equivalent—a loaf of bread. **Belikin Premium** (4.8 percent) boasts a well-balanced body and is brewed with four different types of foreign hops; demand often exceeds supply in many establishments, so order early.

Asking for a simple "beer" will get you a basic **Belikin,** which, when served cold, is no better or worse than any other regional draft. Lastly, the tiny green bottles belong to **Lighthouse Lager,** a healthy alternative to the heavies, but packing a lot less bang for the buck with only 4.2 percent alcohol and several ounces less beer (often for the same price).

All beer in Belize is brewed and distributed by the same company in Ladyville, just north of Belize City (Bowen and Bowen Ltd. also has the soft drink market cornered). Some batches are occasionally inconsistent in quality—if you get skunked, send back your mug and try again. You'll see most Belizeans vigorously wipe the rust and crud from the open bottle mouths with the napkin that comes wrapped around the top—you'd be smart to do the same. Beers in Belize cost anywhere from US$1.50 to US$3

© JOSHUA BERMAN

Creole bar rules on Placencia beach

a bottle, depending on where you are and what size bottle you're getting.

Rum

Of all the national rums, **One Barrel** stands proudly above the rest. Smooth enough to enjoy on the rocks (add a bit of Coca Cola for coloring if you need to), One Barrel has a sweet, butterscotchy aftertaste and costs about US$7 for a liter bottle, or US$3 per shot (or rum drink). Locals often stick to their favorite **Caribbean Rum,** fine if you're mixing it with punch, cola, or better yet, coconut water, *in* the coconut. Everything else is standard, white-rum gut rot.

BITTERS: LOVE POTION NUMBER NINE

"**I**t's good for your penis!" one merchant of this ages-old Garinagu herbal tonic shouted to me as he poured a measured portion of yellowed liquid through a funnel into a recycled pint bottle—he laughed and clenched a fist atop an upraised forearm to emphasize his point. Bitters are made by soaking herbs like *palo del hombre* (man-root) and jackass bitters in 80-proof white rum or gin. The cure-all is used to treat everything from the common cold to cancer, and is sometimes taken as a daily shot to keep your system clean and your urine clear. And of course, bitters are an acclaimed aphrodisiac and sure cure for impotency, according to any vendor of the stuff.

Available under the counter of many a bar and corner store, the local "baby-maker" is also known in the Garifuna tongue as *"gifit,"* and Belizean expats bring it back to the United States by the gallon. The most famous bitters in the country are brewed by "Doctor Mac," a proud and formidable man also known as "Big Mac," on the outskirts of Dangriga. He makes a version for women too (the bottles are labeled either "boy" or "gal"), and you can find his products either at his store in the new area, or at his daughter's "Mackenzie" shop, across the street from the Chaleanor Hotel.

Oh yeah, bitters can get you really drunk, too. Be careful with long-term, regular use though, as some say that one of the ingredients carries trace amounts of arsenic.

Health

BEFORE YOU GO

Resources

Staying Healthy in Asia, Africa, and Latin America, by Dirk G. Schroeder (Avalon Travel Publishing, 2000), is an excellent and concise guide to preventative medicine in the Third World, and small enough to fit in your pack. A bit more unwieldy but still excellent is David Werner's *Where There Is No Doctor* (Hesperian Foundation, 1992).

Consult the Belize page of the American Centers for Disease Control and Prevention (CDC) website, www.cdc.gov/travel/camerica.htm, for up-to-date health recommendations and advice or call their International Travelers Hotline at 404/332-4559 or 877/394-8747. Another excellent resource is the Belize page of www.mdtravelhealth.com. You can also call the Belizean embassy in your country for up-to-date information about outbreaks or other health problems.

Vaccinations

Required: A certificate of vaccination against yellow fever is required for all travelers above one year old and arriving from affected areas.

Recommended: Before traveling to Central America, be sure your tetanus, diphtheria, measles, mumps, rubella, and polio vaccines are up-to-date. Hepatitis A vaccine is recommended for all travelers over age two and should be given at least two weeks (preferably four weeks or more) before departure. Hepatitis B vaccine is recommended for travelers who will have intimate contact with local residents or potentially need blood transfusions or injections while abroad, especially if visiting for more than six months. It is also recommended for all health care personnel. Typhoid vaccine is also recommended for all travelers, available in oral form consisting of four capsules taken on alternate days until completed. At the time of this writing, cholera and polio vaccines are *not* recommended for travelers to Belize.

STAYING HEALTHY

Ultimately, your health is dependent on the choices you make, and chief among these is what you decide to put in your mouth. One longtime resident says staying healthy in the tropics is more than just possible—it is an "art form." Nevertheless, as you master the art, expect your digestive system to take some time getting accustomed to the new food and microorganisms in the Belizean diet. During this time (and after), use common sense: Wash or sanitize your hands often. Eat food that is well-cooked and still hot when served. Avoid dairy products if you're not sure whether they are pasteurized. Be wary of uncooked foods, including shellfish and salads (most high-end restaurants in Belize are very careful and completely safe, but feel free to inspect the kitchen before eating).

Most importantly, be aware of flies, the single worst transmitter of food-borne illnesses. Prevent flies from landing on your food, glass, or table setting. You'll notice Belizeans are meticulous about this, and you should be too. If you have to leave the table, cover your food with a napkin or have someone else wave their hand over it slowly. You can fold your drinking straw over and put the mouth end into the neck of the bottle to prevent flies from landing on it, and put napkins on top of the bottle neck and your glass, too. When you're finished with a dish, ask the waiter to clear it so you have fewer things to guard from the flies.

"Don't drink the water!"

At least one well-meaning friend or relative told you this before you shipped off to Central America, and we agree. Even though most municipal water systems are well-treated and probably safe, there is not much reason to take the chance, especially when purified, bottled water is so widely available and relatively cheap. Avoid ice cubes, unless you're confident they were made with boiled or purified water. Canned and bottled drinks without ice, including beer, are usually safe, but should never be used as a substitute for water when trying to stay hydrated, especially during a bout of diarrhea or when out in the sun.

If you plan on staying awhile in a rural area of Belize, check out camping catalogs for water filters that remove chemical as well as biological

contamination. Alternately, six drops of liquid iodine (or three of bleach) will kill everything that needs to be killed in a liter of water—good in a pinch (or on a backcountry camping trip), but not something you'll find yourself practicing on a daily basis.

Oral Rehydration Salts

Probably the single most effective preventative and curative medicine you can carry are packets of powdered salt and sugar which, when mixed with a liter of water (drink in small sips), is the best immediate treatment for dehydration due to diarrhea, sun exposure, fever, infection, or—say some—a hangover. Particularly in the case of diarrhea, rehydration salts are essential to your recovery. They replace the salts and minerals your body has lost due to liquid evacuation (be it from sweating, vomiting, or urinating), and they're essential to your body's most basic cellular transfer functions. Whether or not you like the taste (odds are you won't), consuming enough rehydration packets and water is very often the difference between being just a little sick and feeling really, really awful.

Sport drinks like Gatorade are super-concentrated mixtures and should be diluted *at least* 3:1 with water to make the most of the active ingredients. If you don't, you'll urinate out the majority of the electrolytes. Gatorade is common in most new gas stations and supermarkets, but rehydration packets are more available and much much cheaper, available from any drug store or health clinic. They can also be improvised even more cheaply, according to the following recipe: mix a half teaspoon of salt, half teaspoon baking soda, and 4 tablespoons of sugar in 1 quart of boiled or carbonated water. Drink a full glass of the stuff after each time you use the bathroom. Add a few drops of lemon juice to make it more palatable.

Sun Exposure

Belize is located a scant 13–18 degrees of latitude from the equator, so the sun's rays strike the earth's surface at a more direct angle than in northern countries. The result is that you will burn faster and sweat up to twice as much as you are used to. Did we mention that you should drink lots of water?

Ideally, do like the majority of the locals do, and stay out of the sun between 10 A.M. and 2 P.M. It's a great time to take a nap anyway. Use sunscreen of at least SPF 30 (Bullfrog's alcohol-based SPF 36 is the authors' choice), and wear a hat and pants. Should you overdo it in the sun, make sure to drink lots of fluids—that means water, not beer—and try not to strain any muscles as you kick yourself for being so stupid. Treat sunburns with aloe gel, or better yet—find a fresh aloe plant to break open and rub over your skin.

DISEASES AND COMMON AILMENTS

Diarrhea and Dysentery

Generally, simple cases of diarrhea in the absence of other symptoms are nothing more serious than "traveler's diarrhea." If you do get a good case, your best bet is to let it pass naturally. Diarrhea is your body's way of flushing out the bad stuff, so constipating medicines like Immodium-AD are not recommended, as they keep the bacteria (or whatever is causing your intestinal distress) within your system. Save the Immodium (or any other liquid glue) for emergency situations like long bus rides or a hot date. Most importantly, drink lots of water! Not replacing the fluids and electrolytes you are losing will make you feel much worse than you need to. If the diarrhea persists for more than 48 hours, is bloody, or is accompanied by a fever, see a health professional immediately. That said, know that all bodies react differently to the changes in diet, schedule, and stress that go along with traveling, and many visitors to Belize stay entirely regular and solid throughout their trip.

Pay attention to your symptoms: Diarrhea can also be a sign of amoebic (parasitic) and bacillic (bacterial) dysentery, both caused by some form of fecal-oral contamination. Often accompanied by nausea, vomiting, and a mild fever, dysentery is easily confused with other diseases, so don't try to self-diagnose. Stool-sample examinations are cheap and can be performed at most clinics and hospitals and are your first step to getting better. Bacillic dysentery is treatable with antibiotics; amoebic is treated with one of a variety of drugs that kill off all the flora in your intestinal tract. Of these, Flagyl is the best known, but other non-FDA–approved treatments like Tinedazol are commonly available, cheap, and effective. Do not drink alcohol with these drugs, and eat something like yogurt or acidophellus pills to refoliate your tummy.

Malaria

By all official accounts, malaria is present in Belize, although you'll be hard-pressed to find anybody—Belizean or expat—who has actually experienced or even heard of a case of it. Still, most travelers choose to take a weekly prophylaxis of chloroquine or its equivalent. The CDC specifically recommends travelers to Belize to use brand name Aralen pills (500 mg for adults), although you should ask your doctor for the latest drug on the market. Begin taking the pills two weeks before you arrive and continue taking them for four weeks after leaving the country. A small percentage of people have negative reactions to chloroquine, including nightmares, rashes, or hair loss. Alternative treatments are available, but the best method of all is to not get bit (see section on mosquitoes later in this chapter).

The risk of malaria is higher in rural areas, especially those alongside rivers or marshes, although malaria-infected mosquitoes breed anywhere stagnant pools of water (of any size, even in an empty bottle cap) are found, including in urban settings.

Malaria works by setting up shop in your liver and then blasting you with attacks of fever, headaches, chills, and fatigue. The onslaughts occur on a 24-hour-sick, 24-hour-improvement cycle. If you observe this cycle, seek medical attention. They'll most likely take a blood test and if positive, prescribe you a huge dose of chloroquine that will kill the bug. Allow time to recover your strength.

Dengue Fever

Dengue, or "bone-breaking fever," is a flu-like, mosquito-carried illness that will put a stop to your fun in Central America like a baseball bat to the head. Dengue's occurrence is extremely low in Belize, but a couple dozen cases are still reported each year. There is no vaccine, but dengue's effects can be successfully minimized with plenty of rest, Tylenol (for the fever and aches), and as much water and *hydration salts* as you can possibly manage. Dengue itself is undetectable in a blood test, but a low platelet count indicates its presence. If you believe you have dengue, you should get a blood test as soon as possible to make sure it's not the hemorrhagic variety which can be fatal if untreated.

HIV/AIDS

HIV and AIDS are a growing problem in Belize. Thankfully, there is an impressive amount of international attention to the problem and awareness and education programs are common. The Peace Corps devotes an entire sector of their country program to this, and the Cornerstone Foundation is another active volunteer organization. When traveling in Belize, do not have unprotected sex, and say no to dirty needles and blood transfusions.

Ciguatera

This is a toxin occasionally found in large reef fish. It is not a common circumstance, but it is possible for grouper, snapper, and barracuda to carry this toxin. If after eating these fish you experience diarrhea, nausea, numbness, or heart arrhythmia, see a doctor immediately. The toxin is found in certain algae on reefs in all the tropical areas of the world. Fish do nibble on the coral, and if they happen to find this algae, over a period of time it accumulates in their systems. The longer they live and the larger they get, the more probable it is they will carry toxin, which is not destroyed when cooked.

Other Sources of Infection

Money can be a source of germs. Wash your hands frequently, don't put your fingers in your mouth, and carry some kind of disinfectant cleaner. When in backcountry cafés, remember that fruits and vegetables, especially those with a thin edible skin (such as tomatoes), are a possible source of bacteria. If you like to eat street vendors' food (and some shouldn't be missed), use common sense. If you see the food being cooked (killing all the grubby little bacteria) before your eyes, have at it. If it's hanging there already cooked and being nibbled on by small flying creatures, pass it by. It may have been there all day, and what was once a nice sterile morsel could easily have gone bad in the heat, or been contaminated by flies. Be cautious of hotel buffets; raw shellfish, potato salad, and other cream-based salads may have been sitting out for hours—a potential bacteria source unless they are well-iced.

Other Diseases

There is moderate incidence of Hepatitis B in Belize. Avoid contact with bodily fluids or bodily waste. Get vaccinated if you anticipate close contact with the local population or plan to reside in Central America for an extended period of time.

Get a rabies vaccination if you intend to spend a long time in Belize. Should you be bitten by an infected dog, rodent, or bat, immediately cleanse the wound with lots of soap, and get prompt medical attention. In Belize, the chief risk is from rabid dogs near the Guatemalan border.

Tuberculosis is spread by sneezing or coughing, and the infected person may not know he or she is a carrier. If you are planning to spend more than four weeks in Belize (or plan on spending time in the Belize jail), consider having a tuberculin skin test performed before and after visiting. Tuberculosis is a serious and possibly fatal disease but can be treated with several medications.

BITES AND STINGS
Mosquitoes and Sand Flies

Mosquitoes are most active during the rainy season (June–Nov.) and in areas with stagnant water, like marshes, puddles, and rice fields. They are more common in the lower, flatter regions of

Belize then they are in the hills, though even in the highlands, old tires, cans, and roadside puddles can provide the habitat necessary to produce swarms of mosquitoes. The mosquito that carries malaria is active during the evening and at night, while the dengue fever–courier is active during the day, from dawn to dusk. They are both relatively simple to combat, and ensuring you don't get bitten is the best prophylaxis for preventing the diseases.

First and foremost, limit the amount of skin you expose—long sleeves, pants, and socks will do more to prevent bites than the strongest chemical repellant. Choose lodging accommodations with good screens and if this is not possible, use a fan to blow airborne insects away from your body as you sleep. Avoid being outside or unprotected in the hour before sunset when mosquito activity is heaviest, and use a mosquito net tucked underneath your mattress when you sleep. Consider purchasing a lightweight backpackers' net, either freestanding or to hang from the ceiling, before you come south—mosquito nets are more expensive in Belize than at home. Some accommodations provide nets, others are truly free of biting bugs and don't need them. If you know where you're staying, ask before you leave whether you'll need a net.

Once in Belize, you can purchase mosquito coils, which burn slowly, releasing a mosquito-repelling smoke; they're cheap and convenient but try to place them so you're not breathing the toxic smoke yourself.

Sand flies don't carry any diseases that we know about, but man do they *suck!* Actually, these tiny midges, or no-see-ums, bite. Hard. They breed in wet, sandy areas and are only fought by the wind (or a well-screened room). Don't scratch those bites!

Chagas' Disease

The Chagas bug *(Trypanosoma cruzi)* is a large, recognizable insect, also called the kissing bug, assassin bug, and cone-nose. It can be as big as a thumb and have a long snout and some kind of dark yellow and black design on their back. In Spanish, it's known as *"chinche,"* but this word is also used for other many other types of beetle-looking creatures. Chagas bugs are present in Belize, found mostly in poor structures of crumbling adobe. The Chagas bug's biggest menace is the disease it carries of the same name. It is a rare ailment passed by the bug to unsuspecting, often sleeping, humans. The Chagas bug bites the victim (usually on the face, close to the lips), sucks its fill of blood, and, for the coup de grâce, defecates on the newly-created wound. Besides the downright insult of being bitten, sucked, and pooped on, two percent of the bug's victims will contract the disease. The first symptoms include swollen glands and a fever that appear one to two weeks after the bite. The disease then goes into a five- to 30-year remission phase. If and when it reappears, Chagas' disease causes the lining of the heart to swell, sometimes resulting in death. There is no cure.

Scorpions, Spiders, and Snakes

Scorpions are common in Belize, especially in dark corners, beaches, and piles of wood. Belizean scorpions look nasty—black and big— but their sting is no more harmful than that of a bee and is described by some as what a cigarette burn feels like. Your lips and tongue may feel a little numb, but the venom is nothing compared to their smaller, translucent cousins in Mexico. Needless to say, to people who are prone to anaphylactic shock, it can be a more serious or life-threatening experience. Everyone has heard that when in a jungle, never put on your shoes without checking the insides—good advice—and always give your clothes a good visual going over and a vigorous shake before putting them on. Scorpions occasionally drop out of thatch ceilings.

Don't worry, despite the prevalence of all kinds of arachnids, including big, hairy tarantulas, spiders do not aggressively seek out people to bite, and do way more good than harm by eating things like Chagas bugs. If you'd rather the spiders didn't share your personal space, shake out your bedclothes before going to sleep and check your shoes before putting your feet in them.

Of the 59 species of snakes that have been identified in Belize, at least nine are venomous, most notably the infamous fer-de-lance (locally called a "Tommygoff") and coral snake. The chances of the average tourist's being bitten are slim. Reportedly, most snakebite victims are children. However, if you plan on extensive jungle exploration, check with your doctor before you leave home. Antivenin is available, doesn't require refrigeration, and keeps indefinitely. It's also wise to be prepared for an allergic reaction to the antivenin—bring an antihistamine and Adrenalin (epinephrine). The most important thing to remember if bitten: *Don't panic and don't run.* Physical exertion and panic cause the venom to travel through your body much faster. Lie down and stay calm; have someone carry you to a doctor. Do not cut the wound, use a tourniquet, or ingest alcoholic beverages.

Botfly

Ah, the lowly botfly! It looks like the common household variety, but this one has developed an unpleasant trick. By depositing eggs on mosquitoes, the botfly allows its young to be transported to an unsuspecting host. As the mosquito feeds, a botfly larva is roused by the body heat of the warm-blooded host and drops onto the unsuspecting human or animal. Burrowing quickly under the skin, the maggot sets up housekeeping. To breathe, it sticks a tiny tube through the skin, and there it stays until one of two things happen: you kill it, or it graduates and leaves home.

A botfly bite starts out looking like a mosquito bite, but if the bit gets red and tender instead of healing, it may be a botfly—get it checked out. Though uncomfortable and distasteful, it's not a serious health problem. To rid yourself of this pesky boarder, Sharon Matola of the Belize Zoo suggests dabbing a glob of Vaseline petroleum jelly over the air hole. This strategy draws out the varmint, intent on home repair but hopelessly mired. It is easy enough, then, to squash the squishy freeloader. Another suggested method, which she credits to Maya guide Gregorio Sho, is especially effective for the head area:

Take a tiny piece of tobacco and stick it in the air hole. Overnight, nicotine destroys the teenage maggot. The next day you can squeeze out the ungrateful boarder at your leisure (à la the nipple scene in Alan Rabinowitz's book, *Jaguar*).

Marine Hazards

When you enter the marine world, you are a strange visitor among thousands of native critters. Most will only injure you if you somehow trigger their defense mechanisms—like if you step on them or grab them.

Anemones and sea urchins live in Belize waters. Some can be dangerous if touched or stepped on. The long-spined black sea urchin can inflict great pain, and its poison can cause an uncomfortable infection. Don't think that you're safe in a wetsuit, booties, and gloves. The spines easily slip through the rubber and the urchin is encountered at all depths. They are more abundant in some areas than in others; keep your eyes open. If you should run into one of the spines, remove it quickly and carefully, disinfect the wound, and apply antibiotic cream. If you have difficulty removing the spine, or if it breaks, see a doctor—*pronto!* Local remedies include urinating on the wound if nothing else is available.

Barracuda, moray eels, and sharks do not appreciate groping hands, and all have ample means to protect themselves. Enough said. As for your snorkel guide who picks up a nurse shark or ray and invites you to pet it, it's probably a better idea to look, not touch, and let him know your feelings before getting in the water—not necessarily because of the danger of attack, but more because we should let these animals alone.

Note that sharks are attracted to blood, certain low-frequency sounds (like those caused by an injured fish), electromagnetic disturbances, and certain shapes and color patterns. Avoid swimming with bleeding wounds. And while barracudas, like other predatory fish, can be excited by fish blood and jerky vibrations, they seem to be more visual hunters. They are likely to snap at something flashy, such as watches and bracelets, so leave your fancy jewelry at home.

A few seagoing critters resent being stepped on and can retaliate with a dangerous wound. The scorpion fish, hardly recognizable with its natural camouflage, lies hidden most of the time on a reef shelf or on the bottom of the sea. If you should step on or touch it you can expect a painful, dangerous sting. If this happens, see a doctor immediately.

If you leave them alone, sting rays are generally peaceful, but if stepped on they will zap you with a tail that carries a poisonous sting capable of causing anaphylactic shock. Symptoms include respiratory difficulties, fainting, and severe itching. Go quickly to the doctor and describe what caused the sting. One diver suggests a shuffling, dragging-of-the-feet gait when walking on the bottom of the ocean. If bumped, the ray will quickly escape, but if stepped on it feels trapped and uses its tail for protection.

Tiny brown, gel-encased globules called *pica-pica* produce a horrible rash; look for clouds of these guys around any coral patch before getting in. Avoid the bottom side of a moon jellyfish, as well as the Portuguese Man-O-War (usually only in March). Sea wasps are tiny, four-tentacled menaces that deliver a sting.

Fire worms (also known as bristle worms) will deposit tiny cactus-like bristles in your skin if touched. They can cause the same reaction as fire coral. *Carefully* scraping the skin with the edge of a sharp knife (as you would to remove a bee stinger) *might* remove the bristles. Any leftover bristles will ultimately work their way out, but you might be very uncomfortable in the meantime. Cortisone cream helps to relieve the inflammation.

Several species of sponges have fine, sharp spicules (hard, minute, pointed calcareous or siliceous bodies that support the tissue) that should not be touched with the bare hand. The attractive red fire sponge can cause great pain; a mild solution of vinegar or ammonia (or urine if there's nothing else) will help. The burning lasts a couple of days, and cortisone cream soothes. Don't be fooled by dull-colored sponges. Many have the same sharp spicules.

Coral

For the hundredth time, don't touch the coral! Many varieties of fire coral will make you wish you hadn't. Cuts from coral, even if just a scratch, will often become infected. Antibiotic cream or powder will usually take care of it. If you should get a deep cut, or if minute bits of coral are left in the wound, a serious and long-lived infection can ensue. See a doctor.

If you should get scraped on red or fire coral you may feel a burning sensation for just a few minutes or up to five days. In some, it causes an allergic reaction and will raise large red welts. Cortisone cream will reduce inflammation and discomfort.

Don't Freak Out!

Don't let these what-ifs discourage you from an underwater adventure. Thousands of people dive in Belize's Caribbean every day of the year without incident. The above list is only to let you know what's out there, not to scare you into remaining on shore or out of the jungle. Know what you're getting into and be sure your guide does as well, and then get into it!

MEDICAL CARE

Although there are hospitals and health clinics in most urban areas and towns, care is extremely limited compared with more developed countries. Serious injuries or illness may require evacuation to another country and you should consider picking up some cheap travel insurance that covers such a need—otherwise, you're looking at US$12,000 just for the transport.

Many Belizean doctors and hospitals require immediate cash payment for health services, sometimes prior to providing treatment. Uninsured travelers or travelers whose insurance does not provide coverage in Belize may face extreme difficulties if serious medical treatment is needed. International Medical Group (www.imglobal .com) is one provider that offers short term insurance specifically for overseas travelers and expats for very reasonable rates.

Belize Medical Associates (5791 St. Thomas St., tel. 501/223-0302, 223-0303, or 223-0304, bzmedasso@btl.net, www.belize medical.com) is the only private hospital in Belize City. They provide 24-hour assistance and a wide range of specialties. Look under "Hospitals" in the BTL yellow pages for an updated listing of other options.

Medications and Prescriptions

Many medications are available in pharmacies in Belize, and some are more strict than others about requiring papers for prescription drugs. Definitely plan on the conservative side: Bring adequate supplies of all your prescribed medications in their original containers, clearly labeled; in addition, carry a signed, dated letter from your physician describing all medical conditions and listing medications, including generic names. If carrying syringes or needles, carry a physician's letter documenting their medical necessity. Pack all medications in your carry-on bag and, if possible, put a duplicate supply in the checked luggage. If you wear glasses or contacts, bring an extra pair. If you have significant allergies or chronic medical problems, wear a medical alert bracelet.

Condoms are cheap and easy to find. Any corner pharmacy will have them, even in small towns of just a few thousand people. Female travelers taking contraceptives should know the generic name for the drug they use.

Bring a Small Medical Kit

At the very minimum, consider the following items for your first aid kit: rehydration salt packets, bandages/gauze, moleskin for blister prevention (duct tape is a fantastic substitute and sticks better), tweezers, antiseptic cream, strong sun block (SPF 30), aloe gel for sunburns, some kind of general antibiotic for intestinal trouble,

acetaminophen (Tylenol) for pain/fevers, eye drops (for dust), birth control pills, condoms, and anti-fungal cream (clorotrimazol). And don't forget a travel-sized orange bottle of Extra Strength Gold Bond Medicated Powder—it makes you feel tingly, light, and dry, and helps prevent fungus, too. Oh yeah.

NATURAL HEALING

In small rural villages, if you have a serious problem and no doctor is around, you can usually find a *curandero*. These healers practice the old, herb-based healing methods and may be helpful in a desperate situation away from modern technology. Locals who live in the dense, jungle areas inhabited by poisonous snakes go to the local "snake doctor," although many advise against it.

You may learn about the grapevine, which provides pure water to cleanse the navel of a newborn infant; the bark of the negrito tree, also called dysentery bark, which treats severe dysentery (and which was sold for high prices by druggists in Europe when pirates discovered it many years back). Tea made from the China root is used for blood-building after an attack from parasites. Another tea made from *ki bix* acts as birth control by coating the lining of the uterus. This is just a tiny sampling of the information shared with visitors.

Due mainly to the influence of Rosita Arvigo, a healer based in the Cayo District, the Belizean government established Terra Nova Medicinal Plant Reserve, referred to in 1993 as the world's first medicinal plant reserve. The 6,000 acres are administered by the Belizean Association of Traditional Healers, dedicated to the preservation of what might be important scientific help in future treatments of illnesses. Seedlings are brought here from threatened areas of the rainforest.

Know Belize

Safety

Know Belize

CRIME

Most of the crime in Belize (besides drug possession and trafficking) is petty theft and burglary. In the rare event that a stranger approaches you and demands your valuable items, remember that things can be replaced!

Staying Safe

It's best not to wear expensive jewelry when traveling. And, don't carry large amounts of money, your passport, or your plane tickets if not necessary; if you must carry these things, wear a moneybelt under your clothes. Most hotels have safety deposit boxes. Don't flaunt cameras and video equipment or leave them in sight in cars when sightseeing, especially in some parts of Belize City. Remember, this is a poor country and petty theft is its number-one crime—don't tempt fate. For more information on security precautions for female travelers, please see the section Special Concerns earlier in this chapter.

It is generally not wise to wander around alone on foot late at night in Belize City. Go out with others if possible, and take a taxi. Most Belizeans are friendly, decent people, but, as in every community, a small percentage will steal anything, given the opportunity. To many Belizeans, foreigners come off as "rich" whether they are or not. The local hustlers are quite creative when it comes to thinking of ways to con you out of some cash. Keep your wits about you, pull out of conversations that appear headed in that direction, don't give out your hotel name or room number freely or where they can be overheard by strangers, and remember—you're not on your own turf, so you're less familiar with everything around you.

A few more tips:

•On any public transport, keep your belongings close by, or at least within sight.

•In emergencies, dial 911 or 90 for police assistance. The number for fire and ambulance is also 90.

island cops

© JOSHUA BERMAN

•Keep your eyes open and be aware of people close by.

•Do *not* bring firearms into the country.

If You Are Robbed

If you are the victim of a crime while overseas, in addition to reporting it to local police, contact your embassy or consulate as soon as possible. The embassy/consulate staff can, for example, assist you in finding appropriate medical care and contacting family members or friends, and will explain how funds could be transferred to you. Although the investigation and prosecution of the crime is solely the responsibility of local authorities, consular officers can help you to understand the local criminal justice process and to find an attorney if needed. From my experience, Belize Police Detectives respond quickly and take these matters—even near-misses—seriously.

Police

Belizean Police can hold somebody for 48 hours with no charges; one U.S. Embassy warden called prison conditions in Belize "medieval." Police officers have been arrested for rape and routinely beat and torture detainees (usually Belizeans). On the whole, most officers are good folks, making the best of a poorly paying job with very few resources. Don't try to bribe them if you're in trouble—you'll only contribute to a more corrupt system that does not need any encouragement.

Illegal Drugs

Belize's modern history began with law-breaking pirates hiding out among the hundreds of cayes, lagoons, and uninhabited coastlines of the territory. The same natural features have made Belize a fueling stopover for **cocaine** traffickers from Colombia. The drug runners' practice of paying off their Belizean helpers with product (in addition to irresistible sums of cash) has created a national market for cocaine and crack with devastating effects, especially in Orange Walk Town and numerous coastal communities.

According to the U.S. State Department, traffickers increasingly use maritime operations in

Know Belize

conjunction with aircraft "wet-drops" or off-loads from sea vessels to smuggle drug shipments into Belizean waters. Cocaine, air-dropped off the coast of Belize, is transported to the Belizean mainland or Mexico by small "go-fast" boats, stored, and then shipped onward to the United States. Occasionally, unintended recipients find this "sea lotto" (also known as "square grouper")—bales of uncut cocaine that are also sometimes dumped overboard by traffickers who are about to get busted—floating in the water.

The United States Drug Enforcement Agency (DEA) is active in Belize—as it is throughout Central America—to battle the flow of cocaine and other illegal drugs; they provide boat patrols, overflights, drug war technology and herbicides, and sniffing dogs at roadside checkpoints.

Marijuana grows naturally and quite well in the soils and climate of Belize, although the country is no longer the major producer it once was. In the early 1980s, "Belizean Breeze" was exported in quantities massive enough to make Belize the fourth-largest pot-producing country in the world. The DEA put an end to that with controversial chemical-spraying programs, which have been known to have a devastating effect on local ecosystems. They seized and destroyed 800 tons of marijuana in Belize in 1983. Nevertheless, small-scale production continues, primarily for the domestic market. It has been argued by some that the job vacuum created by marijuana suppression led directly to Belize's role in the trafficking of cocaine and the subsequent entrance of crack into Belizean communities, a far more deleterious substance than marijuana (which has never killed a single person—ever, and even contains proven medical benefits).

Marijuana prohibition is alive and well in Belize, despite widespread use of the herb throughout the population (not just among the Rastas). The controversial—some would say downright wasteful (with regard to the allocation of public funds)—anti-ganja policy allows harsh penalties for possession of even tiny quantities of *cannabis sativa,* for both nationals and tourists alike. Tightly-wrapped nuggets of buds, usually under two grams, are referred to as "bullets," and possessing even one of these can bring a fine of hundreds of dollars and possible incarceration.

Foreign, hip-looking tourists will most likely be offered pot at some point during their visit. Be careful: The proposal may be a harmless invitation to get high on the beach, or it may be from a hustler or stool pigeon who is about to rip you off and/or get you arrested. In addition, watch out for guys selling pre-rolled joints called *"serias,"* as they are alleged to be laced with crumbled crack cocaine. Use the same common sense you would anywhere in the world, with the added knowledge that Belizean jails are Third World institutions and, needless to say, a major bummer.

Prostitution

Although prostitution is illegal in Belize, the sale of sex is alive and well at a handful of brothels throughout the country, usually on the highways outside major towns. The prostitutes are rarely Belizean and are often working as indentured sex slaves, unwittingly recruited from Honduras, Guatemala, or El Salvador with false promises of legitimate employment. It is undeniable that foreign johns have contributed in no small way to Belize's sex economy. Travelers considering indulging should think seriously about the social impacts that result from perpetuating this institution, and should start by reading the section on AIDS earlier in this chapter.

Money and Measurements

MONEY

Automated Teller Machines (ATMs) are available in nearly all major Belizean towns, but they may operate on different card networks (Plus, Cirrus, etc.) so you may have to try a few to get your card to work. They're also often out of order.

Currency

The currency unit is the Belize dollar (BZE$), which has been steady at BZE$2 to US$1 for some years. While prices are given in US$ in this book, travelers should be prepared to pay in Belizean currency on the street, aboard boats, in cafés, and at other smaller establishments. Everyone accepts U.S. dollars though, as there is a continual shortage in the country, and folks with access to blackmarket changers, who sometimes give considerably more than 2:1, will be eager for your greens.

When you buy or sell currency at a bank, be sure to retain proof of sale. The following places are authorized to buy or sell foreign currency: Atlantic Bank Ltd., Bank of Nova Scotia, Barclays Bank, Belize Bank of Commerce and Industry, and Belize Global Travel Services Ltd. All are close together near the plaza in Belize City and in other cities. Hours are till 1 P.M. Monday–Friday, till 11 A.M. Saturday. You can also change money, sometimes at a rate a bit better than 2:1, at Casas de Cambio. But because Casas de Cambio must charge the official rate, many people still go to the black market, which gives a better rate.

At the Mexico–Belize border you'll be approached by money changers (and you can bet they don't represent the banks). Many travelers buy just enough Belize dollars to get them into the city and to the banks. Depending on your mode of transport and destination, these money changers can be helpful. Strictly speaking, though, this is illegal—so suit yourself. The exchange rate is the same, but you'll have no receipt of sale. If selling a large quantity of Belize

DAY OF REST

Belize is serious about its Sundays. Expect businesses in most parts of the country—even restaurants and cafés—to close on Sundays. The streets empty as well, giving a ghost-town feeling even to places like downtown Belize City. Usually, the only stores and eateries open are Chinese shops, and maybe a few taco stands on the street.

dollars back to the bank, you might be asked for that proof.

Credit Cards and Travelers Checks
Credit cards are taken only at the larger business establishments, so bring travelers checks and cash as well (in small denominations). You will find representatives of Visa, MasterCard, and American Express at the four commercial banks in Belize City; there you can make cash advances against your card.

It's easy to cash and use travelers checks in the more popular destinations.

Tipping
Most restaurants and hotels include the tip on the check; if the tip isn't added to the bill, then 10–15 percent is the norm. It is not customary to tip taxi drivers unless they help you with your luggage. Always tip your tour guide if he or she has made your trip an enjoyable one.

Costs
Make no mistake: Belize is the most expensive country in Central America, and backpackers entering from Mexico, Guatemala, and Honduras are as shocked today as they have always been upon crossing the border. It has always been thus here because of the import-reliant economy and whatever other invisible hands guide such things. Shoestring travelers squeaking by on US$25 a day in Belize are most likely stone sober and eating tacos three times a day;

they are not paying for tours or taxis, and they are surely not diving. They're probably still having a grand old time though, camped out in the bush (or a US$10 room), doing lots of self-guided hiking, paddling, and cultural exploring. It's possible—but all depends on your comfort zone and definition of a good time.

If you've only got a seven-day vacation, though, you won't have to stretch your dollars over as many weeks or months as Susie Backpacker and her dog, Dreddie, and can thus spend more on lodging and activities. Figure at least US$100 per person per day if you want to pay for day trips and don't want to share a bathroom; serious divers or anglers should add a bit more. Weeklong packages at many dive and jungle resorts run between US$1,000 and US$1,600 and go up from there.

Be prepared for some additions on your bills for taxes and service charges:
- Sales tax 9 percent
- Hotel tax 8 percent
- Service charge (a tip placed on a bill) 10 percent
- Airport departure tax US$20

If you use your credit card, it will cost you a little more at most businesses, sometimes 3–5 percent of the bill.

Bank Hours
Many banks are only open till 1 P.M. or 2 P.M. Monday–Thursday, staying open a bit later on Fridays, often closed for lunch, and always closed Saturday afternoons and Sundays.

TIME, WEIGHTS, AND MEASURES
The local time is Greenwich mean time minus six, the same as U.S. central time, year-round (there is no daylight savings time). The electricity is standard 110/220 volt, 60 cycles. Most distances are measured in inches, feet, yards, and miles, although there is some limited use of the metric system.

Communications and Media

MAIL

Posting a letter or postcard is easy and cheap, costing well under US$1, and the stamps are gorgeous. If you visit in the outlying cities or cayes, bring your mail to Belize City to post—it's more apt to get to its destination quickly.

Post offices are located in the center of (or nearby) all villages and cities in Belize, although they usually don't look too post-officey from the outside. When writing letters to Belize, abbreviate Central America as C.A. Be sure to include the periods; otherwise the U.S. Post Office will send your letters to California. You can receive mail in any town without getting a P.O. Box—just have the mail addressed to your name care of "General Delivery," followed by the town, district, and "Belize."

FedEx, DHL, and other international couriers are widely available, and the Mailboxes, Etc. in Belize City (on Front Street, just up from the Water Taxi Terminal) can take care of most of your mailing and package needs.

Sending mail within Belize, you can use either the post office system, or the buses. All Novelo's terminals are experienced at sending letters and packages to destination towns—the recipient can usually pick up the item at the office there, or you can advise them to meet the bus directly.

TELEPHONES

Belize Telecommunications Limited's (BTL's) monopoly on Belizean telephones has been a big news item for years, and was recently sold in a much-publicized stock transfer. How this will affect communications in the future is uncertain. As far as the traveler is concerned, there will always be a way to call home. The most common is to buy a prepaid BTL phone card and punch in the card's numbers every time you borrow a phone or use one of the many pay phones in the country. All towns also have a local BTL office, usually identified by a giant red and white radio tower somewhere very nearby; they can place calls anywhere in the country or world for you and will assign you to a semi-private booth after they've dialed the number. They can also connect you to your homeland phone carrier. See www.btl.net for more information.

Cell Phones

Digicell (www.digicell.bz) offers prepaid temporary service to tourists. Get it at BTL's Airport Service Center, or bring your own GSM 1900 Mhz handset and purchase a SIM pack from any DigiCell distributor nationwide. There are several local cellular services, both analog and digital, and coverage along roadways and in major towns is decent but still improving. One vendor of phones is **Office Essentials** (90 Barracks Rd., Belize City, tel. 501/223-5566).

International Calls

To call out of Belize, dial the International Access Code "00" followed by your country code and then city or area code and the number. The country code for Canada and the United States is "1" and England is "44." Australia is "61." BTL's national phone book has a complete listing of country codes. To reach other countries in Central America, leave out the "00" and dial their country codes as you would the area code in the States. Belize's country code is "501." To receive a call in Belize from the United States, for example, tell the caller to dial "001" to tap into the international network, followed by "501" and your seven digit number. Although they are not toll-free from Belize, 800 numbers are dialed as they are written, preceded by the "00."

INTERNET ACCESS

Web access is widely available throughout the country and is improving all the time. Crappy dial-up connections are now the exception rather than the norm and broadband (DSL, cable, and satellite) is springing up everywhere. Ahead of the pack is San Ignacio, with a handful of extremely modern Internet cafés; San Pedro is up there as well, with Caye Caulker and Placencia close behind. At press time, Placencia offered the only WiFi service, but that's sure to change. If traveling with a laptop, you can usually find a landline to plug into your Ethernet dock at any of the more modern cafés—some have laptop docks already set up, some need to unplug a line from one of their computers. If you're in town for awhile, many Internet businesses have monthly memberships for about US$50 that include unlimited access. You are welcome to sign up for a BTL account if you don't have your own ISP (Internet Service Provider), but that may lead to more headaches then you need and there are many other options.

PUBLICATIONS

Local Newspapers and Magazines

Four weekly and highly politicized papers come out on Fridays (with occasional mid-week editions) and you'll find many a Belizean conducting the weekly ritual of reading their favorite over a cup of afternoon coffee, and then going to happy hour to yap away about the latest scandal. *Amandala* and the *Reporter* seem to be the most objective and respected rags.

Definitely find yourself a copy of *NICH Culture: A Magazine about Belize* (tel. 501/223-4524, nichculture@yahoo.com); although it is published by a government body (NICH is the National Institute of Culture and History), this glossy, oversized quarterly is a brilliantly designed relief from the standard official line of brochure-like propaganda. Features about local customs and characters are illustrated with stunning photography and are ad-free (except for a few self-serving government bits).

In most gift shops, you'll find at least a few colorful Belizean history and picture books put out by **Cubola Productions,** a local publisher specializing in all things Belize, including maps, atlases, short stories, novels, and poems written by Belizeans. Cubola's publications give a great insight into the country.

Foreign News

You will not find the *Herald Tribune* on every newsstand like in other destinations. In fact, you may not find it at all. Check with the Radisson Hotel or Fort Street Guest House in Belize City, where you can sometimes find the *Miami Herald,* a relatively recent *Newsweek,* or the *Times.* **Brodie's** and **The Book Center** also carry American magazines. English-language novels (trashy and otherwise) are widely available in hotel gift shops and many budget accommodations across the country have book exchanges.

MAPS

The most readily available and up-to-date map to Belize is published by **International Travel Maps** (www.itmb.com), whose 1:350,000 map of Belize makes a useful addition to any guidebook—or wall.

All of Belize's most heavily touristed areas create updated town maps, found most often at tourist information booths and car (or golf cart) rental places.

The **Government of Belize Land Department** in Belmopan has detailed topographic maps for the entire country—spendy at US$40 per quad, but vital if you're doing any serious backcountry travel. The British Army and United Kingdom Ordinance Survey have created a number of map series of various scales, but tracking them down will be a challenge.

MORE INFORMATION

The official government ministry is the **Belize Tourism Board** (BTB, US tel. 800/624-0686, Bel. tel. 501/223-1913, fax 501/223-1943, www.travelbelize.org). The BTB offers a unique in-country toll-free help line (800-SERVICE), answered by real people in their marketing department. At the office (on the second level of the Central Bank Building in Belize City), you'll find brochures on a number of reserves and national parks and information on various sections of the country. You'll usually find someone who's willing to talk to you and answer your questions.

The **Belize Tourism Industry Association** (BTIA, tel. 501/227-5717, fax 501/227-8710) is the industry-based association. These folks are also a source of good information about the country—but you will not be directed to a hotel or service that has not paid their annual dues. Still, BTIA sponsors a number of regional booths around the country with helpful maps and brochures.

The **Embassy of Belize** in the United States (2535 Massachusetts Ave. NW, Washington, D.C. 20008, 202/332-9636, fax 202/332-6741) and the **Caribbean Tourism Association** (20 E. 46th St., New York, NY 10017, 212/563-6011 or 800/624-0686) are two more sources of information.

Belize Audubon Society has information about the many parks they manage at their gift shop (tel. 501/223-5004, 8 A.M.–5 P.M. Mon.–Fri.), located in Tourism Village across from Harbor View Restaurant in Belize City.

Without a doubt though, most travelers now conduct all their research online, where they will find a wealth of information, both good and bad. Several notable portals are listed throughout this book and in the Internet Resources.

Suggested Reading

ARCHAEOLOGY

Carrasco, David. *Religions of Mesoamerica: Cosmovision and Ceremonial Centers.* San Francisco: Harper & Row, 1990.

Coe, Michael D. *The Maya.* New York: Thames and Hudson, 1984.

De Landa, Friar Diego. *Yucatan: Before and After the Conquest.* New York: Dover Publications, 1978 (translation of original manuscript written in 1566). The same man who provided some of the best, most lasting descriptions of ancient Maya, also single-handedly destroyed the most Maya artifacts and writings of anyone in history.

Gifford, James. *Prehistoric Pottery Analysis and the Ceramics of Barton Ramie in the Belize Valley.* Cambridge, MA: Peabody Museum of Archaeology and Ethnology, Harvard University, 1976.

Schele, Linda, and David Freidel. *A Forest of Kings: The Untold Story of the Ancient Maya.* New York: William Morrow and Company, Inc., 1990.

Stephens, John L. *Incidents of Travel in Central America, Chiapas and Yucatan* New York: Dover Publications, Inc., 1969 (originally Harper & Bros., New York, 1841). A classic 19th-century travelogue, Stephen's writing is wonderfully pompous, amusing, and incredibly astute—with historical and archaeological observations that still stand today. If you can, find a copy with the original set of illustrations by Stephens' expedition partner.

DIVING AND THE SEA

Burgess, Robert. *Secret Languages of the Sea.* New York: Dodd, Mead, and Company, 1981.

Cousteau, Jacques-Yves. *Three Adventures: Galapagos, Titicaca, the Blue Holes.* Garden City, NY: Doubleday, 1973.

Kuhlmann, Dietrick. *Living Coral Reefs of the World.* New York: Arco Publishing, 1985.

Meyer, Franz. *Diving & Snorkeling Guide to Belize: Lighthouse Reef, Glover Reef, and Turneffe Island.* Houston, TX: Gulf Publishing, 1990.

FICTION/HISTORICAL FICTION

Edgell, Zee. *Beka Lamb.* Portsmouth, NH: Heinemann, 1982. The first internationally recognized Belizean novel, this story of a girl named Beka who is growing up with her country is required reading for all Belizean high schoolers and offers an excellent view of Belizean family life, history, and politics.

Ellis, Zoila, Leo Bradley, Evadne Garcia, Evan Hyde, Lawrence Vernon, Colville Young, and John Walter. *Belizean Writers Series: Snapshots of Belize*. Belize: Cubola Productions, 1994.

Miller, Carlos Ledson. *Belize: A Novel.* www.Xlibris.com, 1999. This historically laden piece of fiction offers an impressively thorough snapshot of Belize over the last 40 years. "Set on a harsh, exciting landscape, this is the compelling story of a family and a nation searching for their identities."

Highwater, Jamake. *Journey to the Sky: A Novel About the True Adventures of Two Men in Search of the Lost Maya Kingdom.* New York: Thomas Y. Crowell, 1978.

King, Emory. *Belize 1798, The Road to Glory.* Belize City: Tropical Books, 1991.

Westlake, Donald. *High Adventure.* New York: Mysterious Press, 1985.

HEALTH AND SAFETY

Arvigo, Rosita and Balick, Michael (foreword by Mickey Hart). *Rainforest Remedies: 100 Healing Herbs of Belize.* Wisconsin: Lotus Press, 1998.

Schroeder, Dirk. *Staying Healthy in Asia, Africa, and Latin America.* Emeryville, CA: Avalon Travel Publishing, 2000.

Werner, David. *Where There Is No Doctor.* Palo Alto, CA: Hesperian Foundation, 1992.

Zepatos, Thalia. *A Journey of One's Own.* Portland, OR: Eighth Mountain Press, 2003. Offers "uncommon advice for the independent woman traveler."

HISTORY AND POLITICS

Barry, Tom. *Belize: A Country Guide.* Albuquerque, NM: Inter-Hemispheric Education Resource Center, 1989.

Bernal, Ignacia. *The Olmec World.* Berkeley, CA: University of California Press, 1969.

Bolland, O. Nigel. *Belize: A New Nation in Central America.* Boulder, CO: Westview, 1986.

Fairweather, Stephen. *The Baymen of Belize.* London, 1992. May be out of print.

Grant, C. H. *The Making of Modern Belize.* Cambridge, England: Cambridge University Press, 1976.

Kerns, Virginia. *Women and the Ancestors: Black Carib Kinship and Ritual.* Urbana, IL: University of Illinois Press, 1983.

Sawatzky, Harry. *They Sought a Country: Mennonite Colonization in Mexico. With an Appendix on Mennonite Colonization in British Honduras.* Berkeley, CA: University of California, 1971.

Setzekorn, William David. *Formerly British Honduras: A Profile of the New Nation of Belize.* Athens, OH: Ohio University Press, 1981.

Shoman, Assad. *13 Chapters of a History of Belize.* Belize City: The Angelus Press, Ltd, 1994. A no-nonsense history of Belize from a fresh, Belizean perspective.

NATURE AND FIELD GUIDES

Being one of the most exhaustively studied tropical countries in the world, Belize boasts a plethora of nature study guidebooks that span every conceivable niche of flora, fauna, and geology. They come in massive, coffee table sizes with color plates, as well as in pocket-size field guides: *Tarantulas of Belize, Hummingbirds of Belize, Orchids of Belize,* and so on.

Beletsky, Les. *Belize and Northern Guatemala: The Ecotravellers' Wildlife Guide.* San Diego, CA: Academic Press, 1999. One of the best, reasonably sized general nature guides to the area, with abundant color plates for all types of fauna.

Lewis, Scott. *The Rainforest Book: How You Can Save the World's Rainforests.* Los Angeles: Living Planet Press, 1990.

MacKinnon, Barbara. *100 Common Birds of the Yucatán Peninsula.* Cancún, Quintana Roo, Mexico: Amigos de Sian Ka'an (Apto. Postal 770, Cancún, Quintana Roo, 77500, Mexico), 1989.

Rabinowitz, Alan. *Jaguar: One Man's Struggle to Establish the World's First Jaguar Preserve.* Washington, D.C.: Island Press/Shearwater Books, 2000 (originally 1986).

Stevens, Katie. *Jungle Walk: Birds and Beasts of Belize, Central America.* Belize: Angelus Press, 1991. Order through International Expeditions, tel. 800/633-4734.

Internet Resources

www.ambergriscaye.com
Official site of Ambergris Caye and a lot more, with links to the whole country.

Belize Audubon Society
www.belizeaudubon.org
Lots of information on the parks BAS manages and general conservation efforts in Belize.

www.belizenet.com
The primary Naturalight website for all things Belize will lead you into their massive network of Belize pages.

Belize Zoo and Tropical Education Center
www.belizezoo.org

www.cayecaulker.org
www.cybercayecaulker.com
www.gocayecaulker.com
Information on Caye Caulker and more.

www.cdc.gov/travel/camerica.htm
www.mdtravelhealth.com
Pre-trip health information and resources.

Diving in Belize
www.scubadivingbelize.com

www.emoryking.com
Home page of Emory King, one of Belize's most prolific author of books and articles, reference, history, etc.

Monkey Bay Wildlife Sanctuary
www.monkeybaybelize.org

www.planeta.com
This is one of the premier ecotourism sites around; look up the Belize page for all kinds of current events and interesting tourism-related articles.

San Pedro Sun
www.sanpedrosun.net
Lots of Belizean news and links from this island newspaper, in addition to the latest Ambergris scoop.

www.studyabroaddirectory.com
www.teachabroad.com
www.volunteerabroad.com
Working, studying, and volunteering abroad information and listings of available positions.

www.toucantrail.com
A comprehensive guide for independent travelers seeking affordable adventure and ac-

commodation with "local flavor."

www.travelbelize.org
Official site of the Belize Tourism Board.

United States Embassy in Belize
www.usembassy.state.gov/belize

Index

Conservation and Preservation

Diving

Recommended Sights

Acknowledgments

First, a tip of the hat to all those who helped with, worked on, and otherwise contributed to the first five editions of *Moon Handbooks Belize;* you created a solid foundation upon which we can only continue to build.

I am deeply grateful to the talented folks who contributed text and photos to this sixth edition. I met photographer Danielle Vaughn in the middle of a wildfire in Montana; this U.S. Forest Service Backcountry Ranger agreed to meet me down south to shoot for a couple of weeks—she ended up with beautiful stock of Belize photos, many of which appear throughout this book. Marine scientist Caryn Self-Sullivan spent several precious vacation days writing about mangroves and manatees, her specialties (and the very things she'd come up to Cayo to get away from). Laurie Smith was only doing her duty (Peace Corps Goals #2 and #3) when she offered to help inform *Moon Handbook* readers about proper reef etiquette, fishing regulations, and snorkel sites around San Pedro. Crissie Ferrara shared images of her backyard in the Toledo District—this gal's a hip, talented, professional photographer and displaced Manhattanite who the Peace Corps sent to PG— check out her website for more amazing travel photography (www.crissieferrara.com). Not only did Judy and Jan Wilson provide photos for the Corozal chapter, they also helped with information, hospitality, a field trip to "Chet," and a great bicycle—thank you!

The good Dr. James Savage, Gentleman Firefighter & Bushman of Mystery, chose Belizean sunshine—specifically, Orange Walk and Belize City sunshine, those being the two areas Big Jim Coyote helped research and write—over his first Alaskan winter. Thanks to my *compa,* Randy Wood, who allowed me to dip into and twist around some of our co-written background text from *Moon Handbooks Nicaragua.*

Big hug-up to Katie Valk, my first contact— and friend—in Belize. I am also grateful to my friends and family who shared a taste of this experience: Mom, Dad, and Grandma Helen (Grandma researched Barton Creek Cave with me on her 85th birthday!); also Rob, Viv, Jody, and—*WHAMO!*—Ze.

Thanks Josh and Melissa for Holiday Cheer (Chanukah hamsteaks) and Cancún rental car info; thanks to the Salamander kids for chilled euphoria. More PCVs: Crissie and Christina Spach for their hospitality and the PG poop; Micki, Kim, and Kristen in San Pedro. Also Nathan Kinkade; Katie Moll; and *el jefe,* Bill Barbieri, who shared his Thanksgiving table with me (and 60 other Peace Corps freeloaders).

Dr. Jaime Awe and Sherry Gibbs were two of the archaeologists that helped me keep track of the many exciting new developments at Belize's Maya sites (they also helped get me to and guide me around some of these sites on their days off— thank you!).

Thanks to Barbara Kasak and Shadow; to Tim, Leif, and Denver at Island Expeditions, and to my body-working saviors round the country: Carrie, Brenda, Marriett, Krista, TP, Harold, and Laurie. An *abrazo* for Mirriam and Laurenz, of course, and for my Green Dragon "office" mates, Isabelle and Megan.

John and Judy Yaeger, my landlords, neighbors, and surrogate parents for a spell, were invaluable. Thanks also to their archaeologist prodigy, Jason Yaeger, for helping with some last-minute questions. While I'm in the Succotz *barrio,* thanks to Tino for the guitar and to the Blue House for perfect space.

Memo, Greg—'ssup.

Thanks to my iBook for waiting until the *day after* I completed my manuscript to crash and die! On the same note, there's a good chance this book would not be in your hands if it weren't for Gary and Yuly Preston at Tradewinds Internet in San Ignacio—instant *amigos* who helped retrieve four months of data. Whew.

To the Belizean environment, I apologize for wasting so many water bottles and non-rechargeable batteries; I promise I'll be better next edition.

To the City of New York and my *primo,* Big Bri Deutsch, thanks for hosting me during the final edits.

My editors at Avalon, Amy Scott and Kay Elliot, as well as Susan Snyder, Olivia Solís, and the rest of the team (it's a big one), have been nothing but fully supportive and a joy to work with. They are the reason this book ends up looking as good as it does. *Gracias.*

This list can go on and on—so many people helped with this edition and shared some of the random moments and adventures that went into the making of it. To everyone I forgot to mention, thanks—until next time . . .

—Joshua Berman

U.S. ~ Metric Conversion

1 inch	=	2.54 centimeters (cm)
1 foot	=	.304 meters (m)
1 yard	=	0.914 meters
1 mile	=	1.6093 kilometers (km)
1 km	=	.6214 miles
1 fathom	=	1.8288 m
1 chain	=	20.1168 m
1 furlong	=	201.168 m
1 acre	=	.4047 hectares
1 sq km	=	100 hectares
1 sq mile	=	2.59 square km
1 ounce	=	28.35 grams
1 pound	=	.4536 kilograms
1 short ton	=	.90718 metric ton
1 short ton	=	2000 pounds
1 long ton	=	1.016 metric tons
1 long ton	=	2240 pounds
1 metric ton	=	1000 kilograms
1 quart	=	.94635 liters
1 US gallon	=	3.7854 liters
1 Imperial gallon	=	4.5459 liters
1 nautical mile	=	1.852 km

To compute Celsius temperatures, subtract 32 from Fahrenheit and divide by 1.8. To go the other way, multiply Celsius by 1.8 and add 32.

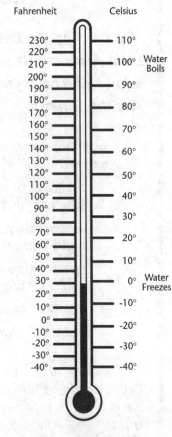

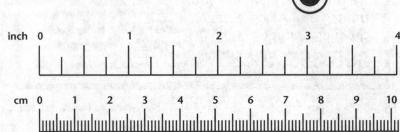

Keeping Current

Although we strive to produce the most up-to-date guidebook humanly possible, change is unavoidable. Between the time this book goes to print and the moment you read it, a handful of the businesses noted in these pages will undoubtedly change prices, move, or even close their doors forever. Other worthy attractions will open for the first time. If you have a favorite gem you'd like to see included in the next edition, or see anything that needs updating, clarification, or correction, please drop us a line. Send your comments via email to atpfeedback@avalonpub.com, or use the address below.

Moon Handbooks Belize
Avalon Travel Publishing
1400 65th Street, Suite 250
Emeryville, CA 94608, USA
www.moon.com

Avalon Travel Publishing
An Imprint of Avalon Publishing
Group, Inc.

AVALON
publishing group incorporated

Editors: Amy Scott, Kay Elliott
Series Manager: Kevin McLain
Acquisitions Editor: Rebecca K. Browning
Graphics Coordinator: Susan Snyder
Production Coordinator: Jacob Goolkasian
Cover Designer: Kari Gim
Interior Designers: Amber Pirker,
 Alvaro Villanueva, Kelly Pendragon
Map Editor: Olivia Solís
Cartographers: Kat Kalamaras,
 Mike Morgenfeld, Ben Pease
Proofreader: Erika Howsare
Indexer: Rachel Kuhn

ISBN: 1-56691-575-9
ISSN: 1533-9130

Printing History
1st Edition—1991
6th Edition—January 2005
5 4 3 2 1

Text © 2005 by Chicki Mallan and Joshua
 Berman.
Maps © 2005 by Avalon Travel Publishing, Inc.
All rights reserved.

Some photos and illustrations are used by permission and are the property of the original copyright owners.

Front cover photo: © Jeff Hunter/The Image Bank/Getty Images

Printed in USA by Malloy Inc.

About the Author

Chicki Mallan

Chicki Mallan discovered the joy of traveling with her parents at an early age. The family would leave their Catalina Island home yearly, hit the road, and explore the small towns and big cities of the United States. The first foreign country she visited, at about age five, was Mexico. Destiny? Since then she has lived in France, Indonesia, and Mexico, and traveled all over Europe, Asia, Africa, Australia, and Central America. In between, she raised eight kids who, after a lot of traveling and living in intriguing places, are now teaching their children what fun it is to travel.

Chicki's first book was published by Moon in 1983; today, she is also the author of *Colonial Mexico, Moon Handbooks Cancún,* and *Moon Handbooks Yucatán Peninsula,* and co-author of *Moon Handbooks Mexico.* Between books, she enjoys her home in California's Sierra Nevada foothills, writing newspaper and magazine articles, and devoting time to her newest hobby, sculpting.

In 1987, Chicki was presented the Pluma de Plata writing award from the Mexican Government for an article she wrote about the coast of the Yucatán Caribbean, which was published in the *Los Angeles Times.*